# Gift-Giving and Materiality in Europe, 1300–1600

# Gift-Giving and Materiality in Europe, 1300–1600

*Gifts as Objects*

Edited by
Lars Kjær and Gustavs Strenga

BLOOMSBURY ACADEMIC
LONDON • NEW YORK • OXFORD • NEW DELHI • SYDNEY

BLOOMSBURY ACADEMIC
Bloomsbury Publishing Plc
50 Bedford Square, London, WC1B 3DP, UK
1385 Broadway, New York, NY 10018, USA
29 Earlsfort Terrace, Dublin 2, Ireland

BLOOMSBURY, BLOOMSBURY ACADEMIC and the Diana logo are
trademarks of Bloomsbury Publishing Plc

First published in Great Britain 2022
Paperback edition first published 2024

Copyright © Lars Kjær and Gustavs Strenga, 2022

Lars Kjær and Gustavs Strenga have asserted their right under the Copyright,
Designs and Patents Act, 1988, to be identified as Editors of this work.

Cover image: Duke of Berry, exchanging gifts and feasting with his family and friends in
January. Illumination from the 15th century manuscript of the 'Tres Riches Heures' of
Jean, Duke of Berry. (© Granger Historical Picture Archive/Alamy Stock Photo)

All rights reserved. No part of this publication may be reproduced or transmitted
in any form or by any means, electronic or mechanical, including photocopying,
recording, or any information storage or retrieval system, without prior
permission in writing from the publishers.

Bloomsbury Publishing Plc does not have any control over, or responsibility for,
any third-party websites referred to or in this book. All internet addresses given in this
book were correct at the time of going to press. The author and publisher regret any
inconvenience caused if addresses have changed or sites have ceased to exist,
but can accept no responsibility for any such changes.

A catalogue record for this book is available from the British Library.

A catalog record for this book is available from the Library of Congress.

ISBN:  HB:     978-1-3501-8369-8
       PB:     978-1-3501-8610-1
       ePDF:   978-1-3501-8370-4
       eBook:  978-1-3501-8371-1

Typeset by Integra Software Services Pvt. Ltd.

To find out more about our authors and books visit www.bloomsbury.com
and sign up for our newsletters.

# Contents

List of illustrations     vi
List of contributors     viii
Preface     xi

Introduction: The matter of the gift  *Lars Kjær*     1

1. 'With this rynge': The materiality and meaning of the late medieval marriage ring  *Anna Boeles Rowland*     17
2. Of ivory, gold and elephants: Materiality and agency of pre-modern chairs as gifts  *Sabine Sommerer*     43
3. Gifts and conflicts: Objects given during the entry of Archbishop Silvester Stodewescher in the Riga Cathedral (1449)  *Gustavs Strenga*     77
4. 'The Polar Winds have driven me to the conquest of the Treasure in the form of the much-desired relic.' (Re)moving relics and performing gift-exchange between early modern Tuscany and Lithuania  *Ruth Sargent Noyes*     103
5. 'The gift' and the living image: Exchange between human and nonhuman actors in fifteenth- to sixteenth-century Prato  *Mads Vedel Heilskov*     133
6. Demoniac's gratitude: Corporeality and materiality of votive offerings to St Nicholas of Tolentino (1325–1550)  *Sari Katajala-Peltomaa*     163
7. Alms boxes and charity: Giving to the poor after the Lutheran Reformation in Denmark  *Poul Grinder-Hansen*     185
8. Taken objects and the formation of social groups in Hamburg, Gdańsk and Lübeck  *Philipp Höhn*     219

Gifts: Concluding Remarks  *Miri Rubin*     249

Index     255

# Illustrations

| | | |
|---|---|---|
| 2.1 | Rome, St Peter, Cathedra Petri, before 875 | 59 |
| 2.2 | Cathedra Petri, detail with Bust of King Charles the Bald | 59 |
| 2.3 | Barcelona, Cathedral Treasury, Throne of Martin I, before 1410 | 60 |
| 2.4 | Throne of Martin I, detail with Dragon | 60 |
| 2.5 | Throne of Martin I, detail with Glass Enamel and Lionhead in the Volute | 61 |
| 2.6 | Madrid, Armeria Real, D. 11, Helmet with Dragon Crest, around 1407 | 62 |
| 2.7 | Kremsmünster, Benedictine Abbey, Art Collections, Inv. OKT 43.2.69, Elephant Chair, 1554 | 63 |
| 2.8 | Elephant Chair, detail with Seat Surface | 63 |
| 2.9 | Elephant Chair, detail with Front of the Scapula's Spine | 64 |
| 2.10 | Paris, Louvre, "Throne", Kohei Nawa, 2018, © Kohei Nawa | SANDWICH Inc. © I.M. Pei / Louvre Museum. | 64 |
| 2.11 | Rome, St Peter, Cattedra Petri, Reliquiary by Gian Lorenzo Bernini, 1666 | 65 |
| 4.1 | Reliquary Chest | 114 |
| 4.2 | The Reliquary of St Maria Maddalena de' Pazzi | 118 |
| 5.1 | Santa Maria delle Carceri | 134 |
| 7.1 | Alms box Svendborg St Nicolai Church | 186 |
| 7.2 | Late-medieval collection plate from Brændekilde Church, Fyn | 188 |
| 7.3 | The interior of the fifteenth-century Holy Ghost House in Copenhagen | 190 |
| 7.4 | Lutheran service depicted on a painted alterfrontal from Torslunde Church on Sjælland 1561 | 192 |
| 7.5 | A medieval monstrance tabernacle in Kerteminde Church on Fyn reused as alms box | 197 |
| 7.6 | Painting from a collection box for the church and for the poor 1633 in St Peter's Church | 198 |
| 7.7 | Inscription over the alms box in Rørvig Church on Sjælland, 1688 | 200 |
| 7.8 | Danish collection plate from *c.* 1600 from an unknown church | 202 |
| 7.9 | Collection plate from Stenløse Church, Sjælland, *c.* 1650 | 203 |

7.10  Collection plate from Slangerup Church, Sjælland, *c.* 1650   204
7.11  Silver plate from an alms box in Sengeløse Church, Sjælland,
       from the early seventeenth century   205
7.12  Two collection plates from 1595 in Søborg Church on Sjælland   206
7.13  Lazarus on the collection plate from Ganløse Church on Sjællland   207
7.14  Painting over the alms box in Helsingborg St Mary's Church, Scania   208
8.1   Map of Hamburg, originally from around 1570   222
8.2   St Mary's church in Gdańsk by Bartholomäus Milwitz   229
8.3   Danish Flag from 1427   235

# Contributors

**PhD Lars Kjær** is Associate Professor of Medieval History at the New College of the Humanities, London. He completed his PhD at the University of Cambridge in 2012. He has worked on elite culture and political life in medieval Denmark and England and the crusades. He edited a special volume of the *Journal of Medieval History* in 2011 with the title *Feasts and Gifts of Food in Medieval Europe: Ritualised Constructions of Hierarchy, Identity and Community*. His *The Medieval Gift and the Classical Tradition: Ideals and the Performance of Generosity in Medieval England, 1100–1300*, was published by Cambridge University Press in 2019.

**PhD Gustavs Strenga** is a researcher at the University of Greifswald and a senior researcher at the National Library of Latvia, where he also previously curated several exhibitions. He has been a post-doc research fellow at the University of Tallinn. He has received his bachelor's degree from the University of Latvia (2004), master's degree from the Central European University (2006) and defended his PhD thesis in the Queen Mary University of London (2014). The history of medieval Livonia, memory studies, gift-giving as a historical phenomenon and book history are his main academic interests.

**Dr Anna Boeles Rowland** is based at the University of Leuven, where she moved after completing her doctorate at the University of Oxford in 2018. Her research focuses on late medieval objects and the people who owned them. In 2019, she edited a special issue of *The Journal of Medieval History*, on 'People, Places and Possessions in Late Medieval England'. She is currently writing her first book, entitled *Marriage Matters: Material Culture and the Gift in Late Medieval England*.

**PhD Mads Vedel Heilskov** is a medieval historian with a background in visual culture. He obtained his PhD degree at the Centre for Scandinavian Studies at the University of Aberdeen, Scotland, in 2018. From 2019 to 2020 he was a postdoctoral researcher at Centre de recherches historiques at the École des hautes études en sciences sociales in Paris, France, with the project titled

*Animated Materiality in the Medieval Catholic West*, funded by the Carlsberg Foundation, and is currently working on the second phase of the same Carlsberg-funded project entitled *Techniques of Life* at The Courtauld Institute of Art in London, UK. His work focuses mainly on medieval religious practices and experiences and the role played by materiality in medieval Christianity. He has published on the topics of religious patronage, gift-giving, devotional practices and materiality in medieval Western Europe, most recently as author in and co-editor of the anthology *Materiality and Religious Practice in Medieval Denmark* (Brepols, 2021).

**Dr Philipp Höhn** is Lecturer at the University of Halle-Wittenberg. His research focuses on the history of maritime violence in the late medieval Baltic and economic anthropology and conflict management in premodern societies more generally. He has also published on the intellectual history of medievalists in the first half of the twentieth century. He is co-editor of *Merchants, Pirates, and Smugglers: Criminalization, Economics, and the Transformation of the Maritime World* (Frankfurt a. M./New York 2019) and has written extensively about the history of the Hanseatic League.

**Dr Sari Katajala-Peltomaa** is Senior Research Fellow at the Academy of Finland Centre of Excellence: History of Experiences at Tampere University. She has specialized in lived religion and canonization processes in the later Middle Ages. Her recent publications include a monograph *Demonic Possession and Lived Religion in Later Medieval Europe* (Oxford: Oxford University Press, 2020), a joint monograph with Raisa Toivo, *Lived Religion and Gender in Late Medieval and Early Modern Europe* (London: Routledge, 2020), and a co-edited volume (with Christian Krötzl) *Miracles in Medieval Canonization Processes: Structures, Functions, and Methodologies* (Turnhout: Brepols, 2018).

**Dr Ruth Sargent Noyes** took her BA (Harvard University) and PhD (Johns Hopkins University) in art history and is currently Marie Skłodowska-Curie EU Senior Research Fellow at the National Museum of Denmark, Copenhagen. Her research takes up the intersection of art, religion and science of the early modern period in its global context, with a special focus on cross-cultural perspectives between Italy and North-Eastern Europe, including Germany, the Low Countries and the Nordic-Baltic region. A 2014 Fellow of the American Academy in Rome, Dr Noyes has received a number of international awards and fellowships. Author of a number of publications, including a recent monograph published by Routledge, she is presently working on topics including relics, epistemic images, hagiography and artistic exchange between historical territories in Italy and the Baltic.

**Dr Sabine Sommerer** is an art historian specializing in medieval art. From 2013 to 2020 she was Senior Researcher and Lecturer for Medieval Art History at the University of Zurich, 2020/21 Guest Fellow at the Bibliotheca Hertziana – Max Planck Institute for Art History in Rome and currently Awardee of the PostDoc-Grant of the University of Zurich. She studied at the Universities of Basel and Freiburg (Germany), held posts as pre-doctoral researcher and teaching assistant at the University of Fribourg (Switzerland) and the Technical University of Dresden, and several PreDoc-Fellowships, including from the Swiss National Science Foundation, and in 2005/06 a residency of the Istituto Svizzero di Roma. In 2012, she published her doctoral thesis about the Trecento murals in the Camera d'Amore in Avio, Trentino, and in 2014 a second monograph in the series Monuments of art and history of Switzerland.' She is currently working on her habilitation project on the materiality and mediality of medieval seats.

**Dr Poul Grinder-Hansen** is curator and senior researcher of the Middle Ages, Renaissance and Numismatics at the National Museum of Denmark. Among his publications are – besides numerous articles – the books *Kronborg. Fortælling om et slot* (Kronborg. The tale of a palace), 2018, *Frederik 2. Danmarks Renæssancekonge* (Frederik 2. The Danish Renaissance King), 2013, *Søren Abildgaard (1718–91). Fortiden på tegnebrættet* (Søren Abildgaard. The Past on the Drawing Board), 2010 and *Danish Middle Ages and Renaissance, National Museum Copenhagen,* 2002. He has been responsible for major special exhibitions, for example Margrete I - Regent of the North. The Kalmar Union 1397–1997 (shown in Denmark, Sweden, Finland and Norway 1996–1998) and The World of Tycho Brahe (2006).

**Miri Rubin** is Professor of Medieval and Early Modern History at Queen Mary University of London. She began her historical studies at the Hebrew University in Jerusalem, completed her PhD at the University of Cambridge and then taught at Oxford. Miri Rubin is the author of several books, including *Corpus Christi: The Eucharist in Late Medieval Culture* (1991), *Mother of God: A History of the Virgin Mary* (2009) and, most recently, *Cities of Strangers* (2020).

# Preface

This anthology explores the interplay between gift-giving and materiality in late medieval and early modern Europe: the possibilities offered by the physical matter of the gift – and the anxieties that this could provoke. This book has its origins in a workshop *Performing Gifts: Rituals, Symbolic Communication and Gift-Giving in Medieval and Early Modern Europe* that took place at Tallinn University on 23–24 August 2019 and was funded by the Estonian Research Council and the Tallinn University.[1] The event drew together scholars from across Europe.[2] In the keynote lectures held by Gadi Algazi and Lars Kjær, following chapters and subsequent discussions, it became clear that many of the participants shared the feeling that more sustained attention to the physical matter exchanged would be desirable, a point emphasized in Miri Rubin's concluding remarks. This anthology gathers together many of the papers from the workshop, together with other contributions on the subject of gifts as material objects.

This book would not have been published without the support of Tallinn University School of Humanities and its staff. Professor Marek Tamm helped to formulate the focus and scope of the workshop and encouraged the publication of the proceedings in a book. Mirjam Uuskari's help was essential for organizing the workshop.

*Editors*
*July 2021, Riga and Cambridge*

## Notes

1   The workshop was funded by Estonian Research Council project MOBJD231 'Economy of Symbolic Exchange. Gift-Giving as a Social, Cultural and Political Practice in Late Medieval Livonia' at Tallinn University and Tallinn University School of Humanities Research Fund.
2   About the workshop, see Gustavs Strenga, 'A Workshop on Gift-Giving in Medieval and Early Modern Europe (23–24 August 2019, Tallinn University)', *Forschungen zur baltischen Geschichte* 15 (2020): 227–9.

# Introduction: The matter of the gift

Lars Kjær

This chapter introduces the contributions below, sets out some of the main themes, and places them against the background of recent scholarly developments, and against ideas about gift-giving current in late medieval and early modern Europe. A word needs to be said at the outset about the chronological scope. In his path-breaking *Essai sur le don*, Marcel Mauss focused attention on the importance of gifts in 'societies of a backward or archaic kind'.[1] Ever since, the assumption that gift-giving is always declining, always less central than 'before', has been hard to shift. In recent decades, however, historians have been challenging these assumptions. Two important anthologies *Negotiating the Gift* (2003) and *Languages of Gift in the Early Middle Ages* (2010) showed that gifts were not archaic features of societies with 'primitive' political systems, but flexible, adaptable tools whose meanings evolved alongside social and political changes.[2] Alongside these general trends in the way historians think about the gift, studies by Natalie Zemon Davies, Ilana Krausman Ben-Amos and Felicity Heal have demonstrated the continuing importance of gifts in early modern France and England.[3] More recent still are a number of fascinating studies of gifts as part of the global exchanges of the early modern world, such as the anthology *Global Gifts: The Material Culture of Diplomacy in Early Modern Eurasia* (2017), and a special issue of the journal *Diplomatica* on *Gift and Tribute in Early Modern Diplomacy: Afro-Eurasian Perspectives* (2020).[4]

This anthology focuses on exchanges within Europe, but looks at material from a wider swathe of European countries like the Baltic and Scandinavia, Italy, Spain and Central Europe. Gift-giving in late medieval and early modern Europe was not an archaic survival, but a vibrant social practice given new urgency by developments in religious and intellectual life, and new possibilities offered by the growth of trade networks as well as by technological developments. For capturing the special fascination of the late medieval and early modern gift, a keen eye for the matter of the gift is helpful.

In the last two decades the study of matter and objects has undergone dramatic developments sometimes described as constituting a 'new materialism'. In Susan Yi Sencindiver's words, this approach is borne out of a 'productive friction with the linguistic turn and social constructionist frameworks' and the prominence given within these to 'language, culture, and representation, which has come at the expense of exploring material and somatic realities beyond their ideological articulations and discursive inscriptions'.[5] Medieval and early modern historians of the gift may well recognize that they too have increasingly become focused on the 'languages and linguistic register' of gift-giving, the 'available vocabularies and recognized modes of applying them'.[6] New materialism promises to make objects, their physical characteristics and their implications central to scholarly discussion. The most ambitious envisage a more radical turn: a 'de-centring of the human'.[7]

There is much that is stimulating about this new turn, not least in the call for greater attention to the material context in which symbolic communication took place.[8] The present anthology is not, however, a work of 'new materialism', certainly not in its most ontologically ambitious form. Our focus is resolutely anthropocentric.[9] We have tried to pay more attention to objects because this allows us to observe the struggles, constraints and anxieties of human actors more clearly. Many of the authors engage, critically, with new materialist scholarship, but this anthology is a product of scholarly traditions that have a complicated relationship with theory.[10] Mayke de Jong quotes an exchange with James A. Brundage that summarizes this approach to theory admirably:

> Historians and magpies have much in common ... We pluck insights, vocabulary and methods from other disciplines when they seem likely to be useful or appropriate to our own concerns and incorporate them into our thinking and writing.[11]

Another aspect of this reserved engagement with critical theory, identified by Arnoud-Jan Bijsterveld in his splendid introduction to scholarship on gift-giving from 2007, is a tendency to consult the work of other historians rather than with the work of scholars from other disciplines.[12] One recent example of such work that speaks to the concerns of many of the essays below, is Chris Wickham's invention of the term 'giftiness' to describe objects that through their particular material qualities and social custom came to be seen as associated with generous exchanges, as opposed to commercial ones. The use of particularly 'gifty' prestige goods enabled, in Janet Nelson's words, 'an in-built symbolic association with "advantages" that pertained to gift giving': loving solidarity, lordly munificence, spiritual excellence and so forth.[13]

The 'gifty' associations of certain classes of objects could be so strong that in certain contexts the failure to act in accordance with expectations, the relationships between individuals and the objects involved could cause scandal. This seems to have been what provoked a breakdown in the relationship between King John of England (d. 1216) and his hired Flemish supporters in the late summer/early autumn 1215. After having made peace with his domestic enemies, John showed the Flemings much less warmth. At the royal castle of Marlborough:

> he did a most villainous thing – he had a great mass of his treasure taken out of the tower and carried into his rooms under the eyes of the Flemish knights, and never gave them one scrap of it.[14]

Furious at being treated so meanly despite their efforts on his behalf, they resolved to return home. What was wrong with John's actions was not only his failure to reciprocate, but his failure to act with the generosity expected of a great lord when great treasure and worthy retainers came into each other's proximity. King John got it wrong, on this and on other occasions, but rulers who heedlessly handed out rewards seemed no less laughable to their elite.[15] Louis IX of France (d. 1270) once confided to his biographer John of Joinville the lesson that his grandfather, Philip II 'Augustus' (d. 1223), had given him on this subject: 'no man can be a good governor of lands unless he knows how to withhold just as firmly as he know how to give.'[16] The web of expectations built up around princes and their possessions placed rulers in a delicate position requiring not so much a mean balance as the ability to shift seamlessly between gushing largesse and a demonstrative turning off of the taps.

Returning to the idea of 'gifty' objects, we should consider the impressions that the sight of noblemen and women decked out in precious rings and drinking from gilded silver cups would have made on medieval observers. Gold rings and silver cups – like the arm-rings of early medieval Scandinavian warlords – were enmeshed in an ongoing story of gift and counter-gift that made them into something more than mere treasure.[17] Worn by an open-handed prince, they became latent instruments of friendly generosity, which might at any time be handed on with a kind smile. In his study of medieval ideals of love and friendship Stephen Jaeger remarked that 'the western nobility always invested as heavily in its emotional life as it did in its jewels'.[18] One might go further and say that it was partly through their intimate association with these ennobling emotions that the treasures of the aristocracy gained their splendour.

Such beneficial readings of noble splendour did not go uncontested. An English poem from the early thirteenth century, *Invectio contra avaritiam*, sought to expose the gift-giving practices of the elite as a mean, self-serving activity:

> The rich give to the rich, so that they may receive again,
> And gifts run into their kin;
> That law is famous, which they have caused to be written,
> If you give to me, I will give to you.

According to the anonymous poet, one of the central vices of his age was that people looked not for truth or virtue, but only for the value of what was offered up as gifts.[19] Such anxieties grew out of ideas rooted in Europe's intellectual legacy about what gifts were or ought to be. In one of the earliest surviving extended discussions of generosity, the *Nichomachean Ethics* (c. 350 BCE), Aristotle identified generosity as a virtue concerned with a balanced attitude towards one's property. But gifts reached beyond this, for 'the liberality of a gift does not depend on its amount, but on the disposition of the giver'.[20] The virtues of the givers and their intentions determined the value of a gift. These ideas were further developed by Stoic writers, most evidently in Seneca the Younger's *De beneficiis* (c. 56–64 CE), the only work wholly dedicated to the question of generosity to survive from antiquity. For Seneca, the most important lesson on generosity was the idea that the thought counted above all: a gift 'consists not of what is done or given, but in the spirit of the giver or doer'.[21] But, alas, 'the ignorant regard only that which meets the eye, that which is handed over and taken possession of'.[22] Seneca was all too aware that his contemporaries often failed to live up to this shining idea of generosity. But nor was this vision of pure generosity restricted to works of moral philosophy: in Ovid's love poems as in the historical and epic works of Virgil and Sallust, we encounter similar celebration of those who look beyond the material gift and disparagement of those who become enthralled to its material worth.[23]

In the first centuries of the Common Era, classical ideals of free generosity encountered a Judeo-Christian tradition that had its own anxieties about physical gifts. The treatment of the story of Cain and Abel in Genesis is revealing.[24] As it stands, the Genesis account is enigmatic:[25]

> Abel was a shepherd, and Cain a husbandman. And it came to pass after many days, that Cain offered, of the fruits of the earth, gifts to the Lord. Abel also offered of the firstlings of his flock, and of their fat: and the Lord had respect to

Abel, and to his offerings. But to Cain and his offerings he had no respect: and Cain was exceedingly angry, and his countenance fell.[26]

The Genesis account of the first gift-offering appears to be all about matter: Abel offered a lamb, and it was accepted; Cain offered grain, and it was rejected. For later commentators this was troubling: surely the Lord did not judge the giver merely by looking at the matter of the gift. The Jewish exegete Philo of Alexandria (d. 50 CE) had sought to find a deeper moral explanation: Cain's central failing was that he loved and esteemed himself above God; this was revealed by his lateness in giving 'in the course of time' and failure to give the first fruits, whereas Abel gave 'the firstlings of his flock'.[27] He had thus transgressed against the instructions to set the first fruits aside for the Lord. More importantly for Philo, however, was that Cain's slowness revealed his ingratitude and self-love. If we are truly grateful to God and attribute our achievements to him, 'we shall run and leap to meet our master'.[28] Philo's focus on Cain's spiritual failure was also taken up in Christian exegesis. Gregory the Great (d. 604), in his *Moralia in Job*, pointed out that since Scripture mentioned Cain before his sacrifices and Abel before his, it was clear that God did not accept 'Abel by virtue of his offering, but by virtue of Abel the gifts offered were well pleasing'.[29] The primacy of intention in determining the value of giving was central to early Christian writing. According to the apostle Paul: 'Every one [should give] as he hath determined in his heart, not with sadness, or of necessity: for God loveth a cheerful giver.'[30] It is perhaps not surprising that Christian writers sought to adopt Seneca, one going so far as to concoct a spurious letter exchange between Seneca and Paul in which they are made to express their mutual admiration.[31]

In the twelfth century direct engagement with classical texts increased, and *De beneficiis* experienced an 'explosion' of interest. The stoic treatise was also extensively reworked to suit the interests of Christian elite audiences in the form of abbreviated manuscripts, *florilegia*, collections of choice sayings by ancient authors, and incorporation into didactic literature. This helped cement the idea in Western European elite culture that virtuous people would consider the thought more than the physical gift.[32] The renaissance saw new interest in Seneca's work: Erasmus of Rotterdam (d. 1536) edited and published *De beneficiis* in 1515 and Martin Luther (d. 1546) drew on Seneca's image of free, intention-focused generosity in formulating his radical re-emphasizing of the freedom of God's gift of grace.[33] Technological change and intellectual fashions conspired to enable Seneca's work to wider audience in more direct form than it had in the Middle Ages; between 1569 and 1614 no less than three translations of *De beneficiis* appeared in English alone.[34]

Throughout the Middle Ages and the early modern period there was a wide audience for the idea that gifts ought to be about more than matter. Yet the physical matter of the gift, their material value, beauty and origins, remained central to social and political life. Arguably, the materiality of gifts was also one of the characteristics that made them so attractive for late medieval and early modern elites. The Habsburg imperial family provides a useful cluster of examples. Fernand Braudel famously stated that for the Habsburgs, rulers of an empire that stretched across three continents, 'Distance was public enemy number one'.[35] Gifts not only helped overcome this but derived further power and glory from it. Gifts from distant lands, especially those whose material substance marked out their exotic qualities, demonstrated the ability to conquer distance. Emperor Charles V (d. 1558) used exotic objects extracted from his far-flung domains to impress his European rivals. None were more spectacular than the Aztec treasures sent by Hernán Cortés (d. 1547). When Cortés's first treasures, including a spectacular golden wheel and featherworks from unfamiliar American birds, arrived in 1520, Charles spun them as gifts, evidence of a powerful and prestigious new alliance. The Venetian ambassador described how: 'His Majesty summoned me for an audience and showed me himself the presents sent to him by the ruler of the lands newly discovered.'[36]

In Sabine Sommerer's chapter below, we see a striking example of the Habsburgs' ability to bridge space through generosity: a young Indian elephant sent to the Portuguese Prince John Manuel (d. 1554), sent on by him to his fiancée Joanna (d. 1573), daughter of Charles V, and then once more to her cousin, Maximilian II of Austria (d. 1576), to serve as the star of Maximillian's entrance into Vienna in 1552. The exotic attraction of this animal was so enduring that even its bones became the object of artistic display and elite self-fashioning after its death. When gifts that matched the Habsburg imperial self-fashioning were not forthcoming, this was a source of frustration: in 1606 one of the Habsburg demands in peace negotiations with the Ottoman Empire was that 'the sultan send gifts worthy of an emperor at last'.[37] Objects originating in the natural resources of a prince's country could be equally useful for princely exchange, especially when further refined through the scientific and artistic craftsmanship of their subjects, as seen in the *Kunstkammer* gifts of Charles V's grand-nephew, Emperor Rudolf II (d. 1612).[38]

Besides imperial grand-standing and displays of humanist learning, the matter of the gift could also be used to send signals and make connections of a very different order. The women of the Habsburg family in particular made use of gifts to emphasize their connection and love for Charles V. 'Wherever he might be', Charles' younger sister, Queen Catalina of Portugal (d. 1578), would send him

> care packages from Lisbon containing delicacies and other gifts that she hoped would please him: scented gloves and embroidered handkerchiefs, ginger and cinnamon, marmalade and conserves that she made herself.[39]

Empress Isabella of Portugal (d. 1539), Charles' wife, matched her sister-in-law's preserves with more romantically charged gifts from her own hand. In 1537, she sent her husband a 'letl'e flower of silke of her owne making, enclosed in a box'. Silk was of course a luxury good, but still, as the English diplomat who reported the gift noted, it 'was not worth a cople of ducketts'.[40] What made the flower important was the fact that the empress had made it with her own hand: a tangible demonstration of love through an act of time-consuming labour that aligned with contemporary ideals of the dutiful, skilled and devoted wife. Here too gifts helped, in a different way, to overcome the challenges of distance.[41]

Sign of love, knowledge, virtue and power, the matter of the gift was central to the many roles that gifts fulfilled in the late medieval and early modern world. In the chapters below we approach exchanged objects from different angles, exploring the ways in which actors utilized the material form of objects to communicate with recipients and wider audiences and how they thought about the role of matter in exchanges human and divine.

\*\*\*

In the first chapter of this book Anna Boeles Rowland explores the 'gifty' object par-excellence: the ring. Rings had long been a cherished token of devotion and alliance. In the later Middle Ages, as Boeles Rowland shows, it became increasingly associated with marriage. The meaning of any individual ring-giving was, however, open to challenge. Unless witnesses could be produced who could testify that the male ring giver had publicly proclaimed the gift to symbolize a desire for marriage, young women, especially those in a vulnerable socio-economic position, risked being accused of having received it – not as an honourable token – but as material reward for sexual favours.

In her chapter Boeles Rowland demonstrates the value of a material perspective for studies of gift-giving. She follows the 'life-cycle' of late medieval marriage rings, from production, over their starring role in courtship and the marriage ceremony, on to the role they played within the marriage and even beyond the death of one of the parties. Looking at the production of rings, Boeles

Rowland highlights the differences in the material objects available to the rich and the poor. While most people would have to make do with mass-produced 'fair rings', the wealthy patronized goldsmiths and were thus able to exercise more agency in the design of wedding rings and the selection of gemstones associated with fidelity and other virtues. But alongside these financial and material considerations, familial sentiments and rituals, such as the passing down of rings as gifts from parents to children, also enhanced their significance. In the marriage ceremony the ring was sprinkled with holy water and was thus 'transformed into something infused with spiritual potential', a small piece of holy matter placed at the heart of the family unit. Equally fascinating is Boeles Rowland's finding of the way in which 'the marital ring remained symbolically charged', even after the death of one of the parties and 'often resisted re-allocation as a simple "ring"'. It became what Rowland calls a 'material mnemonic', playing a key role in commemorating a marriage and a family's history. Sometimes they would be passed down to serve as marriage rings once again, while other rings were returned to the church to serve as a link between the family, their church and their community.

Sabine Sommerer's chapter continues the exploration of the relationship between meaning, matter and memory. Here, however, the focus shifts from the exchanges of ordinary Londoners to the very pinnacle of society. Sommerer studies depictions of chairs as gifts in both literary and narrative sources and looks in details at three surviving chairs. The first is the Cathedra Petri in the Vatican, given by Charles the Bald (d. 877) to St Peter on Christmas Day 875 on the occasion of his imperial coronation. The second, the 'Barcelona Chair', is also believed to have been a royal gift, probably by King Martin I the Humane of Aragon (d. 1410). Gifts of chairs, Sommerer argues, 'embodies' the giver, even more than most gifts because they encouraged audiences to visualize the seated giver upon it: In the case of thrones of course, it was the giver sitting in majesty that would be so visualized, making donations of thrones to churches an act both of humble piety and of royal self-assertion.

The third chair under investigation bears witness to a still more dramatic story of exchange and commemoration, a story that is, furthermore, 'narrated directly through the chair object itself'. The 'Elephant Chair' in the Benedictine Abbey of Krems is a mobile seat constructed out of four elephant bones, commissioned by Sebastian Huetstocker, mayor of Vienna, in 1553. As we saw above, the elephant, originally from India, had been given to Maximilian II for his ceremonial *adventus* into Vienna in 1552, an event that Sebastian had helped organize. When the elephant died the following year, Sebastian was given the bones, which were not only fashioned into a chair but also inscribed with an account of its long journey and images of the ceremonial entry in 1552. With this chair, Sebastian Huetstocker was able both to connect himself to a prestigious chain of exchanges and to preserve the memory of the grand ceremony he had helped arrange for his prince.

Gustavs Strenga continues the exploration of spectacular objects and the way in which they were used to control and preserve the memory of grand ceremonies. Strenga investigates the entry of Silvester Stodewescher (d. 1479) in Riga, as the city's archbishop in June 1449. It was a contentious occasion. Silvester was a burgher's son and the former chaplain of Konrad von Erlichshausen (d. 1449), the Grand Master of the Teutonic Order, and the rivalry between the cathedral chapter of Riga and the Order went back to the early days of the Christian mission in the Baltic in the thirteenth century. Silvester's appointment was a major coup for the Order. During the entry, Silvester had to negotiate his relationship with various parties, both those present, namely the canons of Riga, the secular vassals of the see and the city councillors, and absent, most importantly, his patron Konrad. Silvester had been understandably anxious about the welcome that awaited him, wondering whether the vassals would do to him what the knights of Henry II of England (d. 1189) had done to Thomas Becket, archbishop of Canterbury (d. 1170), three centuries previously. Two weeks after his entry, Silvester wrote a letter that described description of events for Konrad. Gifts play a key role in his account. Strenga shows how the parties used gifts to demonstrate trust and establish the basis for good working relationships as Silvester approached his see. He also captures the joy of the middle-class Silvester catapulted into the rich material surroundings of a prince of the Church. Silvester gives pride of place to one of Konrad's gifts: a gilded and bejewelled cross, containing relics of the Holy Cross, which Silvester placed over his vestments during his entry into the cathedral. The cross was a signal to his new subjects of his powerful connections, but also a signal to Konrad of Silvester's continuing loyalty. Perhaps Silvester feared sharing Becket's fate in another way as well. He did not want, like that other burger's son raised to an archbishopric by a great prince, to be accused of forgetting the gifts of his erstwhile master.[42]

The substance of precious objects and the way in which this, and the objects' biographies, contributed to elite self-fashioning is also central to Ruth Noyes' chapter. This explores the exchange of precious objects between Duke Cosimo III de' Medici (d. 1723) in Florence, capital of the grand Duchy of Tuscany, on the one hand, and Michał Kazimierz (d. 1682) and Mikołaj Stefan Pac (d. 1684) in Vilnius, one of the two capitals of the Polish-Lithuanian Commonwealth, on the other. These princes exchanged 'horses, medicines, furs, ermine, polar bears, amber, ivory, gold, and diamonds' across a distance of over 2,000 kilometres. Noyes studies the rich archival material attesting to these exchanges and their meanings for contemporaries. The materiality of the gifts was rich in significance: the medicine chest sent north was an opportunity to showcase the expertise of the Medici workshops, the Turkish stallion sent south showed Polish-Lithuanian martial success against shared Muslim opponents. Italian parmesan added an exotic flavour to the feasts of the Pac court. As Noyes shows, the distance that the gifts travelled was part of the glory that the exchange brought to the two princely houses. It demonstrated the reach of their power and their ability to pull into their orbit objects, animals and individuals from the other side of the continent.

The most spectacular objects exchanged were relics from the Polish-Lithuanian prince St. Kazimierz Jagiellończyk (canonized 1602) and the Italian noblewoman Maria Maddalena de Pazzi (canonized 1669). Noyes explores how the Pac used amber in Kazimierz's elaborate reliquary and accompanying gifts. They were a 'Baltic translation of the Medicean medicinal chest', demonstrating that the Baltic could match Florentine technology and art. Amber was spectacularly and usefully (to both parties in the exchange) marked as northern. Its intrinsic physical qualities made it 'exegetically suited to reliquaries'. Amber reacted to human touch: becoming warm and acquiring an electric charge, even releasing 'a fragrance redolent of Church incense, the sweet smell ascribed to the incorrupt bodies of saints'.

Holy matter coming alive is also the subject of Mads Heilskov's contribution which investigates the cult of living images in fourteenth- and fifteenth-century Italy, focusing on the cult of Santa Maria delle Carceri in Prato which had miraculously come alive in 1484. Heilskov brings together living images and the ex-voto offerings that supplicants brought to them. These exchanges have been dismissed as manifestations of popular culture and popular religion, distanced from the theological and artistic achievements of Renaissance Italy. Heilskov begins by exploring how the image of the Virgin in Prato was animated, thus acquiring its own particular 'personality'. Heilskov points out that the material context in which the image was found, an old, abandoned prison, became central to the story of the Santa Maria delle Carceri. The transformation of this physical context exemplified its ability to heal and consecrate matter. The relationship between the incarnated image and the material it was made of was ambiguous: on the one hand, there was a determination to present it as a particular manifestation of the Virgin with its own singular story; on the other, copies and representations of the Santa Maria delle Carceri also worked miracles.

Heilskov compares this with the ex-votive offerings, costly offerings but not simply payments in kind. Most of the objects offered were marked by their connection to the supplicant's body. Heilskov sees them as giving 'tangible form to the ephemeral hopes' of the pilgrims. Wax was particularly favoured because its plasticity enabled it 'to mimic the human form and produce a skin-like surface'. Objects that had touched the supplicant or were shaped in their image could work as 'stand-ins' for them: enabling them 'to be eternally present in the proximity of the living image within the walls of the sanctuary', a further doubling and manifestation responding to the miraculous manifestation of the Virgin. Such prestigious commemoration became the object of competition: in 1401 Florence forbade those who were not citizens or members of its greater guilds from placing figurative ex-votos in Florentine Churches.

The relationship between the supernatural and worldly matter, and the commemoration of interactions between the two, is also the focus of Sari Katajala-Peltomaa's contribution. Her chapter focuses on offerings to Saint Nicholas of Tolentino (canonized 1446) and in particular the votive tablets offered up in cases of demonic possession, which became increasingly popular in the fifteenth century. Katajala-Peltomaa argues that these offered opportunities to 'personalize religion, give meaning to past experiences, and narrate them to the surrounding community'. The offerings, a form of gift-exchange, were part of a relationship between the supplicant and the saint, but also with the wider community. It was 'simultaneously personal, private even and shared, public and visible to others', an opportunity to perform and shape one's identity in the eyes of the community. This was particularly important in the case of those who had been previously possessed, as a mark of their reintegration into the community.

As Katajala-Peltomaa points out, these offerings touched on a topic that became the subject of increased debate towards the end of the Middle Ages: 'gifty' exchanges with the divine. Only when infused by the recovering supplicant's spiritual devotion did the material gifts become acceptable as offerings to St Nicholas. This process mirrored the way in which the saint's intervention had driven out the malign spirit from the supplicant's body. Katajala-Peltomaa raises important questions about why tablets were so popular a gift. These were not luxurious objects, and it seems that 'humility was essential when approaching the divine'. Matter was central to the interaction with the divine, but it had to be handled with care so as to offer a message of devotion and respectability.

The place of matter in exchanges with the divine is also central to Poul Grinder-Hansen's chapter. Here, the focus is on charitable giving to the poor in Denmark, and at the heart of a newly created Protestant polity. The Danish Lutheran Church taught, in line with Luther's teachings, that charitable acts such as almsgiving could not make the faithful more acceptable to God. It has often been assumed that this led to a decline in charitable giving in early modern Denmark. But as Grinder-Hansen shows, charitable obligations continued to be important to elite benefactors.

Charity's centrality was made manifest in the many sturdy alms boxes that were placed near the entrance doors to churches. These were often decorated with inscriptions and images stressing the importance of charitable giving, and often presenting ideas more accommodating to the idea of divine reciprocity than the formal theology of the Church allowed. A favourite topic, and one that may have struck a particular note with elite churchgoers, was the figure of Lazarus from the parable of Dives and Lazarus. This tells the story of the rich Dives who went 'clothed in purple and fine linen; and feasted sumptuously every day' but who was condemned to Hell for failing to share his goods with the poor, diseased Lazarus.[43] Whether charity was understood to elicit divine reciprocation or was merely as the 'visible result' of a pure Christian faith, a correct attitude to the poor and to one's material goods was an essential part of virtue. Grinder-Hansen emphasizes a point we have also encountered in Katajala-Peltomaa and Heilskov's contributions: that charitable giving was not only an act conducive for salvation, but also a gesture of social communication. As Grinder-Hansen notes, the placement of the alms box made the act of charity particularly visible to the wider community.

Community and the role of material objects in creating them are also central to our final chapter by Philipp Höhn. This chapter focuses on the role of objects in the formation of identity and community in Hanseatic cities in the later, Middle Ages and especially those that had been 'violently taken'. These, Höhn argues, were just as important for identity formation for mercantile communities as they were for aristocratic families. Höhn focuses on three cases: the weapons and banners seized from the privateer Hans Kniphof by the city of Hamburg in 1525, which were displayed above the pulpit in the cathedral. This display, Höhn argues, was intended to have a stabilizing effect, demonstrating the efforts of Hamburg's elites, whose leadership was by no means uncontested, in protecting their community. The second case, the seizure of a painting of the Last Judgement by mercenaries working for the city of Gdańsk in 1473 under legally dubious circumstances, shows a very different process of commemoration. The circumstances of its capture were not helpful for community building, so it was elided, except within the social circle directly associated with its seizure. It was likely this circle that donated the painting to the church of St Mary in Gdańsk. Höhn's final case study, from Lübeck, concerns the banner of another so-called pirate, a captain in the service of Christian II of Denmark (d. 1559), which had been seized in 1526. This banner was part of a 'topography of objects', which included paintings and practices in the communal heart of the city telling the story of Lübeck's long struggles with the kings of Denmark. Höhn concludes, like Noyes, by urging us to read gifts in context, as 'part of networks of objects, texts and performances', incorporating past and present exchanges and those expected in the future.

Miri Rubin, finally, concludes our volume, as she did the workshop, with reflections on the papers and pointing to further perspectives.

## Notes

1  Marcel Mauss, 'Essai sur le don: Forme et raison de l'échange dans les sociétés archaïques', *L'Année sociologique* 1 (1923–24): 30–186, for an excellent introduction and translation, see Jane I. Guyer, *The Gift: Expanded Edition* (Chicago: Hau Books, 2016), here 58. For a very helpful overview of the historiography of the gift in medieval history – and of scholars' engagement with Mauss, see Arnoud-Jan A. Bijsterveld, *Do ut des: Gift Giving, Memoria, and Conflict Management in the Medieval Low Countries* (Hilversum: Verloren, 2007), 17–50.

2  See especially the introductions: Gadi Algazi, 'Introduction: Doing Things with Gifts', in *Negotiating the Gift: Pre-Modern Figurations of Exchange*, ed. Gadi Algazi, Valentin Groebner and Bernhard Jussen (Göttingen: Vandenhoeck und Ruprecht, 2003) and Janet L. Nelson, 'Introduction', in *The Languages of Gift in the Early Middle Ages*, ed. Wendy Davies and Paul Fouracre (Cambridge: Cambridge University Press, 2010).

3  Natalie Zemon Davis, *The Gift in Sixteenth-Century France* (London: The University of Wisconsin Press, 2000), Ilana Krausman Ben-Amos, *The Culture of Giving Informal Support and Gift-Exchange in Early Modern England* (Cambridge: Cambridge University Press, 2008), Felicity Heal, *The Power of the Gift: Gift Exchange in Early Modern England* (Oxford: Oxford University Press, 2014).

4  *Global Gifts: The Material Culture of Diplomacy in Early Modern Eurasia*, ed. Zoltán Biedermann, Anne Gerritsen and Giorgio Riello (Cambridge: Cambridge University Press, 2018), *Gift and Tribute in Early Modern Diplomacy: Afro-Eurasian Perspectives: Diplomatica* 2 (2020).

5 Susan Yi Sencindiver, 'New Materialism', in *Oxford Bibliographies: Literary and Critical Theory*, ed. Eugene O'Brien (Oxford: Oxford University Press, 2017), for useful introductions, see Stacey Alaimo and Susan J. Hekman, 'Introduction: Emerging Models of Materiality in Feminist Theory', in *Material Feminisms*, ed. Stacey Alaimo and Susan J. Hekman (Bloomington: Indiana University Press, 2008), Diana Coole and Samantha Frost, 'Introducing the New Materialisms', in *New Materialisms: Ontology, Agency, and Politics*, ed. Diana Coole and Samantha Frost (Durham, NC: Duke University Press, 2010) and Samuel Diener, 'New Materialisms', *The Year's Work in Critical and Cultural Theory* (published online 18 June 2020).

6 I cite Gadi Algazi, 'Introduction', 12 and Nelson, 'Introduction', 3 precisely because they have been so influential.

7 Mónica Cano Abadía, 'New Materialisms: Re-Thinking Humanity within an Interdisciplinary Framework', in *Phenomenological Anthropology, Psychiatry, and Psychotherapy in Theory and Practice: Special Issue of InterCultural Philosophy* 1 (2018): 169, see *The Nonhuman Turn*, ed. Richard Grusin (Minneapolis: University of Minnesota Press, 2015).

8 For other calls for more engagement with the material conditions underpinning symbolic communication, see Philippe Buc, *Dangers of Ritual: Between Early Medieval Texts and Social Scientific Theory* (Princeton: Princeton University Press, 2001), 261, Christine Carpenter, 'Introduction: Political Culture, Politics and Cultural History', in *The Fifteenth Century IV: Political Culture in Late Medieval Britain*, ed. Linda Clark and Christine Carpenter (Woodbridge: Boydell & Brewer, 2004), 6.

9 See Susanne Lettow, 'Turning the Turn: New Materialism, Historical Materialism and Critical Theory', *Thesis Eleven* 140 (2017).

10 Literary scholars have characteristically gone further in making objects central to their investigations, see for instance Kellie Robertson, 'Medieval Things: Materiality, Historicism, and the Premodern Object', *History Compass* 5 (2008): 1060–1080 and now Bettina Bildhauer, *Medieval Things: Agency, Materiality, and Narratives of Objects in Medieval German Literature and Beyond* (Columbus: The Ohio State University Press, 2020).

11 Mayke de Jong, 'The Foreign Past: Medieval Historians and Cultural Anthropology', *Tijdschrift voor Geschiedenis* 109 (1996): 323–39, 327 n. 8, see also Janet L. Nelson, 'Introduction', in *Languages of Gift*, 5.

12 Bijsterveld, *Do ut des*, 40.

13 Chris Wickham, 'Compulsory Gift Exchange in Lombard Italy, 650–1150', in *Languages of Gift*, 214; Nelson, 'Introduction', 14.

14 *Histoire des ducs de Normandie et des rois d'Angleterre*, ed. Francisque Michel (Paris: Renouard et cie, 1840), 150–1, English translation in *History of the Dukes of Normandy and the Kings of England by the Anonymous of Béthune*, trans. Janet Shirley (London: Routledge, 2021), 147; John Gillingham, 'The Anonymous of

Béthune, King John and Magna Carta', in *Magna Carta and the England of King John*, ed. Janet S. Loengard (Woodbridge: Boydell Press, 2010), 35–6.

15 See, for instance, John Watts, *Henry VI and the Politics of Kingship* (Cambridge: Cambridge University Press, 1996), 110.

16 Jean de Joinville, *Vie de Saint Louis*, ed. Jacques Monfrin (Paris: Dunod, 1995), 661–2 English translation, *Joinville and Villehardouin: Chronicles of the Crusades*, trans. Caroline Smith (London: Penguin, 2008), 311.

17 On 'biographies of objects', see especially Arjun Appadurai, 'Introduction: Commodities and the Politics of Value', in Arjun Appadurai (ed.), *The Social Life of Things: Commodities in Cultural Perspective* (Cambridge: Cambridge University Press, 1986), 3–63.

18 C.S. Jaeger, *Ennobling Love: In Search of a Lost Sensibility* (Philadelphia: University of Pennsylvania Press, 1999), 5.

19 'Divites divitibus dant, ut sumant ibi, et occurrunt munera relative sibi: lex est ista celebris, quam fecerunt scribi, si tu michi dederis, ego dabo tibi', Thomas Wright's *Political Songs of England: From the Reign of John to That of Edward II*, ed. and trans. T. Wright, introduction by P.R. Coss (Cambridge: Cambridge University Press, 1996), 18.

20 Aristotle, *Nicomachean Ethics*, 4. 1120b 7–11, trans. H. Rackham, *Aristotle in 23 volumes, xix, The Nicomachean Ethics*, Loeb Library (Cambridge, MA: Harvard University Press, 1968), 193.

21 'beneficium non in eo quod fit aut datur, consistit, sed in ipso dantis aut facientis animo.' Seneca, *De beneficiis*, 1.1.3, 1.6.1, trans. John W. Basore, *Seneca: Moral Essays, Volume III* (Cambridge, MA: Harvard University Press), 23. On this, see Miriam T. Griffin, *Seneca on Society: A Guide to De beneficiis* (Oxford: Oxford University Press, 2013).

22 'Inperiti autem id, quod oculis incurrit et quod traditur possideturque, solum notant', Seneca, *De beneficiis*, 1.5.1–6.

23 Neil Coffee, 'Ovid Negotiates with His Mistress: Roman Reciprocity from Public to Private', in *The Gift in Antiquity*, ed. Michael L. Satlow (Malden, MA: Wiley-Blackwell, 2013), Lars Kjær, *The Medieval Gift and the Classical Tradition: Ideals and The Performance of Generosity in Medieval England, 1000–1300* (Cambridge: Cambridge University Press, 2019), 23–35.

24 See Bernhard Jussen, 'Religious Discourses of the Gift in the Middle Ages: Semantic Evidences (second to twelfth centuries)', in *Negotiating the Gift*, 173–92.

25 John Byron, *Cain and Abel in Text and Tradition: Jewish and Christian Interpretations of the First Sibling Rivalry* (Leiden: Brill, 2011), 39.

26 Genesis 4:3–5, all translations from the Bible are from Douay-Rheims. http://www.drbo.org (accessed 18 February 2021).

27 Philo, 'On the Birth of Abel and the Sacrifices Offered by Him and by His Brother Cain', in *Philo in Ten Volumes (and Two Supplementary Volumes)*, vol. 2, ed. and

trans. F.H. Colson and G.H. Whitaker (Cambridge, MA: Harvard University Press, 1968), 52–3, 72, 133–5.
28  Philo, 'On the Birth of Abel and the Sacrifices Offered by Him and by His Brother Cain', 58–9, 64–9, 136.
29  Gregory the Great, *Moralia in Job*, 22.14.21–35, ed. M. Adriaen (3 vols., *Corpus Christianorum Series Latina* 143, Turnhout, 1979), v. ii, 1112.
30  2 Cor. 9:7, on Paul's idea of generosity, see especially: John M. G. Barclay, *Paul and the Gift* (Grand Rapids: Eerdmans Publishing Company, 2015).
31  Griffin, *Seneca on Society*, 164–8.
32  L.D. Reynolds, '*De beneficiis* and *De clementia*', in L.D. Reynolds (ed.), *Texts and Transmission: A Survey of the Latin Classics* (Oxford: 1983), 364, Kjær, *Medieval Gift*, 42–65, 121–49.
33  Risto Saarinen, *Luther and the Gift* (Tübingen: Mohr Siebeck: 2017), 38–57.
34  Heal, *Power of the Gift*, 17.
35  Fernand Braudel, *La Méditerranée et le Monde Méditerranéen à l'Epoque de Philippe II* (Paris: Colin, 1949), trans. by Geoffrey Parker, *Emperor: A New Life of Charles V* (New Haven: Yale University Press, 2019), 382, 653, n. 25.
36  Parker, *Emperor*, 347, Alessandra Russo, 'Cortés's Objects and the Idea of New Spain: Inventories as Spatial Narratives', *Journal of the History of Collections* 23 (2011).
37  Barbara Karl, 'Objects of Prestige and Spoils of War: Ottoman Objects in the Habsburg Networks of Gift-Giving in the Sixteenth Century', in *Global Gifts*, 126.
38  Ivana Horacek, 'The Art of Transformation: *Kunstkammer* Gifts Between Emperor Rudolf II and Elector Christian II of Saxony', *Studia Rudolphina* 13 (2013).
39  Parker, *Emperor*, 219.
40  Parker, *Emperor*, 213, 628, n. 34.
41  For a medieval perspective on elite women's use of objects, see Jitkse Jasperse, *Medieval Women, Material Culture, and Power: Matilda Plantagenet and Her Sisters* (Amsterdam: ARC Humanities Press, 2020).
42  Kjær, *Medieval Gift*, 103.
43  Luke 16:19.

1

# 'With this rynge': The materiality and meaning of the late medieval marriage ring

Anna Boeles Rowland

'What talk you of the posy or the value, You swore to me, when I did give it to you, That you would wear it till your hour of death.' So says Nerissa in Shakespeare's *The Merchant of Venice* upon discovering that her husband Gratiano had carelessly given away the token of her love, a posy ring which he had sworn never to take from his finger. The thoughtless exchange of this ring signifies a deeper lack of commitment, if he can give away this token of fidelity so easily, could he perhaps do the same with his wife? When his wife confronts him, he tries to dismiss her anger by belittling the gift, calling it a 'hoop of gold, a paltry ring' with a posy (the inscription within the inner band of the ring) that was "For all the world like cutlery's poetry, Upon a knife, 'Love me, and Leave me not.'" His argument is that the ring itself was an ordinary and massed produced thing, and therefore without value. Nerissa's response, outlined at the beginning of this chapter, is that this gift was more than its material properties but a symbol of his fidelity and love for her. Similarly, Portia chastises Gratiano for giving away such a precious object, saying 'To part so slightly with your wife's first gift, A thing stuck on with oaths upon your finger, And so riveted with faith upon your flesh.'[1] The ring is described here as a spouse's first gift, and as such it is intimately connected to the relationship of man to wife. It can also be read as a test of loyalty and a gift that demanded to be remembered. To hold someone in mind being in itself an act of fidelity, and Gratiano's actions in giving away this ring are therefore seen as a betrayal of his wife. *The Merchant of Venice* offers an excellent example of how rings could act as symbols for internal values and actions. This play reveals

---

I would like to thank Lars Kjær and Gustavs Strenga for including this chapter in the present volume and for their helpful comments. Thanks are also due to Rachel Delman and Sally Bayley for their insights and suggestions.

the complicated emotions and values attached to the exchange of rings between spouses; in particular, the story of Gratiano's ring aptly illustrates how rings were thought to embody marital sentiments and promises, an act which could transform an ordinary object into something which held the very significance of the marital promise itself. Beginning with some of the cultural ideas expressed in Shakespeare's play, this chapter will examine the culture and practice of the exchange of rings during marriage celebrations in the later Middle Ages to argue that rings played a fundamental role in displaying the marital bond.

In *The Merchant of Venice* the ring is described as something which becomes part of the flesh, and this idea can be traced back to twelfth-century France in a story told by Guibert of Nogent. His story tells of a child bride whose marital ring was so embedded in her finger that she could not remove it.[2] Such descriptions conjure a viscerally grotesque image of the physical intimacy between person and thing as the ring becomes infused with the body of its wearer. In medieval Europe the giving of rings was a common practice to display loyalty and fidelity between friends and lovers, but rings were also ritually given to demarcate marital status.[3] From the twelfth century onwards marriage was created upon the declaration of the words of consent ('I take you') in the present tense, although a legitimate marriage was always followed by an ecclesiastical blessing. We can therefore say that marriage was – at its essence – a lay sacrament created when two people promised to take the other as spouse.[4] By the thirteenth century rings had begun to play an important role in marriage making as a visual and material symbol of marital consent.[5] However, it is not until the fourteenth and fifteenth centuries that we find detailed evidence of the making of marriage of ordinary men and women. Scholarship on later medieval marriage has highlighted how the exchange of rings, and other tokens, acted as socially significant markers of matrimony. In her study of marriage litigation in fifteenth-century Paris, Ruth Mazo Karras has shown that the acceptance of a ring given in the name of matrimony could act as convincing evidence of the existence of a previous contract of marriage.[6] Similarly, Jeremy Goldberg's study of marriage making in late medieval York demonstrates how the gift of rings was used to mark an agreement of marriage.[7] Both show how rings were used as proof of a marital contract and the significance of the gift in defining marital relationships. This chapter aims to address this phenomenon in detail using the marital litigation records from late fifteenth- and early sixteenth-century London. It owes a tremendous debt to Shannon McSheffrey's landmark study of the same. Although the exchange of consent outside the church was considered to be clandestine, McSheffrey has shown that three-quarters of the alleged contracts of marriage in late medieval London were made in extra-ecclesiastical settings, and that many of them were far from clandestine but respectable and an integral part of the making of marriage.[8] The norm therefore was for a couple to exchange present consent – often within a domestic setting – in front of their friends and family who acted as witnesses. The marriage was then publicly ratified by the calling of banns (proclamations in the local parish church of the contract) and then followed by a church blessing, and it was only after this final stage that a couple could cohabitate.

Evidence of these domestic ceremonies of consent is found in the records of the London Consistory Court, a church court whose role it was – in case of a dispute – to determine if someone had agreed to a marriage. This was determined on the basis of statements from those involved in an alleged marriage – would-be spouses, parents, friends and other witnesses.[9] In many ways these accounts can be read as stories – or legal narratives – in which people sought to give an accurate and believable account of what had happened. In the majority of cases their purpose was to uphold a marriage, and therefore, as McSheffrey points out, witnesses 'tended to emphasise the ways in which the "marital" process was normal rather than atypical'.[10] Therefore, whilst the marriages that appeared before the church court were disputed, they were retold to the court as having followed conventional customs. Domestic ceremonies of consent were often presented as ritualized and carefully choreographed events, in which space, gesture and the exchange of gifts played an important role in communicating sincerity and trustworthiness. McSheffrey has argued that whilst rings were exchanged to mark the surety of contract and to mark the progression of a marital relationship, they did not have the preeminent status they now have in modern Western culture.[11] This is undoubtedly true, but nevertheless in later medieval Europe visualizations of the sacrament of marriage, such as in Martianus Capella's *De Nuptiis Philologiae et Mercurii* produced in Norwich around 1400, were often indicated by the groom placing an outlandishly large ring on his bride's finger.[12] Whilst, in southern Europe, the exact moment of a marriage was thought to occur when a ring was placed upon the bride's finger, this event was known colloquially as the 'ring day'.[13] The argument of this chapter is that by using late medieval English court records alongside a variety of different source types, including testamentary records, church treatises, literary sources (romances, plays, etc.) and archaeological finds, we find that the exchange of rings was a powerful visual and material symbol of marital consent, and indeed became a material manifestation of the sacrament of marriage.[14]

This chapter also owes a debt to scholarship on the medieval and early modern gift, which in the last few decades has rejected the homogeneous model of the gift, and instead emphasized the importance of studying the gift in its own – often complex – context.[15] This is aptly surmised by Gadi Algazi in his introduction to 'Negotiating the Gift', in which he urges historians to consider the 'given cultural repertoires of models for shaping interactions' to pay attention to 'available vocabularies and recognised models of applying them'.[16] The categorization of a gift was often centred on social and cultural expectations, in terms of the performative nature of its exchange, and the appropriateness of the social status and character of both the giver and its recipient. This is what Natalie Davis has termed the 'register of the gift', which refers to the language and form of cultural expressions used to exchange gifts – manners, language, etiquette, mode of interaction and so on – and how the descriptions of particular gift-exchanges can add to our understanding of the politics of social relationships and their margins.[17]

The register of the medieval marital gift was one based on specific rituals, words and gestures. The defining featuring being that during the exchange of marital consent ring were often referred to as being given as a token. Tokens were a sub-category of gifts although in practice the meaning between gifts and tokens was often interchangeable. The language of tokens and signs was applied to things that were either hidden or internalized, the exchange of a material token therefore, in the form of a gift, externalized the willing and earnest consent of the couple, and crucial to its public acceptance. In 1495 Richard Fitzjames – who in 1506 was appointed to the bishopric of London to become head of its church courts – made reference in a sermon to 'vysyble synges and outward tokens'.[18] The language of tokens and signs was generally applied to things that were either hidden or internalized. Felicity Heal in her study of the politics of the early modern gift-giving has stated that the token was more explicitly directed to the signalling of intent than a more generic offering. By which she means that, as tokens acted as a manifestation of an internal thought, event or feeling, they were frequently used to advance a relationship in some way. In this context I analyse the gift and acceptance of the marriage ring as a material sign of an internal state of being and intention, that is the acceptance of the marital promise.

My argument will emphasize the significance of material culture in relation to late medieval marriage rings in three ways. Firstly, I will use archaeological finds and documentary descriptions to examine the worth, iconography and materiality of rings – classified as either courtship or marriage tokens – to consider how the physicality of such objects may have added value to the meaning of its exchange as a gift. Secondly, I will look at the ceremony of the exchange of rings as prescribed in the martial mass, as well as similar descriptions in domestic marriage contracts in late medieval London. I argue here that the exchange of rings was part of a communicative performance – involving words, space and gestures – to demonstrate the binding of two people as man and wife. Finally, I will consider what happens after the marriage ceremony had ended, to look at the afterlife of the marital ring. Here we will see how the marital ring remained symbolically charged even after the death of its recipient, and often resisted re-allocation as a simple 'ring'; rather, it retained its status as a material mnemonic of marriage. I have developed the term 'material mnemonic' to describe things that act as conductors of memory and propose that such objects were not just a prompt for memories, but were also implicitly tied to social assumptions, in this case marital fidelity.

## The materiality of the late medieval marriage ring

The material turn has compelled historians of the medieval and early modern gift to re-evaluate their sources and pay closer attention to how the materiality, or 'thingness' of an object, could have a meaning on its exchange as a gift. If a gift was something which was used to express or cement an intention or emotion, then the object was the thing with which this was done. Moreover, after its exchange as a gift it could independently evoke a variety of meanings and emotions over time. A discrete examination of the material gift is thus vital. Whilst materiality is often understood as the physical qualities or 'thingness' of an object, it also refers to the social life of such things and the meaning ascribed to them.[19] Roberta Gilchrist has, however, argued that the physical make-up of particular objects has been side-lined in the study of their social value.[20] The re-construction of the physical object is also constrained by the limitations of the source, as our knowledge of the rings exchanged at marriage is based, in the majority, on the testimony of third-party witnesses. Written accounts of extinct objects pose a problem for a material culture analysis as the very essence of the 'thingness' of objects – weight, texture, taste, smell – is lost to us.[21] As Linda Hurcombe put it, 'these losses reduce the perception of materials as material culture'.[22] The purpose of this section is therefore to re-centre the physicality of medieval-finger rings using archaeological finds and museum catalogue descriptions, from the V&A, Museum of London and the Portable Antiquities Scheme (PAS), alongside descriptions of the rings exchanged in the marital litigation records of the London Consistory. I will first consider the materials and industry that went into their production, how much they cost and where they could be purchased, before finally discussing how certain rings were decorated with stones, iconography and posies to embody marital fidelity.

Material culture scholarship on medieval and early modern finger-rings has so far been largely based on extant examples held in either public or private collections. Although undoubtedly providing useful information about how these rings were made, cut and decorated, such works are almost entirely focused on elite material culture which was deemed valuable enough to preserve and curate.[23] However, our knowledge of medieval finger-rings lower down the social scale has been significantly enhanced by archaeological scholarship on dress accessories, and the recent drive to study the personal significance of possessions, that is their 'use, significance and meaning, rather than their production, exchange or general trends in consumption'.[24]

Finger-rings were made by pouring molten metal in shaped and patterned moulds. They could then be decorated either by directly engraving onto the metal with a small tool or by applying embellishment using a hammer and punch technique.[25] The fastening of stones onto the bezel of a ring only became common from the fourteenth century onwards.[26] Cut stones were not as brilliant as they are today, and stones were often held either by continuous lip of metal or with a simple four or five claw prong setting.[27] Coloured glass was also a popular, and affordable, alternative to precious stones.[28] The process of making a finger-ring was not complicated; instead, their value was tied to the materials with which it was made, and the skill and expertise that went into its decoration. In London rings could be purchased in the shops of coppersmiths and pewters, but also at markets and fairs, and in sixteenth-century England, tokens were also referred to as 'fairings' because of their connections to fairs.[29] More specialized and expensive rings were made and sold by goldsmiths, who sold their wares on Foster Lane, near Cheapside and St. Pauls Cathedral, in the City of London, and which gave the couple (or more usually the man) some form of agency in the design of their wedding rings. Marriage making is best understood as a progress from courtship to the exchange of consent and a church blessing, and the exchange of token reflected this complex progress of negotiation. Rings were given to demonstrate, establish and cement a romantic interest, and we see the type of token often reflecting the stage of a relationship, with cheaper trinkets and dress accessories marking its beginning.[30] The expense of a gift relative to the worth of the person who gave it can therefore be a strong indicator of the importance of the gift and the value of the relationship it was given to represent.

It is rare, however, to find a reference to the value of a ring in the marital litigation records. The exception being John Holder's marital suit against Agnes Chamberlyn in 1471 which gave a valuation of the tokens he had given her, including three gold rings worth 6s 8d each. John Holder's occupation is not recorded, although two of his witnesses were respectively described as a silkwoman and a print maker, both respectable if not prosperous trades.[31] Based on the things he purchased, as part of marriage negotiations, John Holder appears to be towards the top end of the scale. It is impossible to tell whether these prices have been artificially inflated or are a true reflection of their value, but they indicate the high expenditure that *could* be expected as part of the marital process. The identification of rings as either silver or gold is somewhat of a false friend, as excavations of gold finger rings between 1350 and 1450 have shown that their gold content varied between 45 per cent and 75 per cent.[32] The value of a ring was based on the level of precious metal used in its production, but as it is not possible to access this relative value we cannot estimate its worth. As a general rule, gifts of gold or gilt appeared more frequently as a potential marriage advanced.

The value of marriage rings was also tied to their object biography, that is, its life-cycle, cultural markers and entanglement with the events in a person's life.[33] A good example of this is the practice of sons receiving rings from their parents (often their fathers) to be used as a marital ring. In 1483 Thomas Ostrich gave his son (also Thomas) a 'litle ring with a diamond if God fortune him to time coming to wede a woman [and] to geve yt unto her'. The description of this ring further emphasized its symbolic value; 'two rings knit together at the end of a lace and placed in a flat leather box in Thomas Ostrich's study'.[34] This appears to be gimmel ring, a ring made from two intertwined halves and getting its name from the Latin *gemmellus* (twin), and its placement of this ring within a secure box, away from the rigours of daily life, further emphasizes its value to Thomas Ostrich.[35] In London, 1467–1524, there are five cases in which a ring exchanged between a couple was described as a gimmel ring.[36] In four of the cases the exchange of the ring followed an exchange of consent or another form of commitment to matrimony.[37] This suggests that the iconography of the gimmel representing a marital partnership was recognized and adhered to in social practice. Thomas Ostrich's shows that the materiality of this ring was given added value by being bequeathed for use in the making of his son's marriage. The gift of a ring for a child's future spouse, however, shows the importance of family in every aspect of the making of a marriage and indicated that a ring could hold memories beyond its immediate role as a symbol of marriage. The practice of bestowing a lover with a ring given by a parent is also featured as tongue-in-cheek scene in Chaucer's Miller's Tale, in which the Absolon attempts to entice a kiss from Alison with the words 'I haue thee broght a ryng/ My mooder yaf it me/ so god me saue/ Fful fyn it is.' All does not go to plan, however, as Alison's lover Nicholas tries to trick Absolon by sticking his arse out the window for him to kiss instead.[38]

Objects accrue value by their design. The stone in the little ring given to Thomas Ostrich by his father was a diamond; in the Middle Ages diamonds were known for their unbreakable quality which was seen to symbolize the constancy of the marital vow. The thirteenth-century French canonist Guillaume Durand described the diamond as 'unbreakable and love unquenchable, and stronger than death'.[39] The diamond was therefore a popular choice of stone for a marital ring; in 1475 Camilla of Aragon and Constanzo Sforza chose a diamond ring because of its association with abiding love and fidelity.[40] The gift of a diamond ring also occurs in the London marital litigation records, when in 1512 Ann Leventhorp admitted to receiving 'a gold ring with a stone called a diamond'.[41] However, the gift of a diamond ring should not be read as synonymous with marital consent as they could be given as courtship gifts; for example, when the marriage negotiations between Robert Cely and Joan Hart failed in 1480, they demanded she return the courtship gifts he had given her, which included a gold ring with a diamond.[42]

Out of sixty rings mentioned in the marital litigation records twenty are described as enamelled, decorated or otherwise gilded, but only nine are described as having a stone. The predominant description of plain bands does not automatically suggest that these objects did not have any iconographical details. The Museum of London, for example, holds a number of plain gold posy rings, with messages of love inscribed on the inner band, suggesting that these were private messages to be seen by the couple alone.[43] The exchange of posy rings became increasingly common from the fifteenth to the seventeenth centuries (as we have seen in *The Merchant of Venice*),[44] and the inner bands of these rings were inscribed with rhyming words or decorated with symbols, which spoke of private and intimate relationships. This suggests that there was some internal and unexpressed layer of meaning in the symbolism of ring, understood only to the couple in question. Standley has argued that posy rings were popular love tokens because '[whilst] the text would have expressed the giver's sentiment, the circular design of the ring would also perpetuate it'.[45] Messages of fidelity were popular posies: one found in Old Market Street in Usk, for example, read 'CONTINV FAITHFVL'.[46] Some posies had more explicit references to marital choice. For example, a ring found in Cawood, near York, read 'MY BETHROTHED IS WILLING', and another from Bishops Hull (Somerset) was inscribed with the words 'I licke my chois'.[47] The marriage ring given in 1596 by Mary Porredge to her bethrothed John Colyer was inscribed with the words 'yow have my harte till deathe departe', words taken directly from the marital vow.[48] The evidence strongly suggests that finger rings were used as vessels for communication on the importance of marital fidelity and the ethics of marriage. The emphasis on words linked to consent ('willing', 'choice', 'faithful') bears a similarity with the words of marriage consent and wider concepts of marital fidelity. As these inscriptions were on the inner band of the ring, and therefore only known by the couple themselves and the people they showed, they were private and tactile reminders of the fact that a wearer had consented to marriage and should be faithful to their partner.

A ring decorated with a stone, posy or formed of two parts in the case of the gimmel has all been identified as given in the name of marriage in late medieval London. Yet the majority are described by only their material (silver or gold). Reliance on third-party testimony limits an investigation into the relationship between the materiality and meaning of marital rings. However, a material culture perspective emphasizes the importance of making and commissioning of finger rings, and the significant thought and expense that went into buying and selecting a potential marital ring. The stone, decoration and material all held important symbolic significance mirroring contemporary ideas regarding marital fidelity and love. Rings givens by the family often indicate a different sort of value: familial love and sentiment rather than mere economic value. However, the ritual and social context was a complex and fundamental process which turned these things into something which represented the marital bond of two individuals.

## 'With this ring I thee wed'

Special emphasis was placed on the ring during the marriage liturgy. Before it was exchanged it had to be blessed, unless it had been blessed before. The groom placed it on a dish or a book and the priest would then sprinkle it with holy water.[49] The ring was thus transformed into something infused with spiritual potential made sacrament during the speaking of the marital vow 'with this rynge I thee wed and this gold and silver. I the geue and with my body. I the worshipe'.[50] The liturgy transformed the ring into a sacred object, and to reflect this women often bequeathed their marriage rings to churches, which will be discussed in the final section of this chapter. After the blessing the ring was placed on the body of the bride to materially, spiritually and physically bind a couple as man and wife. This exchange was described in the Sarum Missal as thus:

> Then shall the bridegroom places the ring upon the thumb of the bride saying, *In the name of the Father*; then upon the second finger, saying *and of the Son*; then upon the third finger, saying, *and of the Holy Ghost*; then upon the fourth finger, saying, *Amen*, and there let him leave it … because in that finger there is a certain vein which runs from thence as far as the heart; and inward affection, which ought to be fresh between them, is signified by the true ring of the silver.[51]

The materiality of the ring is activated by prayer and the solemnity of the occasion; however, the importance of the body is also a fundamental aspect of this ritual. The placement of the ring on the first, second and third finger mirrored the Lord's Prayer, signalling as Emma Lipton has argued the compatibility of marital affection with the 'the spirituality and grace of the Trinity'.[52] Its final resting place on the fourth finger connected to the heart, the seat of 'inward affection'. In the Middle Ages the heart was seen as the centre of cognition, and self-identity expression of earnest and truthful sentiments was thus seen as coming directly from the heart.[53] In marital litigation records a common formula for the contracting of marriage was 'May you find it in your heart to have me as your husband'.[54] The placement of the marital ring on the fourth finger turned it into a communicative vessel, reminding its wearer of the marital promise whilst also bestowing God's grace given to the ring through its blessing. Descriptions of the marital mass show how ritual infused the marital ring to the body. Marriage was a sacrament, and the ring was the instrument that materially embodied this sacred meaning.

Central to the marital mass was the blessing of the ring and its placement on the body. Prescriptive rather than in-situ evidence; however, we do see that similar weight and significance were placed on rings during domestic contracts of marriage. In 1469 William Love told the court that he had seen Lucy Braggis and Robert Pope exchange words of consent. After these words Robert kissed Lucy and gave her a ring, putting it on her finger whilst saying a blessing, 'in the name of the father and the son and the holy spirit'.[55] Prayer was an elevated form of speech, seen to come directly from the heart.[56] Robert Pope's actions imprinted this ring with a sacramental meaning similar to the performance of the priest during the marriage ceremony described above, animating the ring to embody the bond of marriage.[57] The incorporation of the symbolism of the marital liturgy in a case such as this must be placed in the context of the relationship between the laity and the church in late medieval England. Since the thirteenth century, the church had disseminated the importance of marriage as a sacrament, primarily through sermons, and the material and visual culture of the parish church.[58] Emma Lipton has argued that the growth in lay piety, alongside the power of the middling classes, in the fifteenth century saw an increased interest in the sacrament of marriage as a model for lay spirituality.[59] For late medieval London, Shannon McSheffrey has shown the crucial connection between urban respectability and the making of a proper marriage, and how domestic ceremonies of consent were a fundamental part of civic culture.[60] Open and public publicity of consent was the most crucial factor for the making of marriage in late medieval London, and we see this reflected in the exchange of rings.

But rings could also be used to create false marital testimonies. In the case of the widow Maude Knyff, she denied that she had exchanged contract with Robert Grene and alleged he had stolen a ring from her as false proof of matrimony. To counteract his claim she provided five[61] witnesses to attest to her exchange of consent with Thomas Torald, a self-styled gentleman who in 1469 was given a life grant of 6s 8d per annum for services to the city.[62] This contact took place around the same time as her alleged contract with Robert Grene and was noticeable for its publicity. Joan Bristall recalled how she went to Maude Knyff's house to hear how she was pledged to a certain man and upon arrival she found Thomas and Maude sitting together in the hall at its high table. In many late medieval London homes the hall was the post public place, and it was therefore a popular venue for the exchange of consent.[63] Maude then said to Joan, 'behold, here sits my husband', and Thomas called Maude his wife. The couple then exchanged consent whilst clasping hands. After this, Thomas Torald declared to the assembled witnesses 'behold, Maude, my wife', and Maude replied similarly, 'and you are my husband, behold the sign' (*Et vos estis maritus meus, Ecce signum*); at this point Maude held up the gold ring on her index finger of her right hand (*demonstrando anulum aureum super indicem dextere sue manus*), and they exchanged consent once more.[64] The multiple exchanges of consent and proclamations of marriage represented an extensive public display of matrimony, with the ring used as the external 'sign' of the veracity of consent and marking Maude Knyff's new status as a wife.

Rings played a significant role in domestic consent ceremonies. Here, the legal enforcement of marriage contract relied on the culture of witnessing. Whilst an unwitnessed marriage was still valid if both parties confessed to it, if one of the parties was unwilling a plaintiff needed the evidence from at least two credible witnesses to enforce a match.[65] Late medieval literature frequently included depictions of legal trials to explore both the legal nature of speech and the role of the audience in bearing witness.[66] The N-Town 'Marriage of Mary and Joseph' play (a compilation of religious play texts from East Anglia) draws attention to the culture of witnessing in the making of marriage. The exchange of consent lies at the heart of this text; Joseph says to his bethrothed 'I take the Mary, to wyff' and 'with thys ryng I wedde here ryff'.[67] The Middle English word 'ryff' or 'rif[e]' was an adverb which in this context meant 'openly' or 'manifestly' to communicate to the audience (his witnesses) his sincere willingness to wed.[68] Emma Lipton has argued that the form of his vow in the present tense made this marital contact legally enforceable, thereby highlighting its 'realism' and role of the audience as witnesses, who would presumably also act as witnesses to the marriage of their friends, family and neighbours.[69] The exchange of the ring, however, has been overlooked in Lipton's analysis. Yet, similarly to the N-Town play, in late medieval London rings were usually given after the exchange of marriage consent, often in name or token of marriage. For example, in 1521 Alice Gadbery and Thomas Chamberlyn exchanged consent in the house of William Brocket in front of a number of witnesses. After the exchange of consent, the couple kissed and Thomas gave his new wife a gold ring and placed it on her finger as token of marriage.[70] A token was connected to the signalling of intent, and similarly to the N-Town 'Marriage of Mary and Joseph' was used as a marker of the creation of the marriage bond, and the couple's acceptance of this. Crucially, however, unlike in the marital mass the exchange of rings in extra-ecclesiastical setting not only was tied to the mutually acceptance of the marital sacrament but was also a fundamental part of the culture of witnessing, and used as visible and material evidence of consent itself.

Where the status of a marriage was more ambiguous, the intention behind a ring exchange might also be more ambiguous. Agnes Eston's marriage suit gives a good example of how a ring could act as a false witness of a sincere promise of marriage. In 1494, Agnes Eston was asked by her suitor John Crosby why she did not wear the gold ring he had given her; her reply was that it was not in her power to wear such a thing. John's response was to take the ring, put it on her finger and asked her to wear it for love of him.[71] However, no witnessed – and therefore provable – consent to marriage materialized, thus despite that one of Agnes Eston's witnesses testified that John Crosby had said they were man and wife 'before God' the marriage was void. The context of this story is also very telling; Shannon McSheffrey has shown that John Crosby is likely to have been the son and heir of the London alderman Sir John Crosby and Agnes Eston meanwhile is likely to have been a servant of a far lower social-economic status. McSheffrey has further suggested that John Crosby may have seduced Agnes Eston whilst persuading her, and her employers, of his earnest intentions.[72] Agnes' concern about wearing this gold ring becomes more sympathetic in this context, a gold ring being something which a lowly servant would have felt uncomfortable wearing. John's re-gifting of this ring with his declaration of love appeared to have persuaded her of his intentions, however, misguided.

The receipt of a ring was also used as evidence of marital intention; in marital litigation records, it is often recorded whether a ring was received in gratitude. In 1469 Walter Olyfaunt and John Hornford both agreed that after Thomas Whetely and Joan Wylde had exchanged consent, Joan had gratefully received from Thomas a silver ring.[73] The continued possession of an object was used as evidence of an emotional connection, and thus implicit evidence of matrimony. In 1491 Joan Qualley was said to have received a gold ring from Robert Warde after they had exchanged contract, and a witness to this match said that 'she [Joan] gratefully accepted it and still keeps it with her'.[74] However, as rings were also used during courtship to demonstrate and gain affection, it was often important to demarcate a ring as a token of marriage. For example in 1522, Giles Slater is reported to have placed a 'stone' in a gold ring, which was then presented to Joan Watson by an intermediary who told that Master Giles desired her to 'take this ryng and put it on your finger'; she, however, refused until Giles could make a proper promise of marriage in person.[75] In the marital mass and medieval ceremonies of consent it was the man who gave the ring and put it on the finger of his new wife. Joan Watson's refusal to accept this ring, and put it on her own finger, demonstrates the importance of following the appropriate stages of the marital ritual. Consent had to be publicly exchanged, and it was only then that the new intimacy between man and wife was embodied through the act of placing a ring on the finger.

The first section of this chapter examined how the material object of the ring might embody meanings associated with marital fidelity. However, the creation of the marriage ring as the embodiment of a marital promise was tied to the context of its exchange. In a way it had to transcend its materiality to take on this ritual meaning. In late medieval England warnings were given to young women to avoid ambiguous gifts given in the name of marriage, because such tokens were so intrinsically connected to marriage making they were often erroneously considered to be persuasive evidence of marital intention by the young women, however insincere.[76] Without a properly witnessed exchange, a gift had the potential to cast doubt on the sexual reputation of women who may have accepted a private promise of matrimony alongside a gift and gone to bed with her untrustworthy betrothed. In *The Ring of Truth* Wendy Dolinger refers to something which she calls the 'Slut Assumption', which is that any piece of jewellery a woman owns is perceived as something which she must have gotten via a man either through licit means (in marriage) or illicit (in exchange for sex).[77] Dolinger's argument implies that women are more easily persuaded by the material allure of the gift (its stones, embellishments and so on) than men and therefore more likely to consent to accepting the gift and the obligations it came with.

This idea of women being easily influenced by the physical gift rather than its meaning and virtue has a classical precedent, and this has been extensively discussed in *The Medieval Gift and the Classical Tradition* by Lars Kjær.[78] The exchange of rings therefore had to be conducted publicly and unambiguously. In properly witnessed ceremonies of consent, we see how rings take on the role as a communicative vessel to demonstrate the creation of the marital bond. The final step was the blessing of the ring and its final exchange at the marital mass. Here we see how a ring was infused with the power to act as a mnemonic of the sanctity of the marital vows. We shall now address the role of marriage rings during and at the end of the marital life course.

## The life cycle of marriage rings

In 1530 Andrew Elvynger commissioned a brass monument to himself, his wife Ellen and their children to be placed in the parish church of All Hallows, Barking by the Tower. In this brass we see Andrew and Ellen Elvynger standing in profile facing each other, their hands clasped in prayer. They are dressed modestly in high-necked gowns but made of what appears to be heavy and expensive cloth, and Ellen has a girdle with a set of prayer beads attached to it around her waist. The design of this brass makes it clear that the couple are married, the direction of their gaze and their similar dress are all suggestive of a married couple. Ellen Elvynger is depicted with a kerchief covering her hair, a further indication of her status as a married woman. Most importantly, they are both wearing thick-banded wedding rings, and it is these rings which are in the centre of the brass monument to emphasize their importance. The couple mirror each other, with their rings displayed on the ring fingers of their hands which appear in the foreground: Andrew on his right hand and Ellen on her left. The funeral brass of Andrew and Ellen Elvynger is a visual construction of marital status, one in which the marriage ring played a starring role. However, documentary evidence of the role played by wedding rings during the life-cycle of a marriage is almost non-existent. It is only when spouses are separated (by either death or geographical distance) that we find glimpses of the use and value of marital rings. The materiality and iconography of rings (as discussed in Section 1) give us some indication of didactic role played by rings in acting as material mnemonics of late medieval marital values. This section will focus on the descriptions of rings in Middle English literature and wills, to argue that value and meaning were ascribed to rings its association with distant spouse.

The connection between memory and objects is a strong one in Middle English romance. Here, the recognition token is one of the most prevalent motifs, facilitating plot development, and acting as mnemonic conduits between the protagonists. The mnemonic power of the ring is particularly pronounced in the romance of *King Horn*. The central relationship of the Horn romance is that between Horn and the princess Rymenhild, whom he eventually marries. There are a number of things that set the ring in *King Horn* apart from the marriage rings exchange thus far. Crucially, its exchange is not during a public ceremony of consent (which occurs at the end of the texts) but during a private trothplight ceremony. They exchange private words of marital intention, but Horn says that he will only wed her on the condition that she assists him in becoming a knight; and to help him attain this she gives him a ring. It is also Rymenhild rather than Horn who gives the ring, reversing the gendered expectations of the marital gift register. Nevertheless, like the description of the wedding ring in the *Sarum Missal*, the ring binds the couple together and acts as a reminder of promises made. Throughout Horn's narrative of self-discovery, Rymenhild's ring acts as a powerful mnemonic; it is through looking at this ring that Horn is reminded of his loyalty to her, enabling him to conquer his enemies. Although the couple is separated the ring is described as a manifest mnemonic of their trothplight and a constant reminder to Horn of his promise to return to Rymenhild. The description of the moment when Rymenhild gives Horn the ring explicitly emphasizes her relationship to it:

*Tak nu her þis goldring,*
*God him is þe dubbing;*
*Þer is vpon þringe*
*Igraue Rymenhild þe ʒonge.*
*Þer nis non betere anonder funne*
*Þat eni man of telle cunne;*
*For my luue þu hit were*
*& on þi finger þu him bere:*
*Þe ftones beoþ of fuche grace*

Þat þu ne fchalt in none place
Of none duntes beon of drad,
Ne on bataille beon amad,
Ef thu loke þeran& þenke vpon þi lemman.[79]

There has been much discussion about this ring, much of which has focused on whether or not it was magical. However, all are agreed that the ring was a powerful symbol of the strengthening power of love rather than a purely 'magical' device.[80] Cooper takes the discussion the furthest and compares, in depth, the description of the ring in all three of the *King Horn* manuscripts. Her discussion begins by highlighting a common theme in courtly romances: to have the knight think of his lady during battle and emerge victorious without injury, 'think on me' or 'think on your lemman' became an extremely commonplace motif in such stories.[81] The ring in *King Horn* is, according to Cooper, not magical but a symbol of love, the emotional power of which enables Horn to defeat his enemies.[82] The ring's connection to Rymenhild is enforced in its description. Graceful and unique, the ring appears to personify Rymenhild herself, and also her status as a princess, and the reason that Horn must achieve equality with her; the inscription, 'Rymenhild the yonge', cements the connection between her and the ring.

This ring generates a material presence, a presence in part created by its relationship to its previous owner Rymenhild the Young. We might say that the ring stands for the princess herself. The effect of which reinforces for the reader the physical connection that exists between the ring and the giver. This connection is active and is described as creating a protective power for its bearer, acting as a memory made manifest.[83] One such occasion was immediately after having been given the ring. On his mission to prove his bravery he encounters a ship full of Saracens, and after looking upon his ring, he slays the entire fleet, over a hundred souls.[84] Similarly in *Amoryus and Cleopes*, during the couple's separation Cleopes' ring is transformed into a protective talisman, endowing Amoryus with the ability to defeat the dragon that plagued his father's lands.[85] Such rings are thus more than mnemonic devices but active agents to ensure its wearer could return to their betrothed and fulfil the promise they had made them.

Marital litigation records remind us that marital rings could contain memories of a deceased spouse. In 1470 Maude Knyff was seen embracing Robert Grene around the neck with her right arm, with Robert holding her right hand in his. Robert Grene then took from Maude's left hand a golden ring, and Maude asked him to guard the ring well, out of love for her, because she would not want the ring to be lost, out of love for her deceased husband. It was at this point that the couple exchanged words of consent.[86] The ring in this exchange is treasured beyond its material value because it represented the love Maude had for her previous husband; however, her decision to re-gift this object is also evidence of her consent to leave behind this previous marriage and take Robert as her new spouse. The use and meaning of this marital ring are therefore part of a complex process of emotional negotiation, in which the transition from a former to a new spouse (from old to new loyalties) is communicated through its exchange. The re-gifting of the marital objects to a new spouse was not limited to rings, however. Diane O'Hara has suggested that in early modern England, upon remarriage a widower would give his new wife her predecessors' finest gown, as a 'transfer of sentiment', and relocated marital 'expectation to the new spouse'.[87]

Objects transferred from a previous marriage had to be expunged of former meanings. In 1487 John Ely was reported to have shown his betrothed Agnes Whitingdon a blue gown which had belonged to his wife and which he wished her to wear on the day of their nuptials. The gift of objects associated with a previous marriage symbolized the transfer of marital fidelity, and this was further emphasized when they were exchanged during important ritual moments (the speaking of words of consent and the church blessing), which suggests that such objects had to be expunged of their previous meaning. Roberta Gilchrist has argued that objects which had been used as part of the sacrament became consecrated materials which had special rules regarding their disposal.[88] One such method was to translate its meaning from one spouse to another. However, we shall now see how marital rings were disposed at the end of life.

Anthropologists have observed that important personal possessions were often kept within the family.[89] This was often because, as Annette Weiner and Marcel Mauss have proposed, objects are irrevocably linked to, or even inalienable, from their owners and that memories cannot be eradicated by death or new ownership.[90] Memories and associations fade with the passage of time; however, testamentary evidence demonstrates that marriage rings were important objects, which were thus bestowed with great care. In April 1495 the will of the London widow Agnes Sibott was proved at the commissary court in St Paul's Cathedral. Agnes had married William Sibott after his first wife had died, and in her will she bequeathed to her step-daughter Elizabeth a violet furred gown, a girdle harnessed with silver and Elizabeth's mother's wedding ring'.[91] Agnes Sibott makes a further bequest to her own daughter, Joan Sibott, to whom she gives 'a green gown, a girdle of violet harnessed with silver, my wedding ring, and a pair of coral beads gaudied with silver'. At the time of her death Agnes Sibott possessed not only her own wedding ring, but also that of her husband's former wife. Agnes Sibott's bequest shows how the mnemonic and emotional importance of such objects was emphasized by the intimacy of a familial relationship; in this case Agnes Sibott recognized that her step-daughter would value the ownership of her mother's wedding ring. A century earlier in 1395 Lady Alice West of Hampshire bequeathed her son 'a rynge with which I was aspoused to God, wuch were my lords his faderes.'[92] This bequest shows two important things. Firstly, it demonstrates how family memory was kept alive through material culture, and the important role that women played in the continuation of genealogical legacies.[93] Secondly, it presents the marital ring as a sacred object – a perception that is central to all these examples, and this leads us to the final section of this chapter which examines the bequest of marital rings to ecclesiastical institutions.

Roberta Gilchrist has argued that the gift of some of the most significant biographical objects from the private context of the medieval household to the public context of the parish church can be seen as surprising.[94] However, it is important to remember that spiritual power in the Middle Ages was ascribed to consecrated objects.[95] This chapter has shown how marriage rings were made and perceived as active embodiments of marriage and therefore resisted being reassigned as an everyday dress accessory. At the end of the marital life course we saw how this meaning was dispersed either by being transferred into a new marital relationship, given as treasured possessions to family members, or returned to the church. An example being Agnes Petygrewe from Somerset, who in 1509 gave her wedding ring to her parish church in Publow.[96] Katherine French has argued that the gift of more personal domestic items to the parish church was more often practised by women, and these items were things which were often connected to the rituals of life, not least marriage rings but also wedding girdles and paternoster beads.[97] French has shown how women often requested that their bequests adorn a particular saint, with St Katherine and St Mary both being popular recipients. In 1500 it was recorded that the statue of St Mary at Pilton in Somerset possessed a mantle adorned with fourteen rings.[98] This mantle would have clothed the saint on their feast day and been carried during processions within the parish. Gilchrist has encouraged us to read such votive offerings as 'not merely votive offerings' but 'biographical objects which conjoined the lifecycle of the person with that of their church and community' which also transmitted divine energy through its physical contact with the image of the saint.[99] The bequest of a marital ring which was so personally connected to a person's life course and identity was at the same time an intimate gift with a desire to be close to divinity but also the return of a sacramental object to its most appropriate place, the church – perhaps even the place where it had been given as part of the marital vow.

## Conclusions

Marriage in the Middle Ages was a culturally and socially embedded process, and this was reflected in the exchange of rings. This chapter has looked at the life cycle of the medieval marital ring and concluded that each part of its life-cycle was a fundamental part of the overall gift. Rings were first chosen and decorated to symbolize the values associated with marriage, and surviving archaeological evidence shows how the words of marital consent could be etched on posy ring or embodied by *fede* and gimmel rings. At the point of marriage rings were given to visually communicate the willing and wholehearted consent of the marrying couple, acting as material manifestations of the creation of the sacred bond of marriage. The final part of the marrying process was the church blessing, and here we see how rings were transformed into sacred objects; this process animated them creating a spiritual link between its wearer, its giver and the heavens to act as a reminder of the sanctity of marriage. Memory of the gift and what it represented remained important throughout the life course of these objects and the people who wore them; we see this in literary sources and the bequest of marriage rings in wills. Rings retained their identity as objects and were carefully disposed of either within the family or to parish churches as material mnemonics of the deceased. However, marriage rings were also important as personal and intimate reminders of family members, as well as the history of the marital line. Throughout this chapter we have seen how marriage rings were often given to children either for their own future marriage or as a reminder of a departed parent. The (re)gift of marriage rings within the family gives us glimpses into the cultural perception of marriage, not only as a divinely ordained sacrament, but an everyday reality: one in which ties of kinship and affection were mediated via everyday objects.

## Notes

1 William Shakespeare, *The Merchant of Venice*, ed. Bernard Lott (London: Longham 1964), 5.1. lines 146–68. For further discussion on the relationship between the ring and the body in *The Merchant of Venice* see Wendy Doniger, *The Ring of Truth: And Other Myths of Sex and Jewelry* (Oxford: Oxford University Press, 2017), 107–9.

2 Elizabeth Van Houts, *Married Life in the Middle Ages, 900–1300* (Oxford: Oxford University Press, 2019), 80–1.

3 Rings and other tokens were also given in flirtation or friendship, and the categorization of the gift as marital or not was dependent on the register of its

exchange. This is a subject which I plan to expand on in my forthcoming book *Marriage Matters: Consent, Material Culture and the Exchange of Gifts in Late Medieval Society* hopefully to be published in the near future.

4   Emma Lipton, *Affections of the Mind: The Politics of Sacramental Marriage in Late Medieval Literature* (Notre Dame: University of Notre Dame Press, 2007), 115.

5   In *The Ring of Truth* Wendy Doniger recently examined the extremely rich variety of literary depictions touching on the relationship between jewellery (in particular rings), sex and the sexes, and which continues to be (re)told throughout history. Doniger, *The Ring of Truth*, 1.

6   Ruth Mazo Karras, *Unmarriages: Women, Men and Sexual Unions in the Middle Ages* (Philadelphia: University of Pennsylvania Press, 2012), 178.

7   P.J.P. Goldberg, *Women, Work, and Life Cycle in a Medieval Economy: Women in York and Yorkshire c. 1300–1520* (Oxford: Clarendon Press, 1992), 239.

8   Shannon McSheffrey, *Marriage, Sex and Civic Culture in Late Medieval London* (Philadelphia: University of Pennsylvania Press, 2006), 239.

9   The London Consistory Court was based at St Pauls Cathedral, and this chapter is based on the four surviving deposition books held in the London Metropolitan Archives (LMA) covering the years 1467–1524.

10  McSheffrey, *Marriage*, 12.

11  McSheffrey, Marriage, 61.

12  Bodley. MS. Canon. Misc. 110. fol., 123r. The Bodleian Libraries, University of Oxford.

13  Deborah Youngs, *The Life Cycle in Western Europe, c. 1300–c. 1500* (Manchester: Manchester University Press, 2006), 140.

14  In *The Ring of Truth* Wendy Doniger recently examined the extremely rich variety of literary depictions touching on the relationship between jewellery (in particular rings), sex and the sexes, and which continue to be (re)told throughout history. Doniger, *The Ring of Truth*, 1.

15  For an overview of this discussion see Lars Kjær, *The Medieval Gift and the Classical Tradition, Ideals and the Performance of Generosity in Medieval England, 1100–1300* (Cambridge: Cambridge University Press, 2019), 4–5.

16  Gadi Algazi, 'Introduction: Doing Things with Gifts', in *Negotiating the Gift: Pre-Modern Figurations of Exchange*, ed. Gadi Algazi, Valentin Groebner and Bernhard Jussen (Göttingen: Vandenhoeck und Ruprecht, 2003), 13.

17  Natalie Zemon Davis, *The Gift in Sixteenth-Century France* (London: The University of Wisconsin Press, 2000), 14–16.

18  Felicity Heal, *The Power of the Gift: Gift Exchange in Early Modern England* (Oxford: Oxford University Press, 2014), 31.

19  Janet Hoskins, *Biographical Objects: How Things Tell the Story of People's Lives* (London: Routledge, 1998), 195.

20  Roberta Gilchrist, 'The Materiality of Medieval Heirlooms: From Sacred to Biographical Objects', in *Mobility, Meaning & Transformation of Things: Shifting Contexts of Material Culture through Time and Space*, ed. Hans Peter Hahn and Hadas Weiss (Oxford: Oxbow Books, 2013), 3–4.
21  Rachel M. Delman and Anna Boeles Rowland, 'Introduction: People Places, and Possession in Late Medieval England', *Journal of Medieval History* 45:2 (2019): 131–3.
22  Linda M. Hurcombe, *Archaeological Artefacts as Material Culture* (London: Routledge, 2007), 109.
23  Marian Campbell, *Medieval Jewellery in Europe* (London: V&A, 2009); Diana Scarisbrick, *Jewellery. Makers, Motifs, History, Techniques* (London: T&H, 1989).
24  Eleanor R. Standley, *Trinkets & Charms: The Use, Meaning and Significance of Dress Accessories. 1300–1700* (Oxford: School of Archaeology, 2013), 7. See also, Roberta Gilchrist, *Medieval Life: Archaeology and the Life Course* (Woodbridge: The Boydell Press, 2012), 114–54.
25  Marian, *Medieval Jewellery*, 10.
26  Scarisbrick, *Jewellery*, 35.
27  Campbell, *Medieval Jewellery*, 16.
28  Standley, *Trinkets & Charms*, 89.
29  Diana O'Hara, *Courtship and Constraint: Rethinking the Making of Marriage in Tudor England* (Manchester: Manchester University Press, 2000), 67–8.
30  O'Hara, *Courtship and Constraint*, tables 4–5, Standley, *Trinkets & Charms*, 33.
31  Anne F. Sutton, 'Alice Claver, Silkwoman (d.1489)', in *Medieval London Widows, 1300–1500*, ed. Caroline M. Barron and Anne F. Sutton (London: Hambledon Press, 1994), 129–42.
32  Geoff Egan, *Dress Accessories, c.1150–c.1450* (Woodbridge: The Boydell Press, 2002), 327.
33  Gilchrist, *Medieval Life*, 11–13.
34  Lesley Boatwright, Moira Habberjam and Peter Hammond, ed., *The Logge Register of Prerogative Court of Canterbury Wills, 1479–86*, vol. 2 (Knaphill: Richard III Society, 2008), 218–20.
35  Scarisbrick, *Rings*, 18.
36  The descriptive used in the records was, gemew. OED 3: A double ring.
37  The cases which included an exchange of a gimmel ring are as follows: LMA DL/C/09065, *Beatrice Smyth C John Crote*, 35r-35v; *Nicholas Sager c. Elisabeth Leg*, 47r-v; *Alice Billingham c. John Wellis*; LMA DL/C/09065B 8r-v; *Mark Patenson c. Margaret Flemmyng*, 80r-v; LMA DL/C/206, *William Cutt c. Katherine Ridley*, 291v-292r.
38  'The Miller's Tale, lines 3794–6', in *The Riverside Chaucer*, ed. F.N. Robinson (Oxford: Oxford University Press, 2008), 76.
39  Rachel Church, *Rings* (London: V&A Pub., 2011), 18.

40  Diana Scarisbrick, *Rings: Jewelry of Power, Love and Loyalty* (London: Thames & Hudson, 2007), 17–18.
41  '*unum[m] anulu[m] aure[m] eu[m] lapide vocat diamond*', LMA DL/C/206, 174v and 187v.
42  The other gifts included a girdle of gold with a buckle, a pendant of silver and gilt and a tippet of damask. Alison Hanham, *The Celys and Their World: An English Merchant Family of the Fifteenth Century* (Cambridge: Cambridge University Press, 1985), 88.
43  An example of which can be seen in Joan Evans, *English Posies and Posy Rings: A Catalogue with an Introduction* (London: Oxford University Press, 1931), 14.
44  Scarisbrick, *Rings*, 17–18.
45  Standley, *Trinkets & Charms*, 34.
46  Standley, Trinkets & Charms, table 3.1, 34; and a deformed copper alloy ring dated to the late middle ages was found in Oxfordshire and inscribed with the words '… IKE MY CHO'. PAS BERK-7B7F25.
47  Another common posy was AUTRE NE VEUX (I wish for no other). Gilchrist, *Medieval Life*, 239; and Scarisbrick, *Rings*, 18.
48  O'Hara, *Courtship and Contraint*, 83.
49  McSheffrey, *Marriage*, 45.
50  A. Jeffries Collins, ed., *Manuale ad usum percelebris ecclesiae Sarisburiensis*, Henry Bradshaw Society 91 (Chichester: Moore and Tillyer, 1958), 48.
51  *The Sarum Missal in English*, trans. Frederick E. Warren (London: De La More Press, 1911), 147–8.
52  Emma Lipton, *Affections of the Mind*, 110.
53  Danielle Westerhof, *Death and the Noble Body in Medieval England* (Woodbridge: The Boydell Press, 2008), 53; Heather Webb, *The Medieval Heart* (New Haven: Yale University Press, 2010), 21, and 32–3; and Victoria Blud, 'Emotional Bodies: Cognitive Neuroscience and Mediaeval Studies', *Literary Compass* 13 (2016): 461.
54  McSheffrey, *Marriage*, 19.
55  LMA DL/C/205, 33r-34r.
56  C.M. Woolgar, *The Senses in Late Medieval England* (London: Yale University Press, 2006), 90–1.
57  *Manuale ad usum percelebris ecclesiae Sarisburiensis*, 48. For an English translation see Jacqueline Murray, ed., *Love, Marriage and Family in the Middle Ages: A Reader* (Omskirk: Thomas Lyster, 2001), 261–70.
58  Christine Peters, 'Gender, Sacrament and Ritual: The Making and Meaning of Marriage in Late Medieval and Early Modern England', *Past and Present* 169 (2000): 65–6; David d'Avray, *Medieval Marriage: Symbolism and Society* (Oxford: Oxford University Press, 2015), 1–2, 8–10, and 18–20.
59  Lipton, *Affections of the Mind*, 2.

60  McSheffrey, *Marriage*, 164–89.
61  DL/C/205, 62v-63r, 63v-64v, 64v-65r, 65v, 67r-68v, and 68v-69v.
62  CLBL, 82 and CLRO, Journal 7, 185v. In McSheffrey, *Marriage*, n15, 237.
63  McSheffrey, *Marriage*, 124.
64  LMA DL/C/205, 67r-68v.
65  James A. Brundage, *Medieval Canon Law* (London: Longman, 1995), 132.
66  Emma Lipton, 'Marriage and the Legal Culture of Witnessing', in *The Cambridge Companion to Medieval English Law and Literature*, ed. Candace Barrington and Sebastian Sobecki (Cambridge: Cambridge University Press, 2019), 202.
67  The Marriage of Mary and Joseph, lines 309–322, in *The N-Town Play*, vol. 1, ed. Stephen Spector (Oxford: Oxford University Press, 1991), 103–4.
68  MED, rif) adv. (a) Widely; ben runnen ~, to be widespread; (b) openly, clearly, manifestly.
69  Lipton, 'Marriage and the Legal Culture of Witnessing', 204.
70  LMA DL/C/207, and 79r-81r.
71  LMA DL/C/09065, 201v-202r.
72  McSheffrey, *Marriage*, 71.
73  LMA DL/C/205, 52v-53r.
74  Quem annulum dicta Johanna gratanter recepit et ad huc retinet eundem penes se. LMA DL/C/09065, 7r.
75  LMA DL/C/207, 129r-130r.
76  This is a complex subject and emerges from a much larger work on gender, sexuality and the gift, hopefully to be published in the near future.
77  Doniger, *The Ring of Truth*, 20–2.
78  Kjær, *The Medieval Gift*, see in particular the discussion of Dido, 26 and Ovid, 30–2.
79  'Take now this gold ring/ God him is the dubbing (adornment)/ There is upon the ring/ Engraved "Rymenhild the young"/ There is non better under the sun/ That any man can tell of/ For my love thou it wear/ And on thi finger thou him bear/ The stones being of such grace/That thou shall not in any place/ Of no blows be afraid/ Nor in battle go mad/ If thou looketh upon it/ and think upon your bethrothed/beloved.' Joseph Hall, ed., *King Horn: A Middle-English Romance* (Oxford: Clarendon Press, 1901), C lines 563–76, 33.
80  This ring has been described as a 'talisman' by Barron and Stevens, a 'wonder-working' ring by Hibbard and, intriguingly, as 'somewhat magical' by Berry. W.r. J. Barron, *English Medieval Romance* (London: Longman, 1987), 67; John Stevens, *Medieval Romance: Themes and Approaches* (London: Hutchinson and Co., 1973), 43; Laura Hibbard, *Medieval Romance in England* (New York: Burton Franklin, 1960), 92; and Mary Hynes Berry, 'Cohesion in King Horn and Sir Orfeo', *Speculum* 50 (1975): 660.

81  Helen Cooper, *The English Romance in Time: Transforming Motifs from Geoffrey of Monmouth to the Death of Shakespeare* (Oxford: Oxford University Press, 2004), 150.
82  Cooper, *English Romance in Time*, 150.
83  This connection with memory was also fundamental to the medieval Jewish marriage ring, the bezel of which was in shape of a miniature building, which is most likely to be the Second temple in Jerusalem destroyed in 70 CE, the design acting to preserve the memory of the destruction of the temple and Jerusalem (fundamental to the identity of Jews living in the Diaspora) during the marital life course. Maria Stürzebecher, 'The Medieval Jewish Wedding Ring from the Erfurt Treasure: Ceremonial Object or Bride Price?' in *Erfurter Schriften zur Jüdischen Geschichte, Band 6: Ritual Objects in Ritual Contexts* (Jena: Bussert & Stadeler, 2020), 72.
84  'He lokede on Þe ringe, & Þo3te on rimenilde. He flo3 Þer on hafte, on hundred bi Þe lafte'. Hall, ed., *King Horn*, C lines 613–616, 35. A similar event occurs after Horn has been banished, and when he defeats Saracen giant, C lines 873–5, 49.
85  John Metham, *The Works of John Metham: Including the Romance of Amoryus and Cleopes*, ed. Hardin Craig, EETS (London: Oxford University Press, 1916), 53–4.
86  LMA DL/C/205, 60v-61r.
87  O'Hara, *Courtship and Constraint*, 84.
88  Gilchrist, 'The Materiality of Medieval Heirlooms', 11–13.
89  Gilchrist, 'The Materiality of Medieval Heirlooms', 9.
90  Annette Weiner, *Inalienable Possessions: The Paradox of Keeping-while-Giving* (Berkeley: University of California Press 1992), 8–12; and Marcel Mauss, *The Gift: The Form and Reason for Exchange in Archaic Societies*, trans. W.D. Halls (London: Routledge, 1990), 13–16.
91  'My violet gown furred, girdle harnessed wit silver and her moders wedding ring'. LMA 0971/8, 124r.
92  Frederick J. Furnivall, ed., *The Fifty Earliest English Wills in the Court of Probate, London* (London: Trübner & Co, 1964), 135.
93  The Important Role Women Played in Sustaining Family Memory, often using Objects as 'Pegs for Memories', has been extensively discussed by Elisabeth van Houts in *Memory and Gender in Medieval Europe, 900–1200* (Basingstoke: Palgrave Macmillan, 1999), 148–9 and 193–20. See also Bronach C. Kane, *Popular Memory and Gender in Medieval England: Men, Women and Testimony in the Church Courts, c.1200–1500* (Woodbridge: The Boydell Press, 2019), 137–71 and Matthew Innes, 'Keeping It in the Family: Women and Aristocratic Memory, 700–1200' in *Medieval Memories: Men, Women and the Past, 700–1300*, ed. Elisabeth van Houts (London: Routledge, 2001), 17–35.
94  Gilchrist, 'The Materiality of Medieval Heirlooms', 9.
95  Gilchrist, *Medieval Life*, 250.

96 TNA PROB 11/16/309. With thanks to Rachel Delman for this reference.
97 Katherine L. French, *The Good Women of the Parish: Gender and Religion after the Black Death* (Philadelphia: University of Pennsylvania Press, 2008), 41, and Janet S. Loengard, '"Which may be said to be her own": Widows and Goods in Late Medieval England', in *Medieval Domesticity: Home, Housing and Household in Medieval England*, ed. Maryanne Kowaleski and P.J.P. Goldberg (Cambridge: Cambridge University Press, 2008), 162–76.
98 French, *The Good Women*, 43.
99 Gilchrist, *Medieval Life*, 250.

# 2

# Of Ivory, Gold and Elephants: Materiality and agency of pre-modern chairs as gifts

Sabine Sommerer

As a primordial symbol of power and dignity, the gift of a chair usually belongs to the royal sphere. The elitist milieu in which chairs circulated as gifts had great impact on their materiality, distinguished by particularly precious embellishments of gold, silver, ivory and gems. However, the emblematic nature of thrones of authority has always lent an inherently stereotypical undertone to the gift, whether real or described in written accounts. A passage from Chrétien de Troyes' *Erec and Eneide* (around 1165), where Arthur and Guinevere, the King and Queen of Britain, each receive a lavishly decorated folding chair from the knight Bruiant, is likewise anticipatory and paradigmatic: Chrétien de Troyes describes two new and beautiful white ivory thrones in the great hall, admires the great skill and subtlety of their designer and also the exclusive material – instead of wood, everything was made of gold and pure ivory.[1] Obviously, the chairs were given a certain exotic appeal since they came with unique structural features: the feet showed a singular figurative combination and, with the inclusion of crocodiles, a display of extraordinary animal creatures.[2]

Indeed, such concise descriptions of the materiality and design of gifted chair objects are rather rare. Yet, the rhetoric of superlatives is symptomatic: the two thrones are made only from the finest material (*nule rien de fust / se d'or non ou d'ivoire fin*), the subtlest and newest design (*bien fez et nués*) and the utmost skill (*sanz nule faille […] taillé de grant fin*). It goes without saying that the gift-giving

---

I would like to thank editors and participants of the workshop for the most inspiring questions and comments; a warm thank goes especially to Gadi Algazi. For very helpful discussions, literature and photos concerning the Barcelona Chair, I would like to thank Marc Sureda i Jubany, Xavier Barral i Altet, Mn. Robert Baró, Joan Domenge Mesquida, Marta Serrano Coll, Henriette Wiltschek and Ramon Pujades Bataller. This article also benefited greatly from helpful corrections by Carola Jäggi and Louise Chapman. It has mainly been written during my research stay as PostDoc Fellow at the Bibliotheca Hertziana–Max Planck Institute for Art History in Rome (project number BH-P-20-28), for which I would like to thank its director Tanja Michalsky.

of these most precious thrones honoured the king and queen, as recipients. But it also honoured the giver, bestowing the gift's change of hand with a brilliant reciprocity. Marcel Mauss's principle of reciprocity and especially his point that some of the giver's identity may live on in the gift[3] also applies to the agency of gifted chairs, as these artefacts allude to their donors and make them present in various ways. I argue that gifting chairs is about embodying the giver, as expressed in the artefact's materiality and decoration.

The following analysis of premodern gifted chairs in the Western Occident including today's Austria, Italy, Spain and England contributes to the study of the diverse and complex language of gifts. Hereby, the focus shall not so much be on 'actors that used, spoke and wrote about gifts'.[4] Instead, it falls on the question of how the chairs were structurally and materially conceived and acted as agents of representative strategies. Following Cecily Hilsdale, who has urged especially art historians to explore the visual strategies of gift-exchange on the basis of texts, objects, images and spatial environments,[5] I ask how the objects themselves, made out of the most precious materials and decorated with images and texts, expressed royal agendas of power and hierarchy. In a first step, I investigate the materiality of the chair gifts mentioned in written sources. I then discuss in greater depth the semantics of the chair as well as its material and memorial value, focusing on three preserved royal gifts. This selection of chair gifts corresponds to the actual preservation of such chair *realia* and ranges from the ninth to the sixteenth century. Thus, this chapter considers all gifted medieval chair artefacts known to me to date.

## Chair gifts in written sources

By virtue of their forms, iconographies and materials, chair gifts act as memory stores that are part of the surrounding performance. This becomes evident in the earliest described example of a chair gift, which dates back to the fourth century: around 384, Saint Jerome (347–420) received some gifts including a *sella,* given from the young widow Marcella, a disciple he met in Rome sometime after 382. In his letter of thanks, Jerome comments on the memorial value by noting how gifts and letters are generally able to provide comfort in the absence of bodies. He then speaks of chairs, in particular: '[…] seats are designed in such a way that a virgin does not direct her steps to the outside […]' and '[…] your gifts also go well with us: sitting goes well with being lazy […]'.[6] In addressing the generic affordance of chairs to sit along with their sedative nature, Jerome touches on a symptomatic aspect of chair gifts. By connecting the chair directly to his disciple and friend Marcella, he is comforting himself by imagining her sitting on that chair like the virgins he is talking of in his letter. Almost like a contact relic, the chair gift comes with a special aura. We can only assume that Jerome wrote this against the background of empty funerary chairs in early Christian burial chambers, since a written reflection on the embodiment of objects does reveal itself to us only half a millennium later: In his treatise on the nature and meaning of relics, the *Flores epytaphii sanctorum* (Flowers for the tombs of the saints) of around 1100, Thiofrid († 1110), abbot of the Benedictine Abbey of Echternach, explains relics as corporeal media. He also speaks of the message that runs through the relics and can have a healing effect by the power of God flowing from body to body.[7] Also Jerome sees Marcella's Chair as embodied object with healing capacities. As Marcellas presence has literally taken possession of the chair, the gift brings to the fore what is distant and invisible.

As this example also makes clear, gifted chairs carry an intrinsic memorial value, as a manifestation of the presence of a person, and their giver in particular. While memorial value clearly plays a major role in this early Christian example, no word is given by Jerome about the design and material of the chair itself.

Other historical sources provide descriptions of chair gifts that can be dated back to sometime between the tenth and the thirteenth centuries. These descriptions follow a similar pattern. Generally, no great importance is attached to describing the chairs in detail. Yet they often mention typology and material, albeit in terms that do not vary greatly. On the other hand, the uniformity of these topical descriptions is sometimes reflected in terminology. For example, there are no clear distinctions between typological and functional denominations. In most cases, seat-related terms such as *thronum* and *cathedra* are used as synonyms. Thus, the seat of a king and a *faldistorium* might both be termed *cathedra* at the same time.[8] What we can deduce from these sources is that in most cases, writers are describing mobile chairs, such as faldistories. In Ademar of Chabannes' (988–1034) *Chronica*, Charles the Simple (879–929) is said to have given a silver or silver-plated folding chair (*faltestalium argentatum*) to the abbey church of Saint Martial in Limoges around 922–923.[9] As Ademar tells us, Charles had confiscated this chair together with other loot (*de spoliis*), such as liturgical textiles and books kept in the chapel of his counter-king Robert I (866–923).

In his *Chronaca Veneziana*, the Venetian chronicler John the Deacon (965/70–1018?) mentions another donated chair, *cathedra elephantinis artificiose sculpta tabulis*, made with artistically sculpted ivory panels.[10] Doge Pietro

Orseolo II (991–1009), for whom John was Ambassador, donated this precious chair to Otto III (980–1002) in mid-December 1001.[11] The chair must have been one of numerous objects passed between the two protagonists with the intent of sealing an alliance between the Emperor and the Doge.[12] There has been much speculation about the identity of this artefact.[13] I do not engage in this discussion, but instead emphasize once again that the rhetoric of the superlative is used to manifest hierarchies: John the Deacon describes the gift-exchange as a kind of competition in which his favourite, the Doge, outclasses Otto III. The chronicler allows Doge Orseolo to win the 'gift-duel',[14] coming up with larger and more valuable gifts. An ivory chair seemed to be the most suitable medium for this challenge.

Set with precious stones and made of costly material, the chairs were equally useful as pawn items and gifts after victory in battle. As a gesture of gratitude for financial support enabling victory in the Battle of Benevento in 1266, Charles I of Anjou (1298–1328) donates a golden folding chair – confiscated as war spolium – to pope Clemens IV (around 1200–1268). Saba Malaspina describes the gift in his *Chronica*, which was written at the Roman Curia between 1283 and 1285. In the third book, the chronicler details Charles' victorious campaign against Manfred of Sicily and dedicates a few lines to the chair gift.[15] Malaspina mentions the typology of the chair (*facistorium*), its golden material (*aurea*), the casting as method of production (*massa conflatam*) and, with the overall adornment of magnificent precious pearls (*margaritis coruscantibus undique circumseptam*), also its decoration. We can assume though, the chair was not made of pure gold but of gilded bronze, like the Dagobert Chair from Saint-Denis or the gilded silver chair from Barcelona discussed below. Although we no longer have any material evidence of this chair today, its later vita can be traced in inventory entries such as the one of pope Boniface VIII (1235–1303) of 1295. As part of the papal treasury, the precious chair – which was repeatedly pawned and redeemed throughout its lifetime – must have made stops in Perugia and Assisi. After 1311, all traces of it are finally lost.[16]

As we have seen so far, the gifted chairs mentioned in written sources were mobile. In most cases the highly valuable objects were donated from a king either to a religious institution or to an individual historical person. About the origin of the chairs we only know that they were sometimes looted as spoils and then gifted as such. Not mobile though, but still bearing a spolia, the so-called 'Chair of St. Peter', a throne in San Pietro di Castello, the Episcopal Church of Venice, is another example of a gifted chair. According to the chronicle of

Andrea Dandolo (1307–1354), the Byzantine Emperor Michael III (r. 842–867) donated a *cathedram marmoream* to Doge Giovanni Partecipazio (r. 829–836), which was then placed behind the main altar in San Pietro.[17]

In the following, I concentrate on three gifted chair objects that like the just mentioned 'Chair of St. Peter' came to us as *realia*. They show how memorial *and* material value played an equally central role in their conception. Furthermore, they may illustrate how these two components relate to one another and the extent of their mutual dependence.

## Rome, Barcelona, Vienna – A chair from the King

The oldest preserved chair gift[18] – the Cathedra Petri in the Vatican (Figure 2.1) –has received the most attention from scholarship. It changed hands on a symbolic date: on Christmas Day in 875, Charles the Bald (823–877) donated the chair to St. Peter on the occasion of his imperial coronation.[19] Since 1666, the Cathedra is encased in a baroque reliquary by Gian Lorenzo Bernini (1598–1680), raised high in the apse of the Vatican Basilica (Figure 2.11).[20] While one of the two copies now stands in the Treasury of St. Peter, the original throne has left its chair-shaped shell only three times since its concealment. The last time was in 1968, for a lengthy and intensive scientific analysis.[21] Measuring 137 cm in height, 85.5 cm in width and 65.2 cm in depth, the Cathedra Petri consists of three components. The first is a seat made of oak wood (height: 66.2 cm) with a gable-shaped backrest dated dendrochronologically to the middle of the ninth century.[22] The second is an oaken panel on the front side, to which partly reused and elaborately decorated ivory panels are attached, dendrochronologically and stylistically dated to around 860.[23] The third is a supporting wooden structure from pine, dendrochronologically dated in 1235 and added as a carrying device.[24]

Both the seat and the backrest are divided by arcades while the throne gable in the filling reveals three oval openings. All external surfaces of the throne are decorated with ivory strips that are partly worked à jour and 'applied over a metallic sheet of gilded copper, so that in the gaps of the decoration the gilding of the background, still clearly recognisable in some parts, shone through'.[25] The panels visible from the front display a lavish figural richness. Fighting scenes between armed men, animals and hybrid creatures can be found in both the sculpted ivory strips and the eighteen ivory panels on the front of the throne seat (Figure 2.1). Here, the two upper rows show – to an unprecedented detailed extent for Carolingian art – the twelve labours of Hercules,[26] while the third shows six hybrid creatures. These plaques are richly decorated with ornaments and figural representations using an engraving technique whereby the engravings still show remnants of polychrome colour. These small fragments suggest that larger areas, especially the bodies of the main figures, were once covered with gold foil appliqués inserted into the flat recesses.[27] With this chryselephantine combination, the Cathedra Petri is the only surviving chair decorated with ivory *and* gold in the tradition of the old testamentary Solomonic Throne described in 1 Kings, 10.18: 'Then the king made a great throne covered with ivory and overlaid with fine gold […]'.[28]

Because we lack a written source for either the gift or its donor, the bust of a ruler (Figure 2.2) on the horizontal ledge in the gable gains even greater importance. The majority of researchers identify the moustachioed bust, wearing a crown, and holding a sphere and sceptre, with Charles the Bald.[29] He is assumed to be the giver of the Cathedra along with the Bible at S. Paolo fuori le mura.[30] Physiognomic similarities can be drawn either with the King's effigy in the initial miniature from the Codex Aureus, created in Charles' court school, or with the equestrian statuette of Charles the Bald in the Louvre that dates to about the same time and was created in a workshop in Metz.[31] Because of the divergent dating of the chair and the wooden panel on the front of the seat with the Hercules tablets, it has been assumed that the Cathedra Petri was primarily created as a throne for Charles the Bald and only secondarily became a gift for St. Peter. From the twelfth century onwards then, its function changed again, since it was believed to be the original cathedra (*ipsa cathedra*) of St. Peter himself. As such, it was venerated as a super relic and dislocated several times within Old St. Peter's Basilica.[32] It is certainly no coincidence that the function and use of donated chairs could change before and after the act of donation, as I will further elaborate below.

In the treasury of the Cathedral of Barcelona, evidence has existed since 1421 of a tower monstrance. The monumental, so-called *custodia* consists of three distinct parts. The first part is an ostensory displaying the consecrated host, the Blessed Sacrament. In 1480, a second part, a gilded cathedra (Figure 2.3) was added to carry this monstrance.[33] Then, a third part – two gilded crowns – was fixed to the back of the throne. Since only a posthumous entry in the treasury register of 1492 mentions the chair as a gift of King Martin I the Humane of Aragon (†1410), the chair's attribution to a specific donor remains uncertain.[34] However, the existence of the chair in the cathedral treasury and its function as a bearer of the ostensorium is noteworthy enough. This function is likely the reason why the chair was preserved in the cathedral treasury. Unlike many other cimelia of the treasury, the monumental piece survived the Spanish Civil War (1936–1939) while exhibited in exile in Paris, first in the exhibition 'Art catalane du Xe au XVe siècle' in the Jeu de Paume and until 1940 in the exhibition rooms of the Maisons-Lafitte.[35] Remarkable though is the fact that only the secular elements with crowns and thrones were on display. As we can see from the photographs, the crowns were also exhibited in Paris. Also believed to be a gift of Martin I, their royal aura was intended to represent the Spanish Crown as the ruling insignia.[36] In fact, postfactual legends surrounding its origin and provenance are as much a part of the chair as its noble material and unique appearance; they were certainly encouraged by the chair itself. Regarding the Barcelona Chair, no clear statements can be made about the concrete function and attribution of the chair gift as sources remain too meagre.[37] Thus, a detailed description – somewhat neglected in research, especially with respect to the animals depicted on the throne – seems indispensable, especially given our interest in materiality.

Typologically, the chair is a folding chair or *faldistorium*: several hinges placed at different levels show that it was possible to fold the side rests and demount parts of the chair (Figure 2.4).[38] A source from 1413 mentions the costs 'to transfer the cathedra on which the King celebrated the courts to the Valencians in Segorb and to bring it from Segorb to Castelló.'[39] Assuming that this concerns indeed the cathedra in question, transported from Valencia to Segorb and from there to Castelló, leads to the interesting consequence that the chair was used as a ceremonial seat. Its folding abilities as well as its dimensions – 1.24 m in height, 0.59 m in width and 0.47 m in depth[40] – would allow this. In addition to that, the chair is made from gold-plated silver and bestowed with a light, graceful structure through a mass-work construction with several openings. Structurally and materially, the Barcelona Chair seems to be closely related with the so-called Coronation Chair in Westminster Abbey.[41] Commissioned by Edward I (1239–1307) in 1297, the latter chair consists of a backrest with gables, corner posts, tracery and a three-storey structure.[42] Aside from their structure, the two chairs are very similar in gilding and glass decoration. The Barcelona Chair is equally decorated with polychrome inlays on the inside, as indicated by a few fragments of transparent blue glass.[43] The sides of the armrests form concave curves, all ending in pointed trefoils shaped into tendrils with a lion head at each centre (Figure 2.5). A dragon sits right in front of the lower volute as if taking advantage of the last remaining free space on the rest (Figure 2.4). The lions are displayed on the armrests. Thus, they are connected to them in a manner analogous to the planned gilded leopards for the Coronation Chair,[44] perhaps roughly alluding to the Biblical Solomonic Throne in 1 Kings 10.19: 'On both sides of the seat were armrests, with a lion standing beside each of them.'

The dragons instead refer to the heraldic animal of the Aragon, an etymologic allusion that also arises through the onomastic alliance of *dragó* and *Aragó*.[45] Because of the dragon, researchers have considered Martin's father, Peter the Ceremonious (1319–1387), as commissioner of the chair,[46] but it seems to me that Martin's many other commissions make him the more plausible candidate. One of these objects is a helmet with the monumental dragon crest made in Mallorca around 1407, which is now in the Armeria Real of Madrid (Figure 2.6).[47] With the gift of a gilded chair to the Cathedral of Barcelona, it seems Martin was acting against his predecessors' habit of self-crowning. This tradition was not an Aragonese invention, since in 1229 already King Frederic II (1194–1250) crowned himself in Jerusalem in 1229, but Martins grandfather Alphonse the Benign (1299–1366), certainly influenced by that, was the first Aragonese King, who did not allow the archbishop to put the crown on him.[48] This was repeated in 1336 by Alphonse's son Peter the Ceremonious, who even went one step further by refusing to allow the archbishop to adjust the crown after the self-coronation. Moreover, he did not divide unction and coronation into two masses as his father did, but compromised the archbishop by requiring him to attend the king's self-coronation in person after the anointing.[49] After all, Peter was furthermore very concerned to generate iconographic representations via liturgical books with precious illuminations, commissioned by himself.[50] With similarly ambitious aspirations, Martin also took the path of self-crowning and had it documented through artistic media.

By making this chair his second emblem and also on behalf of other commissions, as e.g. the so-called *Rollo de Poblet*,[51] we can conclude that Martin I must have accorded a special role to the semantics of the chair, as well as to throning more generally as a sovereign act.[52] The *cadira* in the treasury of the Cathedral of Barcelona is thus an object of luxury and royal insignia, not only due to its precious material and artistic nature, but also because it was a very personal sign of King Martin I. As a gift to the Cathedral, it substituted his office and person. In addition, the gift of the chair acted as a mediator to God by visualizing the presence and memory of the donor. This was all the more important, since Martin I had no heirs.

While the chair gifts discussed above represent uninscribed objects, with our next example we will encounter a seat whose biography is not primarily elucidated by external evidence as written sources. Rather, the chair's vita and raison d'être are narrated directly through the chair object itself. The so-called Elephant Chair in the Benedictine Abbey of Kremsmünster is a mobile seat constructed out of four elephant bones (Figure 2.7).[53] In 1554 it was commissioned by the Vienna mayor Sebastian Huetstocker (†1557), who had previously received the elephant bones as a gift. That these are indeed the bones of a pachyderm can be deduced not only from their size, but also from their engravings. Huetstocker did not only attempt to secure his commemoration after death by means of a chair, he even went one step further by manifesting the chair's function through scripture and images on the seating surface. As we will see, the *sella* declares itself materially as well as through text and image as a memorial object.[54]

The prehistory begins with the journey of an Indian elephant,[55] born around 1539, that was shipped on the first of two fleets sailing between 1540 and 1559 to the Portuguese court at Lisbon around 1550.[56] From Lisbon, the Indian elephant had to walk the lengthy distance to Burgos in northern Spain. The barely ten-year-old animal was sent on behalf of the Portuguese Infant Joan Manuel (1537–1554) to his promised bride Joanna (1535–1573), the daughter of the Spanish King Charles V (1500–1558).[57] Even before the marriage took place in 1552, the elephant had already left Burgos as it was handed over to the bride's cousin and brother in law, Maximilian of Austria (1527–1576), in July/August of 1551.[58] Maximilian took the elephant on an even longer voyage from Valladolid heading northwards to accompany his *adventus* into Vienna on Saturday, 7 May 1552.[59] Maximilian's entry was staged as part of the festivities celebrating his return,[60] and never before had the city seen an elephant. The parade was organized by his younger brother, Ferdinand II (1529–1595), together with the mayor of Vienna Sebastian Huetstocker.

But the pompous arrival of the famous elephant was soon matched by the dishonour of his death. Because of bad living conditions, he died the following year. The bones of the elephant's right shoulder blade and front leg were presented to Sebastian Huetstocker,[61] who then had them made into a tripod chair in 1554. The shoulder blade served as seat surface, the other bones as frame being mounted individually on a turned wooden stand. The *sella* measures 82 cm in height, 89 cm in width and 55 cm in depth.[62] The bones were engraved, in a way that the orientation helped the spectator to define the front of the chair. The chair legs are covered in heraldic and floral decor, with two coats of arms representing the most important protagonists of the 1552 *adventus*: the crowned arms of Maximilian II appear on the right, while the arms of his spouse Maria appear on the left. The coat of arms on the back rest refers to the lineage of the Vienna city councillor's familiy, the Huetstocker.[63] Figures and text further decorate the upper face of the large blade bone (Figure 2.8) and the front of the scapula's spine, which extends from the underneath (Figure 2.9). There, the oblong space of the spine is filled with a kind of procession: First, an elephant is depicted walking from right to left. We see his saddle, a castle-like platform with a harness (*howdah*), behind him a man clothed in contemporary attire standing to the right. Because of its central position and oversized buckle, the castle-like saddle is especially emphasized.

Two further figures are flanking the inscription on the seat surface (Figure 2.7). The one standing to right is clothed with a long, exotic fur-coat, while the figure to the very left is clothed in a contemporary Renaissance style. Turned towards the centre, this man is pointing with a stick to a long inscription in the middle. The inscription is depicted as written on the outspread elephant's hide, reporting the pre-history and genesis of the three-legged stool. The detailed description of the event is of the most important sources for the festal entry and parade in 1552:

'CVM.ILLVSTRISS(*imus*): PRINCEPS.MAXMILIANVS:/
REX.BOEHEMIAE.ARCHIDVX.AVSTRIAE.ETC.VNA/
CVM.REGIA.CONIVGESVA.MARIA.CAROLI.V.ROM(*anorum*)./
IMP(*eratoris*).FILIA.DVOBVSQ(ue).REGIIS.LIBERIS.VIENNAM.EX./
HISPANIIS.ANNO.MDLII.DIE.VII.MENS(*is*): MAII.VEN/
IRET.ELEPHANTEM.INDICVM.SECVM.ADDVXIT./
QVI.ELEPHAS.INCVRIA.RECTORIS.DIEXVIII.MENS(*is*):/
DECEMB(*ris*): ANNI.SVBSEQVENTIS.IN.SVBVRBIO./
VIENNENSI.MORITVR.EMORTVI.PONDVS.CEN/
TENARIORVM.XLII.LIBRARVM.LXXIII.FVIT./
EXCVIVS.OSSIBVS.MIHI.SEBASTIANO./
HVETSTOCKER.TVNC.TEMPORIS.CON/
SVLI.VIENNENSI.D(*omi*)NVS.FRANCISCVS./
DELASSO.SVPREMVS.STABVLI.REGII.PRAEFEC/
TVS.IVSSV.REGIS.ARMVS.DEXTER.DONOM/
ISSVS.EST.EX.QVO.HANC.SELLAM.MEM/
ORIE.ERGO.F[*ieri*].F[*eci*]./1554.'

This is to translate as:

When his Serene Highness Prince Maximilian, King of Bohemia, Archduke of Austria etc. came along from Spain to Vienna with his royal wife Maria, daughter of the Roman Emperor, Charles V, and their two royal children, on the seventh of the month May in the year 1552, he brought with him an Indian elephant. This elephant died because of carelessness of his keeper in the following year on the eighteenth of the month December in the suburb of Vienna. At his death he weighed 42 Centner and 73 Pound. From its remains, and on the order of the king, there was given to me, Sebastian Huetstocker, at that time mayor of

Vienna, by Francisco Delasso, the supreme equerry, a gift of the right arm, from which I had this chair made for the sake of memory. 1554.[64]

The inscription recounts the date of the arrival and death of the animal, then talks about how the recipient of the elephant bones gift – Huetstocker, the Mayor of Vienna – made this chair from them. It further notes the year of production, 1554, and ascribes a memorial purpose to the chair. The first figure in the inscription is clearly the patron Sebastian Huetstocker, who may also be the figure in front of the elephant hide (Figure 2.7). Thus, the images and text do not merely record the life and death of the elephant, but also his afterlife in the form of transmutation into a chair.

## Semantics, material and memorial values

As we have seen, ceremonial chairs are imbued with stately semantics. They are distinctive[65] objects per se, separating the seated person from surrounding bystanders. It is not uncommon for seats to be elevated by a pedestal and only accessible via steps, distinguished with a footstool (*suppedaneum*), or flanked by low-lying rows of benches (*subsellia*). The hierarchically determined location of the chairs within an architectural context is also relevant to their meaning. It is no coincidence that seats in the interior of a church are located in specific places such as the presbytery, baptistery or crossing; there, they are usually in close proximity to sacral hot spots (the altar, *confessio*, images of the Virgin Mary, the baptismal font or pulpit, etc.) or on visually or liturgically important axes as the apex of the apse. Sometimes, these spatial areas are further accentuated by the interior design. Chairs are also objects of *dignitas*, in connection with the semantics of *distinctio*, as they are distinguished by the people sitting on them. Their occupants hold dignified offices and/or sit in dignified clothing during official acts. These events usually have a ceremonial character, in that they are regulated normatively, and occur in the context of collective ritual acts.

For the above-mentioned chairs, stately semantics are supported *materialiter*. In fact, both the material and its decorated surface interact competitively with the identity/individuality, the body and the memory of the donor. The immense material value on the one hand and the high standards behind the artistic décor on the other play a pivotal role. In material terms, the Cathedra Petri appears as chryselephantine *Sedes Salomonis*. On the other hand, the imperial intentions of the West Frankish King Charles the Bald are further iconographically reflected in the gable of the throne, where zodiac signs on the sloping beams are flanked by personifications of *Sol* and *Luna*, respectively *Gaia* and *Oceanus* (Figure 2.1). Other astrological personifications refer to a heavenly and cosmological sphere, thus offering Charles protection and legitimacy.[66] With this universal claim to *deificatio*, that is to assimilation as a Christ-like king (*rex christianus*),[67] the fact that Charles the Bald presented his chair to St. Peter seems to fit in perfectly with the Franconian and Carolingian tradition of gift-making. Charles' grandfather Charlemagne (747–814) and great-grandfather Pippin (751/2–768) also gave prominent gifts to St. Peter: Around 761, Pippin donated an altar mensa that was erected in close proximity to the tomb of St. Peter.[68] With the unprecedented exposition of the donated altar at the holiest place in the Memorial Basilica, Pippin's proximity to the Pope was commemorated in liturgical acts. Each time, Pippin was sanctioned anew. Charlemagne likewise offered costly gifts to St. Peter and did not fail to record his offerings in writing so they might be remembered for all eternity. In an inscription on a donated altar cloth (*in pallio altaris*), he immodestly implies that this was not the only gift he had offered to St. Peter.[69] On the occasion of his coronation on Christmas Day in 800, Charlemagne had donated a silver altarpiece and precious liturgical vessels to the *memoria in eternum*.[70] These included a chalice with the inscription KAROLO, and a votive crown for the ciborium. The silver altar and crown are clear references to the Emperor Constantine (†337), who did not bequeath such gifts to St. Peter himself but used them primarily to glorify his donated Memorial Church and in particular his self-positioning as a direct representative of God.[71] If we imagine, for example, the effect of the crown hanging from the ciborium represented on the casket of Samagher in the National Archaeological Museum of Venice (*c.* 440 AD) we can see how the liturgical foundations of the altar and the crown embody the donor at the tomb of St. Peter.[72] The demand for incorporated immanence could hardly be better met.

Divine assimilation is thus clearly expressed in the gift itself, which also clarifies the divine legitimacy of the gift-giver's power. In a very similar manner, we might envision Charles the Bald standing *in personam* at the altar with his cathedra as a deputy. His image on the backrest personalized the chair gift, and in a reciprocal effect the donor was embodied in an object-like way as he became and remained immanent – and thus present within the scene. Just as Charlemagne inscribed his chalice gift with KAROLO, Charles the Bald immortalized himself with his own image. Flanked by two geniuses offering him crowns, his image again reminds the viewer of his divine legitimacy.

The inviting character of the chair further articulates semantic facets of meaning resulting from the inherent ability of a chair to afford sitting.[73] Given that the chair provides a space for sitting,[74] one imagines the possessor or donor seated upon it. If we assume that Martin the Humane was indeed the giver of the Barcelona Chair, its properties, e.g. the royal iconography and materiality, strengthen this assumption all the more.[75] The combination of the four lions and two dragons is remarkable because they operate at different heraldic levels: the lions are presented as heads only, and figure *pars pro toto* as a symbol of royal majesty. But as whole figures, the dragons act even more punctually by embodying the personal emblem of Martin I. This doubling serves as a heraldic sensitization, generally expressing Martin's royal descent (through the lions) and specifically his personal legitimacy as a sovereign (through the dragons). In sum, the heraldic signs are unique markers of Martin's personage. Together with the distinctive semantics of the chair, they position him as owner of the chair by suggesting corporeality.

The Coronation Chair provides analogous representation of an enthroned king that plays a major role in his imaginary embodiment within the chair itself. Belonging to the chair's original decoration, the iconography culminates with a monumental portrait of the enthroned king on the inner backrest.[76] Thus, the physical structure of this chair and its materiality are remarkably interwoven. Literally spoken, the *corporeality* of the chair makes the *corpus realis* evident by showing a king, presumably Edward the Confessor, sitting on it. A similar pattern occurs with the Barcelona chair, where the communicative qualities of the object become evident through the function, semantics and materiality of the chair: aside from the royal and dynastic heraldry the exclusive properties of the Barcelona Chair are closely related to that of the Coronation Chair. Alluding to the king as the rightful possessor of the chair, they make him structurally and materialistically present.[77] This can also be applied to the Cathedra Petri: while the material and formal properties of the Cathedra Petri and the Barcelona Chair indicate their royal origin, the placement of portraits or heraldic signs in prominent positions serves to remind the viewer of a specific person.

In our third example of the Kremsmünster chair, the embodiment of the donor is also evoked structurally, materially and iconographically. Here, the memorial claim is additionally communicated through text. In contrast to the Cathedra Petri and the Barcelona Chair, the vita of the Kremsmünster chair involved three giftings: the first was in 1542, when the Portuguese prince John Manuel wanted to present the elephant as a gift to his promised bride Joanna in Burgos. The second was in 1549 when, probably out of more pragmatic reasons, the animal came to Joanna's sister Maria and her husband Maximilian II of Austria to Valladolid.[78] The third was after the death of the elephant, when the mayor of Vienna received the elephant's right front leg from Maximilian II in 1553. The third giver was thus not only human. Special accentuation of this unusual, twofold donor was therefore necessary, which is manifested within the chair object itself in distinct modalities: through the bony structure of the *sella*, the material visibility of the bones as carriers of the whole chair and of images and not least through text and the engraved images themselves. Remarkably, also Maximilian is represented by heraldic devices *and* scripture on the chair. The gifted object interlaces him with the act of gift-giving in a way that illuminates the significance of his person: not aside from the written text, his coat of arms is featured on rather accentuated spots of the chair such as the right leg of the *sella*. This contributes to the *memoria* of the memorable event, namely, the *adventus* of the later emperor into Vienna.

The purpose of the chair gift as memorial object, as visualized here in text and image, raises further questions. We might wonder whether the Elephant Chair was ever intended for sitting rather than viewing. Was it intended to enrich a hypothetical Kunst- or Wunderkammer of Huetstocker as an exotic symbol of his rank?[79] Since there are no historical accounts describing either how Huetstocker used the chair or where it was displayed, many questions remain regarding the chair's function and display. Thus, the information provided by the chair itself regarding its function and *raison d'être* becomes all the more important. Once the chair reveals its purpose as a memorial object, we are returned to the semantics of chairs. Why did Huetstocker make a chair from the curious gift of bones? Assuming the *sella* was not just a pragmatic solution to the problem of producing something meaningful from a gifted set of bones, I would like to conclude in more general terms with the following question: why were chairs given away?

## Conclusion

Chairs were popular as elite gifts and as such became meaningful status symbols. Chair gifts were made with the most precious materials, the highest artistic quality, and rich iconographic programs. Aside from the *realia* that continue to exist in part today, many chair gifts exist only in written records. Both the material value and the artistic claim of the chair were topical, and often went hand-in-hand with the creation of legends regarding the gifted chairs. Thus, the attribution of preserved chair-*realia* to a prominent donor often originates in a postfactual myth. When dealing with gifted chairs, then, one inevitably encounters the problem of questionable attribution. And yet, sources mentioning chair gifts clearly show that these chairs played an essential role in the historic world politics and diplomacy. Their significance was instrumentalized not least for personal salvation and *memoria*.

Characteristics of elite materiality, stately semantics and memorial potential are all inherent to the chair objects discussed here. In elaborating on each, I have tried to show the extent to which the chairs proved particularly suitable agents in the diplomatic relations of the Frankish, Aragonese and Habsburgian rulers. That these strategies still worked in Early Modern times becomes evident with the iron and silver chairs, that were gifted to Emperor Maximilian II in 1564 and to Queen Christina of Sweden (1626–1689) in 1640 on the occasion of their coronations.[80] Equally, they are present in the monumental 'Throne' installed in the pyramid of the Louvre in 2018, created by the Japanese artist Kohei Nawa for the 160th anniversary of diplomatic relations between France and Japan (Figure 2.10). As with medieval dynamics, Nawa's throne is an authoritarian status symbol equated with the semantics of power through use of the most precious materials such as gold leaf and platinum foil applications and the latest artistic techniques as 3D-modelling.[81] The decisive factor of material presence and its potential to stage the divine light becomes even clearer when compared with Bernini's reliquary for the Cathedra Petri (Figure 2.11).

The three chairs examined above are intrinsically imbued with stately semantics. As objects of distinction with the capacity to afford seating, they suggest corporeality and – to come back to Cecily Hilsdale – are thus 'powerful mediating agent[s] in social […] dynamics' best suited to 'underscore memoria'.[82] Each chair gift is a mobile object with no ties to a specific location or purpose. As such, chairs could undertake long journeys, assume new functions and carry other cultural connotations. Each gifted chair also became part of a gift chain, passing from hand-to-hand across their respective lifetimes. They thus passed through different geographical, cultural and social contexts, as well. For example, the raw material of the Kremsmünster *sella*, derived from an elephant, that travelled from Goa to Lisbon, Valladolid, and up to Vienna. Yet, it also passed through different social classes, as the bone of the elephant's right leg departed royal stirps to become a chair for the mayor of Vienna. Finally, it passed through the different contexts for donation. As foreseen marital gift naturally also imbued with diplomatic intentions, the elephant was sent from the Portuguese to the Spanish court before leaving the marital context entirely when it was handed over to Maximilian II. With an equally diplomatic intent, the latter then bequeathed the right front leg bone to the mayor of Vienna. Similarly, the Cathedra Petri and the Barcelona Chair left their secular and royal contextual origins behind when they were dedicated to a sacral destination. The two chairs thus reached the end of the gift chain since, according to Cecily Hilsdale, 'once dedicated to the saints [a gift] cannot be deaccessioned from its sacred role'.[83] The diplomatic function and social role of the chairs became spiritual.[84] These transfers and transformations were only made possible by the mobility of the seats. The mobility of the chairs enabled them to be used in collective ritual acts, such as liturgical ceremonies and processions. The temporary physical presence of the gift giver was then expanded into a permanent presence through proximity to the saint.

The biographies of these gifted artefacts coincide with those of a celebrated medieval gift, the Eleanor Vase[85], which King Louis VII (†1180) gave to Abbot Suger of Saint Denis (1081–1151) on the second occasion of gifting.[86] After reframing the object with a filigree mount in gold, silver and precious jewels (*gemmis auroque ornato*[87]), the Abbot introduced it into a new, sacral context by dedicating it to the saints at the abbey. Along with the chain of gifting (*donationis seriem*) the distinct hierarchy of the recipients can be traced by means of Suger's inscription on the vase.[88]

Our chair gifts, too, passed through various stages over the course of their lifetimes, undergoing processes of transmuting and becoming object conversions. This becomes most obvious in the Kremsmünster chair, where furthermore also the re-enactment of the gift-giving is illustrated materially as well as through image and text. The figurative representations and heraldic devices positioned on the *sella* provide clear 'trace[s of] its genealogy of exchange'.[89] The chair was supposed to fulfil the function of a biographical memorial object and serve as a reminder of an event of importance for its patron. The successful parade and the good relationship Huetstocker subsequently entertained with the royal court legitimized and confirmed his prominent position within Viennese society. The *sella* reminds us of the practice of exotic animal gifts, exchanged since antiquity among the highest religious and secular dignitaries.[90] In addition, we can trace a direct reference to the materiality of the chair: by its tattooing in a literal sense, the act of recollection is triggered not only by text and image on the seat, but also through its real and visualized matter, the elephant's bones and the depicted hide. As performative aspect of commemoration,[91] the recognizability of individual elements is pivotal within material and thus also memorial value, since their agency is based on an imaginative reconstruction of their production.

The materiality, authoritarian semantics and royal genealogy of the Cathedra Petri, the Barcelona Chair and the Kremsmünster *sella* bear witness to their value as a gift, likely ensuring their preservation up to the present day. While the paragone between semantic and material value was inherent in all the discussed chairs at their creation and had roughly balanced out at the time of the gifting, it had to be negotiated anew in the further course of these chair rites.

*Of Ivory, Gold and Elephants* 59

**Figure 2.1** Rome, St Peter, Cathedra Petri, before 875. Source: Margherita Guarducci, La Cattedra di San Pietro nella scienza e nella fede, Rome 1982, pl. IV. © Public domain.

**Figure 2.2** Rome, St. Peter, Cathedra Petri, before 875, detail with Bust of King Charles the Bald. Source: Margherita Guarducci, La Cattedra di San Pietro nella scienza e nella fede, Rome 1982, pl. VII. © Public domain.

**Figure 2.3** Barcelona, Cathedral Treasury, Throne of Martin I, before 1410. © Cathedral of Barcelona, photo: Guillem F. Gel.

**Figure 2.4** Barcelona, Cathedral Treasury, Throne of Martin I, before 1410, detail with dragon. © Cathedral of Barcelona, photo: Guillem F. Gel.

**Figure 2.5** Barcelona, Cathedral Treasury, Throne of Martin I, before 1410, detail with glass enamel and lionhead in the volute. © Cathedral of Barcelona, photo: Guillem F. Gel.

**Figure 2.6** Madrid, Armería Real, D.11, Helmet with dragon crest, also known as king Martin's crest, around 1407. © Patrimonio Nacional, Real Armería, 10000028.

*Of Ivory, Gold and Elephants* 63

**Figure 2.7** Kremsmünster, Benedictine Abbey, Art Collections, Inv. OKT 43.2.69, Elephant Chair, 1554. © University of Applied Arts Vienna, Thesis of Henriette Wiltschek 2012/13, photo: Peter Kainz.

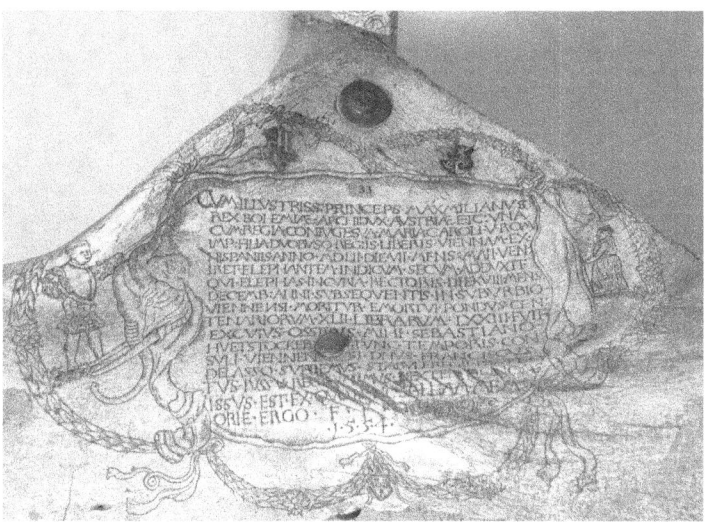

**Figure 2.8** Kremsmünster, Benedictine Abbey, Art Collections, Inv. OKT 43.2.69, Elephant Chair, 1554, detail with seat surface. © University of Applied Arts Vienna, Thesis of Henriette Wiltschek 2012/13, photo: Peter Kainz.

**Figure 2.9** Kremsmünster, Benedictine Abbey, Art Collections, Inv. OKT 43.2.69, Elephant Chair, 1554, detail with front of the scapula's spine. © Stift Kremsmünster, photo: Stefan Kerschbaumer.

**Figure 2.10** Paris, Louvre, "Throne", Kohei Nawa, 2018, © Kohei Nawa | SANDWICH Inc. © I.M. Pei / Louvre Museum.

**Figure 2.11** Rome, St Peter, Apse, Cattedra Petri, Reliquiary by Gian Lorenzo Bernini, 1666 © Photo: Sailko, CC BY 3.0 (public domain).

## Notes

1 'En la sale ot. ii. faudestués d'ivoire […]. N'i avoit nule rien de fust, se d'or non et d'ivoire fin. Antaillié furent de grant fin, car li dui manbre d'une part orent sanblance de liepart, li autre dui de corquatrilles. Uns chevaliers, Bruianz des Illes, en avoit fet de l'un seisine le roi Artus et la reïne.' See David Staines, *The complete Romances of Chrétien de Troyes* (Bloomington/Indianapolis: Indiana University Press, 1990), 83, lines 66867–66880.

2 The original text leaves it ambivalent as to whether the leopards and crocodiles decorated the foot of a chair in full figure or half each.

3 Marcel Mauss, *Die Gabe: Form und Funktion des Austausches in archaischen Gesellschaften*, trans. Eva Modenhauer (Frankfurt: Suhrkamp, 1990), 36–9; 143–50.

4 Lars Kjaer, *The Medieval Gift and the Classical Tradition: Ideals and the Performance of Generosity in Medieval England, 1100–1300* (Cambridge: Cambridge University Press, 2019), 5.

5   Cecily Hilsdale, 'Gift', *Studies in Iconography* 33 (2012): 171–82, here 173.
6   '[…] *sellae ut foras pedes virgo non moveat* […] *munera vestra convenient: sedere aptum est otiosis* […].' Cited from: *Saint Jérome Lettres*, ed. and trans. Jérôme Labourt (Paris: Société d'édition 'Les Belles Lettres', 1951), 95–6; on the exegesis of Jerome's letters cf. Hartmut Beyer, '*Nesciunt muta esse munera sapientis*. Geschenkexegese und Geschenktheorie in der lateinischen Epistolographie des Mittelalters', in *Geschenke erhalten die Freundschaft. Gabentausch und Netzwerkpflege im europäischen Mittelalter*, ed. Michael Grünbart (Berlin: LIT Verlag, 2011), 13–51, at 31–5.
7   Michele C. Ferrari, 'Gold und Asche. Reliquie und Reliquiare als Medien in Thiofrid von Echternachs "Flores epytaphii sanctorum"', in *Reliquiare im Mittelalter*, ed. Bruno Reudenbach and Gia Toussaint (Berlin: Akademie Verlag, 2011), 61–74, at 63. On the presence of saints in reliquaries see Amy G. Remensnyder, 'Legendary Treasure at Conques: Reliquaries and Imaginative Memory', *Speculum* 71:4 (1996): 884–906.
8   To name but two examples: *cathedre seu faudastorii aurei preciosis lapidibus*: Louis de Mas-latrie, 'Perte et rachat du trône de l'empereur Frédéric II', *Bibliothèque de l'École des chartes* 23 (1862): 248–55, here 251–2 and 254–5; *cathedra sive faudistorium*: Percy E. Schramm, *Kaiser Friedrichs II. Herrschaftszeichen* (Göttingen: Vandenhoeck & Ruprecht, 1955), 82.
9   'Et de spoliis, quae ceperat Carolus, s. Marciali, sicut voverat, id est de capella Rotberti regis: evangelium, dalmaticam, faltestalium argentatum, vestimentum integrum sacerdotale preciosum, duos libros, vexillum ex veste auro texta unum.' Ademar: Hist III, cap. 22. Monumenta Germaniae Historica, Scriptores 4, 215. Percy E. Schramm, *Herrschaftszeichen und Staatssymbolik*, vol. 3 (Stuttgart: Anton Hiersemann, 1956), 1097.
10  'Eo tempore duo imperialia ornamenta auro miro opere acta cesar per Iohannem diaconum Petro suo compatri duci, unum ex Papiensi, aliud ex Ravennati urbe, dono transmisit. Cui dux recompensationis gratia cathedram elephantinis artificiose sculpta tabulis per eundem diaconum Ravennae direxit. Quam avide suscipiens, in eadem urbe conservandam reliquit.' Johannes Diaconus, *Chronicon Venetum et Gradense*, Monumenta Germaniae Historica, Scriptores 7, 34.
11  Giovanni Monticolo, *Chronache Veneziane Antichissime*, vol. 1 (Roma: Forzani 1890), 164. Otto III took over the confirmation godparenthood for Orseolo's three-year-old and third son Piero in 996, whose name then was changed in 'Otho/Ottone'.
12  A half year before, Orseolo already presented an ivory chair (*eburneum sedile cum suo subsellio*) to Otto III, which he unwillingly accepted (*licet invitus*). Luigi Andrea Berto, *Giovanni Diacono Istoria Veneticorum* (Bologna: Zanichelli Editore, 1999), lib. IV, n. 59, 198–201. Orseolo's gift-offensive went together with his request of Otto's godparenthood also for Orseolo's daughter. Otto has agreed and consolidated in a perfect way the loyalty bond (*ad perfecte namque fidei vinculum confirmandum*). Berto, *Diacono Istoria*, 198.

13  Hans Graeven, 'Fragment eines frühchristlichen Bischofsstuhls im Provinzial-Museum zu Trier', *Bonner Jahrbücher* 105 (1900): 147–63, at 160.
14  Knut Görich, 'Heimliche Herrscherbegegnung: Kaiser Otto III. besucht Venedig (1001)' in *Venedig als Bühne. Organisation, Inszenierung und Wahrnehmung europäischer Herrscherbesuche*, ed. Romedio Schmitz-Esser, Knut Görich, Jochen Johrendt (Regensburg: Schnell & Steiner, 2017), 51–66, at 63.
15  '[…] *rex Karolus de copiosa et preciosa, quae jam in ejus dominii cesserat […], necnon facistorium Caesaris, sedem imperialem aurea massa conflatam, margaritis corruscantibus undique circumseptam, […], domino Clementi sanctae memoriae summo pontifici pro grandis et cari muneris oblatione transmittit.*' Saba Malaspina, *Storia delle cose di Sicilia (1250–1285)*, ed. Francesco de Rosa (Cassino: Francesco Ciolfi, 2014), 132–5, see also *Die Chronik Des Saba Malaspina*, ed. Walter Koller and August Nitschke (Hannover: Hahnsche Buchhandlung, 1999), lib. III, n. 14, 177 (Monumenta Germaniae Historica, SS 35).
16  Norbert Kamp, 'Die Herrscherthrone im Schatz der Kardinäle 1268–1271', in *Festschrift Percy Ernst Schramm*, vol. 1, ed. Peter Classen and Peter Scheibert (Wiesbaden: Steiner, 1964), 157–74. According to Franz Ehrle, 'Der "constantinische Schatz" in der päpstlichen Kammer des 13. und 14. Jahrhunderts', *Archiv für Literatur- und Kirchengeschichte des Mittelalters* 4 (1888): 191–200, at 197, we must assume that by 1311 the folding chair was disassembled; see also Percy E. Schramm, 'Ein verschollener Thron (*faldistorium*) Friedrichs II.' in Schramm, *Herrschaftszeichen*, 86–7. For the inventories of 1295 and 1311 with further literature, see Christiane Elster, *Die textilen Geschenke Papst Bonifaz' VIII. (1294–1303) an die Kathedrale von Anagni. Päpstliche Paramente des späten Mittelalters als Medien der Repräsentation, Gaben und Erinnerungsträger* (Petersberg: Michael Imhof Verlag, 2018), 100–2.
17  The throne, composed from marble and sandstone, bears Kufic inscriptions on the front and rear side of its backrest, a spolially reused, probably Seljuk funerary stele. In 1591 the throne was removed to the south nave of the church. Areli Marina, 'From the Myth to the Margins: The Patriarch's Piazza at San Pietro di Castello in Venice', *Renaissance Quarterly* 64:2 (2011): 353–429, at 396; Vincenzo Strika, *La 'cattedra' di S. Pietro a Venezia. Note sulla simbologia astrale nell'arte islamica*, Naples: Tipografia Don Bosco, 1978; Rebecca Müller, Sic hostes Ianua frangit. *Spolien und Trophäen im mittelalterlichen Genua* (Weimar: VDG: 2002), 65; Stefano Carboni, *Venice and the Islamic World, 828–1797* (New Haven: Yale University Press, 2007), cat. no. 87; Christian Forster, 'Inschriftenspolien. Ihre Verwendung und Bedeutung im Mittelalter', in *Verborgen, unsichtbar, unlesbar – zur Problematik restringierter Schriftpräsenz*, ed. Tobias Frese et al. (Berlin: De Gruyter, 2014), 143–67, here 159–60.
18  It remains open whether the marble throne in Metz Cathedral, reused from an ancient or late antique column, was a gift to Bishop Chrodegang (742–766)

from King Pippin (714–768), who had assisted the Bishop with the cathedral's refurbishing (*cum adiutorio Pippin regis*), e.g. the altar, choir screen and triumphal arch. Cf. Mechthild Schulze-Dörlamm, 'Zeugnisse der Selbstdarstellung von weltlichen und geistlichen Eliten der Karolingerzeit (751–911)', in *Aufstieg und Untergang. Zwischenbilanz des Forschungsschwerpunktes 'Studien zu Genese und Struktur von Eliten in Vor- und Frühgeschichtlichen Gesellschaften'*, ed. Markuss Egg and Dieter Quast (Mainz: Verlag des Römisch-Germanischen Zentralmuseums, 2009), 153–215, at 157, 158 with fig. 3 and 207.

19  For the donations of Charles' grandfather Charlemagne, on the occasion of his coronation on Christmas day exactly seventy-five years earlier.

20  Hugo Brandenburg, *San Pietro. Storia di un monumento* (Milan: Jaca Book, 2015), 286–99; Marcello Fagiolo, *Roma barocca. l protagonisti. gli spazi urbani, i grandi temi* (Rome: De Luca, 2013), 97–103; Sebastian Schütze, 'Werke als Kalküle ihres Wirkungsanspruchs: die Cathedra Petri und ihr Bedeutungswandel im konfessionellen Zeitalter', in *Sankt Peter in Rom 1506–2006*, ed. Georg Satzinger and Sebastian Schütze (Munich: Hirmer, 2008), 405–25.

21  *La cattedra lignea di San Pietro in Vaticano*, ed. Michele Maccarrone (Rome: Tipogr. Poliglotta Vaticana, 1971); Michele Maccarrone et al., *Nuove ricerche sulla cattedra lignea di S. Pietro in Vaticano* (Rome: Tipogr. Poliglotta Vaticana, 1975). The two Vatican monographs were followed only by essays, but no more monographic studies on the Cathedra Petri. As a consequence, research had to concentrate on not very good photographs of uncleaned ivory works, and the throne itself could not be studied in its original form since then.

22  Elio Corona, 'Indagine dendrochronologica', in *La cattedra lignea*, 165–72; Antonio Ferrua, 'Esame strutturale e archeologica, in *La cattedra lignea*, 113–19; Marisa Alessio, 'Datazione con il metodo di carbonio-14', in *La cattedra lignea*, 173–85; Vittorio Federici, 'Esami chimici', in *La cattedra lignea*, 185–90.

23  Before the panel with the ivory plaques was secondarily attached, also the chair's front side was arcaded. According to dendrochronological analysis, the substrate, a two-winged diptych, was made in eastern France (presumably in Lorraine). Ernst Hollstein, 'Die Cathedra Lignea von St. Peter im Vatikan', in *Nuove ricerche sulla cattedra,* 79–103, at 103; Ernst Hollstein, 'Zur dendrochronologischen Regionaldiagnose der Eichenhölzer der Cathedra Lignea von St. Peter im Vatikan', *Römische Quartalschrift* 75 (1980): 206–7.

24  Elio Corona, 'Ricerche dendrocronologiche sul rivestimento ligneo (gabbia) della Cattedra di S. Pietro', *Memorie del Museo Tridentino di scienze naturali* 22 (1979): 37–47, mentions besides pine also parts from chestnut and ash wood, see 37 and 46–7.

25  Pietro Romanelli, 'La decorazione in avorio', in *La cattedra lignea*, 191–216, here 191.

26  Rebecca Müller, 'Mythenrezeption in karolingischer Zeit. Bilder, Texte, und Bilder in Texten', in *Mittelalterliche Mythenrezeption. Paradigmen und Paradigmenwechsel*, ed. Ulrich Rehm (Vienna: Böhlau Verlag, 2018), 81–104, at 92; Müller further

demonstrates, how the ivory panels dominate the perception of the cathedra in structural, topological and material terms; see also Ulrich Rehm, *Klassische Mythologie im Mittelalter. Antikenrezeption in der bildenden Kunst* (Vienna: Böhlau, 2019), 93–8.

27 Rainer Kahsnitz, 'Der Nachtragsband zu Goldschmidts Elfenbeincorpus', in *Atlanten des Wissens. Adolph Goldschmidts Corpuswerke 1914 bis heute*, ed. Kai Kappel, Claudia Rückert and Stefan Trinks (Berlin: Deutscher Kunstverlag, 2016), 118–35, here 126.

28 Stefan Trinks, 'Eingehüllt in Gold und Bein – die *techné* des Chryselephantin als 'Mitstreit' im Mittelalter, *Zeitschrift für Kunstgeschichte* 79 (2016): 481–507, especially 493–5 on the Cathedra, as a special case of drilled and gold-inlaid ivory. For medieval artefacts of the Salomonic Throne in the Christian West, see Allegra Iafrate, *The Wandering Throne of Solomon. Objects and Tales of Kingship in the Medieval Mediterranean* (Leiden: Brill, 2016), 215–57.

29 Raffaele Garrucci, *Storia della arte cristiana nei primi otto secoli della Chiesa*, vol. 6 (Prato: F. Giachetti & G. Guasti, 1880), 12. Percy E. Schramm, 'Die Cathedra St. Petri in der Peterskirche zu Rom', in *Herrschaftszeichen*, 694–707, at 700–702; Percy E. Schramm, 'Kaiser Karl der Kahle der Stifter des Thrones in St. Peter', in *La cattedra lignea*, 277–93, at 277–9; Lawrence Nees, 'Charles the Bald and the Cathedra Petri', in *Charles the Bald: Court and Kingdom*, ed. Margaret T. Gibson and Janet L. Nelson (2nd ed., Aldershot: Variorum, 1990), 340–7; Nikolaus Staubach, *Rex Christianus. Hofkultur und Herrschaftspropaganda im Reich Karls des Kahlen. Teil 2: Die Grundlegung der 'religion royale'* (Vienna: Böhlau, 1993), 292; William Diebold, 'The Ruler Portrait of Charles the Bald', *Gesta* 76:1 (1994): 6–18. Albeit emphasizing the new type of portrait of Charles the Bald, Anne-Orange Poilpré confines her study of the portrait of Charles the Bald on thrones to manuscripts and does not discuss the Cathedra Petri. Anne-Orange Poilpré, 'Le portrait royal en trône sous le règne de Charles le Chauve: l'espace constraint de la royauté', in *L'image médiévale. Fonctions dans l'espace sacré et structuration de l'espace cultuel*, ed. Cécile Voyer and Éric Sparhubert (Turnhout: Brepols, 2011), 325–40.

30 'Karolus […] in die nativitatis Domini beato Petro multa et pretiosa munera offerens […].' Monumenta Germaniae Historica, Scriptores rer. Germ. 5, 1883, ad anno 876: Hincmarus Remensis, Annales Bertiniani. Schramm, 'Cathedra', 705.

31 Percy Ernst Schramm, *Die deutschen Kaiser und Könige in Bildern ihrer Zeit: 751–1190* (Munich: Prestel, 1983), 50–62.

32 Michele Maccarrone, 'Die Cathedra Sancti Petri im Hochmittelalter. Vom Symbol des päpstlichen Amtes zum Kultobjekt (II)', *Römische Quartalschrift* 76 (1981): 137–72, here 165–6; Sible de Blaauw, *Cultus et decor. Liturgia e architettura nella Roma tardoantica e medievale*, vol. 2 (Vatican City: Biblioteca Apostolica Vaticana, 1994), 721; Diego Giovanni Ravelli, *La solennità della Cattedra di San Pietro nella Basilica Vaticana. Storia e formulario della Messa* (Rome: CLV, Edizioni liturgiche,

2012), 187–8; and recently Carola Jäggi, 'Cathedra Petri und Colonna Santa in St. Peter zu Rom. Überlegungen zu „Produktion" und Konjunktur von Reliquien im Mittelalter', in *Erzeugung und Zerstörung von Sakralität zwischen Antike und Mittelalter*, ed. Armin F. Bergmeier et al. (=*Distant Worlds Journal* 1 (2016)): 109–31, at 122–4; Sabina Rosenbergová, 'The Myth of the Cathedra Petri', in *Re-thinking, Re-making, Re-living Christian Origins*, ed. Ivan Foletti et al. (Rome: Viella, 2018), 333–44, at 341–4.

33   Holger Guster, Die Hostienmonstranzen des 13. und 14. Jahrhunderts in Europa (unpublished doctoral thesis, University of Heidelberg, 2009), 269–73; Núria de Dalmases, *Orfebreria catalana medieval: Barcelona 1300–1500* (Aproximació a l'Estudi), vol. 1 (Barcelona: Editat per l'Institut d'Estudis Catalans, 1992), 298–302 and soon to be published: Ramon Pujades Bataller, 'Una sala del tron sense tron monumental', in Ramon Pujades Bataller, *Un cor en pedra: el Palau Major de Barcelona (924–1954)* (Barcelona: MUHBA, forthcoming).

34   'Item visitavit cathedram argenti que fuit bone memorie regis Martini, nunc vero continuo manet in altari maiori Sedis ad sustendandum custodiam maiorem ponderis incamerata ducentarum trium marcharum et IIIIor unciarum. (…) Item pese la cadira d.argent daurade la qual stà continuadament en lo tabernacle al altar maior, qui serveix a portar la dita custòdia lo dia de Corpore Christi ab una basa […]'. Maria J. Torres I Ferrer, 'Una nova aportació per a l'estudi del tresor de la Seu de Barcelona: L´inventari de 1492 Lambard', *Estudis d'art medieval* 9 (1996): 207–29, at 223 and 229.

35   *L'art Catalan du Xe au XVe siècle*. Exhibition Catalogue Jeu de Paume des Tuileries (Paris: Gauthier-Villars, 1937); and recently: Eva March, 'Guerra, propaganda y nacionalismo catalán en el París de 1937', *Acta/Artis. Estudis d'Art Modern* 4/5 (2016–2017): 205–37.

36   March, 'Guerra', 220, with fig. 10.

37   For the chair's function as an episcopal cathedra, see Francesca Español, 'Silla y custodia. Ostensorio turriforme', in *Maravillas de la España medieval. Tesoro sagrado y monarquía*, ed. Isidro G. Bango Torviso (Junta de Castilla y León: Caja España, 2001), 289–93.

38   Schramm, 'Der silberne Thron des Königs Martin I. des Humanen von Aragon (1396–1410) in Barcelona', in *Herrschaftszeichen und Staatssymbolik*, 937–8, here 938.

39   '[…] per desfer la cadira en la que lo Rey celebrava les corts als Valencians en Segorb e de portarla de Segorb a Castelló'. Manuel Trens, *Las custodias españolas* (Barcelona: s.n., 1952), 33.

40   For the written communication of the dimensions I would like to thank Imma Ferrer, Arxiu Capitular de Barcelona.

41   The structural similarity of these two chairs has already been pointed out by Schramm, 'Der silberne Thron', 938 and Paul Binski, *Westminster Abbey and the*

*Plantagenets. Kingship and the Representation of Power 1200–1400* (New Haven: Yale University Press, 1995), 136.

42  Percy E. Schramm, 'Der hölzerne Thron König Edwards I. von England (1299) in Westminster mit dem Steinsitz der schottischen Könige', in *Herrschaftszeichen und Staatssymbolik,* 928–37; Paul Binski, 'A "Sign of Victory": The Coronation Chair, Its Manufacture, Setting and Symbolism', in *The Stone of Destiny: Artefact and Icon,* ed. Richard Welander, David Breeze and Thomas Owen Clancy (Edinburgh: Society of Antiquaries of Scotland, 2003), 207–22; and recent James Alexander Cameron, '*Sedilia in choro sunt fracta*: The Medieval Nomenclature of Seating in Churches', *Journal of the British Archeological Association* 168 (2015): 111–30, here 120–2; Warwick Rodwell, *The Coronation Chair and Stone of Scone* (London: Oxbow Books, 2013).

43  De Dalmases, *Orfebreria*, 299.

44  For the Account Books of 1299–1300, see Rodwell, *Coronation Chair*, 36. For the symbolic of lions on thrones, see Peter Seiler, 'Richterlicher oder kriegerischer Furor? Untersuchungen zur Bestimmung der primären Bedeutung des Braunschweiger Burglöwen', in *Heinrich der Löwe. Herrschaft und Repräsentation,* ed. Konstanzer Arbeitskreis für Mittelalterliche Geschichte e.V. (Ostfildern: Jan Thorbecke Verlag, 2003), 136–79, here 159–75.

45  Amadeo Serra Desfilis, 'A Search for the Hidden King: Messianism, Prophecies and Royal Epiphanies of the Kings of Aragon (circa 1250–1520)', *Arts* 143:8 (2019): 1–28, here 17.

46  Schramm*, 'Der silberne Thron',* 937; Joan Molina Figueras, 'Memoria visual de una dinastía. Pedro IV El Ceremonioso y la retórica de las imágenes en la corona de Aragón (1336–1387)', *Anales de Historia del Arte* 23 (2013): 219–41, at 231.

47  Juan Bautista Crooke Y Navarrot, *Catálogo Histórico-Descriptivo de la Real Armería de Madrid* (Madrid: Hauser y Manet, 1898), 139–41; Jaume Riera I Sans, 'Els heralds i les divises del rei Martí (1356–1410)', *Paratge Quaderns d'Estudis de Genealogia Heràldica Sigil·lografia i Nobiliària* 14 (2002): 41–61, at 54; Encarna Montero Tortajada, 'Noticias sobre la escultura en papel en Valencia y la Corona de Aragón durante la Baja Edad Media', in *Escultura Ligera. I Jornadas Internacionales de Escultura Ligera*, ed. Gemma Contreras (Valencia: Institut Valencià de Conservació, Restauració i Investigació, 2017), 99–108, at 100–1.

48  For the aragonese tradition of self-coronation, see Jaume Aurell and Marta Serrano-Coll, 'The Self-Coronation of Peter the Ceremonious (1336): Historical, Liturgical, and Iconographical Representations', *Speculum* 89:1 (2014): 66–95.

49  Aurell/Serrano-Coll, 'Self-Coronation', 73–6.

50  Aurell/Serrano-Coll, 'Self-Coronation', 84–94.

51  This genealogical roll (1409–1410) was given to the Cistercian monastery of Poblet, which was the royal burial grounds for the Aragonese. There, beside numerous portraits of his predecessors, *Martí Rey* is shown as the only seated

king. Amadeo Serra Desfilis, 'La historia de la dinastía en imágenes: Martín el Humano y el rollo genealógico de la Corona de Aragón', *Locus Amoenus* 6 (2002–2003): 57–74, at 70.

52  There again appears to be a connection to the English Crown or to the activities of Edward's I, as he also had commissioned a genealogical roll, whose two parts are preserved in: Oxford, Bodleian Library, ms. Bodl. Rolls 3 and London, British Library, Cotton Galba Charter XIV.4. Desfilis, 'Martín el Humano', 64.

53  Kremsmünster Abbey, Art Collections, Inv. OKT 43.2.69. Henriette Wiltschek, 'Ein postmortaler Beinbruch. Zur Klebung und Konservierung eines gravierten Knochenobjekts: Der Elefantenstuhl aus Stift Kremsmünster', *Österreichische Zeitschrift für Kunst und Denkmalpflege* 67:1/2 (2013): 123–9; Henriette Wiltschek, *Der Elefantenstuhl aus Stift Kremsmünster (1554). Zur Klebung und Konservierung eines gravierten Knochenobjekts* (Thesis, University of Applied Arts Vienna, 2013). I would like to thank the author for making the unpublished typescript available to me. For the latest publications to the *sella* see also Annemarie Jordan Gschwend, 'Die Elefanten der Königin', in *Elfenbeine aus Ceylon. Luxusgüter für Katharina von Habsburg (1507–1578). Exhibition Catalogue Museum Rietberg Zurich*, ed. Johannes Beltz (Zurich: Rietberg Museum, 2010), 127–37, at 132–35 and Annemarie Jordan Gschwend, 'Stuhl aus den Knochen Süleymans', in *Elfenbeine aus Ceylon*, 140–57.

54  Still fundamental for the differentiation and definition of *memoria* as a social act in which the presence of the dead is constituted and a community of commemorators and commemorated is created: Otto Gerhard Oexle, 'Memoria und Memorialbild', in *Memoria. Der geschichtliche Zeugniswert des liturgischen Gedenkens im Mittelalter*, ed. Karl Schmid and Joachim Wollasch (Munich: Willhelm Fink Verlag, 1984), 384–440. This chapter also relies on Oexle's concept of the 'memorial image' (*Memorialbild*) introduced for artefacts that evoke memory through iconography. On *memorabilia* (*Erinnerungsstücke*) see Stephan Albrecht, *Die Inszenierung der Vergangenheit im Mittelalter. Die Klöster von Glastonbury und Saint-Denis* (Munich: Deutscher Kunstverlag, 2003), 14–6 and Markus Späth, *Verflechtung von Erinnerung. Bildproduktion und Geschichtsschreibung im Kloster San Clemente a Casauria während des 12. Jahrhunderts* (Berlin: Akademie-Verlag, 2007), 22–4. Philippe Cordez, *Schatz, Gedächtnis, Wunder. Die Objekte der Kirchen im Mittelalter* (Regensburg: Schnell & Steiner, 2015), uses the term 'memorial objects' to describe artefacts that were permanently linked to the memory of a person through an inscription on the object or a mention in a written source.

55  The name *Suleiman*, often given for this elephant, cannot be traced in contemporary sources. Thus, further elaborations on its historical or political meaning, as in Annemarie Jordan Gschwend, *The story of Süleyman. Celebrity elephants and other exotica in Renaissance Portugal* (Zurich: A. Jordan Gschwend, 2010), are to be read with caution.

56  Ferdinand Opll, "'… ein(e) vorhin in Wien nie gesehene Rarität von jedermann bewundert". Zu Leben, Tod und Nachleben des ersten Wiener Elefanten', *Jahrbuch des Vereins für Geschichte der Stadt Wien* 60 (2004): 229–73, at 240–1.
57  Opll, 'Rarität', 241.
58  Opll, 'Rarität', 240.
59  For the travel route, see Opll, 'Rarität', 243–6.
60  Stephan Oettermann, *Die Schaulust am Elefanten. Eine Elephantographie Curiosa* (Frankfurt: Syndikat, 1982), 36, 102, mentions that Emperor Frederick III was supposed to receive an elephant as diplomatic gift from John II of Portugal in 1486, but this animal died on its travels in southern Germany, and thus never reached Vienna. See also Opll, 'Rarität', 67.
61  The elephant's remains continued to live on as exotic attractions and were presented as gifts to new owners. The animal was skinned and stuffed, exhibited in Vienna and Munich until it fell victim to rot in a damp cellar in 1945. The taxidermy mount was exhibited in Vienna for nineteen years, until in 1572 Maximilian II presented it to his brother-in-law Albert V, Duke of Bavaria, for his *Kunstkammer* in Munich. There, the mount survived until 1945, when it decayed in a damp storage room. In Munich, the taxidermy mount was exhibited at various locations: in 1928 it was moved from the exhibition rooms of the Alte Akademie to the Bavarian National Museum, where in 1942, it was deposed in the museum cellar during the Second World War and finally decayed in 1945. Ferdinand Opll, 'Etwas bisher noch nie Geschautes. Leben, Tod und Nachleben des ersten Wiener Elefanten', in *Tiere unterwegs. Historisches und Aktuelles über Tiererwerb und Tiertransporte*, ed. Dagmar Schratter and Gerhard Heindl (Vienna: Braumüller, 2007), 65–93, at 75.
62  Wiltschek, 'Elefantenstuhl', 125.
63  For the heraldic description of the 'Hutstockerische Wappen', see Franz Karl Wissgrill, *Schauplatz des landsässigen Nieder-Österreichischen Adels vom Herren- und Ritterstande von dem XI. Jahrhundert an, bis auf jetzige Zeiten*, vol. 4 (Vienna: Franz Seizer, 1800), 472.
64  The english translation is my own inspired by the German translation from Opll, 'Leben, Tod und Nachleben', 89, in deviation from Jordan Gschwend, 'The story of Süleyman', 64, who reads *in curia rectoris*, instead of *incuria rectoris*. See Hubert Reitterer, 'INCURIA RECTORIS. Zum Tod des ersten Wiener Elefanten', in *Studien zur Wiener Geschichte* (Vienna: Selbstverlag des Vereins für Geschichte der Stadt Wien, 2005), 333–5.
65  This term hails from a socio-anthropological context: Pierre Bourdieu, *La distinction. Critique sociale du jugement* (Paris: Les Editions de Minuit, 1979), in accordance with the concept of habitus proffered by Norbert Elias, Über den Prozess der Zivilisation. Soziogenetische und psychogenetische Untersuchungen. Band 2: Wandlungen der Gesellschaft: Entwurf zu einer Theorie der Zivilisation

(Basel: Verlag Haus zum Falken, 1939). On distinction in the sacred space by means of an elevated bishop's cathedra, see Eric Palazzo, *L'évêque et son image* (Turnhout: Brepols, 1999), 69.

66  To the Cathedra Petri as *Acheiropoieton*, see Trinks, 'Chryselephantin', 494.

67  Staubach, *Rex Christianus*, 283–334, especially 294.

68  Franz Alto Bauer, 'Herrschergaben an St. Peter', *Mitteilungen zur Spätantiken Archäologie und Byzantinischen Kunstgeschichte* 4 (2005): 65–91, at 82–3.

69  '*Petre* […], *tu Caroli clemens devoti munera regis Suscipe, quae cupiens obtulit ipse tibi.* […]'. Lorscher Sylloge, ICUR II, 147, n. 9, Monumenta Germaniae Historica, Poet lat. 1, 106–7, n. 14.

70  '[…] *et patena aurea maiore cum gemmis idversis, legente KAROLO* […]'. Lib. Pont II, 7–8.

71  Bauer, 'Herrschergaben', 70.

72  Jas Elsner, 'Concealment and Revelation: The Pola Casket and the Visuality of Early Christian Relics', in *Conditions of visibility*, ed. Richard Neer (Oxford: Oxford University Press, 2019), 74–110.

73  In 1979, the psychologist James J. Gibson has introduced the term *affordance*, studying the psychology of materials and things: Their 'composition and layout […] constitute what they afford. If so, to perceive them is to perceive what they afford.' James J. Gibson, *The Ecological Approach to Visual Perception* (New York: Tyalor & Francis Group, 2015), 119.

74  According to Don Norman, *Design of Everyday Things* (New York: Basic Books, 2013), 11: 'the term affordance refers to the perceived and actual properties of the thing, primarily those fundamental properties that determine just how the thing could possibly be used. […] A chair affords ("is for") support and, therefore, affords sitting.'

75  Parallels can also be found, with the abovementioned gifts of Pippin, Charlemagne and Charles the Bald, as the donor is in search for the assimilation with the divine assimilation. This is expressed particularly well in the Barcelona chair: here we have a core with the Blessed Sacrament – the consecrated host – which rests on the royal throne crowned with crowns. While the crowns clothe the sacred, the throne forms the basis of the divine institution.

76  Marie Louise Sauerberg, 'The Polychromy of the Coronation Chair: A detailed study', in Rodwell, *Coronation Chair*, 77–104, especially 82–4.

77  The crowns attached to the chair after 1480 will only have strengthened this impression.

78  Opll, 'Rarität', 241.

79  Opll, 'Rarität', 263, speculates about the chair as an expression of rank ('Ausdruck repräsentativen Standesdenkens') without implying any physical use of the seat.

80  The amber chair, which Emperor Leopold I received from the Elector Friedrich Wilhelm von Brandenburg in 1678, is quite well researched as a diplomatic agent or modern chair gift. Not only does this chair bear witness to valuable materials and elaborate design, but with its Hercules plates it also approaches iconographically medieval chair gifts, such as the Cathedra Petri. Susanne Netzer, 'Bernsteingeschenke in der preussischen Diplomatie des 17. Jahrhunderts', *Jahrbuch der Berliner Museen* 35 (1993): 227–46, here 233–5; Winfried Baer, 'Ein Bernsteinstuhl für Kaiser Leopold I. Ein Geschenk des Kurfürsten Friedrich Wilhelm von Brandenburg', *Jahrbuch der Kunsthistorischen Sammlungen in Wien* 78 (1982): 91–138; and 130, for the two above-mentioned chairs for Maximilian and Christina.

81  In the description of the work the artist connects the throne with royalty, monarchy and other 'instances of power and authority (that) have rules'. http://kohei-nawa.net/works/throne (accessed 20 April 2021).

82  Hilsdale, 'Gift', 174.

83  Hilsdale, 'Gift', 178.

84  Hilsdale, 'Gift', 178.

85  Musée de Louvre, MR 340.

86  George T. Beech, 'The Eleanor of Aquitaine Vase: Its Origins and History to the Early Twelfth Century', *Ars Orientalis* 22 (1992): 69–79; Philippe Buc, 'Conversion of Objects', *Viator. Medieval and Renaissance Studies* 28 (1997): 99–143, about the Eleanor Vase 125–7.

87  *De administratione*, §280. Cited from: *Abt Suger von Saint Denis. Ausgewählte Schriften. Ordinatio. De consecratione. De administratione*, ed. Andreas Speer and Günther Binding (Darmstadt: Wissenschaftliche Buchgesellschaft, 2000), 366–7.

88  *Abt Suger von Saint Denis*, 366–7; Beech, 'Aquitaine Vase', 370; Hilsdale, 'Gift', 174.

89  Hilsdale, 'Gift', 174.

90  Elephants as diplomatic gifts were given to Charlemagne in 802; to Henry III. in 1255; to René of Anjou in 1477 and to Leo X. in 1514, cf. Oettermann, *Schaulust*, 97–104; Avinoam Shalem discusses exotic animals as gifts in their cross-cultural context, see Avinoam Shalem, 'Objects as Carriers of Real or Contrived Memories in a Cross-cultural Context', *Mitteilungen zur spätantiken Archäologie und byzantinischen Kunstgeschichte* 4 (2005): 101–19; See also: Oleg Grabar, 'The Shared Culture of Objects', in *Byzantine court Culture from 829 to 1204*, ed. Henry Maguire (Washington D.C.: Dumbarton Oaks Research Library and Collection, 1997), 115–29. Exotic gifts and animals are also mentioned in I Kings, 10:1–3, when Queen of Sheba visited King Solomon in his royal court in Jerusalem accompanied by '(…) camels laden with spices, great quantities of gold, and precious stones. (…)'.

91  Remensnyder, 'Imaginative Memory', 886.

# 3

# Gifts and conflicts: Objects given during the entry of Archbishop Silvester Stodewescher in the Riga Cathedral (1449)

Gustavs Strenga

Late medieval ceremonial entry (*adventus*) was an urban phenomenon that usually involved townspeople, their political representatives – members of the city's government – and a lord. As a ritual it was already practised in the early Middle Ages, based on a Roman imperial tradition, and it continued well into the early modern period, being present in the political life of almost every European city. Ceremonial entries – royal advents, princely and episcopal entries – could be used to mark a new ruler taking power.[1] Moreover, an entry was meant to create or reinstate the relationship between a lord and his subjects, to mutually and publicly confirm 'their privileges and duties with an exchange of rights'.[2] This was important for political legitimacy. Entries had to demonstrate the unity and stability of a political relationship between a city and its lord.[3] Yet they also had the potential to be volatile situations in which existing conflicts could resurface and ritual ceremonies could turn into violent clashes.[4] As will be seen in this chapter, entries were events that were heavily influenced by political contexts during which people with different backgrounds, intentions and aims met. The participants could experience a conflicting spectrum of emotions: joy, suspicion, excitement and even fear for their lives.

In recent decades medieval royal and princely entries have been thoroughly researched.[5] However, the aspect of gift-giving during entries has been less well examined. Gift-exchange was an essential element of the festive urban entries of medieval rulers and bishops.[6] Gifts as 'media of communication'[7] helped to establish or symbolically strengthen the relationship between a lord who

This article has been written with the support of the Estonian Research Council during the Mobilitas Pluss project MOBJD231 'Economy of Symbolic Exchange. Gift-Giving as a Social, Cultural and Political Practice in Late Medieval Livonia' at Tallinn University.

entered a city and his subjects. Gifts were an integral part of medieval politics and diplomacy; they helped to mediate conflicts, create, consolidate and stabilize political relationships between partners,[8] and during the entries they fulfilled exactly these functions. Yet, as Martina Winkler points out: 'gifts were and are media of communication that can convey offers of peace and friendship, but are also suitable for communicating provocations and generating conflicts.'[9] During entries gifts were usually given in specific 'ritualized moments', frequently by several groups or their representatives.[10] These were public acts in which objects high in value were given to a ruler and they were reciprocated with objects or other immaterial acts (privileges, oaths, etc.).[11] The objects given or exchanged during entries share similarities with diplomatic gifts. Gifts exchanged between rulers showed the wealth, status and power of a giver and had to demonstrate respect to a recipient.[12] Gifts given as part of an entry also had to be costly and of high quality in order to both adequately represent a giver and show respect for a recipient.

An audience and need for representation were features of every medieval political gift.[13] However, in the case of gifts given during the ceremonial entries of lords, the audience for the gift-giving had as important a role as the objects themselves. The audience, that is those who observed the ritual activities during the entry, read and interpreted the symbolic meanings of objects given.

Gifts were both given and returned during ceremonial entries. However, such direct reciprocity cannot be observed in the case study presented in this chapter. Marcell Mauss' concept of a gift reciprocity has been a central notion here – gift given creates a countergift.[14] Yet both anthropologists and medievalists have argued that not every gift created obligations and reciprocity.[15] Gifts remained gifts even if they were never returned.

This chapter focuses on the gifts given during a bishop's entry into his cathedral in mid-fifteenth-century Northern Europe. Episcopal ceremonial entries were an equally widespread phenomenon in medieval Europe as the entries of secular rulers.[16] In some cities, like Florence, for centuries the episcopal entries followed almost the same practices and traditions of a secular entry rite.[17] The case study analysed here offers a unique example from late medieval Livonia. In late June 1449, the new archbishop of Riga, Silvester Stodewescher, travelled from Prussia, where he had been the chaplain and chancellor of the Teutonic Order's Grand Master. This was not a routine entry. As Hartmut Boockmann has shown, it was an entry of an archbishop appointed to office thanks to political scheming in an environment where his appointment was not desired by his subjects.[18] During the entry Silvester faced danger while meeting people whom he did not know and who saw him as an enemy. Silvester entered into a space – Livonia and the cathedral of Riga – in which he had never been and where he was an alien. This was an event in which ceremonial pomposity and excessive luxury intertwined with lack of trust and fear of imminent death. Silvester's entry revealed conflicts he (potentially) and the Teutonic Order definitely had with the cathedral chapter, his vassals and the city council. This entry is unique because an elaborate report of this event has survived, a letter from Silvester to his patron[19] – the Grand Master of the Teutonic Order Konrad von Erlichshausen (r. 1441–1449).[20] Dated 5 July 1449, two weeks after the entry, the letter is a self-narrative, a self-testimonial, an ego document,[21] in Boockmann's view – a document that provides many details relating to social history and the human condition of the narrator, his fears and hopes.[22] There are numerous references to the objects or services given to Silvester Stodewescher in this text and it reveals the material world of late medieval ceremonial entry in the Northern Europe. Yet, as has been demonstrated by Boockmann and will be shown further in this chapter, this was not a lord's entry into a city itself: Stodewescher ceremoniously entered the cathedral compound within the city walls but did not go to the city hall and meet the councillors.

Medieval entries were material experiences that had to mediate political messages as well as performances during which appearance and representation mattered. The entries demanded splendour, pomp and excessive luxury that represented the power and resources of the two sides involved in the process. Every detail in ceremonial activities was essential. Usually luxurious and expensive objects were chosen for representation, which were bought specially for the occasion and often used only once, such as costly cloths for a baldachin.[23] The objects used as gifts during the entries were also expensive, exclusive, sometimes even exotic, and had a symbolic meaning.

This chapter analyses the gifts given during Silvester's entry and one of the main questions here is: how or whether at all gifts changed and influenced relationships and how they reflected Silvester's relationships with his subjects – the cathedral canons, his vassals, and city of Riga – and his patron, the Grand Master of the Teutonic Order? The second question that motivated to conduct this case-study is: how the material form of the objects given carried specific messages and symbolic meanings? Yet in order to understand these acts of gifting and the relationships in which the objects were given, the context of Silvester's appointment – internal Livonian political relationships and centuries old political feuds – is fundamental. Although gift terminology was not used in the main source for this chapter – the letter of Silvester Stodewescher to the Grand Master – the context makes it clear that these were gifts; the meaning of the objects given was negotiated in particular situations when they were given or exchanged.[24] Gifts initiated and shaped Silvester's relationships with his partners and subjects, most of whom had opposed his appointment.

## Before Silvester Stodewescher's entry

The whole process of Silvester's appointment as the archbishop of Riga was interwoven with political scheming and exchanges of material goods. The quest for the archbishop's seat began on 5 April 1448 when the archbishop of Riga, Henning Scharpenberg (e. 1424–1448), died, leaving the most important ecclesiastical office in Livonia vacant.[25] Only a few weeks later, the Grand Master of the Teutonic Order began his efforts to convince Pope Nicolas V (p. 1447–1455) to appoint his chancellor Silvester Stodewescher as the new archbishop of Riga.[26] The struggle to secure Silvester's appointment in the papal curia was costly. The primary protagonists in this process were the Grand Master of the Teutonic Order himself and the Order's main representative in Rome – the Procurator General, who corresponded on this matter regularly.[27] Klaus Militzer has described in detail the financial interactions the Order undertook in order to provide the necessary resources for Silvester's appointment and he has pointed out that the Teutonic Order invested an impressive sum – 6240 Rhenish Guldens – in Silvester's appointment.[28]

Gifts played an essential role in achieving Silvester's appointment. Most of the more than six thousand Rhenish Guldens went to the expenses of the Procurator General in the papal curia. A third of the sum was spent on gifts and bribes. The Procurator General acquired gifts for the pope, two cardinals and *nepos* of Cardinal Protector of the Teutonic Order; a further sum of 1100 ducats was allocated for the payments to the curial officials that could be described as bribes.[29] This is not extraordinary because in the Middle Ages illicit gifts were frequently made in order to acquire offices.[30] The Teutonic Order had experience in curial politics and in gaining the support of the curial officials, cardinals and the popes themselves, including making use of material incentives.[31] The knowledge of internal dealings was essential since the late medieval and early modern papal court was an environment in which gifts and bribes played an important role in decision making.[32] Objects and money given by the Procurator General in summer and autumn of 1448 apparently worked well and helped the Teutonic Order to achieve its goal. However, according to Militzer, the attempts in the curia to appoint Silvester could be seen to be financially undisciplined squandering of money.[33]

The Grand Master of the Teutonic Order triumphed in this political game. On 9 October 1448 the pope named Silvester Stodewescher as the next archbishop of Riga.[34] Before that, in April 1448, the cathedral chapter had elected the bishop of Lübeck, Nikolaus Sachow as the new archbishop of Riga.[35] Yet the opposition to the Order's plans was unsuccessful. Nikolaus Sachow did not dispute Silvester's later appointment, thus it was more difficult for the cathedral chapter to oppose the Order's intentions.[36] The Riga cathedral chapter appealed to the pope against Silvester's appointment, yet the Order's procurator in Rome effectively countered the chapter's efforts to hinder Silvester from becoming the archbishop of Riga.[37] In March 1449 Silvester's opponents gave in. Under certain conditions[38] the chapter and vassals accepted Silvester as the archbishop of Riga.[39] Silvester in turn granted a charter stipulating that he would abide by all the privileges and rights of both the cathedral chapter and vassals.

Silvester did not come from an influential noble or merchant family, but he had connections, which helped him to follow a career that only the medieval church could offer for a man of his standing.[40] Silvester was the son of a burgher of Thorn (Toruń) in Prussia. He studied law or theology in Leipzig (1427–1433), becoming *magister atrium,* and was later member of *Collegium Beatae Virginis* there. He was connected to the Teutonic Order already during his studies – the Grand Master Konrad Erlichshausen seems to have financed his studies. When Silvester returned to Prussia in 1441, he joined the Order and from then on was chaplain and chancellor of the Grand Master in Marienburg (Malbork).[41] Silvester and the Grand Master were apparently close. Silvester owed his whole career to Konrad von Erlichshausen. The letters sent by Silvester to the Grand Master reveal their close personal bond.[42] There is one word used numerous times in Silvester's letter of 30 May 1449 that characterizes the whole relationship; Silvester Stodewescher calls himself a creature of God and the Grand Master (*seyne unde euwer creature*) and in the next sentence writes 'I, creature of your majesty' (*ich, euwer hachwirdikeit creature*).[43] The Grand Master was more for Silvester than just a patron – he was his creator.

By the appointment of the Grand Master's 'creature' as the new archbishop, the Teutonic Order aspired to take over the cathedral chapter of Riga and thus the archbishop's office and the Church of Riga itself. Since the late thirteenth century, the Order had tried to gain the upper hand in relations with the Rigan archbishops and the city, the Order's main political adversaries, and even had defeated them in a civil war (1297–1330).[44] The Order's first attempt to take over the office of archbishop and the cathedral chapter was successful. In 1393 the Order's man was appointed as the archbishop of Riga – a nephew of the

Grand Master Konrad of Wallenrode, Johann of Wallenrode (e. 1393–1418). In 1394/97 he successfully incorporated the cathedral chapter in the Teutonic Order, when it accepted the Order's statutes.[45] However, in 1423/26 the chapter returned to the Augustinian statutes, stopped wearing the habits of the Teutonic Order (1426/28) and after 1436 it definitely no longer belonged to the knightly corporation.[46] Silvester's appointment was important for the Teutonic Order because it represented an opportunity to regain what had been lost and establish their power over an institution that had caused numerous problems in the past – the church of Riga. As Klaus Eberhard Murawski and Boockmann argue, Silvester had obligations towards the Teutonic Order.[47] Silvester had to follow an agenda set by the Grand Master in order to reintegrate the cathedral chapter into the Teutonic Order.[48] Silvester's mission in Riga was clear, yet he still had to enter his cathedral and receive his consecration in the September of 1449.[49] The entry itself did not make him archbishop; that happened months after the entry, when he was consecrated.[50]

## Giving in absence. Silvester Stodewescher's arrival in his realm and objects given by the cathedral chapter

Though usually gifts during late medieval and early modern entries were exchanged in presence, Silvester's *adventus* reveals very different practices of giving and the entry's description offers plenty of dramatic moments in which given objects or offered services played a certain role. These practices tell something about Silvester's relationships with those who gave him objects.

Altogether five relationships were represented during Silvester's entry and referred to in his letter to the Grand Master of 5 July 1449.[51] During his entry Silvester was met by the canons of Riga cathedral chapter and the archbishop's vassals. Three other partners were not present physically but played an important role in the entry: the city councillors of Riga, Konrad von Erlichshausen, the Grand Master of the Teutonic Order and the Master of the Livonian branch. Three of these five relationships involved giving of objects, a further involved an exchange of services and privileges, and the remaining one included no gifting or offering of services. In his letter Silvester mentions utensils given by the cathedral chapter, a gift from the Grand Master, the gifts from the Riga city council and services offered by his vassals – the local noblemen.[52] Closer study of the gifts given during this entry reveals the complicated and dramatic relationships that existed between the new archbishop and his partners. Remarkably, none of the objects given to Silvester during the entry were given in person; they were all sent to him through servants and messengers. So there was no direct gift-exchange like that which would have taken place during other ceremonial entries, for example, those of the Teutonic Order's Livonian Masters in Reval (Tallinn) during the fifteenth and early sixteenth centuries.[53] The indirect nature of the giving, combined with the absence of some gifts that could have been expected, shows the complexity of Silvester's entry and the difficult and dramatic circumstances under which it took place.

Silvester Stodewescher was a foreigner and unfamiliar with Livonia.[54] His journey from Prussia to Riga in the early Summer of 1449 was his first visit to the province. The entry was carefully prepared, both politically and ceremonially. Before that, in the spring of 1449, the two sides – the Grand Master and new archbishop and the cathedral chapter and the noblemen of the archbishop's territories – had reached an agreement: thus there was some kind of guarantee that Silvester would not be received as an enemy in Riga.[55] Yet, in Silvester's mind there were two possible outcomes: one in which he would be festively received; the other in which he would be slaughtered. And his death, in Boockmann's view, seemed the most likely outcome for Silvester himself.[56] Andris Levāns argues that Silvester's whole episcopate depended on his ability to attest his authority and justify his right to it;[57] therefore, the entry was an opportunity to demonstrate his ability to be not only a 'creature' of the Grand Master, but a political figure with whom his opponents should reckon with and a figure that they should be able to negotiate with and trust in.

When Silvester entered Livonia – near the river Lyva (Līva), in the south of Courland – and on the way to Riga, travelling through territories controlled by the Teutonic Order, he was under the protection of the Livonian branch's officials, as the Grand Master had requested.[58] The first incidence of objects being given to Silvester took place in Hasenpoth (Aizpute), Courland, some 180 kilometres westwards of Riga, when the chapter's representatives were sent to the new archbishop with numerous objects. Silvester in his letter described how: 'The provost of my church [Dietrich Nagel], the cathedral canons and the noblemen sent to me to Hasenpoth a chaplain and a servant with silver [altar] vessels, books and other valuables, both to serve at the altar and table, the gilded chalice, bowls [for washing hands], dishes and [patens], all of silver, in a good condition.'[59] Were these objects, brought to Silvester in Hasenpoth, actually gifts, as they have been interpreted in the historiography?[60] It is possible that these valuables came from the Rigan archbishops' treasury (objects which Silvester inventoried in Riga and described further in his letter) and were delivered to

Silvester for his use.⁶¹ Yet, these objects and services of a chaplain and servant allow themselves to be interpreted as gifts. Objects sent by the provost, the cathedral chapter and vassals served to create mutual trust.

Though the cathedral chapter's provost Dietrich Nagel was not present in Hasenpoth and did not hand the objects to Silvester in person, these were not anonymous gifts. Silvester Stodewescher and Dietrich Nagel already knew each other; they had met in Marienburg a few months before.⁶² Nagel, originating from Hannover, was an influential man, who had spent a few years in Rome. During the 1430s he had represented the Church of Riga in Rome and at the Council of Basel and by 1442 had become the provost of the cathedral chapter.⁶³ Because of Nagel's experience, skills and knowledge, this relationship was essential for Silvester. Nagel, though opposing the Teutonic Order and initially also the new archbishop, became important for the archbishop's political efforts because of his experience in Livonian politics, his rhetorical skills and in-depth knowledge of the episcopal archive.⁶⁴ In 1449, the success of entry was also important for Nagel in his efforts to safeguard the interests of the cathedral chapter. It is possible to speculate that Nagel might have been aware that he could more effectively influence Stodewescher's policies through close cooperation with the new archbishop.

In the handing over of the objects, Dietrich Nagel and the cathedral canons showed that they trusted Silvester and displayed their intention of gaining the new archbishop's trust. Although these objects could have belonged to the recipient (that is to his office), they can also be described as 'preliminary presents' that were made to initiate a relationship or show the good intentions of the receiving party.⁶⁵ For example, during the third entry of the Teutonic Order's Livonian Master Wolter von Plettenberg (r. 1494–1535) into Reval (1525) the city's envoys greeted him when he was still 30 kilometres from Reval, gifted him with Rhenish wine and pleaded with him to renew the city's privileges in return.⁶⁶ The objects given to Silvester in Hasenpoth marked a peaceful beginning of the new archbishop's relationship with Dietrich Nagel, the cathedral canons and his vassals. Despite this, as Silvester's description of future events showed, tension remained and the new archbishop did not feel completely safe in this relationship.

Silvester Stodewescher must have been astonished by the pomp and material splendour he experienced during the entry. He wrote that ships waited for them near Riga on the river Duna (Daugava) and the largest ship he boarded was decorated with expensive cloths and so well-furnished inside 'that also the pope or emperor could travel with it'.⁶⁷ As Boockmann points out, Silvester, the son of a burgher, official and clergyman in the Grand Master's court, transcended the possibilities offered by his comparatively humble origins and in one day became a prince.⁶⁸

Just before entering the city, like other rulers during their entries, Stodewescher spent a night close by – in a castle on the island of Dalen (Dole) in the river Duna – and entered the city the next morning.[69] On Sunday, 22 June, two days before the feast of St John the Baptist, the entry into the city finally took place. Silvester was greeted by a crowd. Silvester claimed that townspeople formed a line more than a mile long to greet him before the city and that a baldachin was erected just outside the city walls.[70] The crowds expected such an event during medieval ceremonial entries, since it was an opportunity to see their lord.[71] To emphasize the pomp with which he had been received, Silvester also added that 2000 horses were gathered to greet him.[72] Just in front of the city wall, under the baldachin, Stodewescher met local clergymen, school boys and friars, before being greeted by the cathedral canons, his closest subjects, partners and fiercest opponents. All the details we know about this entry show that Silvester entered his cathedral and not the city itself, only the cathedral premises and the archbishop's castle that were both located next to the city wall.

## A gift from the patron. The Grand Master's gilded cross and Silvester's entry in the cathedral

The whole description of the entry was written for one man – the Grand Master of the Teutonic Order, who had given Silvester not only this episcopate but also a very special gift. Silvester's tone in his letters to the Grand Master was one of exaggerated humbleness. Silvester signalled to his patron that he owed a great deal to the Grand Master and, as Boockmann puts it, acted as the Grand Master's vassal.[73] As already explained above, Silvester and Konrad von Erlichshausen were apparently close, and the new archbishop must have been aware that he was in Riga only because of the Grand Master of the Teutonic Order. Before coming to Livonia, Silvester received several valuable gifts from his patron. In the letter to the Grand Master of 30 May 1449, the one in which Silvester Stodewescher referred to himself as the Grand Master's 'creature', he reported that he had received many letters, documents and valuables he had asked for from his patron. In the text Stodewescher mentioned one particular object sent by the Grand Master – a gilded cross, richly ornamented with precious stones and relics of the Holy Cross and others.[74] The objects given by the Grand Master show his trust in Silvester; however, the cross with gems and relics had a special role to play during Silvester's entry in the cathedral. In the letter of 5 July, Silvester described how he prepared for the entry in front of the cathedral, after the cathedral canons had presented the text of an oath sworn by his predecessors.⁷⁵ 'After that I dressed a surplice made from silk, I did put on an almuce and hanged a cross that your grace sent to me, and followed the procession until the cathedral doors,' he wrote.⁷⁶ Dressed in expensive ritual clothes and with a cross on his chest, Silvester was ready to enter his own cathedral.

Silvester was wearing the cross given to him when, just before entering the cathedral doors, he took an oath as his predecessors had done.⁷⁷ Then Silvester entered the cathedral. The *Te Deum* was sung as the new archbishop ascended a throne constructed for the occasion, just like in episcopal enthronization ceremonies in the German bishoprics.⁷⁸ After that the mass was celebrated. The cross was on Silvester's chest at all times during the ritual entry into the cathedral, mass and oath giving ceremonies, clearly visible for everyone who looked at him. The cross with its relics designated the new archbishop's body, which was in constant contact with the relics.

The richly decorated gilded cross with relics worn by Silvester was not just a decorative element – it was a media of communication. The entry into the cathedral was a performance that had numerous audiences: his opponents – the cathedral canons and individuals bound to the chapter; the noblemen who were the archbishop's vassals; the representatives of the Teutonic Order's Livonian branch; and indirectly, mediated through a letter, the Grand Master of the Teutonic Order. It is plausible that the audience present in the cathedral, especially the cathedral canons and the representatives of the Teutonic Order, who had communicated with Silvester while he travelled to Riga, knew whom this cross was a gift from. Undoubtedly the cross was a public sign of Silvester's allegiance to the Grand Master, a challenge to his opponents who were once again reminded that Stodewescher was, as Boockmann has put it, 'the agent of their largest enemy'.⁷⁹ It had also a symbolical meaning for Silvester himself; the letter can be seen as a rewriting of this performance for the sake of his patron, in which the cross is given a central role and can be interpreted as the means for Stodewescher to demonstrate that he remembers his patron.

## A gift of a service? Silvester meets his vassals

After the mass the vassals gave an oath to the new archbishop. In the letter Silvester described the fear that he experienced. The vassals took out a ritual sword with a gilded sheath for the oath.⁸⁰ According to Boockmann, when Silvester saw the swords, he anticipated his own death in the cathedral, experiencing a similar fate to St Thomas Becket (1119/20–1170).[81] However, despite Silvester's fear, no one intended harming him and even the sheaths of the swords did not touch his body.

A meal followed in which the new archbishop took part along with the cathedral canons and several noblemen. Though one may have expected gifts to be given by the noblemen, no material gifts were handed over. Instead, the noblemen offered Silvester their services; the noblemen told him that they themselves would serve him during the meal (*sie welden [m]ir selbst czu tische dienen*), explaining persistently that Silvester had nothing to fear for.[82] Boockman points out that fear of poisoning or being stabbed by knives used for cutting meat may have made Silvester reluctant.[83] Yet the noblemen insisted and Silvester gave in. Silvester, as he himself later wrote, understood from many speeches and signs that they were motivated by love (*ausz liebe meyneten*); therefore, he let the noblemen serve him. This practice of noblemen serving at the table of their lord resembled instructions to the prince-electors in the Golden Bull of 1356, according to which they had to serve food for the king at table during the festive coronation meal.[84] The noblemen gained honour by serving their lord and these services at the table could be interpreted as non-object, invisible gifts.[85] In contrast to the other instances where the objects were given to Silvester, here there was mutual face-to-face communication. For the noblemen communication with the new archbishop was essential because they were bound in a lord-vassal relationship. As Jesse Hurlbut argues, during the entries of the Burgundian dukes gifts from a city were exchanged for the duke's oath;[86] here the noblemen's services may have been exchanged for favours delivered by the archbishop. On the next day, in a ritual ceremony in the refectory of the cathedral cloisters, Silvester re-confirmed their fiefs after each nobleman laid their hat, belt and weapon on the ground, got on their knees, begged the archbishop to give as a fief their heritage received from a father and were kissed by him.[87] Though services are usually overlooked as gifts due to their immateriality services, here it is evident that an exchange of services and privileges took place between Silvester and his vassals, the same vassals who shortly before had so frightened him in the cathedral.

## Gifts given in absence. The city of Riga and their gifts to the new lord

The final but no less important partners the new archbishop received gifts from were the Riga city councillors. For both parties this was a crucial relationship; the city was waiting to have their rights and privileges reconfirmed by the new archbishop and Silvester was aware of Riga's political and economic importance and the problems it could cause.[88] On Sunday, 22 June, Silvester sent a message to the city council after the festive meal, pleading with them to pardon all offenders who had been fined and banned from the city by erasing their records from the city's account books.[89] The pardoning of offenders was frequently practised during rulers' entries in other European cities and, following Silvester's request, the city council of Riga pardoned them and released prisoners.[90] Following this, the city council sent the archbishop a red scarlet cloth (*eyn roth scharlach*), a twelve- or fourteen-squirell furs (*czwelff ader 14 czymmer schone groewerck*), and a cask of 'good Rhenish wine' (*vas grosser wen eyn ohme mit gudem Reynischen weyne*).[91] The city's account register reveals that a considerable sum – 85 Riga marks – was spent on these gifts to Silvester.[92] These were similar gifts to those given by the city council when Silvester's predecessor Henning Scharpenberg entered the city for the first time in 1424. During his entry the city gifted Scharpenberg with cloths, pelts and wine and in addition gave him a red bishop's headgear (*ene rode musse*).[93] The gifts of Riga city councillors to the new archbishops were valuable and, as it seems, certain practices of gift-giving were repeated even after the quarter of century that separated Henning's and Silvester's entries.

Gift-exchange was an integral part of episcopal entries in European cities and objects were usually exchanged between bishops and city governments in person.[94] Yet, during Silvester Stodewescher's entry the gifts of the city council were 'sent' (*santen dornoch mir*) to the archbishop, not presented by the representatives of the council in person.[95] Was the non-presence of the city councillors in the archbishop's castle a sign of mistrust? Should have he gone to the city council on the day of his arrival (June 22), when he already had a full schedule (entry into the cathedral, oaths, the festive meal)? Does the fact that gifts from the city council were not made in person demonstrate that there was something unusual in the relationship between Silvester and the Riga city council? Their representatives met the new archbishop in person weeks later when three city councillors went to his consecration – 'coronation' (*kroninge*) – in the archbishop's residence, the castle of Ronneburg (Rauna) located some 100 kilometres northeast from Riga, most likely carrying gifts with them, because the expenses recorded were high for such a short journey.[96] In normal circumstances the archbishop would be consecrated in his cathedral. When the previous archbishop Henning Scharpenberg was installed (*kroninge*) in 1424, most likely in his cathedral, the city council presented him with wine worth 28 Riga marks;[97] yet it remains unknown if they had met Henning

Scharpenberg in person beforehand and given gifts directly to him. In Silvester's case it is not clear whether the city councillors by sending their initial gifts were demonstrating a cautious attitude towards the 'creature' of the Teutonic Order or following a tradition for the city councillors not to meet a new archbishop in the city, but to meet him in person and exchange gifts only when he was consecrated.

One late medieval ceremonial entry in Riga demonstrates very different practices of gifting that only emphasize the exceptionality of Silvester's entry. After the treaty of Kirchholm (1452) that established the shared lordship of the Teutonic Order's Master and the archbishop over Riga,[98] the ceremonial entries of the Master took place in the city. In 1495, the new Master of the Livonian branch, Wolter von Plettenberg, entered Riga for the first time, accompanied by '450 horses and armed men'.[99] On the next day he went to the town hall and, after the oath was given by the councillors, the two parties exchanged gifts. Plettenberg gave the burgomaster 'a beautiful ring (*boch*) [decorated] with a sapphire' and the councillors gifted the Master with three kinds of spices – ginger, *barkenkrutt* and *kruserkrum* – and three kinds of wine – claret, malmsey and Rhine wine; additional portions of wine, bread, beer and oats were later sent to the castle where the Master was staying.[100] Here such elements as the physical presence of the lord, the oath and gifts exchanged were part of the same ceremonial episode. Likewise, the gifts were exchanged in person, offering a space for symbolic interaction and ritual.

Although the practices of the city's political leaders for meeting their lord for the first time may have changed between 1449 and 1495, the most likely explanation is that the communication between Silvester and the councillors in 1449 – the gifts given in absentia and without any return gifts – was exceptional. The distance between the two parties becomes even more evident when the *adventus* of 1449 is compared with numerous entries of Wolter von Plettenberg in early sixteenth-century Reval, during which he had festive meals with the city councillors and received gifts, such as a large silver gilt goblet with the city's coat of arms (1525).[101] The political situation in 1449 – the archbishop being the man of the Teutonic Order – influenced the gift-giving practices during the entry of Silvester. Possibly the city councillors in 1449 were aware of Silvester's intention to share his power over the city with the Order's Master and saw him as someone detrimental to the city's interests.[102]

Wine, as given by the city council to Silvester in 1449, was a typical urban political gift. Though food and drinks were gifted across medieval society,[103] wine was a political liquid that helped the elites to establish and maintain political relationships.¹⁰⁴ According to Valentin Groebner, 'wine gifts were also inextricably linked with the demonstration of political legitimacy'.¹⁰⁵ Wine was also frequently used as a gift during princely entries.¹⁰⁶ Wine was a usual gift for official guests in late medieval Riga, both foreign – Lithuanian and Russian envoys – and local – Livonian bishops and officials of the Teutonic Order; wine frequently appears in the fifteenth-century account records of the city council.¹⁰⁷ The records of the city of Reval further show that wine was the most common commodity gifted, constituting 40 per cent of all gifts given by the city council to its guests.¹⁰⁸ Wine was a more prestigious beverage than beer, which was also was frequently gifted by urban governments.¹⁰⁹

The gifts given by the city council during Silvester's entry have to be seen as a beginning of a relationship in which objects were repeatedly gifted, following certain traditions and patterns. In 1451, when the relationship between the city and the archbishop was tense, the city council repeatedly gave gifts of wine, herring and honey.¹¹⁰ During Silvester's episcopate, the city council sent wine, beer, bread and oats to their archbishop almost annually at Easter in the 1450s and 1460s; in 1468 these foodstuffs given to Silvester were recorded in the account book as 'gifts' (*an wyne, bere vnde brodt tor giffte*).¹¹¹ As in other late medieval cities,¹¹² the city councillors of Riga used luxurious gifts to their possible political allies as effective political tools. Livonian bishops received expensive gifts when they arrived in the city. In 1468 or 1469, when Jodocus Hoenstein, bishop of Oesel (1458–1469/1471) arrived in Riga on the route home from Rome, 62 marks were spent 'for the gifts and friendship' (*tor giffte vnde fruntechopp*).¹¹³ When Johann Bertkow, bishop of Dorpat (1473–1485), entered the city in 1473, a marten coat (*eyner marthen suben*) and Rhenish wine were bought as gifts for him.¹¹⁴ The foodstuffs given almost annually to Silvester Stodewescher for decades after his entry in Riga were routine gifts that were sometimes supplemented with additional gifts in situations when the relationship between the archbishop and city became strained.

The entry ceremonies ended on Monday (the oaths of the cathedral canons and re-distribution of the fief), but in his letter to the Grand Master Silvester went on to describe his first steps in Riga and the first political decisions he made.¹¹⁵ According to his own letter, after his entry into the city on 25 June Silvester Stodewescher visited the Master of the Teutonic Order in Kirchholm (Salaspils). The Master of Teutonic Order in Livonia was absent from the entry and offered the new archbishop no material objects or services. The absence can be explained by illness on the part of the Master, Heinrich Vinke von Overberg (1438–1450).¹¹⁶ However, other officials of the Livonian branch similarly gave no gifts to the new archbishop, even though the Order's officials and brethren were the first to receive Silvester when he had just crossed the border of Livonia and the Master's representatives were present during the entry.[117] It could be assumed that Silvester Stodewescher simply omitted the gifts given by the representatives of the Livonian branch in his letter to the Grand Master; however, this seems unlikely because of the very detailed account he gives. Yet, it is otherwise difficult to explain the absence of gifts from the Livonian branch.

## Conclusions

Silvester Stodewescher died on 12 July 1479, thirty years after his entry in Riga. Around 1469 he had transformed from a chaplain and candidate of the Teutonic Order into the archbishop who followed in steps of his predecessors and fought with his former patrons.[118] The man who had become the archbishop of Riga due to the financially and diplomatically resourceful efforts of the Teutonic Order died as a captive in the castle of Kokenhusen (Koknese), having been incarcerated there by the same corporation.[119] Ironically, the 'creature' of the Order's Grand Master Konrad von Erlichshausen, who died months after Stodewescher's arrival in Riga, had become the Order's fiercest enemy. The Order even took revenge on the archbishop's dead body; the journey of Silvester Stodewescher's remains from Kokenhusen to Riga, where he would be buried in the cathedral, took a month in the summer heat.[120]

The gift-giving practices during this entry demonstrate that it was an exceptional event and most of the relationships Silvester was involved in were fragile. The practices were different from those during other Livonian rulers' entries for which sources survive. A reason for that was the long-term enmity between the Teutonic Order and its opponents: Stodewescher's predecessors in the office, the cathedral chapter, the city of Riga and the noblemen. The enmity was only reinforced by Silvester's appointment. There was a fragility of relationships and mistrust involved in giving of the objects. The objects given during this particular entry did not change the relationships, but the objects worked as instruments in establishing trust, strengthening relationships and overcoming volatility – they changed something. However, as seen in the case of the objects sent to Silvester Stodewescher, by his cathedral chapter, its provost and the noblemen when he was in Hasenpoth, these gifts did not fully convince him of the givers' good intentions. As a result, when the noblemen were giving their oath to the new archbishop in the cathedral of Riga and used a sword with a naked blade, Silvester thought that he might be killed.

Silvester Stodewescher was the Teutonic Order's candidate; moreover, he was an agent of the Grand Master. He became the archbishop because of the Order's successful lobbying in the papal curia, superseding Lübeck's bishop, Nikolaus Sachow, who had been elected by the Riga cathedral chapter. It was the Grand Master's direct involvement in the Livonian affairs, his attempt to regain the Teutonic Order's control over the cathedral chapter of Riga. The expensive gift of a gilded cross with precious stones and relics given to Silvester Stodewescher by the Grand Master was a sign of the new archbishop's allegiance and functioned as such during Silvester's entry in the cathedral. Its materiality (relics) as a holy object hanging on his chest also served to transform the new archbishop.

Gifts are not always material objects. Services can equally be seen as gifts. During Silvester Stodewescher's entry, the noblemen, the archbishop's vassals, offered to serve him at table during the festive meal that followed the mass and oath ceremonies conducted after Silvester's entry in the cathedral. The new archbishop was hesitant at first, probably afraid of poisoning or being stabbed, but accepted their efforts as sign of love after the noblemen's assurance.

A certain trait characterizes all instances of giving objects in this case. All material gifts were made in absentia and in most of the instances there was absence of reciprocity. According to his own description of the entry, Silvester Stodewescher did not give or return any gifts. The cathedral chapter, its provost and the noblemen sent objects to the new archbishop when he was in Hasenpoth, yet we do not know whether he gave gifts to the cathedral canons and the noblemen. Most likely Silvester did not make a counter-gift to the Grand Master for him gifting him a cross with precious stones and relics; the archbishop returned this gift in the form of personal loyalty to the Grand Master and pursuing aims set by him.

It is evident that the relationship between Silvester and Riga city councillors was complicated and the fact that the new archbishop did not meet the city councillors and did not exchange gifts with them upon his arrival to Riga has to be seen as an exception. The gifts that were sent were comparable to those sent by the city council when the previous archbishop, Henning Scharpenberg, entered Riga in 1424. The city councillors met Silvester Stodewescher in person only when they attended the archbishop's consecration in Ronneburg in September of 1449 and most likely offered him gifts on that occasion. Though Silvester Stodewescher and the city councillors did not exchange gifts in person, as, for example, during the entry in Riga of Wolter von Plettenberg in 1495, the Master and the city councillors did: it was a relationship in which gifts were given for decades. The city council's account book reveals gifts sent by the city to the archbishop during moments of crisis in their relationship and on the occasion of various feasts.

Silvester Stodewescher was an important actor on the Livonian political stage. His entry onto it in June 1449 was the spectacular beginning of political and personal drama that involved a mix of uncertainty, fear, princely pomp and numerous rituals. Those whom Silvester, according to his letter to the Grand Master, eared during the entry became his friends and allies, yet those who acted as his patrons in 1449 turned into his enemies and incarcerators.[121]

## Notes

1   Philippe Buc, *The Dangers of Ritual: Between Early Medieval Texts and Social Scientific Theory* (Princeton: Princeton University Press, 2001), 39; Marie-Claude Canova-Green, Jean Andrews, and Marie-France Wagner, ed., *Writing Royal Entries in Early Modern Europe* (Turnhout: Brepols, 2013).
2   Peter Johanek and Angelika Lampen, 'Adventus. Studien zum herrscherlichen Einzug in die Stadt. Zur Einführung', in *Adventus. Studien zum herrscherlichen Einzug in die Stadt*, ed. Peter Johanek and Angelika Lampen (Köln: Böhlau, 2009), vii–xvi, vii.
3   Peter Arnade, *Realms of Ritual: Burgundian Ceremony and Civic Life in Late Medieval Ghent* (Ithaca: Cornell University Press, 1996), 129.
4   Johanek and Lampen, 'Adventus', vii.
5   Valentin Groebner, *Liquid Assets, Dangerous Gifts: Presents and Politics at the End of the Middle Ages*, trans. Pamela E. Selwyn (Philadelphia: University of Pennsylvania Press, 2002), 34; Michail A. Bojcov, 'Ephemerität und Permanenz bei Herrschereinzügen im spätmittelalterlichen Deutschland', *Marburger Jahrbuch für Kunstwissenschaft* 24 (1997): 87–107; Andreas Bihrer, 'Einzug, Weihe und Erste Messe. Symbolische Interaktion zwischen Bischof, Hof und Stadt im Spätmittelalterlichen Konstanz. Zugleich einige Methodische Ergänzungen zu den Ergebnissen der aktuellen Adventusforschung', in *Symbolische Interaktion in der Residenzstadt des Spätmittelalters und der Frühen Neuzeit*, ed. Gerrit Deutschländer, Marc von der Höh and Andreas Ranft (Berlin: Akademie Verlag, 2013), 65–88, 72; Arnade, *Realms of Ritual*, 145; Buc, *The Dangers of Ritual*, 42, 71–7.
6   This is a selection of publications on medieval and early modern ceremonial entries: Andrew Brown, *Civic Ceremony and Religion in Medieval Bruges c. 1300–1520* (Cambridge: Cambridge University Press, 2011); J. R. Mulryne, Maria Ines Aliverti and Anna Maria Testaverde, ed., *Ceremonial Entries in*

*Early Modern Europe: The Iconography of Power* (Farnham: Ashgate, 2015); Neil Murphy, *Ceremonial Entries, Municipal Liberties and the Negotiation of Power in Valois France, 1328–1589* (Leiden: Brill, 2016); Mikhail A. Boytsov, 'The Healing Touch of a Sacred King? Convicts Surrounding a Prince in Adventus Ceremonies in the Holy Roman Empire during the Fourteenth to Sixteenth Centuries', *German History* 33:2 (2015): 177–93; Canova-Green, Andrews and Wagner, *Writing Royal Entries in Early Modern Europe*; Alois Niederstätter, 'Königseinritt und -gastung in der spätmittelalterlichen Reichsstadt', in *Feste und Feiern im Mittelalter. Paderborner Symposion des Mediävistenverbandes*, ed. Detlef Altenburg, Jörg Jarnut and Hans-Hugo Steinhoff (Sigmaringen: Thorbecke, 1991), 491–500.

7   On gifts during medieval rulers' entries, see Jesse D. Hurlbut, 'The Duke's First Entry: Burgundian Inauguration and Gift', in *Moving Subjects: Processional Performance in the Middle Ages and the Renaissance*, ed. Kathleen Ashley (Amsterdam: Rodopi, 2001), 155–86; Mario Damen, 'Princely Entries and Gift Exchange in the Burgundian Low Countries: A Crucial Link in Late Medieval Political Culture', *Journal of Medieval History* 33:3 (2007): 233–49; on gifts during the episcopal entries, see Maureen C. Miller, 'The Florentine Bishop's Ritual Entry and the Origins of the Medieval Episcopal Adventus', *Revue d'Histoire Ecclésiastique* 98:1–2 (2003): 5–28, 5; Maureen C. Miller, 'Why the Bishop of Florence Had to Get Married', *Speculum* 81:4 (2006): 1055–91; Jacek Maciejewski, 'Nudo Pede Intrat Urbem: Research on the Adventus of a Medieval Bishop through the First Half of the Twelfth Century', *Viator* 41:1 (2010): 89–100.

8   Mark Häberlein, 'Geschenke und Geschäfte: Die Fugger und die Praxis des Schenkens im 16. Jahrhundert', in *Faszinierende Frühneuzeit: Reich, Frieden, Kultur und Kommunikation 1500–1800; Festschrift für Johannes Burkhardt zum 65. Geburtstag*, ed. Wolfgang E. J. Weber (Berlin: Oldenbourg Verlag, 2008), 135–50, 137; Groebner, *Liquid Assets*, 141.

9   Arnoud-Jan Bijsterveld, 'The Medieval Gift as Agent of Social Bonding and Political Power: A Comparative Approach', in *Medieval Transformations. Texts, Power, and Gifts in Context*, ed. Esther Cohen and Mayke De Jong (Leiden: Brill, 2001), 124–56, 124, 138; Ulf Christian Ewert and Jan Hirschbiegel, 'Mehr als nur der Schöne Schein. Zu einer Theorie der Funktion von Luxusgegenständen im Zwischenhöfischen Gabentausch des späten Mittelalter', in *Materielle Grundlagen der Diplomatie: Schenken, Sammeln und Verhandeln in Spätmittelalter und Früher Neuzeit*, ed. Mark Häberlein and Christof Jeggle (Konstanz: UVK Verlagsgesellschaft, 2012), 33–58, 57; Evelyn Korsch, 'Geschenke im Kontext von Diplomatie und symbolischer Kommunikation. Der Besuch Heinrichs III. in Venedig 1574', in *Materielle Grundlagen der Diplomatie: Schenken, Sammeln und Verhandeln in Spätmittelalter und Früher Neuzeit*, ed. Mark Häberlein und Christof Jeggle (Konstanz: UVK Verlagsgesellschaft, 2012), 103–22, 103.

10  Martina Winkler, 'Die Macht der Gaben – Ein Kommentar', *Jahrbücher für Geschichte Osteuropas* 63:1 (2015): 99–108, 104.
11  Arnade, *Realms of Ritual*, 28.
12  Hurlbut, 'Duke's First Entry', 174.
13  Arnd Reitemeier, *Außenpolitik im Spätmittelalter: die diplomatischen Beziehungen zwischen dem Reich und England 1377–1422* (Paderborn: Schöningh, 1999), 446; Ewert and Hirschbiegel, 'Mehr als nur der Schöne Schein', 41.
14  Gadi Algazi, 'Introduction: Doing Things with Gifts', in *Negotiating the Gift: Pre-Modern Figurations of Exchange*, ed. Gadi Algazi, Valentin Groebner, and Bernhard Jussen (Göttingen: Vandenhoeck & Ruprecht, 2003), 9–27, 18.
15  Marcel Mauss, *The Gift: The Form and Reason for Exchange in Archaic Societies*, trans. W.D. Halls (London: Routledge, 2002), 10–23.
16  Annette Weiner, *Inalienable Possessions: The Paradox of Keeping-While-Giving* (Berkeley: University of California Press, 1992); James Laidlaw, 'A Free Gift Makes No Friends', *Journal of the Royal Anthropological Institute* 6:4 (2000): 617–34; Gadi Algazi, 'Some Problems with Reciprocity', *Endoxa: Series Filosóficas* 15 (2002): 43–50; Algazi, 'Introduction', 10.
17  Andreas Schmidt, *'Bischof bist Du und Fürst': die Erhebung geistlicher Reichsfürsten im Spätmittelalter – Trier, Bamberg, Augsburg* (Heidelberg: Universitätsverlag Winter, 2015); Kerstin Hitzbleck, 'Die Einzüge der Bischöfe von Halberstadt in Mittelalter und Frühneuzeit', in *Adventus. Studien zum herrscherlichen Einzug in die Stadt*, ed. Peter Johanek and Angelika Lampen (Köln: Böhlau, 2009), 229–66; David Rivaud, *Entrées épiscopales, royales et princières: dans les villes du Centre-Ouest de la France XIVe - XVIe siècles* (Genève: Droz, 2013); Miller, 'The Florentine Bishop's Ritual Entry', 5–28; Bihrer, 'Einzug, Weihe und Erste Messe', 65–88; Miller, 'Why the Bishop of Florence Had to Get Married', 1055–91; Maciejewski, 'Nudo Pede Intrat Urbem', 89–100.
18  Miller, 'Florentine Bishop's Ritual Entry', 15.
19  Hartmut Boockmann, 'Der Einzug des Erzbischofs Sylvester Stodewescher von Riga in Sein Erzbistum im Jahre 1449', *Zeitschrift Für Ostforschung* 35 (1986): 1–17.
20  Hermann Hildebrand, ed., *Liv-, Est- und Kurländisches Urkundenbuch*, vol. 10 (Riga: J. Deubner, 1896) (hereafter, LUB 10), no. 628; Boockmann, 'Einzug des Erzbischofs Sylvester Stodewescher', 1–17.
21  Klaus Eberhard Murawski, *Zwischen Tannenberg und Thorn: Die Geschichte des Deutschen Ordens unter dem Hochmeister Konrad von Erlichshausen 1441–1449* (Göttingen: Musterschmidt, 1953), 71–118; Klaus Eberhard Murawski, 'Konrad von Erlichshausen (Ellrichshausen)', in *Die Hochmeister des Deutschen Ordens 1190–1994*, ed. Udo Arnold (Marburg: Elwert, 1998), 128–30.
22  Sabine Schmolinsky, 'Selbstzeugnisse im Mittelalter', in *Das dargestellte Ich: Studien zu Selbstzeugnissen des späteren Mittelalters und der frühen Neuzeit*, ed. Klaus Arnold, Sabine Schmolinsky, and Urs Martin Zahnd (Bochum: Winkler, 1999),

19–28; Sabine Schmolinsky, *Sich schreiben in der Welt des Mittelalters: Begriffe und Konturen einer mediävistischen Selbstzeugnisforschung* (Bochum: Winkler, 2012).

23  Boockmann, 'Einzug des Erzbischofs Sylvester Stodewescher', 5.
24  Bojcov, 'Ephemerität und Permanenz', 88.
25  Algazi, 'Introduction', 12–13.
26  Gert Kroeger, *Erzbischof Silvester Stodewescher und sein Kampf mit dem Orden um die Herrschaft über Riga* (Riga: Kymmels Buchhandlung, 1930), 150.
27  Kroeger, *Erzbischof Silvester Stodewescher*, 161; LUB 10, no. 431.
28  William Urban, 'The Diplomacy of the Teutonic Knights at the Curia', *Journal of Baltic Studies* 9:2 (1978): 116–28.
29  Klaus Militzer, 'Die Finanzierung der Erhebung Sylvester Stodeweschers zum Erzbischof von Riga', in *Zentrale und Region: Gesammelte Beiträge zur Geschichte des Deutschen Ordens in Preussen, Livland und im Deutschen Reich, aus den Jahren 1968 bis 2008*, ed. Klaus Militzer (Weimar: VDG, 2015), 113–29, 124.
30  Militzer, 'Finanzierung der Erhebung Sylvester Stodeweschers', 124–5.
31  Florin Curta, 'Merovingian and Carolingian Gift Giving', *Speculum* 81:3 (2006): 671–99, 691; Bruce Buchan and Lisa Hill, *An Intellectual History of Political Corruption* (London: Palgrave Macmillan, 2014), 74.
32  On gifts and bribes in the diplomacy of the Teutonic Order, see Urban, 'Diplomacy of the Teutonic Knights', 119, 120, 125; Hartmut Boockmann, 'Nachrichten über die Diplomatie des Deutschen Ordens aus dem "Tresslerbuch"', in *Balticum. Studia z Dziejów Polityki, Gospodarki i Kultury XII–XVII Wieku. Ofiarowane Marianowi Biskupowi w Siedemdziesiąta Rocznice Urodzin*, ed. Zenon Hubert Nowak (Torún: TNT, 1992), 67–78, 69–70; Nele Kaestner, 'Tiere als Mittel der Repräsentation und Diplomatie im Deutschen Orden im Lichte des Marienburger Tresslerbuches (1399–1409)', in *Perzeption und Rezeption: Wahrnehmung und Deutung im Mittelalter und in der Moderne*, ed. Joachim Laczny and Jürgen Sarnowsky (Göttingen: V&R Unipress, 2014), 67–106.
33  Catherine Fletcher, *Diplomacy in Renaissance Rome: The Rise of the Resident Ambassador* (Cambridge: Cambridge University Press, 2015), 145–67; Geoffrey Barraclough, 'The Making of a Bishop in the Middle Ages: The Part of the Pope in Law and Fact', *The Catholic Historical Review* 19:3 (1933): 275–319, 302.
34  Militzer, 'Finanzierung der Erhebung Sylvester Stodeweschers', 125–7.
35  Boockmann, 'Einzug des Erzbischofs Sylvester Stodewescher', 2–3.
36  Anja Voßhall, 'A Matter of Distance? The Bishops and the City of Lübeck in the Late Middle Ages', in *A Companion to Medieval Lübeck*, ed. Carsten Jahnke (Leiden: Brill, 2019), 166–84, 169–70.
37  Kroeger, *Erzbischof Silvester Stodewescher*, 155; Boockmann, 'Einzug des Erzbischofs Sylvester Stodewescher', 3.
38  Kroeger, *Erzbischof Silvester Stodewescher*, 157–8.

39  The cathedral chapter had to keep their Augustinian habit and the possessions of the church shall not be mortgaged to the Order.
40  Kroeger, *Erzbischof Silvester Stodewescher*, 159.
41  Boockmann, 'Einzug des Erzbischofs Sylvester Stodewescher', 5.
42  Bernhart Jähnig, 'Hochmeisterkaplan und Hochmeisterkanzler – die Leiter der Hochmeisterkanzlei in Marienburg 1309–1457', in *Kancelarie krzyżackie: stan badań i perspektywy badawcze*, ed. Janusz Trupinda (Malbork: Muzeum Zamkowe, 2002), 149–66, 160–1, Boockmann, 'Einzug des Erzbischofs Sylvester Stodewescher', 2.
43  LUB 10, no. 619; no. 628.
44  LUB 10, no. 619; Boockmann, 'Einzug des Erzbischofs Sylvester Stodewescher', 6.
45  Manfred Hellmann, 'Der Deutsche Orden und die Stadt Riga', in *Stadt und Orden. Das Verhältnis des Deutschen Ordens zu den Städten in Livland, Preußen und im Deutschen Reich*, ed. Udo Arnold (Marburg: Elwert, 1993), 1–33; Bernhart Jähnig, 'Der Kampf des Deutschen Ordens um die Schutzherrschaft über die livländischen Bistümer', in *Ritterorden und Kirche im Mittelalter*, ed. Zenon Hubert Nowak (Torún: UMK, 1997), 97–111.
46  Bernhart Jähnig, *Johann von Wallenrode O. T. Erzbischof von Riga, Königlicher Rat, Deutschordensdiplomat und Bischof von Lüttich im Zeitalter des Schismas und des Konstanzer Konzils (um 1370–1419)* (Bonn: Verlag Wissenschaftliches Archiv, 1970), 18; Bernhart Jähnig, 'Die Verfassung der Domkapitel der Kirchenprovinz Riga. Ein Überblick', in *Kirchengeschichtliche Probleme des Preussenlandes aus Mittelalter und früher Neuzeit*, ed. Arnold Bartetzky and Bernhart Jähnig (Marburg: Elwert, 2001), 53–72, 70; Boockmann, 'Einzug des Erzbischofs Sylvester Stodewescher', 2.
47  Jähnig, 'Verfassung', 70; Boockmann, 'Einzug des Erzbischofs Sylvester Stodewescher', 2.
48  Murawski, *Zwischen Tannenberg und Thorn*, 170; Boockmann, 'Einzug des Erzbischofs Sylvester Stodewescher', 4.
49  Murawski, *Zwischen Tannenberg und Thorn*, 170.
50  Kroeger, *Erzbischof Silvester Stodewescher*, 160, 164.
51  Boockmann, 'Einzug des Erzbischofs Sylvester Stodewescher', 14.
52  LUB 10, no. 628; Boockmann, 'Einzug des Erzbischofs Sylvester Stodewescher', 7–16.
53  LUB 10, no. 628, 466, 467, 469.
54  Paul Johansen, 'Ordensmeister Plettenberg in Reval', *Beiträge zur Kunde Estlands* 12:4–5 (1927): 100–15; Anu Mänd, 'Signs of Power and Signs of Hospitality. The Festive Entries of the Ordensmeister into Late Medieval Reval', in *The Man of Many Devices, Who Wandered Full Many Ways: Festschrift in Honor of János M. Bak*, ed. Balázs Nagy (Budapest: Central European University Press, 1999),

281–93; Nicholas W. Youmans, 'Rituals of Mobility and Hospitality in the Teutonic Knights', *East Central Europe* 47:1 (2020): 39–66, 52–3.
55 LUB 10, no. 617; Andris Levāns, 'Die lebendigen Toten. Memoria in der Kanzlei der Erzbischöfe von Riga im Spätmittelalter', in *Kollektivität und Individualität: der Mensch im östlichen Europa: Festschrift für Prof. Dr. Norbert Angermann zum 65. Geburtstag*, ed. Karsten Brüggemann, Thomas M. Bohn and Konrad Maier (Hamburg: Kovac, 2001), 3–35, 22.
56 Kroeger, *Erzbischof Silvester Stodewescher*, 159; Murawski, *Zwischen Tannenberg und Thorn*, 169.
57 Boockmann, 'Einzug des Erzbischofs Sylvester Stodewescher', 5.
58 Andris Levāns, 'Politiskās organizācijas modeļi viduslaiku Livonijā, 13.–16. gadsimts. manifestācijas un leģitimācijas formas', in *Latvieši un Latvija: Valstiskums Latvijā un Latvijas valsts – izcīnītā un zaudētā*, vol. 2, ed. Tālavs Jundzis un Guntis Zemītis (Rīga: Latvijas Zinātņu akadēmija, 2013), 52–76, 69.
59 LUB 10, no. 617.
60 'Meyner kirchen probyst [Dietrich Nagel], thumhern unde manschafft die santen mir enkegen bis czum Haszenpott eynen capplan unde diner mit silberem gerete, buchern unde anderem cleynot beyde czum altar unde tische dienende, also obirgulte koppe, bedackte stotczen, credencien, becken unde schallenen, alle silberen, eyne gute notdrofft.' LUB 10, no. 628, 466.
61 Kroeger, *Erzbischof Silvester Stodewescher*, 162.
62 LUB 10, no. 628, 469; Boockmann, 'Einzug des Erzbischofs Sylvester Stodewescher', 14.
63 Kroeger, *Erzbischof Silvester Stodewescher*, 159.
64 Brigide Schwarz, 'Prälaten aus Hannover im spätmittelalterlichen Livland: Dietrich Nagel, Dompropst von Riga († Ende 1468/Anfang 1469), und Ludolf Nagel, Domdekan von Ösel, Verweser von Reval († Nach 1477)', *Zeitschrift für Ostmitteleuropa-Forschung* 49 (2000): 495–532, 500–5, 511.
65 Mihkel Mäesalu, 'Historical Memory as the Cause of Conflict in Medieval Livonia', *Vestnik of Saint Petersburg University. History* 64:3 (2019): 1014–30, at 1016–17, 1019, 1021, 1027; Levāns, 'Die lebendigen Toten', 9–11; Kroeger, *Erzbischof Silvester Stodewescher*, 151.
66 Natalie Zemon Davis, *The Gift in Sixteenth-Century France* (Madison: University of Wisconsin Press, 2000), 26.
67 Johansen, 'Ordensmeister Plettenberg in Reval', 104; Mänd, 'Signs of Power and Signs of Hospitality', 282–3.
68 LUB 10, no. 628, 466.
69 Boockmann, 'Einzug des Erzbischofs Sylvester Stodewescher', 5.
70 Arnade, *Realms of Ritual*, 129; Johansen, 'Ordensmeister Plettenberg in Reval', 104; Kroeger, *Erzbischof Silvester Stodewescher*, 162.

71  LUB 10, no. 628, 467; Boockmann, 'Einzug des Erzbischofs Sylvester Stodewescher', 10.
72  Mänd, 'Signs of Power and Signs of Hospitality',
73  Boockmann, 'Einzug des Erzbischofs Sylvester Stodewescher', 9.
74  Boockmann, 'Einzug des Erzbischofs Sylvester Stodewescher', 4.
75  'Ich habe iczunt [..] etliche briffe, schriffte unde besunder vorhoffte unde grosz gebetene cleynot, als eyn obirgult, wol gezciret mit edeln gesteynen crewcze mit anderen gar tewerbarem heilgthum, mit namen von dem heiligen holcze, unde andrer entpfangen.' LUB 10, no. 619; Boockmann, 'Einzug des Erzbischofs Sylvester Stodewescher', 6.
76  Boockmann, 'Einzug des Erzbischofs Sylvester Stodewescher', 9.
77  'Dornoch czag ich an eyn korrackell von seyde gemacht unde nam doruff eyn almucium unde hing vor mich das crewcze, das mir euwer gnode sante, unde folgete der procession bis an die thunkirchenthor.' LUB 10, no. 628, 467.
78  LUB 10, no. 628, 467; Boockmann, 'Einzug des Erzbischofs Sylvester Stodewescher', 11.
79  Schmidt, 'Bischof bist Du und Fürst', 242.
80  Boockmann, 'Einzug des Erzbischofs Sylvester Stodewescher', 4.
81  LUB 10, no. 628, 467; Boockmann, 'Einzug des Erzbischofs Sylvester Stodewescher', 5, 11.
82  Boockmann, 'Einzug des Erzbischofs Sylvester Stodewescher', 11.
83  LUB 10, no. 628, 467–8; Boockmann, 'Einzug des Erzbischofs Sylvester Stodewescher', 12.
84  Boockmann, 'Einzug des Erzbischofs Sylvester Stodewescher', 12.
85  Bernd Schneidmüller, 'Inszenierungen und Rituale des spätmittelalterlichen Reichs. Die Goldene Bulle von 1356 in westeuropäischen Vergleichen', in *Die Goldene Bulle: Politik – Wahrnehmung – Rezeption*, ed. Ulrike Hohensee et al. (Berlin: De Gruyter, 2008), 261–97, 281; Paul Töbelmann, 'Dienst und Ehre: Wenn der Herzog dem Kaiser den Braten schneidet', *Zeitschrift für Historische Forschung* 37:4 (2010): 561–99, 568; Boockmann, 'Einzug des Erzbischofs Sylvester Stodewescher', 12.
86  Algazi, 'Some Problems with Reciprocity', 44; Algazi, 'Introduction', 12.
87  Hurlbut, 'The Duke's First Entry', 171–5.
88  LUB 10, no. 628, 468; Boockmann, 'Einzug des Erzbischofs Sylvester Stodewescher', 14.
89  Levāns, 'Politiskās organizācijas modeļi viduslaiku Livonijā', 70.
90  LUB 10, no. 628, 469.
91  LUB 10, no. 628, 469; Boockmann, 'Einzug des Erzbischofs Sylvester Stodewescher', 14–15; Levāns, 'Politiskās organizācijas modeļi viduslaiku Livonijā', 70.
92  LUB 10, no. 628, 469; Boockmann, 'Einzug des Erzbischofs Sylvester Stodewescher', 15.

93 'Item 85 mark geschenket dem biischoppe van Rige an wande werke vnd 1 ame wyns.' August von Bulmercq, ed., *Kämmerei-Register der Stadt Riga 1348–1361 und 1405–1474* (Leipzig: Duncker & Humblot, 1909), 241, 9.
94 *Kämmerei-Register der Stadt Riga*, 153, 4; 157, 42.
95 Bihrer, 'Einzug, Weihe und Erste Messe', 65; Miller, 'The Florentine Bishop's Ritual Entry', 5.
96 LUB 10, no. 628, 469.
97 *Kämmerei-Register der Stadt Riga*, 240, 86; Rūta Brusbārde, 'Stadt zweier Herren. Die Ratsherren der Stadt Riga im Spannungsfeld zwischen dem Erzbischof und dem Meister des livländischen Ordenszweiges (1415–1470)', in *Das mittelalterliche Livland und sein historisches Erbe = Medieval Livonia and Its Historical Legacy*, ed.Ilgvars Misāns, Andris Levāns, and Gustavs Strenga (Marburg: Herder-Institut, 2022), 151–59, 154.
98 *Kämmerei-Register der Stadt Riga*, 153, 9.
99 Jähnig, 'Der Kampf des Deutschen Ordens', 104; Kroeger, *Erzbischof Silvester Stodewescher*, 169–81.
100 Leonid Arbusow Sen., *Liv-, est- und kurländisches Urkundenbuch*, section 2, vol. 1 (Riga: J. Deubner, 1900), (hereafter LUB 2/1), no. 158.
101 LUB 2/1, no. 158; Anu Mänd, *Urban Carnival: Festive Culture in the Hanseatic Cities of the Eastern Baltic, 1350–1550* (Turnhout: Brepols, 2005), 194–5.
102 Johansen, 'Ordensmeister Plettenberg in Reval', 105; Mänd, 'Signs of Power and Signs of Hospitality', 283–4.
103 Kroeger, *Erzbischof Silvester Stodewescher*, 171.
104 Chris Woolgar, 'Gifts of Food in Late Medieval England', *Journal of Medieval History* 37:1 (2011): 6–18, 10.
105 Mario Damen, 'Giving by Pouring: The Function of Gifts of Wine in the City of Leiden (14th–16th Centuries)', in *Symbolic Communication in Late Medieval Towns*, ed. Jacoba van Leeuwen (Leuven: Leuven University Press, 2006), 83–100, 99; Susan Rose, *The Wine Trade in Medieval Europe: 1000–1500* (London: Bloomsbury, 2013), 130; Groebner, *Liquid Assets*, 23; Hurlbut, 'The Duke's First Entry', 171.
106 Groebner, *Liquid Assets*, 23.
107 Damen, 'Princely Entries and Gift Exchange in the Burgundian Low Countries', 237–40.
108 *Kämmerei-Register der Stadt Riga*, 122, 307.
109 Juhan Kreem, 'Gäster i Revalunder Medeltiden: Gåvor och Mottagare i Stadens Räkenskaper', *Historisk Tidskrift för Finland* 83 (1998): 492–506, 476; Anu Mänd, 'Animals as Presents in Late-Medieval Livonia', in *Animaltown: Beasts in Medieval Urban Space*, ed. Alice M. Choyke and Gerhard Jaritz (Oxford: BAR Publishing, 2017), 59–65, 60.
110 Damen, 'Giving by Pouring', 86.

111 *Kämmerei-Register der Stadt Riga*, 248, 249, 250; Brusbārde, 'Stadt zweier Herren', 154.
112 *Kämmerei-Register der Stadt Riga*, 264, 272, 282, 286, 289, 300, 307, 307, 318, 319.
113 Groebner, *Liquid Assets*, 15–49.
114 *Kämmerei-Register der Stadt Riga*, 310.
115 *Kämmerei-Register der Stadt Riga*, 332.
116 LUB 10, no. 628, 469–70; Boockmann, 'Einzug des Erzbischofs Sylvester Stodewescher', 14–16.
117 Lutz Fenske and Klaus Militzer, *Ritterbrüder im livländischen Zweig des Deutschen Ordens* (Köln: Böhlau, 1993): 912; Kroeger, Erzbischof Silvester Stodewescher, 163.
118 LUB 10, no. 628, 466, 467.
119 Kroeger, *Erzbischof Silvester Stodewescher*, 220–79; Boockmann, 'Einzug des Erzbischofs Sylvester Stodewescher', 16.
120 Kroeger, *Erzbischof Silvester Stodewescher*, 274–6.
121 Gustavs Strenga, *Remembering the Dead: Collective Memoria in Late Medieval Livonia* (PhD Thesis, Queen Mary University of London, 2013), 189.

# 4

# 'The Polar Winds have driven me to the conquest of the Treasure in the form of the much-desired relic.' (Re)moving relics and performing gift-exchange between early modern Tuscany and Lithuania

Ruth Sargent Noyes

## Introduction: 'Polar Treasure'

This chapter is framed around the sacred relics of the bodies of saints which marked the beginning and end of an early modern transcultural exchange of luxury gifts between Counter-Reformation Italy and the Baltic. Slaves, horses, medicines, furs, ermine, polar bears, amber, ivory, gold and diamonds comprised some of these gifts. Collectively, they constituted a transcultural potlatch that climaxed and collapsed in reciprocal *translatio*, the ritual relocation of relics of saints and holy persons.[1] This exchange demonstrated a bilateral preoccupation with material expressions of largesse, instantiated courtly dynastic ideals and notions of place and history, and entangled members of Tuscan and Lithuanian dynasties and a cadre of intermediaries over 2,000 kilometers and two decades in the late seventeenth century. This 'relic diplomacy' worked through the negotiation of gifts, exchanges and acquisitions of saints' relics to ally and align those involved with European powers and the divine. Following other avid relic-seeking sovereigns of the period such as King Philip II of Spain, patrons' deep religiosity and its material instantiation by means of collecting relics and their attending physical containers (reliquaries) not only consolidated and maintained diplomatic, social, affective and spiritual relationships, but were also crucially constitutive of premodern paradigms of legitimate righteous rule, particularly in contexts of reform or instability.[2] According to Catholic Counter-Reformation theology reaffirming the cult of relics and saints against Protestant attacks, relics enabled the galvanic diffusion of supernatural aura through material traces, thanks to the proximity and multiplicity of their heavenly avatars, the saints, to the Divine.[3] Relics were considered not only (or even mainly) symbols of power, prestige and piety, but actual *conductors* of divine grace, much like metals conduct electricity.[4]

In January 1677 Grand Duke Cosimo III de' Medici (1642–1723) penned the following exultation:

> The Polar Winds have driven me to the conquest of the Treasure in the form of the much-desired relic of the holy King [sic] *Casimiro*, with which I already see myself rewarded, when I will sail through the danger of a thousand obstacles and difficult abysses before arriving at its possession. Words cannot express the joy that floods my heart reading the dispatch from Vilnius.[5]

Cosimo was the penultimate patriarch of a dynasty that dominated peninsular politics for two and a half centuries, and since 1670 ruler of the Grand Duchy of Tuscany, a Habsburg imperial fief and historical territory covering part of west-central Italy with its capital in Florence.[6] The grand duke's jubilant message was in reply to a missive from Vilnius, one of the capitals (along with Krakow) of the historical territory of the Polish-Lithuanian Commonwealth. This dualistic state consisting of the Grand Duchy of Lithuania and the Crown of the Kingdom of Poland was ruled by a common elected monarch and covered areas of present-day Lithuania, Poland, Latvia, Belarus and Ukraine.[7] The dispatch from the Grand Duchy was on behalf of the recently nominated bishop of Vilnius Mikołaj Stefan Pac (1626–1684), scion of the powerful Pac (or Pacowie) clan. Their rise to pre-eminence in the Baltic paralleled that of the Medici in Italy, and by the 1660s the Pac were the Polish-Lithuanian King's main political allies and held all important positions in Lithuanian government.[8]

Framed with the rhetoric of seafaring conquest, Cosimo's letter inflected complex period discourse that wove together at times conflicting images of the Nordic-Baltic sea region that on one level framed Europe's far north-eastern borderlands as frigid and frightening wasteland.[9] On another level, the region was conceptualized as Europe's neo-crusader 'Indies' abundant in environmental resources and spiritually fecund with souls for conversion.[10] It was also fashioned as *Antemurale Christianitatis* (Bulwark of Christendom) protecting western Catholicism against manifold heretical threats.[11] In hagiography, it likewise figured *locus sanctus* guarding a numinous resource, the bodies of its Christian saints and martyrs. It was the latter that the Tuscan grand duke had been promised over two years earlier. Specifically, Cosimo was desirous for the body (or a piece thereof) of royal Polish-Lithuanian saint Kazimierz Jagiellończyk (1458–1484, canonized 1604), his name translated in Italian as *Casimiro*.[12] Kazimierz's relics were closely guarded by the chapter of Vilnius cathedral. A documented request in the chapter archives registered in October 1677 'in the presence of the nominee' Mikołaj Stefan Pac, addressed to Cosimo III de' Medici according to his family's self-styling in Latin as *Magnus Ducatus Etruriae* (Grand Duchy of Etruria), conveyed their eventual consent. However, there was an important qualification: 'By sending the relics [of St. Kazimierz Jagiellończyk] to the prince of Etruria, the chapter chose to have granted the relics of St. Maria Maddalena de' Pazzi.'[13]

The Vilnius chapter thus solicited an equally precious relic from the newly canonized Florentine Carmelite nun Caterina de' Pazzi, known as Suor Maria Maddalena (1566–1607, canonized 1669). The Tuscan grand duke and his mother Grand Duchess Vittoria della Rovere actively promoted the cult of this Tuscan noblewoman and mystic at Santa Maria degli Angeli on the south side of the river Arno.[14] The ceremonial trade of bodily remains of the pair of holy elites reified a strong node of entente interconnecting Italo-Baltic prerogatives during a watershed period of broader Counter-Reformation bidirectional interest.[15] The Medici set their sights on Poland-Lithuania and the Pac courted Italian state and religious powers, even as both their houses and dominions began approaching a horizon of degeneration.[16] I demonstrate that the natural substances used to fabricate the reliquaries charged with concretizing the translation of the Italo-Baltic relics' meanings between their respective contexts evoked notions of time, place and their shifting relation to history, as well as history's own malleability.

What follows explores how the respective Tuscan and Lithuanian relics could be leveraged from multiple viewpoints to manifold political, martial, spiritual and ideological ends, instantiating a hermeneutical borderland wherein intercultural selfhood and cultural geographies might be negotiated. In these borderlands, I argue, could be found the juncture of Pac and Medici interests, converging on a pair of saints whose holiness was especially constituted through the incorrupt corporeal integrity of their bodies. This mutual exchange helped to reaffirm and realign their interests on the regional and trans-European stage, despite the reality that both elite families and their respective territories faced existential political and patrimonial threats, as if their apotropaic gifts might ward off the inevitable dissolution of their familial lines and state autonomy in the next century. Together they discursively forged an unbroken chain stretching backward along the axis of human chronology to re-embody Italy's connection to the Baltic through the special potency of relics of vaunted integral saints like Jagiellończyk and Pazzi, famed for the miraculous incorruption of their bodies even after death. Lastly, I explore how a re-examination of their little-known gift-exchange can contribute to a revisionist transregional history that reconsiders conventional understandings of cultural dynamics between ostensibly far-flung regions of Europe specifically and perceived centres and their purported peripheries more generally.

## 'Relic diplomacy'

Cosimo III de' Medici's avid desire for the Pac to give him a piece of *Casimiro* was apparently first expressed in coincidence with and perhaps in connection to undertakings for both families. The grand duke had his own ambitions for the Commonwealth royal election. The Medici promoted family members for royal election as king of Poland-Lithuania, and to this end positioned Italian secretaries and informants like Lorenzo Domenico de' Pazzi at Commonwealth courts.[17] With his great-aunt Constance of Austria the Queen of Poland and Grand Duchess of Lithuania as consort of King Sigismund Vasa III, Cosimo III himself intended to participate in the 1669 and 1673 Commonwealth elections after the death in 1667 of his uncle Mattias de' Medici (among the most favoured candidates for the throne). He would later renounce in favour of the candidature of his thirteen-year-old brother, Francesco Maria de' Medici.[18] Cosimo's crusade for a relic of Prince Kazimierz was sustained by a profound Counter-Reformation religiosity that manifested in an avid appetite for the rarest holy relics. This was a fervour shared and fostered by his grandmother Maria Maddalena and mother Vittoria della Rovere.[19] Together they amassed within the *Cappella delle Reliquie* (Chapel of Relics) completed in the Palazzo Pitti in 1616 a breath-taking collection of first-class relics, together with reliquaries grouped according to material in special display cabinets for rock crystal, ebony, silver and amber.[20]

In 1673, Mikołaj Stefan Pac won the nomination to the Vilnius episcopate. However, the same Vilnius chapter with custodianship of Jagiellończyk's remains also opposed his thorny episcopate. Mikołaj had problematically annulled his marriage to take up the priesthood late in life, browbeat the chapter's members in a contest for authority, and struggled to gain papal ordination (granted only in 1682), to this end making multiple trips to Italy in the 1670s to negotiate with the pope and recruit allies.[21] Pac concurrently reformed stewardship of the Vilnius cathedral treasury's sacral furnishings and holy relics, where Kazimierz held pride of place, as an expression of his faith and close connection to the divine, to legitimate his ecclesiastical authority and claim to spiritual hegemony.²² In this context the question of who held jurisdiction over the saint's relics became a heated point of contention, and delayed the fulfilment of the Medici's desire for a relic for years.

The same year that Mikołaj Stefan Pac began his struggle with the cathedral chapter, a significant 1673 Polish-Lithuanian military victory against the Ottoman Turks at the battle of Chocim (Khotyn) brought honour and prestige to the embattled new bishop's cousin, Lithuanian Grand Hetman (i.e. commander of the armed forces) Michał Kazimierz Pac (1624–1682). Their new circumstances inaugurated a campaign of self-fashioning whereby the Pac framed themselves as northern heirs to Roman ancient martial and spiritual glory, part of broader period ethnogenesis mythologizing Lithuania as the successor to ancient Rome.²³ The Pac increased their socio-cultural capital and consolidated their influence by forging an Italian familial double origin story privileging parallel Roman imperial and Florentine patrician pedigrees. On the one hand they linked their aristocratic origins to the ancient Roman Palemon of the Po river valley of Etruria (also the invented *locus* of Medicean power) who during the reign of Nero fled north.²⁴ On the other, they asserted common parentage with none other than the saintly Maria Maddalena de' Pazzi, a claim grounded in the onomastic relation between family names.²⁵ Around this same time the restoration of the Kazimierz reliquary chapel in Vilnius was complete,²⁶ followed by construction of a new Pazzi reliquary chapel in Florence.²⁷ This presented a special opportunity for Pac self-promotion, as they constructed Florentine kinship through cultural patronage and religious foundations cultivating a special devotion to the cult of their saintly Florentine kin.²⁸ When visiting Florence on one of his Italian sojourns, the would-be Vilnius bishop made a pilgrimage to Santa Maria degli Angeli to pay homage to his sanctified relative, pledging financial support for her cult and likely negotiating in person the potential exchange of relics.²⁹

The holiness of both saints involved resided especially in their incorrupt corporeal integrity, as their corpses supposedly defied natural decay. Such a miraculous corporal manifestation suggested that the subject was divinely exempt from the physical process of decomposition, and became increasingly commonplace as a sign of sanctity in seventeenth-century hagiography.³⁰ The phenomenon was also tied to their status as nonviolent spiritual martyrs or 'martyrs of the spirit' who battled against temptation rather than physical dangers, symbolized iconographically by the motifs of the white lily and white crown denoting carnal abstinence, mystical purity and spiritual suffering.³¹

Verification of the wondrous incorruptibility of the remains of both saints occurred on the occasion of ceremonial translations of their relics (Kazimierz in 1604, Maria Maddalena in 1608).³² Their intact cadavers were closely guarded within reliquary chapels as apotropaic talismans for their respective cities and communities, and potent conduits channelling supernatural thaumaturgic curative powers. In 1634 the Carmelite nuns begrudged an amputated finger to generate critical Vatican support for her canonization only at Pope Urban VIII's insistence.³³ In 1672 the Vilnius chapter denied an appeal for a relic from the Polish-Lithuanian King himself.³⁴

## Slaves, stones, beasts and cheese

Bishop nominate Pac's difficult position in Vilnius necessitated years of ongoing epistolary exchanges amongst himself, the Tuscan grand duke, the Vilnius chapter, Jesuits, papal nuncios, and Italian agents and secretaries in Poland-Lithuania to negotiate the mutual gifting of relics. Concurrently, Cosimo III traded gifts with Grand Hetman Michał Kazimierz Pac. Pac apparently initiated the exchange in 1675, the same year that Medici solicitations of a relic reached Vilnius. He dispatched to the Florentine court a young Turkish slave boy captured in the 1673 battle of Chocim (Khotyn), recalling Pac's role in defeating Ottoman forces.³⁵ In early modern Italy slavery was closely associated with North-eastern Europe and Eurasia, source of Tartar, Cossack, Muskovite and Turkish prisoners of war.³⁶ Tuscany maintained thousands of prisoners of war to power the galleys out of its slave and trading port of Livorno, where the Medici also imported critical supplies of Baltic grain from primarily Poland-Lithuania.³⁷ Thus, Pac's gift of human *spolia* gestured not only to Medicean maritime power, but also its direct connection to and indeed dependence on the Baltic. The boy also reified the common Tuscan-Lithuanian 'Turkish threat' to propagandistic ends while currying specifically to Cosimo's pious proclivity for using such captives to exercise power in displays of religiosity. A contemporary noted that he also taught 'Christian doctrine to three Cossack children, aged 7 to 12, who have been sent to him as a gift by the bishop of Krakow'.³⁸

The discursive effectiveness of Pac's living gift was confirmed when in early 1676 Cosimo replied in kind with 'a chest encrusted with stones, and filled with medicines' 'to use for the needs of [the Hetman's] soldiers in the combats of war … [and as] an example of the labors of my Gallery [*Galleria*]'.³⁹ This represented a serial Medicean product advertising the grand-ducal conglomerate workshops within the Palazzo Pitti, the so-called *Galleria dei Lavori* (Gallery of Works). The *Galleria* under Cosimo III promoted art and science at the highest level and included a *spezzieria* (pharmacy) and *fonderia* (alchemical laboratory), as well as artists' workshops – most notably the *Opificio di Pietre Dure* (Workshop for Hardstone).[40] Together these various experts produced the so-called *casse* or *cassette* (medicinal chests), like that presented to Pac. Such chests constituted a renowned Medicean commodity to increase imperialist medical expertise associated with the grand-ducal house and build alliances with other European courts through the sharing of this knowledge in material form. These objects were presented with such frequency in the seventeenth century that the *casse* presented in a standardized form comprising up to eighteen compartments, each containing a medicinal therapeutic sourced via a global network of agents collecting exotic *naturalia*. These included notably Baltic amber, found in a number of Medici pharmacopeia.[41]

The description of the Grand Hetman's chest (now lost) as 'encrusted with stones' strongly suggests it was from the Gallery's *Opificio di Pietre Dure*, the premier grand-ducal workshop for the production of *pietre dure* or hardstone artworks. These entailed a highly detailed, complex inlay process whereby expert artists created pictorial compositions with thin slices of marble and imported exotic hardstones. The technique often embellished objects for courtly use gifted to members of the European nobility as materializations of Medicean technical ingenuity and worldwide diplomatic ties.[42] As if to reinforce such cultural messaging, in 1676 or 1677 Tuscan-born Medici court artist Michele Arcangelo Palloni (1642–1712) migrated to Lithuania to work under the aegis of the Pac.[43] Among Palloni's first Lithuanian commissions were a portrait likeness of Hetman Pac to be gifted back to Cosimo.[44] He later completed an extensive programme of mural paintings decorating the church at the important Pažaislis monastery (near present-day Kaunas, Lithuania), founded by Lithuanian Grand Chancellor Krzysztof Zygmunt Pac, brother of Bishop Mikołaj Stefan Pac and cousin of the Grand Hetman.[45] This project included a fresco cycle for a Pazzi reliquary chapel, most notably a near life-size depiction of the ritual display and *translatio* of her wondrously intact body.[46]

About a decade later, Palloni completed a pendant to this painting in Vilnius at the behest of Jan Kazimierz Sapieha (1637–1720), who became Grand Hetman of Lithuania on Pac's death and sponsored the redecoration of the reliquary Chapel of St. Kazimierz in Vilnius cathedral. The chapel had been completed in the 1630s under the oversight of Lithuanian Grand Treasurer and Deputy Chancellor Stefan Pac (1587–1640), father of Mikołaj Stefan Pac. The lavish construction was designed and built by Italian architects Matteo Castelli (*c.* 1555–1632) and Costante Tencalla (1593–1646).[47] During the Deluge Kazimierz relics were spirited away by retreating Lithuanian troops and occupying Muscovite forces wreaked damage on the cathedral, largely destroying the chapel's decorative program.[48] Following the 1666 restoration of Jagiellończyk's body, Palloni was engaged in the 1690s to restore the holy prince's reliquary sanctuary to its rightful glory. The project included a mural similarly depicting the miraculous incorruption of his corpse, reinforcing typological connections between the two saints and linking the Vilnius chapel to Pažaislis as complementary *loca sancta*.

Palloni was almost certainly sent as a Medici protégé and a Tuscan counterpoint to the Turkish slave, capable of demonstrating and disseminating the conquering power of a patently Florentine aesthetic and cultural programme at the Baltic courts. This 'artistic invasion' also expanded the prestige of his new Lithuanian patrons as international arbiters of taste and demonstrated both their means and ambitions, as typically only rulers of the highest order could afford to maintain court artists. In this regard, it bears note that the Pac economized by sharing the artist amongst themselves, and that Palloni ultimately did not remain in their exclusive employ. Likewise noteworthy is the fact that the status of the premier geographic centre of art in this period had largely shifted away from Florence, to the Roman and French courts. Thus, Palloni and his art served as gifts that to a certain extent served to mask the limitations of their giver and receivers.

Something similar could be said for the next instalment in the Medici-Pac exchange: horses, among the ultimate courtly gifts. Early in 1677 Medici-Pac agents managed despite difficult winter conditions to arrange overland delivery of a *cavallino Polacco* (Polish pony) and *cavallo Turco* (Turkish stallion) fitted with Turkish saddle and tack from the grand hetman's own stables, together with *una divota gallentaria di ambra* (a devout knick-knack made of amber).[49] All of these gifts satisfied Medici period taste for hippological, Islamic martial and spiritual *exotica*, yoking together the mastery of nature, violent conquest and spiritual battle.[50] Cosimo gifted in return a crucifix from his *Galleria* and soon after (at the Hetman's behest) Italian-bred horses.[51] The so-called Polish pony was likely a Lithuanian *Žemaitukas* (Eng. Samogitian).[52] This uniquely Baltic regional rarity surely enhanced the Medici stables.[53] The stallion of Turkish stock (much sought-after amongst European elites) vaunted as *spolia* contributed bellic prestige.[54] It could also serve for breeding in rivalry with renowned equine studs in Mantua and Naples, who historically held primacy over Tuscany in all things horse-related.[55]

The import of these gifts can be read against early modern hippological court culture and 'horse diplomacy' through the gifting of such equine rarities.[56] This reflected broader cultural practices of zoological exchange that played a vital role in forging diplomatic and, through breeding, pseudo-dynastic ties among far-flung ruling elites.[57] Equine culture was equally important from the Hetman's perspective, as top military commander within a conglomerate Commonwealth where power dynamics were constantly renegotiated and elite masculinity constructed through martial horsemanship.[58] He maintained his own herds in competition with Turkish and Russo-Muscovite 'Argamak' (from a Tartar word) horses,[59] and the well-known stud farms of the Lithuanian Grand Dukes.[60] He also doubtless emulated his predecessor Grand Hetman Krzysztof Mikołaj Dorohostajski (1562–1615), who in 1603 authored Baltic Europe's first hippological treatise.[61] Thus it is no surprise that Michał Kazimierz Pac, while expressing thanks and obligation for the crucifix, in 1679 also eagerly requested both 'an exquisite Neapolitan stallion, not an old horse and good for both war and stud', and 'two Neapolitan mares for breeding'.[62] Pac furthermore solicited 'four *forme* of parmigiano', indicating parmesan cheese commonly associated with the Duchy of Parma, a Habsburg fief presided by Cosimo's cousin Ranuccio II Farnese (1630–1694).[63] While cheese may seem a curious thing amongst the other luxury goods in this Medici-Pac exchange, it makes sense under the rubric of items for an aspirational court such as that of the Pac, where each 30–40 kg *forma* gave ample evidence of the reach of the Hetman's illustrious connections and literalized courtly conspicuous consumption.[64] One can imagine a sumptuous fête hosted at one of Hetman Pac's palaces, where a tour of the stables would be followed by a visit with court artist Palloni sketching guests' portraits, inspection of the luxury items from the grand-ducal *Galleria* and banquet where the monstrous cheeses were dramatically served.

That the horses had piqued Cosimo's particular passion for collecting exotic fauna sourced via a global network of agents is confirmed by his eager solicitation in 1679 of more *animalia*. His request included sixty so-called *pelle di dante*, cervine pelts of Eurasian deer or antelope used to prepare cream-colored chamois leather for courtly finery such as gloves, shoes and other accoutrements. He also wanted 'two large white bear [*orso bianco*] pelts, which here will be a most admirable rarity'.[65] Earlier in the century the Polish monarch was famous for wearing polar bear and ermine pelts to keep warm in his royal carriage.[66] By summer 1679 further arrangements were underway to procure for Cosimo live specimens: a polar bear and a pair of *zibellini*, white or dark-furred ermine or sable.[67] These treasures were almost certainly destined for the new *Serraglio degli animali rari* (Menagerie of rare animals) constructed between 1677 and 1680 within the Boboli Gardens adjacent to Palazzo Pitti.[68] The new grand-ducal menagerie revived Medicean cultural politics of collecting *animalia*, which the dynasty had a long history of acquiring as gifts from prestigious rulers as living symbols of Medici might.[69] Collecting and breeding zoological wonders at court enacted period notions of racial and geo-ethnic difference as well as nature versus nurture, social engineering and dynastic durability.[70] The polar bear was not only an exceptionally rare example of charismatic 'mega-fauna', but also tested the Pac's connections in the Nordic-Baltic region, much like the cheese and Neapolitan horses tested Medicean networks on the peninsula. While the bears were not indigenous to Lithuania, they could still be sourced in this period from southern Norway, part of the Dano–Norwegian Realm, or from Siberia via Muskovy.[71]

Sable and ermine – desirable both alive and as pelts – were intrinsically linked to the history of western European colonization of and relations with the Baltic, fuelled for centuries by a robust trade in furs.[72] White ermine had a dual symbolic meaning, signalling the possessor's wealth, status, connections and dominion over nature, and symbolizing fidelity, purity, moderation and clemency. As an embodied fur item of clothing it was an emblem derived from ancient natural histories and medieval bestiaries and disseminated in the Renaissance via widely circulated printed emblem books and the Italian noble Order of the Ermine.[73] Vestments ornamented with more than seventy dangling black-tipped ermine tales worn by Medici grand dukes for their coronation enrobed the grand-ducal body within a network of privileged associations.[74] *Zibellini* also figured on or as objects connected with marriage, as its associated virtues of chastity and fidelity imbued its material form with immaterial notions of dynastic stability.[75]

Period usage of the term *zibellino* itself could denote both an animal belonging to the weasel, or mustelid family, and a women's luxury fur accessory fashioned from its pelt and worn as or attached to girdles.[76] These accessories, according to natural scientific discourse associating mustelids with fecundity and period notions of sympathetic magic, functioned as an apotropaic amulet ensuring fertility, safe pregnancy and easy childbirth. Seventeenth-century Medici women in fact prescribed amongst themselves 'a girdle made of an animal from Poland, which has allowed many women who were in danger of miscarriage to give birth successfully', almost certainly just such a fur piece.[77] The animal's ability to reproduce rapidly and prolifically, despite inhabiting prohibitively cold Baltic regions, suggested that it could help suppress the cold female humoral nature and promote conception. This suggests that the Medici sought *zibellini* to promote manifold dynastic ends: Cosimo had justified concerns about future viable male heirs (in fact he would be the last such of his line). Thus he likely gifted some of the Lithuanian mustelid pelts to Medici women for use as fertility talismans. Their phylactery potential operated in concert with pharmaceutics' humoral efficacy, and relics' thaumaturgical powers.[78]

## Gifting incorruption

In the midst of exchanges with Hetman Pac, word reached Cosimo in January 1677 via the Jesuits that a Kazimierz relic was forthcoming, prompting his triumphant paean cited in the opening of this chapter.[79] In October the grand duke learned through multiple channels that thanks to lobbying efforts by the Jesuit superior general, papal nuncio, Italian royal secretary to the Polish monarch and King Jan III Sobieski himself, the Vilnius cathedral chapter deigned to concede him 'the relic of St. Casimir so ardently desired by Your Most Serene Highness, which Monsignor Bishop [Pac] wishes to send to you directly: it consists of a piece of the saint's shinbone [*stinco*].'[80] It was removed from the silver coffin safeguarding his remains on 27 October 1677and furnished with an illuminated parchment authentic certificate testifying to the details of the bone's ceremonial *translatio*. The authentic underscored its exceptional extraction from 'the relics of the intact body' of Kazimierz.[81] The single largest relic of the Baltic prince known today was however not dispatched immediately. It was placed in a silk-embellished cypress casket, inside a silver chest and over the course of the next year a third reliquary chest was manufactured of ivory, wood and amber in the coastal port city of Gdańsk (Danzig)[82] (Figure 4.1).

In October 1678 the precious treasure journeyed south accompanied by an amber crucifix and ensemble of amber altar furnishings, arriving in Florence shortly before Christmas 1678.[83] The outermost Gdańsk casket measured an impressive 35.5 cm wide, 58 cm long and 20 cm high. It consisted of a wood frame overlaid with complex inlay composed of thin intricately carved plaquettes of various shades of amber and ivory pieced together as a three-dimensional mosaic. Fabricated according to a distinctly archaizing stylistic register and iconographic program, the casket presents as a three-dimensional pastiche of individual parts that appear as *spolia* repurposed from much older objects, including florid carved appliqués, faux gems and cabochons, all fashioned from amber.[84] The ivory (perhaps sourced from Sibero-Russian walrus) was long associated with devotion, avidly collected by the Medici, and often featured

**Figure 4.1** Gdańsk (Danzig) workshop. Reliquary of St. Kazimierz Jagiellończyk, c. 1677–1678. Wooden core, amber, silver, ivory, metal. 35×56×20 cm. Florence, Palazzo Pitti (Tesoro dei Granduchi). © Public domain.

together with amber in Baltic-made objects of the period. Here it appeared in twenty-five carved reliefs on the four sides and top in iconic vignettes illustrating biblical episodes of the incarnation (Annunciation, Visitation) and portraying early Christian and medieval saints (Lawrence, Francis, Christine, Barbara, Margaret of Antioch, Catherine of Alexandria), as well as winged cherubim. The effect evokes medieval ivory caskets often used as reliquaries.[85] Pairs of addossed figures of evangelists (Peter or Paul and John) and early bishops (Augustine and Ambrose) guard the front opening and verso, their stiff frontal posture and linear carving also evocative of medieval sculpture. Spiral Solomonic columns at the four corners miniaturized a signature feature of Baroque sacral architecture associated with Constantinian Rome.[86]

The Baltic casket's mode of re-contextualizing fragmentary 'originals' within a palimpsestic assemblage inflected Italian Baroque forms in patently Baltic materials. The pastiche related to the past in form, style and language, thematizing the temporal passage between venerable and modern in a way that reanimated the grandeur of the past in honour of both dynasties. Their munificence was punctuated by reliefs of the Medici escutcheon (the so-called *palle*), and four Florentine *gigli* (fleur-de-lis) equally reminiscent of Pac heraldic lilies and symbolic of the saint's spiritual martyrdom.[87] The reliquary's 'amber antiquarianism' also invested with an aura of venerability the links between these dynasties and the cult of the saint inside, whose canonization was in fact only finalized in 1604. He was made present by the sculpted equestrian figurine of Kazimierz, his sword and shield and stiff posture reminiscent of the centuries-old *Vytis* emblem of the Lithuanian Grand Duchy.[88] The elaborate artwork represented a Baltic translation of the Medicean medicinal chest from the grand-ducal Galleria. As a relic chest, it represented not only the technological and artisanal equal to the Florentine *pietre dure*, but also the thaumaturgic equivalent to the prophylactic medicines contained within the grand-ducal *casse*, some of which themselves contained amber.[89] One train of early modern natural history theorized amber's marine origin. As rejoinder to the Medici *casse*, the Prussian-made reliquary achieved with indigenous materials a spectacular display of technical mastery over raw nature and a dazzling visual effect comparable to Florentine *pietre dure* hardstone artworks. Bishop Pac had chosen the perfect rejoinder to the martial gifts first exchanged between his Hetman cousin and Cosimo III de' Medici: for a slave, he dispatched a holy warrior; for pharmaceutical unguents, a spiritual salve; for gems from the earth, a stone thought to come from the sea; for ostentatiously modern artistry, a superlative work of art that professed its own antiquity.

That amber was prominent across the Pac-Medici gift-exchange was in keeping with amber diplomatic gift-giving to promulgate the rare and storied substance as the patrimony of the Baltic elite.[90] Medicean affinity for the prized substance manifested not only in collecting and displaying amber, engaging with it in religious ceremonial, and incorporating it in medicines, but also the discursive obfuscation of its Baltic provenance.[91] By the time Cosimo received the long-awaited relic in its amber container, the Medici had amassed in the *Cappella delle Reliquie* well over thirty amber items, and a visit to the *Tesoro dei Granduchi* in the Palazzo Pitti today reveals a veritable encyclopaedia of amber objects.[92] His house had also constructed for over a century a discursive 'Italianization of amber' mythologizing its native peninsular origins in the Po river valley of ancient Etruria over the actuality of amber deposits on the Prussian littoral.[93] That Etruria likewise represented the mythological seat of the Pac line points to amber's particular agentive properties as a heterotemporal and heterotopic material, imbued with the potential to forge in reverse as it were links in an unbroken chain that stretched back along the axis of human chronology, retroactively reaffirming common dynastic origins and the transhistorical unity of the cult of saints. Amber's generative materiality evoked notions of deep time and the present, foreign and local, thus translating the meaning of the Jagiellonian relic between respective contexts. Amber's material hermeneutics made it exegetically suited to reliquaries: enlivened when handled, it underwent an invisible but sensible physical transformation triggered by and evocative of human flesh, bodying forth the presence of the saints. Amber retained warmth, conserved a static charge (amber in Greek is *electron*, ἤλεκτρον) and released a fragrance redolent of Church incense, the sweet smell ascribed to the incorrupt bodies of saints, and the common expression of holy persons 'in odor of sanctity'.[94]

In June 1679, six months after receiving the Kazimierz relic, the grand duke personally welcomed Bishop Pac, who was travelling south on another trip to Rome to negotiate his papal confirmation. He stopped in Florence to deliver his cousin Michał Kazimierz Pac's gifts of *pelle di dante*, polar bear pelts, and (perhaps) a portrait of the Grand Hetman painted by Michele Arcangelo Palloni at Cosimo's behest (the live bear apparently never materialized).[95] He also pledged financial support towards the new reliquary chapel in Borgo Pinti underway for staging the lavish 1685 *translatio* of Pazzi's inviolate body to a marble and *pietre dure* altar.[96] This was a costly undertaking spearheaded by Cosimo and the Dowager Grand Duchess, who commissioned a magnificent gold filigree crown encrusted with over six hundred precious gems to be manufactured in the grand-ducal *Galleria* and embellish the saint's inviolate remains during the *translatio* ceremony.[97]

In the wake of Pac's visit and in conjunction with his success winning Vatican confirmation, in August 1682 the grand duke wrote of the imminent delivery of his own gift of relics to the Pac. These came from the body of Maria Maddalena de' Pazzi, 'ornament and bulwark of my Homeland [Tuscany] as well as splendor of Your Illustrious family [Pac]'. Cosimo underscored the great importance of the remains, 'no matter how small of Her Holy Body', for the propagation of the saint's fame in the Baltic. He wrote:

> Thus it is with great faith that I dare to send this to Your Eminence [Bishop Pac], namely a tooth and a few hairs of the Saint, presuming that You are fully aware of the absolute impossibility of obtaining [such relics]. Given that the Saint's own body completely intact and each and every part fully clothed in incorrupt and supple flesh, according to the marvellous disposition of Divine Providence ... it has not been and is not appropriate for the Holy Apostolic See to violate such remarkable integrity, not even for the solemn demands of canonization.[98]

The relics were dispatched from Florence later that same year. They arrived around Christmas in Vilnius, whence Bishop Pac wrote in January 1683 to express thanks for 'the most precious gift [*Dono*] of the relics of S. Maria Maddalena de Pazzi, with which Your Most Serene Highness with singular generosity has deigned to grow in this city and Diocese devotion to this great saint and multiply within me obligations to Your Most Serene Highness'.[99] Reading the timing of this gift against missives reminding Pac of his promised patronage in support of Pazzi's cult in Florence suggests that Medicean reciprocity was tied to both Pac's episcopal confirmation and his vowed sponsorship. This vow was apparently still unfulfilled on Pac's death in 1684, when Vilnius cathedral records logged the transfer of the Pazzi relics from the magnate's private palace to the cathedral treasury, signalling the end of the decade-long power struggle between chapter and bishop.[100]

The reliquary of St Maria Maddalena de' Pazzi was made in 1682 of gold, enamel, rock crystal and more than 120 diamonds (Figure 4.2).[101] At a mere 13 cm high it stands less than half the height of the amber reliquary casket of St Kazimierz Jagiellończyk. Its authors were Medici goldsmiths Giovanni Comparini and Giuseppe Vanni, who also worked on the jewelled crown for Pazzi's *translatio*. Their Pazzi reliquary was a tiny trophy reflective of the war, diplomacy, political struggles and crusader rhetoric surrounding its creation. Conceived as a miniature ostensory, the reliquary safeguards contents so miniscule as to verge on the invisible. Their presence within the crystal globe is attested by the enamel inscription on the crowning banderole, 'DENS ET CAPILLI S[ANCTAE] MARIAE MAGD[ALENAE] DE PAZZI'. Despite its small size, this tour-de-force of the Medici *Galleria* in fact showcased a range of metallurgical and lapidary techniques. The artists' technical mastery revealed the floral forms sublimated in the baroque Solomonic column and translated the architectonic monumentality inhering in reliquary design into a diminutive florid style and floral iconography that disclosed the thaumaturgic prolificacy of its contents.

Its three legs evocative of foliage and plumage terminate in a hexagonal ring, reflecting the centuries-old Medici symbol of a gold and diamond ring surmounting three feathers or plumes.[102] Enamel covers much of the gold's surface in the form of floral and vegetal motifs, three-dimensional enamel lilies framing a single tooth and entwined with faint hairs, crown, fleur-de-lis, banderol and cross. Rendered by fusing ground glass to a metal substrate in imitation of precious stones, this technically demanding medium was long associated with exegesis of the Divine 'refiner's fire' and used for ecclesiastical

**Figure 4.2** Giovanni Comparini, Giuseppe Vanni, Medici Granducal Workshops (Gallery of Works in semi-precious hardstone). Reliquary of St Maria Maddalena de' Pazzi, 1682. Cast, chased and enameled gold; ground rock crystal (quartz); opaque enamels, diamonds. 13 cm h. Vilnius, Cathedral Treasury (Church Heritage Museum). © Public domain.

objects and reliquaries.[103] All was encrusted with faceted diamonds, from the Greek ἀδάμας (*adámas*, 'unconquerable, invincible'). These gems articulated both the relics' talismanic potency as 'ornament and bulwark' of grand-ducal dominion and its curative power, gesturing to the lapidary medicine that played an essential role in early modern cultures of *materia medica*.[104] The monstrance defending and ostending Pazzi's fragmentary avatars seemingly blooms from the stem surmounted by a petal-like capital. Composed of two hemispheres, its translucent globe looks like glass, but was in fact sculpted by court lapidary Giuseppe Antonio Torricelli from the clearest quartz in the *Opificio di Pietre Dure* charged with hardstone mosaic production in the *Galleria*.[105] Torricelli was trained in the glyptic arts associated with Roman antiquity, revived in Renaissance Italy and pursued to perfection in the Medici workshops. Here, Torricelli and others specialized in producing unparalleled crystal clear reliquary receptacles that imitated venerable *spolia*.[106]

Maria Maddalena's dazzling crystal globe inflected temporal notions, much like Kazimierz's glimmering amber casket. What is more, following Pliny's Natural History, early modern gemology maintained precious stones were formed of congealed liquid under the earth's surface. Rock crystal constituted a special case, formed of the purest water deeply frozen as ice and over time converted into a hard limpid mineral.[107] Thus crystal, like amber, was ultimately aqueous in origin and essence. The etymological derivation of the term crystal was from the Greek κρύσταλλος (*krústallos*), itself a derivation of κρύος (*krúos*), meaning cold. This made rock crystal a 'cold' substance complementary to 'warm' amber in period scientific theory. The substance thus ontologized the female humoral state appropriate to its saint and the frigid climate of the gift's Baltic destination. It also hinted, however, at the relics' numinous fertile potential to overcome – even conquer – their sex and the inhospitable environment of their future home. Through pious engagement, the precious remains could disseminate the saint's fame and aura in the north. Perhaps Cosimo hoped that whereas the *zibellini* had failed to increase his family's fecundity, 'his' relic could instead figuratively 'procreate' and cultivate the fame of the Medici line in the north.

## Conclusion: 'Relic states'

As the Tuscan-Lithuanian gift-exchange concluded in a celebration of piety, prolificacy and permanency, the families involved presided over dynastic horizons and religio-political hegemons in an increasingly irrevocable state of collapse. Hetman Pac died in 1682 without heirs and Bishop Pac in 1684, while Cosimo lived to see his patrimonial line extinguished. That all the precious offerings in the Medici-Pac case demonstrated a bilateral preoccupation with gifts ontologizing not only rarity and luxury but also purity, fertility, hegemony and longevity suggests a link between the significance of the substance of gifts and the status of a 'realm [that] was becoming a somewhat Ruritanian shadow of its former self'.[108] From the Medicean perspective, the grand duke had obtained a significant primary relic of a prince from a kingdom he himself designed (if only briefly) to rule, who numbered amongst the last pre-Tridentine saints raised to the altar by a Medici pope, and whose name rendered in Italian as *Casimiro* was a near homophone to the favourite grand-ducal name Cosimo. This offered a pious lens through which to inflectively legitimize his line's *translatio imperii* realigning interests in the north, even as the relatively minor power of the Tuscan Grand Duchy was outpaced on the global stage and their bloodline approached extinction.[109] From the perspective of the Pac, obtaining a relic of a newly canonized noble Florentine descended from a common family line offered a pious lens through which to inflectively legitimize their own *translatio imperii*. This helped to realign their interests within a religiously divided polity and within greater Catholic Europe, even as the Commonwealth reeled from the series of mid-seventeenth-century Swedish and Russian military campaigns collectively known as the Deluge and their house also faced discontinuation.[110]

In this context, the Baltic and Italian reliquaries, however apparently different, in fact represented complementary parts of a mutually transformative system, 'intelligible only through the relationships that unite them'.[111] Both resonated with Counter-Reformation lapidary and bodily models of hagiography, predicated on the Pauline invocation in I Peter 2:4–8 of the saints as 'living stones' pieced together like a mosaic into a virtual edifice, the Celestial Jerusalem, built with the bodies of the saints themselves, and representative of the transhistorical institution of the Church founded on Christ as cornerstone, an edifice simultaneously realized at the end of human history and existing eternally beyond it.[112] Delimited by common boundaries of religiosity and generosity and patterns of cultural production and engagement with objects, Cosimo and the Pac mapped a virtual territory beyond themselves. Their promulgation of complementary models of sanctity, embodied by their shared saints delimiting the notional survival of a transregional Roman *imperium* as ideological relic and consecrated in cultural discursive practices, synchronically reached back through history to operate the proverbial engine of human history in reverse, reaffirmed retroactively the unity of both the cult of saints and their dynastic interests.[113]

In articulating these transcultural temporal dynamics, the very material and hermeneutical mutability of the gifts exchanged as religious, political and cultural indexical signs evinces their crucial and malleable role as not only symbols of common fictionalized pasts, but also diplomatic agents crucial to communal identity formation amongst ruling elites.[114] They shaped culturally distinct representation within and between evolving early modern European states, exposing the reliance of a self-styled centre that was grand-ducal Tuscany on its so-called artistic periphery, grand-ducal Lithuania. Revisiting their little-known exchange of gifts can contribute to productively problematizing conventional understandings of cultural dynamics between West-Southern and East-Northern Europe specifically and perceived centres and their purported peripheries more broadly.[115] This Italo-Baltic case study might also contribute to recent much-needed recalibrations gauging 'the demarcation between substantive cultural exchange and the sorts of movements and negotiations that were routine within any society'.[116] Thus this chapter raises the question if the Medici-Pac gifts represent a cross-cultural study, or if the regions under discussion were in fact part of a broader and substantially coherent early modern culture.

In reality the miraculous corporal state of both holy persons involved was neither without contest nor without threat. In Florence, Pazzi's corpse was subjected to repeated expert autopsies and questions surrounded the supernatural nature of its preservation, with some suggestions that the Carmelites may have secretly embalmed the remains. Scepticism surrounding her body was so great that Maria Maddalena's remains became a target of derision by period Protestants.[117] In Vilnius, the multiple rushed relocations of St Kazimierz Jagiellończyk's corpse during mid-seventeenth-century military conflicts had reduced his relics from miraculously intact to fragmentary. Their dissolute state may be one reason why the cathedral chapter was so reticent to re-open the reliquary casket containing what was left of the prince.[118] The crucial stabilizing role of gifts constituting bonds amongst networks of mutual exchange and reciprocation within and between constituencies likewise reaffirmed the vaunted integrity of their holy avatars, to re-embody Italy's connection to the Baltic through the special potency of relics of vaunted integral saints like Jagiellończyk and Pazzi. These processes pointed to a mode of relationality between saint and state, such that the translations of the status and conditions of the bodies of these saints might be diachronically and synchronically mapped against the transformations undergone by the Lithuanian and Tuscan realms. Throughout the endurance and disaggregation of both, *translatio* evinces the representational labour that such ritually relocated relics perform over time in the space of ritual, wherein the fragile condition of saint and state might be masked by a variety of media and measures.[119]

## Notes

1. Regarding the conceptual leveraging of the potlatch see Claude Lévi-Strauss, *The Way of the Masks*, trans. S. Modelski (Seattle: University of Washington Press, 1982). For relic *translatio* see Hans-Jakob Achermann, 'Translationen heiliger Leiber als barockes Phänomen', *Jahrbuch für Volkskunde* 4 (1981): 101–11; Martin Heinzelmann, 'Translation (von Reliquien)', *Lexikon des Mittelalters* 8 (2002): 947–9.
2. Guy Lazure, 'Possessing the Sacred: Monarchy and Identity in Philip II's Relic Collection at the Escorial', *Renaissance Quarterly* 60 (2007): 58–93.
3. Helen Hills, *The Matter of Miracles: Architecture and Holiness in Baroque Naples* (Manchester: Manchester University Press, 2015). On agentive properties ascribed to holy matter see also Mads Heilskov's chapter in this volume.
4. A recent helpful theoretical overview of research about relics in the Christian West with bibliography can be found in Georges Kazan and Tom Higham, 'Researching Relics: New Interdisciplinary Approaches to the Study of Historic and Religious Objects', in *Life and Cult of Cnut the Holy: The First Royal Saint of Denmark*, ed. Steffen Hope et al. (Odense: Syddansk Universitetsforlag, 2019), 142–67.
5. Rome, Archivum Romanum Societatis Iesu (hereafter ARSI), Epistolae Externorum, vol. 36, 1r-v, 32r-v. For relevant archival sources pertaining to the exchanges taken up in this chapter see records preserved in Florence, Archivio di Stato Firenze (hereafter ASF), f. Mediceo del Principato: 1529–1753 (hereafter MP), 4489–4494, especially 4492, 298r-v, 442r-v, 561r, 604r, 697r; 4493, 602r-v, 603–604, 608r-v, 609r-v. For an overview of aspects taken up in the present study see Aušra Baniulytė, 'Italian Intrigue in the Baltics: Myth, Faith, and Politics in the Age of the Baroque', *Journal of Early Modern History* 16 (2012): 23–52.
6. Elena Fasano Guarini, 'COSIMO III de' Medici, granduca di Toscana.' Dizionario Biografico degli Italiani 30 (1984). https://www.treccani.it/enciclopedia/cosimo-iii-de-medici-granduca-di-toscana_(Dizionario-Biografico)/ (accessed 11 January 2021). A classic study of grand-ducal Tuscany under the late Medici remains Harold Acton, *The Last Medici* (London: Cardinal, Sphere Books Ltd, 1988).
7. A helpful Anglophone introduction to the Grand Duchy of Lithuania is Norman Davies, *Litva: The Rise and Fall of the Grand Duchy of Lithuania: A Selection from Vanished Kingdoms* (New York: Penguin, 2013). For the early modern Baltic region see David Kirby, *Northern Europe in the Early Modern Period. The Baltic World 1492–1772* (London and New York: Longman, 1990).
8. For the Pac see Robert Frost, *After the Deluge: Poland-Lithuania and the Second Northern War, 1655–1660* (Cambridge: Cambridge University Press, 1993), 80–90 and passim; Aušra Baniulytė, 'The Pazzi Family in Lithuania: Myth and Politics in the European Court Society of the Early Modern Age', *Medium aevum quotidianum*

58 (2009): 41–57; Andrej Kotljarchuk, *In the Shadows of Poland and Russia: the Grand Duchy of Lithuania and Sweden in the European Crisis of the Mid-17th Century* (Huddinge: Södertörns University, 2006), 271–2. Pac relations with Italy and the Medici have been taken up in a number of important multilingual studies by Aušra Baniulytė and Anna Sylwia Czyż cited throughout this chapter.

9   For a recent collection of studies in premodern representations and perceptions of far northern Europe (including the Baltic), including helpful bibliography, see Dolly Jørgensen and Virginia Langum, ed., *Visions of North in Premodern Europe* (Turnhout: Brepols, 2018). See also Eleanor Rosamund Barraclough, Danielle Marie Cudmore and Stefan Donecker, ed., *Imagining the Supernatural North* (Edmonton: University of Alberta Press, 2016).

10  For the Baltic as commodity frontier see Jason Moore, '"Amsterdam Is Standing on Norway," Part I: The Alchemy of Capital, Empire and Nature in the Diaspora of Silver, 1545–1648', *Journal of Agrarian Change* 10:1 (2010): 33–68; Jason Moore, '"Amsterdam Is Standing on Norway" Part II: The Global North Atlantic in the Ecological Revolution of the Long Seventeenth Century', *Journal of Agrarian Change* 10:2 (2010): 188–227. For the Baltic as Indies of Europe see Stefan Donecker, 'Est vera India septemtrio: Re-imagining the Baltic in the Age of Discovery', in *Re-forming Texts, Music, and Church Art in the Early Modern North*, ed. Tuomas M.S. Lehtonen and Linda Kaljundi (Amsterdam: Amsterdam University Press, 2016), 393–419.

11  Paul Srodecki, *Antemurale Christianitatis: Zur Genese der Bollwerksrhetorik im östlichen Mitteleuropa an der Schwelle vom Mittelalter zur Frühen Neuzeit* (Husum: Matthiesen Verlag, 2015).

12  For Casimir in the present context see Sigita Maslauskaitė-Mažylienė, *Šventojo Kazimiero atvaizdo istorija XVI–XVIII a* (Vilnius: Lietuvos nacionalinis muziejus, 2010). A recent exhibition at the Church Heritage Museum Vilnius commemorating the relic exchange treated in the present essay resulted in the important multilingual publication by Sigita Maslauskaitė-Mažylienė, *Masterpieces of the History of the Veneration of St. Casimir: Lithuania – Italy* (Vilnius: Bažnytinio paveldo muziejus, 2018).

13  Jan Kurczewski, *Kościół Zamkowy, Czyli Katedra Wileńska W Jej Dziejowym, Liturgicznym, Architektonicznym I Ekonomicznym Rozwoju*, 3 vols. (Vilnius: Nakład I Druk J. Zawadzkiego, 1908–1916), III: 229.

14  Clare Copeland, *Maria Maddalena de' Pazzi: The Making of a Counter-Reformation Saint* (Oxford: Oxford University Press, 2016); Adelina Modesti, *Women's Patronage and Gendered Cultural Networks in Early Modern Europe: Vittoria della Rovere, Grand Duchess of Tuscany* (New York: Routledge, 2020), 225–41. For Pazzi in the Lithuanian context see Aušra Baniulytė, 'Šv. Marijos Magdalenos de'Pazzi kultas Lietuvos baroko kultūroje: atvaizdai ir istorinė tikrovė', *Darbai ir dienos* 53 (2010): 225–58.

15 On the potency of relics and their attending ceremonies and rituals see also Gustavs Strenga's essay in this volume.
16 For an overview of Italo-Baltic connections over the longue durée see Riccardo Casimiro Lewanski, ed., *La via dell'Ambra. Dal Baltico All'Alma Mater. Atti Del Convegno Italico-Baltico* (Bologna: Università degli Studi, 1994); Piero Bugiani, 'From Innocent III to Today—Italian Interest in the Baltic', *Journal of Baltic Studies* 38:2 (2007): 255–62. For Italo-Lithuanian culture see Aušra Baniulytė, 'Italai XVI–XVII a. Lietuvos Didžiosios Kunigaikštystės kasdieniame gyvenime', in *Lietuvos etnologija*, ed. Auksuolė Čepaitienė (Vilnius: Lithuanian Institute of History, 2005), 75–96; Daiva Mitrulevičiūtė, ed. *Lietuva-Italija: šimtmečių ryšiai* (Vilnius: Išleido Nacionalinis muziejus Lietuvos Didžiosios Kunigaikštystės valdovų rūmai, 2016). For connections between the Holy See and Poland-Lithuania in the early modern period see especially the work of historian Gaetanio Platania, e.g. *Polonia e Curia Romana: corrispondenza tra Giovanni III Sobieski, re di Polonia con Carlo Barberini protettore del Regno* (Viterbo: Sette Città, 2011).
17 Aušra Baniulytė, 'Gli italiani alla corte dei "Pazzi" in Lituania: mito e politica nel Seicento barocco', *Archivio storico italiano* 168 (2010): 325–48.
18 Antonio Panella, 'Candidati italiani al trono polacco. I Medici', *Rassegna Nazionale* 16 April 1917: 269–79.
19 Riccardo Gennaioli and Maria Sframeli, eds., *Sacri Splendori: Il Tesoro Della 'Cappella Delle Reliquie' in Palazzo Pitti* (Livorno: Sillabe, 2014), 244–7; Riccardo Spinelli, *Le Committenze Sacre Di Cosimo III De' Medici: Episodi Poco Noti o Sconosciuti (1677–1723)* (Florence: Edifir Edizioni Firenze, 2019).
20 Alice E. Sanger, *Art, Gender and Religious Devotion in Grand Ducal Tuscany* (Burlington: Ashgate, 2014), 71–92; Gennaioli and Sframeli, *Sacri Splendori*, 243–338; Modesti, *Women's Patronage and Gendered Cultural Networks*, 205–42.
21 Andrzej Rachuba, 'Mikołaj Stefan Pac', *Polski Słownik Biograficzny* (Wroclaw: Zakład Narodowy im. *Ossolińskich*, 1979), 24: 738. For the chapter's opposition see Kurczewski, *Kościół zamkowy czyli katedra wileńska*, 225–45.
22 Anna Sylwia Czyż, 'Pamięć o poprzednikach i kłótnie z kapitułą, czyli o działalności biskupa Mikołaja Stefana Paca na rzecz skarbca katedry wileńskiej', *Humanities and Social Sciences* 23 (2018): 9–30.
23 Joanna Orzeł, 'From Imagination to Political Reality? The Grand Duchy of Lithuania as a Successor of Rome in the Early Modern Historiography (15th–18th centuries)', *Open Political Science* 1 (2019): 170–81.
24 Aušra Baniulytė, 'Pacai ar Pazzi? Nauja Palemono legendos versija LDK raštijoje', in Istorijos Rašymo Horizontai, *Senoji Lietuvos literatūra* 18, ed. Aušra Jurgutienė and Sigitas Narbutas (Vilnius: Lietuvių literatūros ir tautosakos institutas, 2005), 140–66; Anna Sylwia Czyż, 'Włosi w kręgu rodziny Paców', in *Stan badań nad wielokulturowym dziedzictwem dawnej Rzeczypospolitej*, vol. 6, ed. Wojciech

Walczak and Karol Łopatecki (Białystok: Instytut Badań Nad Dziedzictwem Kulturowym Europy, 2013), 175–96.

25  Aušra Baniulytė, 'Šv. Marijos Magdalenos de'Pazzi kultas Lietuvos baroko kultūroje: atvaizdai ir istorinė tikrovė', *Darbai ir dienos* 53 (2010): 225–58.

26  For the Casimir Chapel see Piotr Jamski, 'Kaplica św. Kazimierza w Wilnie i jej twórcy', *LDK sakralinė dailė: atodangos ir naujieji kontekstai. Sacred art of Grand Duchy of Lithuania: discoveries and new contexts*, Acta Academiae Artium Vilnensis 51 (2008): 91–112.

27  Aleksandra Koutny-Jones, *Visual Cultures of Death in Central Europe: Contemplation and Commemoration in Early Modern Poland-Lithuania* (Leiden: Brill, 2015), 173–5; Modesti, *Women's Patronage and Gendered Cultural Networks*, 225–41.

28  Anna Sylwia Czyż, 'Fundacje artystyczne rodziny Paców. Stefana, *Krzysztofa Zygmunta i Mikołaja Stefana. 'Lillium bonae spei at antiquitate consectarum'* (Warsaw: Wydawnictwo Naukowe UKSW, 2016).

29  For Pac's pilgrimage and pledge see ASF, MP, b. 4494, 731r-v, 744r-745v, 749r-750v, 755r-v. See also Baniulytė, 'Šv. Marijos Magdalenos de'Pazzi', 232; Giovanni Matteo Guidetti, 'Il reliquairio di santa Maria Maddalena de'Pazzi a Vilnius e l'attività di Giovanni Comparini e Giuseppe Vanni per la corte di Toscana: nuovi documenti', *Bollettino della Accademia degli Euteleti della Città di San Miniato* 79 (2012): 197–215.

30  Bradford Bouley, 'Negotiated Sanctity: Incorruption, Community, and Medical Expertise', *The Catholic Historical Review* 102:1 (2016): 1–25.

31  Ruth Sargent Noyes, *Peter Paul Rubens and the Counter-Reformation Crisis of the Beati Moderni* (New York: Routledge, 2018), 184–5.

32  Virgilio Cepari, *Vita della serafica vergine s. M.M. de' P. fiorentina... con l'aggiunta cavata da' processi formati per la sua beatificazione e canonizazione dal padre Giuseppe Fozi* (Rome: Bernabò, 1669), 377–8.

33  Copeland, *Maria Maddalena de' Pazzi*, 76–7, 154–5.

34  Vilnius, Wróblewski Library of the Lithuanian Academy of Science, Manuscript department, f. 43, b. 646, l. 1; Maslauskaitė-Mažylienė, *Masterpieces of the history of the veneration of St. Casimir*, 64.

35  Baniulytė, 'Italai XVI–XVII a. Lietuvos Didžiosios Kunigaikštystės kasdieniame gyvenime.'

36  Sally McKee, 'Domestic Slavery in Renaissance Italy', *Slavery & Abolition* 29:3 (2008): 305–26; Anti Selart, 'Slavery in the Eastern Baltic in the 12th-15th Centuries', in *Serfdom and Slavery in the European Economy, 11th–18th Centuries*, ed. Simonetta Cavaciocchi (Florence: Firenze University Press, 2014), 351–64.

37  Salvatore Bono, 'Schiavi musulmani sulle galere e nei bagni d'Italia dal XVI al XIX secolo', in *Le genti del mare Mediterraneo*, ed. Rosalba Ragosta (Naples: Lucio Pironti, 1981), 2: 837–75; Corey Tazzara, 'Port of Trade or Commodity Market?

Livorno and Cross-Cultural Trade in the Early Modern Mediterranean', *Business History Review* 94:1 (2020): 201–28.
38. In Anna Maria Massinelli and Filippo Tuena, ed., *Treasures of the Medici* (London: Vendome Press, 1992), 176. For the Baltic context of the socio-cultural utility of the motif of the Turkish threat see Alan V. Murray, 'Saracens of the Baltic: Pagan and Christian Lithuanians in the Perception of English and French Crusaders to Late Medieval Prussia', *Journal of Baltic Studies* 41:(2010): 413–29. For the Medici context see studies in Francesco Freddolini and Marco Musillo, ed., *Art, Mobility, and Exchange in Early Modern Tuscany and Eurasia* (New York: Routledge, 2020).
39. ASF, MP, b. 4492, fols. 293 r-v, 294r-295v, 297r-v, 955v.
40. Leon Satkowski, 'The Palazzo Pitti: Planning and Use in the Grand-Ducal Era', *Journal of the Society of Architectural Historians* 42:4 (1983): 336–49. For artistic activities see Annamaria Giusti, 'The Grand Ducal Workshops at the Time of Ferdinando I and Cosimo II', in *Treasures of Florence: The Medici Collection 1400–1700*, ed. Cristina Acidini Luchinat (Munich: Prestel, 1997), 115–43. For pharmaceuticals see Ashley Lynn Buchanan, 'The Politics of Medicine at the Late Medici Court: The Recipe Collection of Anna Maria Luisa de' Medici (1667–1743)' (PhD dissertation, University of South Florida, 2018).
41. Buchanan, 'The Politics of Medicine', 30–2, 128–9. For further bibliography regarding amber see below.
42. Annamaria Giusti, *Pietre Dure and the Art of Florentine Inlay* (London: Thames and Hudson, 2006).
43. ASF, MP, 4493, 430v. For Palloni see Giovanni Matteo Guidetti, 'Additional Information about the Sources of Michele Arcangelo Palloni's Artistic Language', *Acta academiae artium Vilnensis* 51 (2008): 75–89.
44. Thus far such a portrait has not been identified. See ASF, MP, 4493, 430v.
45. Mindaugas Paknys, *Pažaislio vienuolyno statybos ir dekoravimo istorija* (Vilnius: LKTI, 2013).
46. Eighteenth-century records for Pažaislis described 'Relikwiarz duży hebanowy ze półeczkami srebrenemi I trzema osóbkami, w którym są dwa Vella S. Marii Magdaleny de Pasis, olejek w ampułce, kawałek habitu szarego za szkłem lokowane.' ('large ebony reliquary with silver small shelves and three figurines on top, in which there are two *Vella* of S. Maria Magdalena de Pazzi, oil in an ampoule, a piece of gray habit'). Vilnius, Wroblewskis Library of the Lithuanian Academy of Sciences, f. 43-9919, 'Pažaislio vienuolyno ir bažnyčios inventorius, sudarytas 1797', 20–1. See Baniulytė, 'Šv. Marijos Magdalenos de'Pazzi', 234; Czyż, 'Włosi w kręgu rodziny Paców', 186. For the decorative program see Anna Sylwia Czyż, 'Treści ideowe wystroju kościoła i klasztoru w Pożajściu', in *Kameduli w Warszawie 1641–2016: 375 lat fundacji eremu na Bielanach*, ed. Karol Guttmejer i Anna Sylwia Czyż (Warsaw: Miasto Stołeczne, 2016), 305–36.

47  For Castelli and Tencalla see especially the work of Mariusz Karpowicz, e.g. *Matteo Castello. L'architetto del primo barocco a Roma e in Polonia* (Lugano: Edizioni Ticino Management, 2003); Mariusz Karpowicz, *Artisti ticinesi in Polonia nella prima metà del Seicento* (Lugano: Edizioni Ticino Management, 2002), 135–53. For the Jagiellończyk reliquary chapel see Piotr Jamski, 'Kaplica św. Kazimierza w Wilnie i jej twórcy'; Giorgio Mollisi, ed., *Gli artisti del lago di Lugano e del Mendrisiotto nel Granducato di Lituania (dal XVI al XVIII sec.)* (Lugano: Edizioni Ticino Management, 2013), 29–31; Koutny-Jones, *Visual Cultures of Death in Central Europe*, 173–5.
48  Laimonas Briedis, *Vilnius, City of Strangers* (Vilnius: Baltos Lankos, 2008), 55–6.
49  ASF, MP, 4492, 318r-v; 4493, 313r, 321r.
50  Federica Gigante, 'Medici Patronage and Exotic Collectibles in the Seventeenth Century: The Cospi Collection', in *Art, Mobility, and Exchange in Early Modern Tuscany and Eurasia*.
51  ASF, MP, 4493, 435.
52  Bonnie L. Hendricks, *International Encyclopedia of Horse Breeds* (Norman: University of Oklahoma Press, 1995), 448–9.
53  Sarah G. Duncan, 'Stable Design and Horse Management at the Italian Renaissance Court', in *Animals and Courts,* ed. Mark Hengerer and Nadir Weber (Berlin: De Gruyter, 2020), 129–52.
54  Hedda Reindl-Kiel, 'Ottoman Diplomatic Gifts to the Christian West', in *The Ottoman Orient in Renaissance Culture. Papers from the International Conference at the National Museum in Krakow*, ed. Robert Born and Michał Dziewulski (Krakow: National Museum in Krakow, 2015), 95–118.
55  Mackenzie Cooley, 'Marketing Nobility: Horsemanship in Renaissance Italy', in *Animals and Courts*, 111–28.
56  Peter Edwards et al., ed., *The Horse as Cultural Icon: The Real and the Symbolic Horse in the Early Modern World* (Leiden: Brill, 2011); Magdalena Bayreuther, 'Pferde in der Diplomatie der Frühen Neuzeit', in *Materielle Grundlagen der Diplomatie: Schenken, Sammeln und Verhandeln in Spätmittelalter und früher Neuzeit*, ed. Mark Häberlein and Christof Jeggle (Konstanz: UVK-Verl.-Ges., 2013), 227–56.
57  Nadir Weber, 'Lebende Geschenke. Tiere als Medien der frühneuzeitlichen Außenbeziehungen', in *Medien der Außenbeziehungen von der Antike bis zur Gegenwart*, ed. Peter Hoeres and Anuschka Tischer (Wien: Böhlau Verlag, 2017), 160–80. For animal gifts in the Medici milieu see Angelic Groom, *Exotic Animals in the Art and Culture of the Medici Court in Florence* (Leiden: Brill, 2018). For the Baltic context see Anu Mänd, 'Horses, Stags and Beavers: Animals as Presents in Late-Medieval Livonia', *Acta Historica Tallinnensia* 22:1 (2016): 3–17.
58  Przemyslaw Gawron, 'Royal Horse Guard: Polish-Lithuanian Commonwealth in the Vasa Period, 1587–1648', in *Las caballerizas reales y el mundo del caballo*, ed. Juan Aranda Doncel and José Martínez Millán (Córdoba: Edicioneslitopress, 2016), 283–96.

59  For Argamaki horses see A.M. Kleimola, 'Cultural Convergence: The Equine Connection between Muscovy and Europe', in *The Culture of the Horse: Status, Discipline, and Identity in the Early Modern World*, ed. Karen Raber and Treva J. Tucker (New York: Palgrave Macmillan 2005), 45–62.

60  Austėja Brasiūnaitė, 'Stud Farm of the Grand Duke of Lithuania: Traditions and the Importance of the Horse in Warfare and Messenger Service 14–16 Century', in *Las caballerizas reales y el mundo del caballo*, 167–78.

61  Krzysztof Dorohostajski, *Hippika to jest księga o koniach, potrzebna i krotochwilna młodości zabawa, przez Krzysztofa Dorohostajskiego ku pożytkowi ludzi rycerskich na jasność wydana* (Krakow: Andrzej Piotrowczyk, 1603).

62  Florence, ASF, MP, 4493, 435.

63  Mario Zannoni, *Il Parmigiano Reggiano nella storia* (Parma: Silva Editore, 1999), 45 ff.

64  For a similar case involving the Medici gifting cheese see Brian Brege, 'Making a New Prince: Tuscany, the Pasha of Aleppo, and the Dream of a New Levant', in *Art, Mobility, and Exchange in Early Modern Tuscany and Eurasia*.

65  ASF, MP, 4493, 431r.

66  See e.g. papal nuncio Mario Filonardi in 1637, 'His Majesty was alone in a carriage drawn by three horses, with the pelt of a white bear on his lap and a cape lined with ermine fur' ['Sua Maestà era solo in slitta tirata da tre cavalli, con una pelle d'orso bianco tra le gambe et in dorso un'ungarina foderata di zebellino…']. Rome, Biblioteca Vaticana, Barb. Lat. 6598, f. 23r-v.

67  ASF, MP, 4493, 435v.

68  On the gifting of large 'charismatic megafauna' see also Sabine Sommerer's chapter in this volume.

69  Groom, *Exotic Animals in the Art and Culture of the Medici Court*, 95–111.

70  See studies in 'Identity and Self-Definition', in *The Culture of the Horse*, 223–349.

71  For a cultural history see Michael Engelhard, *Ice Bear: The Cultural History of an Arctic Icon* (Seattle: University of Washington Press, 2017).

72  Janet Martin, *Treasure of the Land of Darkness: The Fur Trade and Its Significance for Medieval Russia* (Cambridge: Cambridge University Press, 1986); Thomas Noonan and Roman Kovalev, 'The Furry 40's. Packaging Pelts in Medieval Northern Europe', in *States, Societies, Cultures, East and West. Essays in Honor of Jaroslaw Pelenski*, ed. Janusz Duzinkiewicz (New York: Ross, 2004), 653–82.

73  Leah R. Clark, *Collecting Art in the Italian Renaissance Court: Objects and Exchanges* (Cambridge: Cambridge University Press, 2018), 158–207.

74  Karla Langedijk, 'A New Cigoli: The State Portrait of Cosimo I De' Medici, and a Suggestion concerning the Cappella De' Principi', *The Burlington Magazine* 113:823 (1971): 575–9.

75  James Beck, 'The Dream of Leonardo da Vinci', *Artibus et Historiae* 14:27 (1993): 188–9.

76 Tawny Sherrill, 'Fleas, Furs, and Fashions: Zibellini as Luxury Accessories of the Renaissance', in *Medieval Clothing and Textiles*, ed. Robin Netherton and Gale R. Owen-Crocker (Woodbridge: Boydell Press, 2006), 2:121–50.

77 Sheila Barker, 'Christine de Lorraine and Medicine at the Medici Court', in *Medici Women. The Making of a Dynasty in Grand Ducal Tuscany*, ed. Giovanna Benadusi and Judith C. Brown (Toronto: Centre for Renaissance and Reformation Studies, 2015), 154–80.

78 Jacqueline Marie Musacchio, 'Weasels and Pregnancy in Renaissance Italy', *Renaissance Studies* 15:2 (2001): 172–87.

79 Rome, Archivum Romanum Societatis Iesu (hereafter ARSI), *Epistolae Externorum*, vol. 36, fol. 1r-v, 32r-v; in *Masterpieces of the History of the Veneration of St. Casimir*, 65–6.

80 ASF, MP 4493, fols. 470r-v, 472 r-v, 602r-v.

81 Florence, Archivio della Basilica di San Lorenzo, 73. See *Sacri Splendori*, 270, 93–6.

82 Rachel King, 'The Shining Example of "Prussian Gold": Amber and Cross-Cultural Connections between Italy and the Baltic in the Early Modern Period', in *Materiał rzeźby: Między techniką a semantyką*, ed. Aleksandra Lipińska (Wrocław: Wydawn Uniwersytetu Wrocławskiego, 2009), 456–70.

83 Rome, ARSI, *Epistolae Externorum*, vol. 36, fol. 32r-v. See also Florence, ASF, MP 4493, fol. 492r, 608r-v, 609r-v and Guardaroba Medicea, n. 802 Guardaroba del taglio, 594.

84 *Sacri Splendori*, 266–7; *Masterpieces of the History of the Veneration of St. Casimir*, 74–6.

85 For the Nordic-Baltic region and Siberia as sources of ivory in this period see M. Rijkelijkhuizen, 'Whales, Walruses, and Elephants: Artisans in Ivory, Baleen, and Other Skeletal Materials in Seventeenth- and Eighteenth-Century Amsterdam', *International Journal of Historical Archaeology* 13:409 (2009): 409–29; for Medici ivory collections see Eike D. Schmidt, 'Cardinal Ferdinando, Maria Maddalena of Austria, and the Early History of Ivory Sculptures at the Medici Court', *Studies in the History of Art* 70 (2008): 158–83. For comparison to Byzantine ivory caskets see Anthony Cutler, 'On Byzantine Boxes', *The Journal of the Walters Art Gallery* 42/43 (1984–1985): 44–6.

86 J. B. Ward Perkins, 'The Shrine of St. Peter and Its Twelve Spiral Columns', *Journal of Roman Studies*, XLII (1952): 21–33.

87 Anna Sylwia Czyż, 'The Symbolic and Propaganda Message of the Heraldic Programmes in Two 17th-Century Marriage Prints (Epithalamia) of the Pacas Family', *Knygotyra* 73 (2020): 79–93.

88 Juozas Galkus, *Lietuvos Vytis: albumas* (Vilnius: Vilniaus dailės akademijos leidykla, 2009).

89 On curative properties ascribed to amber in this period see Rachel King, 'Whale's Sperm, Maiden's Tears and Lynx's Urine: Baltic Amber and the Fascination for It in Early Modern Italy', *Ikonotheka* 22 (2009): 168–79.

90 Susanne Netzer, 'Bernsteingeschenke in der preussischen Diplomatie des 17. Jahrhunderts', *Jahrbuch der Berliner Museen* 35 (1993): 227–46; Rachel King, 'Whose Amber? Changing Notions of Amber's Geographical Origin', *Ostblick* 2 (2014): 1–22.

91 For Medicean amber theorizing see Tomasz Grusiecki, 'Foreign as Native: Baltic Amber in Florence', *World Art* 7:1 (2017): 3–36.

92 Kerstin Hinrichs, 'Bernstein, das 'Preußische Gold' in Kunst- und Naturalienkammern und Museen des 16.-20. Jahrhunderts' (PhD dissertation, Humboldt.-Universität Berlin, 2007), 266–9.

93 For early modern Italy as a source of amber see Rachel King, 'Finding the Divine Falernian: Amber in Early Modern Italy', *V&A Online Journal* 5 (2013). http://www.vam.ac.uk/content/journals/research-journal/issue-no.-5-2013/finding-the-divine-falernian-amber-inearly-modern-italy/ (accessed 14 January 2021).

94 Rachel King, 'The Beads with Which We Pray Are Made from It: Devotional Ambers in Early Modern Italy', in *Religion and the Senses in Early Modern Europe*, ed. Christine Göttler and Wietse de Boer (Leiden: Brill, 2013), 153–75.

95 ASF, MP, filza. 4493, fol. 431r. It remains unclear from the documents if the Hetman's portrait was indeed complete and gifted at this time. No such surviving portrait has yet been identified today in Medici collections.

96 His promise could be interpreted as a kind of votive offering in thanks for his successful confirmation as bishop. On ex-votos see also Sari Katajala-Peltomaa's contribution in this volume.

97 For Pac's pilgrimage and pledge see ASF, MP, b. 4494, 731r-v, 744r-745v, 749r-750v, 755r-v. For Medici patronage of the Pazzi chapel and *translatio* see Modesti, *Women's Patronage and Gendered Cultural Networks*, 225–41.

98 ASF, MP 4494, fol.731r-v.

99 ASF, MP 4494, fol. 743r.

100 Baniulytė, 'Šv. Marijos Magdalenos de'Pazzi', 54–5.

101 ASF, Guardaroba Medicea, n. 880, Guardaroba del atglio, *Filza di conti 1681–1682*, inserto 6, n. 528. See Guidetti, 'Il reliquairio di santa Maria Maddalena de'Pazzi a Vilnius', 197–200; *Sacri Splendori*, 274–5; *Masterpieces of the History of the Veneration of St. Casimir*, 78–9.

102 Heather L. Sale Holian, 'Family Jewels: The Gendered Marking of Medici Women in Court Portraits of the Late Renaissance', *Mediterranean Studies* 17 (2008): 148–82. On the manifold valences of rings as gitfs per se, see Anna Boeles Rowland's essay in this volume.

103 Barbara Drake Boehm and Elisabeth Taburet-Delahaye, ed., *Enamels of Limoges, 1100–1350* (New York: The Metropolitan Museum of Art, 1996).

104  Marieke Hendriksen, 'The Repudiation and Persistence of Lapidary Medicine in Eighteenth-Century Dutch Medicine and Pharmacy', in Gems in the Early Modern World. *Europe's Asian Centuries*, ed. Michael Bycroft and Sven Dupré (Cham: Palgrave Macmillan, 2019), 197–220.

105  Annamaria Giusti, 'Torricelli, Giuseppe Antonio', *Grove Art Online*. https://www.oxfordartonline.com/groveart/view/10.1093/gao/9781884446054.001.0001/oao-9781884446054-e-7000085746 (accessed 12 October 2020).

106  Letizia Arbeteta, *Arte transparente. La talla del cristal en el Renacimiento milanés* (Madrid: Prado Museum, 2016).

107  Annibale Mottana, 'Italian Gemology during the Renaissance: A Step toward Modern Mineralogy', in *The Origins of Geology in Italy*, ed. G.B. Vai and W.G.E. Caldwell, *Geological Society of America, Special Paper* 411 (2006): 1–21.

108  Quoting Stella Fletcher, 'The Medici Family', *Oxford Bibliographies in Renaissance and Reformation*. https://www.oxfordbibliographies.com/view/document/obo-9780195399301/obo-9780195399301-0260.xml (accessed 14 January 2021).

109  Lia Markey, *Imagining the Americas in Medici Florence* (University Park, Pennsylvania: Pennsylvania State University Press, 2016).

110  Frost, *After the Deluge*.

111  Lévi-Strauss, *The Way of the Masks*, 93.

112  Stefania Tutino, '"For the Sake of the Truth of History and of the Catholic Doctrines": History, Documents, and Dogma in Cesare Baronio's Annales Ecclesiastici', *Journal of Early Modern History* 17:2 (2013): 125–59.

113  Noyes, *Peter Paul Rubens and the Counter-Reformation crisis of the Beati moderni*, 55–7.

114  For an exploration of these concepts in a different context, see Philipp Höhn's contribution.

115  Tomasz Grusiecki, 'Going Global? An Attempt to Challenge the Peripheral Position of Early Modern Polish-Lithuanian Painting in the Historiography of Art', *The Polish Review* 57:4 (2012): 3–26.

116  Kristoffer Neville, *The Art and Culture of Scandinavian Central Europe, 1550–1720* (University Park, Pennsylvania: The Pennsylvania State University Press, 2019), 12.

117  Bradford A. Bouley, *Pious Postmortems: Anatomy, Sanctity, and the Catholic Church in Early Modern Europe* (Philadelphia: University of Pennsylvania Press, 2017), 105–8.

118  Briedis, *Vilnius, City of Strangers*, 55–6.

119  Echoing Pamila Gupta, *The Relic State: St Francis Xavier and the Politics of Ritual in Portuguese India* (Manchester: Manchester University Press, 2014), 13–14.

# 5

# 'The gift' and the living image: Exchange between human and nonhuman actors in fifteenth- to sixteenth-century Prato

Mads Vedel Heilskov

This chapter seeks to elucidate the complex interplay between humans, images, objects and the divine – all considered living, efficacious or capable of agency – that took place in the exchanges between votary – a person who had made a vow to a sacred entity, often in exchange for a service – and living images in late fifteenth- and early sixteenth-century Italy. It examines the role of exchange of favours, images and objects as instrumental in the construction and affirmation of images and objects as living agents through which humans and the divine were able to interact. The fifteenth and early sixteenth centuries in Italy saw a rise in the cult of living images – that is in the cultic devotion to images that had miraculously acquired life. Soon after an image had miraculously acquired life, a wave of miracles normally followed and pilgrims began to flock at the site. In their wake, a sanctuary would be built around the image to accommodate the masses.[1] Pilgrims usually brought gifts to the image in hope of or in thankfulness for the overcoming of various hardships, often as votive offerings. These could take almost any form imaginable, but were generally in some way connected either to the body of the votary or to the miracle that was granted or hoped for, thereby giving tangible form to the ephemeral hopes, desires or thankfulness of the votaries.[2] The living image and the practice of votive offering were therefore interconnected phenomena in Italy (and elsewhere) in the late medieval period. However, their mutual relationship has not yet been scrutinized, as scholarship tends to focus on either one of the two without considering their interdependence.

This research was supported by The Carlsberg Foundation.

I will closely examine the exchanges that took place between votaries and the Santa Maria delle Carceri in Prato (Figure 5.1), Tuscany, at the end of the fifteenth century following the image's miraculous animation in 1484. Not only is this example of cultic devotion to a living image emblematic for its typological kind; its genesis and the practices and exchanges that followed are also extraordinarily well illuminated thanks to two miracle collections from the 1480s and 1505 respectively, as well as other documents. Both miracle collections were transcribed and published by Anna Benvenuti in 2005.[3] The latter miracle collection, written by jurist and promoter of the Marian cult in Prato Giuliano di Francesco Guizzelmi (1446–1518), is the richest in terms of detail. It collects ninety-four miracles, many of which were witnessed by Guizzelmi himself or by known citizens of the town and most examples will therefore be extracted from this collection.[4] These examples are not seen in isolation as individual occurrences, but as dynamic chains of actions and reactions set in motion and perpetuated by exchanges between human and nonhuman actors. Following a contextualization of the topic in previous research, the argument falls in three segments: analysing first the becoming of the miraculous image and the spread

**Figure 5.1** The Santa Maria delle Carceri in its current setting in Prato, Tuscany. © Mads Vedel Heilskov.

of its cult, then the distributed personhood of divine and human actors through their replication in images and objects that were exchanged and circulated as well as able to act on their own accord, and finally the exchange that took place between these living materials as they were assembled together within the sacred space. The analysis shows that exchanges of vows, favours, objects and images falling within the register of 'the gift' were built into the very understanding of what constituted a living sacred entity and that exchange, usually by means of material mediation, was the central mode of communication between humans and the divine.

## Contextualization: Research History

While ex-votos (offerings to fulfil a vow) and living images were interlinked in fifteenth- and early sixteenth-century Italy, their treatment in scholarship has been more parallel than connected: both phenomena have in common that they have been labelled as representations of popular culture and thereby separated from the formal history, philosophy and liturgy of the Christian church. The heuristic categorization of votive offering as a practice favoured by the unlearned happened already in late antiquity and the early medieval period, when it was criticized as a pagan practice in opposition to the Christian faith.[5] During the fifteenth and sixteenth centuries, as votive offering spread in the Christian West, not least in Italy, it was again heavily criticized by both Catholic and Protestant theologians for being idolatrous, especially at sanctuaries of living images. In the following centuries, during the Enlightenment, it was primarily seen as a backwards and simpleminded practice.[6] This view was carried into the professional historical writing during the modern breakthrough, where ex-votos were dealt with within the broader framework of folklore studies.[7]

Scholarship on the cult of living images shares the same characteristics. Living images were often criticized for being fake or idolatrous by ecclesiastical authorities already during the Middle Ages.[8] During the sixteenth century, they were condemned as idolatrous by both Catholics and Protestants.[9] Then, in the Enlightenment, the medieval European cult of living images was compared to African tribes' 'childish' belief in the efficacy of images and was understood within the newly formulated concept of 'fetish'.[10] In the wake of the modern breakthrough, the cult of living images was used to frame the Middle Ages as the antithesis of modernity. Within church historical and liturgical studies in particular, it was used by both Protestant and Catholic scholars to show how the uneducated and blatantly anti-modern medieval people had misunderstood the Christian teachings or, indeed, how greedy clerics had misused the good faith of the uneducated masses to trick them into donating their belongings under the false pretence of miraculous occurrences.[11] Therefore, the cult of living images too has traditionally belonged to the study of popular culture and folklore.

The characterization of both these categories as representations of popular beliefs carried over into the historical anthropology and history of mentalities during the mid-twentieth century, which fostered a renewed interest in popular culture with a 'history from the bottom' approach.[12] Scholars like André Vauchez and Jean-Claude Schmitt mainly focused on popular piety from a historical-anthropological angle seeking to write a history of the people through their ritual practices.[13] This one-sided focus on rituals turned images and objects into passive components in the actions carried out by humans. In contrast to the predominant historical-anthropological approach of his contemporaries, art historian David Freedberg focused on the efficacy of the images as something emanating from themselves rather than the rituals and devotions that surrounded them. Freedberg, moreover, included living images, pilgrimage tokens and ex-votos in his study, although they were treated in separate chapters. While to some extent paving the way for the recent new materialist approach, Freedberg was preoccupied with the image as a visual category rather than as a material one (as were his contemporaries), thus largely ignoring the talismanic function and potency attached to pilgrimage tokens and ex-votos as material objects.[14]

Because of their heuristic categorization within folklore studies and the history of popular culture, living images and ex-votos have also played a marginal role in the broader history of Christianity and Christian art.[15] This situation has not been helped by the conceptual framework of 'the Renaissance' which has privileged a particular humanist (in its historical meaning) understanding of culture, art and religion at the expense of practices and art that do not fit within that paradigm. This has, for instance, led Hans Belting to conclude that the cult image saw a crisis during the fifteenth and sixteenth centuries, although the opposite is well attested[16]; and ex-votos have largely been ignored by art historians, even when they could be attributed to the most famous artists of the Renaissance.[17] The concept of the Renaissance itself has led scholars to privilege new breakthroughs in art, technology, religion, politics etc. over continuities.[18] Therefore, the new ideas and practices of a few artists and intellectuals have been made to represent the outlook and mentality of entire populations.[19] This general picture changed around a decade ago, when the ontology-focused approach of 'new materialism' was increasingly applied by medievalists to their subject matters and source material, not least in the wake of Caroline Walker Bynum's *Christian Materiality* (2011).[20] The matter of agency has marked the study of religion in the past decade in particular.[21] With 'new materialism', scholarship has realized that the presence of things, in any context, causes a particular experience of the world and provokes a reaction: objects in interaction with spaces, bodies and minds are thus seen as able to effect action and change.[22]

As useful as this realization is, it is lacking in terms of providing a proper understanding of how differences in power or agency between groups of humans and nonhumans have been structured and formed over the course of history to effect different modes of experience in different agents.[23] In the context of the social reality of fifteenth- to sixteenth-century Italy, we cannot ignore that consumption was a significant part of the material framework of the religious life, not least in the practice of votive offering, where the elite would spend vast amounts of wealth on ex-votos made of noble metals, precious stones and exotic fabrics.[24] Even wax, often used for ex-votos, was unaffordable for most.[25] Moreover, the focus on 'things' and their power can obscure the role of human agency. So while the realization following 'new materialism' that the medieval religious practices took place in a world of objects that participated actively in shaping the minds and social reality of people has contributed with valuable new insights, it comes with an inbuilt blindness regarding the human experience and the importance of ritual practice for the images' and objects' ability to obtain potency.

The main points reached through this review of previous scholarship are that ex-votos and living images have both primarily been interpreted as phenomena external to formal Christian practice and they have both been categorized as representations of popular culture. Combined with the consequences of the conceptual framework of the Renaissance, both phenomena have been marginalized. The view that ex-votos and living images belonged to popular culture was integrated in the historical anthropology, where they became entryways into the study of medieval popular religion, not least through the study of rituals, for instance in the context of religious festivals and spectacles. While this framework largely ignored the agency of images and objects, the current new materialist trend largely ignores the human actions that images and objects participated in. Moreover, ex-votos and living images, as well as pilgrimage tokens and other types of devotional *Kleinkunst* have (with a few exceptions) been treated as separate phenomena.[26] They have thereby been detached from each other, although they arguably functioned together in complex interactions and exchanges.

On this background, the current study places itself in the intersection between the historical-anthropological study of rituals and the new materialist study of object agency and thing-power. By focusing on the actions carried out in interaction between human, material and divine entities, I treat them as equally able to act and interact, thus bridging the divide between the purely anthropological and the purely material approaches. I direct my focus towards exchange as this was the main communicative situation where humans, nonhumans and the divine met and interacted.

## Obtaining personhood

The miraculous animation of the image of the Virgin Mary took place on the 6th of July 1484,[27] when an eight-year-old boy named Jacopino d'Antonio was chasing a cricket at the old ruined prison on the outskirts of the town of Prato. Only a month after the miraculous animation of the image had taken place, the commune of Prato wrote to Pope Sixtus IV (1414–1484) to get a permission to erect a sanctuary around it. Just two months later, on 12 September 1484, the newly appointed Pope Innocent VIII (1432–1492) issued a bull granting the commune the rights of patronage over the sanctuary, stating that it was now independent of parish control and local ecclesiastical jurisdiction. Then, on 9 October 1484, the process of building the sanctuary was initiated.[28] By 20 April 1485 plans had been submitted and the committee that was appointed by the commune initially chose the design by Giuliano da Maiano (1432–1490). The construction thus began only to be put on hold. The design was abandoned and, at the invitation of the commune of Prato, none other than Lorenzo de' Medici (1449–1492) selected a new design by Giuliano da Sangallo (1443–1516) who signed the contract with the commune on the 9th of October 1485.[29]

The process of making the site an officially recognized place of pilgrimage was thus very quick and effective, which attests the importance of having such a site for the town, its economy and identity. Significantly, it was crucial for the commune to keep the economy and legal issues free of any parochial ties from the early onset, probably because this would grant them a significant economic advantage. The pattern of the miracle narrative as well as of the political, economic and architectural actions and decisions that were made to initiate and enhance the cult largely follows that of other cult places in fifteenth- and sixteenth-century Italy, such as Todi and Montepulchiano.[30] The Prato example is, however, very well attested in the sources, making it a suitable entryway for the present study.

The older miracle collection has a rather short description of the miraculous animation and largely leaves out any details of pilgrimages to the site. Its anonymous author, known as pseudo-Andrea di Giuliano del Germinino, does, however, begin his description by mentioning how the divine grace radiates from the miraculous image, fills up the priests and citizens of Prato and elsewhere and works wonders for them. Then, after briefly describing the miraculous transformation of the image and its ability to sweat, bleed and weep, it states that the image of the Virgin manifests itself for anyone who is in need, poor or weary, and that anyone who is thirsty for the living water from the Virgin shall recommend themselves to her. It then concludes that the following list of miracles is a trusty investigation of when, how and for what these trustworthy people received mercy. The introduction ends with a plea to the reader to have faith in the veracity of these accounts.[31] In other words, it is implied that the working of wonders is connected to pilgrimage and that the purpose of collecting the miracles was to disseminate the cult and affirm its veracity for potential (gift-bearing) pilgrims.

Guizzelmi's miracle collection gives a much fuller account of the events; those leading up to the miraculous transformation as well as those taking place afterwards, thus describing the chain of actions and reactions in great detail. In fact, it first meticulously gathers the sacred history of Prato, from the acquisition in 1141 of a miracle-working relic of the Virgin Mary's belt, the Sacra Cintola, which was kept at Prato's principal church, the Pieve of Santo Stefanoto[32], and the miraculous animation of a figure of the Virgin that took place in 1348 and again in 1399 during the Bianchi devotions.[33] Then it goes on to describe the state of the old prison where the miraculous animation of Santa Maria delle Carceri took place. The prison and its floors, walls, tunnels and yards are described in great detail, with much effort put into its staging as an abandoned and desolate place that was in ruins and taken over by wild animals.

We learn that the painted figure was very old, although its style suggests that it was painted during the Trecento (fourteenth century).[34] It was intact, according to Guizzelmi, and showed the Virgin Mary with the infant Christ in her arms. Christ had a swallow in his hand and wore a yellow robe. The Virgin held a flower in her right hand. She and the Christ child were flanked by Saint Leonard, advocate of prisons, on their right side and Saint Stephen, advocate for the people of Prato, on their left. He concludes his description by saying that this is the form in which the image is seen and painted today and for all eternity and in which it has made an 'impression' (*formata*) on many and has been shown all over the world.[35] He then goes on to describe the curiosity that the miracle sparked in people and the questions they had.[36]

Only after this setting of the scene does Guizzelmi begin the actual description of the miraculous animation of the image, which provides many additional details to the older miracle collection. Firstly, the boy, Jacopino, is described as a shapely child who was white, blond and shaped like an angel. As he was guided by the cricket, he saw the figure of the painted Virgin and her son that was placed on this bad spot and immediately kneeled before her with his hands folded to give his devotion to her. There he then saw the Virgin put her living baby with the living swallow in his hand down into the prison beneath her and anoint/cleanse (*nectare*) the place three times with her hand. Then she went back onto the wall with her son and became a painting again. Afraid, Jacopino went home to his mother and told her of the miracle he had witnessed, but she did not believe him. This happened twice more. He then went back to the prison for a third time and sat down to admire the image.

While he sat there, a man tried to carry him away, which he failed to do as he did not have the strength to carry him. A thirteen-year-old boy named Nicolo di Guidetto Guidetti from Florence passed by and asked what he was doing. Jacopino then asked Nicolo if he did not see the lights and what the Virgin was doing. Nicolo did not see anything, but returned later to the place anointed by the Virgin. Here, he saw an infinite number of people clad in white with white candles in their hands. He then became fatally ill and, while on his deathbed, he would comfort his parents telling them that he was with the many people in white robes carrying candles that he had seen and that they were coming for him. He said this repeatedly, and as he died, his father declared that he had given a son to the Virgin.

At night, while this was taking place, Jacopino still sat in front of the image. As people began to worry about him, a priest in service of the Bishop of Pistoia named Messer Giovanni Celmi arrived, and Jacopino told him what he had witnessed. Jacopino's words moved the people who were gathered there and they began to recite these miracles. Following this incident, many people began to see the figure transform and weep, open and close her eyes, sweat blood and other wonders and people soon began to flock at the site bringing candles, candelabras and charitable gifts while pleading for mercy and weeping ostentatiously.[37]

Throughout Guizzelmi's foundation narrative we encounter motifs of conversion, transformation and transfer entangled with one another in discourses of contagious and sympathetic magic.[38] Within these discourses, exchange was the central mediator that enabled sacrality to be obtained, transferred and passed on between divine, material and human agents. The place is described as a bad spot on Earth where nature reigns and civilization is absent.

Only by the consecration by the living Virgin herself could this deserted place be transformed. This way, the site was converted by the divine agency of the Santa Maria delle Carceri through threefold consecration, but was also described in phrases that resonate with tropes often used in monastic foundation narratives.[39] This notion is further underlined by the use of 'claustro' (cloister/enclosed place) in its description.

Completely uninhabitable for humans, the prison was in the throes of chaos; a state that 'offended the eternal God' (*offendeva lo eterno Dio*). In fact, the only thing that remained intact and untouched by the forces of evil was the image and the large window it was placed by. Its preservation was itself a sign of the divine agency radiating from it. In that way, the place itself played a role in the miraculous events it hosted. One might say that the ruined and unfriendly frame of the site surrounding the painting played an important role in conditioning the boy's experience, giving the painting an aura of elevated wholeness among the fragments.

In this setup, clearly resting on biblical narratives,[40] the ruined and deserted prison formed the perfect background for a conversion on several levels; of the site, the image, the child and many other people throughout the narratives of the miracle collection. In other words, the initial conversion had to take place at a site that was outside the human sphere and overtaken by evil, and this triumph of all that was perceived as civilized and good over that which was perceived as lost and vile became the pillar on which the sanctuary and cult rested. The site was, moreover, able to obtain the consecration through the contagious touch of the Virgin and permanently hold it, effectively making it a *brandeum* (contact relic).[41]

The description of the image itself is preoccupied with the way it was perceived by the community and with the way it had made an impression on it already from the onset. Its (perceived) antiquity and state of preservation stood in contrast to its surroundings and made Jacopino notice it. Moreover, the living image was not simply the Virgin Mary, that is, the divine prototype. It was the Santa Maria delle Carceri, a particular identity acquired through its ability to act on its own and interact with pilgrims and devotees in various forms of communication and exchange. Throughout the miracle collection, the image is referred to by its full name and is continuously construed as an independent 'person'.[42] In that way, the Santa Maria delle Carceri was her own person and an *exuvium* (thing stripped from a body, here in the extended meaning of remnant, relic, cast-off, fragment or detached part of a person or even objects belonging to someone and thus associated with them) of the Virgin Mary's *distributed personhood* (personhood distributed in the milieu or agency beyond the body-boundary, often through *exuviae*) simultaneously.[43]

From its initial animation, we see how the responses of devotees are construed as appropriate in accordance with the decorum of pilgrims at a sacred site. The child is described as an angelic character whose innocence emanates from his behaviour and appearance. His appearance as a character of light is carried on into the narrative of lights radiating from the image and the figures clad in white that carried candles in Nicolo's death-bed visions, forging a metaphorical concordance between the image and its ideal worshippers. Both boys' narratives involve their parents, but while Jacopino's mother is described as a woman of little faith who, as Peter denied Jesus before the Passion, dismisses her son's visions three times, Nicolo's father accepts that his son's life is given up to the Virgin. This metaphorical tie between the death of a boy, the coming to life of the image and the vison of pilgrims is remarkable because its various aspects all rely on discourses of gift-exchange.

Nicolo's father offered his son to the Virgin in a manner that closely resembles the miracle narratives where children, as we shall see below, were given to the Virgin as votive effigies. This can be understood in Christological terms, meaning that the life of Nicolo was sacrificed in exchange for the image coming to life in order to work its wonders for the common good. The logic is clear; the life of an ideal devotee is sacrificed for the image to obtain life. If we see the giver as Nicolo himself, then the gift did not only contain part of him, it *was* him. If we see the giver as Nicolo's father, then the gift certainly also contained part of its giver. In both instances, the act resembled the death of Christ on the cross, seen from the perspective of Christ on the one hand and from his grieving mother on the other.

Furthermore, the visions that frame this part of the narrative give a preview of the cult that arose after the miraculous animation and show us what was expected of the ideal pilgrim: she/he was to dress in a white robe (no doubt inspired by the aforementioned Bianchi devotions), carry candles (one of the most common gifts offered by pilgrims at shrines[44]) and offer gifts to the cult image.[45] At the end of the miracle narrative, the events were authenticated and formalized. The involvement of Messer Giovanni Celmi, who was not only an ordained priest but also acting on the authority of the bishop of Pistoia, meant that the Church itself authenticated the miracle. To further underline the veracity of his story, Guizzelmi let this final part of the narrative play out in front of witnesses.[46] In this way, the conversion of the site, the image, the initial ideal devotees (Jacopino, Nicolo and the white clad devotees of Nicolo's visions) and the people all came together in the final gesture that authenticated the miraculous transformation of the image and the site.

It is thereby clear that transformation took place as a sequence of actions and reactions on several levels in several human and nonhuman agents when the image of the Virgin came to life and a cult was established. The site itself was converted as the image broke free of its material boundary and consecrated it, making it ready to receive pilgrims. The first witnesses were also transformed and in each their way freed from earthly boundaries. Jacopino went to the prison without permission, freeing himself from the confinements of school as well as his mother's doubts to devote himself to religious meditation, whereas Nicolo was freed in a much more dramatic fashion from his earthly shell as his soul was claimed by the white clad apparitions. In his description of these interlinked processes of transformation and breaking of boundaries, Guizzelmi repeatedly includes witnesses and deals with peoples' reception, testifying over and over that this all happened at the will of God and so the cultic activities at the site are continually justified. In Guizzelmi's narrative of the process of the living image's animation and its conversion of both the site and the humans that were implicated, exchange was the central element that allowed sacrality to be mediated and circulated. Exchange, then, realized the breaking down of the ontological boundary that separated living and dead matter.

## Distributing personhood

The relationship between the sacred prototype, the living image and humans took on further complexity when images began to be exchanged among them after the living image was consolidated as a miracle performing cult image. In many of the miracles recorded by Guizzelmi, votaries used images and objects of different kinds in their communication with the living image. Some of these depicted the living image itself and were made out of either paper or lead; some had a talismanic nature after they had touched it. In exchange for the miracles performed by the image, often through its *exuviae* or 'avatars', votaries would offer images of themselves or of particular body parts made of different materials (i.e. wax, wood, silver), or different paraphernalia attached to the miracle (i.e. an olive branch, a shirt, bandages, crutches). These images and objects were not necessarily one-to-one replicas of their prototypes, but rather stood for them indexically, sometimes through mimetic artistic techniques, sometimes by touch or direct involvement in the occurrence, and sometimes by association (i.e.

length, weight).⁴⁷ In these exchanges, images and objects worked as stand-ins for the sacred prototype, for the living image, for humans as well as for miracles, and became mediators between these different agents and catalysts for further miraculous occurrences.⁴⁸ The mediating images and objects of different kinds thereby became actors in their own right and were able to contain both actors and actions.

After the image had miraculously animated, word that it also performed miracles spread swiftly. Pilgrimage tokens and paper images soon were made, and people in need of a miracle began to flock to Prato. On 5 August 1484, only approximately two months after the image animated, a certain Sancti di Simone da Sogliano, castellan for Count Carlo Malatesta, went from Florence where he had been hospitalized for eighteen months at the Sancta Maria Nuova Hospital to Prato, accompanied by a poor man seeking to have his leg healed from a fetid wound that had rendered him crippled and unable to walk without crutches. He vowed himself to the Santa Maria delle Carceri and promised to give a large wax image of himself in her honour in return for her help. His leg, however, failed him on the way and he had to stop one kilometre outside Prato. There he saw an image of the Madonna painted on paper amidst the branches of an olive tree. He devotedly recommended himself to the Santa Maria delle Carceri in front of the image and was instantly cured. He then walked to the shrine and publically told about his miraculous healing. As a sign of this miracle, the living image was crowned with an olive wreath.⁴⁹

The power of the living image was thus evoked through mimetic representation and was activated without the need of anything but the votary devotedly recommending himself to it. The replica was thus every bit as powerful as the original and could act as a mediator between the votary and the divine entity and as a catalyst for divine intervention. The opposition between truth and deception, original and replica was effectively broken down in the votive situation. Guizzelmi does not tell whether or not the promise of placing a large wax ex-voto by the image was in fact fulfilled, but the crowning of the image with an olive wreath shows that the act of vowing oneself to the image in hope of a miracle, as well as the act of performing the miracle could be contained and preserved within a symbolic object that was mimetic of the circumstance of the miracle. In this particular instance it did not represent any particular material value. Instead, emphasis is put on the aspect of publically promoting the miraculous image rather than on the exchange of wealth. Gift-giving discourses permeates the narrative nonetheless.

The 'gift' of healing took place through Sancti's surrogate body in the form of a wax effigy that was able to contain his personhood. To some extent, the significance of all of the objects that became efficacious in this exchange depended on the intent to give in order to receive. The paper 'avatar' of the Santa Maria delle Carceri, who herself was an avatar of the Virgin Mary, worked because it was activated by Sancti's pious intent to give.[50] The wreath of olive branches was a signal that the pious intent to give was rewarded with a miracle; a material sign of both sides of the contractual obligation between agents that was able to contain the entirety of the miraculous occurrence in one prominently placed symbol. The sympathetic magic that took place in Sancti's healing worked on several levels: images and persons were replicated, and intentions, actions and personhood were contained within pictorial and material avatars that acted vicariously for their prototypes. The production of all these levels of meaning ultimately depended on discourses of gift-giving.

While the paper image that facilitated Sancti's miraculous recovery worked sympathetically through its mimetic quality, contagious magic plays a significant role in a number of miracles in Guizzelmi's collection. Throughout the collection, both paper and other types of replicas of the Santa Maria delle Carceri, most prominently pilgrimage tokens made of lead, frequently acted as efficacious agents that were able to contain the essence of the living image. In some of the miracles involving different types of images that had touched the living image, Guizzelmi himself plays an active part. As cult-promoter, he had access to these treasured *brandea*, and their circulation was a central part of his efforts to disseminate the cult. This adds another level to the capacity of images and objects to capture and distribute personhood and their ability to acquire efficacy through contagious magic.

One miracle where various images that had touched the living image play an active role involves a colleague of Guizzelmi's, messer Bartholomeo, who was guardian at the legal office in Pisa. He had been sick with a fever for fourteen months, but in May 1485 Guizzelmi took a figure of the Santa Maria delle Carceri made of paper and placed it on him.[51] Then Guizzelmi took a lead amulet that had touched the Madonna and told him to put it around his neck. He did so with great devotion and prayed to the Santa Maria delle Carceri for mercy. He instantly recovered and never had a fever again for the rest of his life.[52] In another case, in June 1485, demonic possession led a certain mona Piera to faint and exhibit strange behaviour. Guizzelmi offered her husband a 'Virgin Mary of lead' (*una vergine maria di piombo*) that looked like and had touched the living image. Piera was held down by several women as her husband placed the amulet around her neck, and they all prayed for mercy. The husband vowed that he would visit the living image and give thanks if the Virgin could exorcize the demons. The demons left the body and the husband kept his vow.[53]

Here, an image on paper and lead amulets that were *brandea* worked separately and in conjunction. In the first example, a form of reciprocal relationship between the images was manifested through gesture: the paper image was placed on Antonio, while he put the lead amulet around his neck himself. We thereby see a strategy involving two elements: the intercessory prayer by Guizzelmi, manifested by his gesture of placing the image on Antonio vicariously asking the Virgin for mercy, and Antonio's own prayer for mercy, manifested by him placing the amulet around his neck while uttering a prayer. We moreover see an additive strategy where sacrality increases through the adding up of efficacious images. The other example shows us that verisimilitude was of importance for the efficacy of the amulet – it depicted the Santa Maria delle Carceri and not simply a generalized Virgin Mary. The same is true of the miracle that follows in Guizzelmi's collection. In July 1485, a young man from Florence named Giovannantonio was ill from cancerous boils in and around the genitals and, given up by doctors, he was nearing the end of his life. Giovannantonio's father, Carlo, put a lead amulet which was made in the similitude of the image and had touched it around his son's neck. Meanwhile, both father and son recommended and vowed themselves to the image and promised to place the 'son in wax' (*figliuolo di cera*) by her. As soon as the amulet was placed around Giovannantonio's neck, he began to recover and the father fulfilled the vow.[54]

Pilgrimage tokens could also be worn as protective amulets. For instance, on an unspecified date in 1486, a certain Angnolo, who was disabled after an accident thirty years prior, was wearing a lead image of the Santa Maria delle Carceri on his clothes as he fell from a horse and down a slope. During his fall he could hear his bones break and then, upon remembering that he wore his protective amulet, he recommended himself to the Virgin. As he landed, he got up completely uninjured and even free of the previous injury as well.[55] In this case, the votary recommending himself to the Virgin was the catalyst for the miracle and so far, the act of praying, vowing oneself and handling the talismanic devices in various ways succeeded in activating the sacred images. In other instances, however, amulets acted on their own accord as *apotropeia* able to repel evil. An example of this form of pure object agency involves Guizzelmi himself. On 30 May 1486 he was kicked by a mule but suffered no injury because he wore a lead amulet that had touched the image on his clothes.[56]

Counter-gifts in return for miracles often took the form of images or symbolic objects that worked in their own right, making the votaries present in proximity of the living image. Although there is no explicit mention of a counter-gift in exchange for miraculous healing in a little more than half of the miracle stories (49 out of 94), we can, given the generalized mention of publically giving thanks to the image, expect that some form of gift was offered in most instances. Some examples, however, make this dynamic of giving and counter-giving abundantly clear; in the case of the abovementioned Giovannantonio, a wax effigy was to be placed in the sanctuary in proximity of the living image. The wax effigy was a rather obvious replica of the votary and worked explicitly as stand-in (although examples from other places show us that wax replicas could be done with more or less effort invested in their verisimilitude to their giver, an aspect that was dependent on the amount of money spent). Others offered stand-ins that worked in a less visually explicit way. These could be loaves of wax or candles that had the same length or weight as their prototype or things that had touched the votary or were associated with them, that is *exuviae*.[57]

For instance, in September 1485, a certain Giovanni who lived in Bologna vowed that he would offer the weight in wax of his child, Simone, to the image if she cured him of his disease. As soon as the vow was made, the miracle occurred and the child was cured. One year later, Giovanni went to Prato to satisfy his vow. We are told that the amount corresponded to 75 pounds, a sum worth more than 75 libre. Giovanni, moreover, left the shirt that Simone wore when the miracle took place at the sanctuary in order to publically manifest the mercy he had received from the Virgin in front of the general public.[58] Another pilgrim, a Giovanni from Pescia, promised to go to a sculptor and give the Madonna six libre worth of wax in June 1486. As he did this, he also left his bandages and sling in the oratory of the sanctuary as public manifestations of the mercy he had received.[59]

In the first example, the weight stands for the son and represents a monetary value too. As the wax was not sculpted, it would have been re-used by the guardians of the sanctuary. It was therefore important for the father to leave a lasting avatar of his son at the sanctuary which he reached through the use of *exuviae*. The bandages and sling had the same purpose. Contagious and sympathetic magic thus worked in reverse too; an object that had touched or was associated with the votary was able to stand-in for them, contain their personhood and enable them to be eternally present in the proximity of the living image within the walls of the sanctuary.[60]

Votaries and miracles could also be present by way of two-dimensional images. In fact, votive panels depicting miracles, sometimes as whole storylines and sometimes as particular scenes, were popular throughout the medieval and early modern period in the entire catholic West and beyond.[61] In Guizzelmi's collection, this practice is encountered in an example of the most ostentatious type of miracles: the resurrection from the dead. The miracle took place on 24 March 1486 via the mediation of a paper image of the Santa Maria delle Carceri. A fifteen-year-old boy named Girolamo from Carpenera had died and his father, Jacopo, witnessed the dead boy's brother in his room kneeling in front of a paper image of the Santa Maria delle Carceri. Jacopo joined his son in prayer and they both vowed and recommended the dead boy to the image. The votaries' plead was so heartfelt that Girolamo was instantly raised from the dead. The resurrection took place in front of witnesses who immediately ran to the father's house to tell him that his son was resurrected. This miracle led to great festivities and approximately a year later, on 15 July 1487, Jacopo and Girolamo went together on a pilgrimage to Prato and donated ten gold florins to the image alongside a painted votive panel of the dead son.[62]

Not only did the family pay a lot in gratitude for the miraculous resurrection, they also let the boy – in his dead form – rest perpetually in the company of the Virgin, just as the father and brother had promised during their prayer. This example also tells us about the use of images during domestic devotion. Such paper images were common and we know from Guizzelmi's own *memoriale* that he purchased prints on paper of the Santa Maria delle Carceri on one of his trips to Florence in May 1490.[63] These were then circulated around the public to promote the cult, and as shown through many of the examples cited above, such images as well as the likewise serially produced and circulated pilgrimage tokens made of lead played a central part in peoples' religious practice, both at home and in public.

In short, replicas working as extensions of both divine and human actors were used, exchanged and worked individually and together in complex ways. Such complexities can be witnessed in the miracle that cured Guizzelmi's own nephew, Lactantio, in March 1487 and in which Guizzelmi played a central part. At that time Lactantio was eight months old and unable to eat due to illness. Guizzelmi recommended him to Santa Maria delle Carceri and the crucifix in the Pieve. He took a lead figure of the Virgin, had it touch the living image and then hung it around his nephew's neck while reciting the Pater Noster and Ave Maria. As the image touched the boy's neck, he instantly recovered.

Guizzelmi then professed that if the boy stayed well, he would have his replica made in new wax that weighed the same as the child at this very moment, corresponding to the worth of ten libre, and have it covered in silver and offer it to the Virgin. The following year, as the child was still well, the silver-covered wax-baby was made and placed in the vicinity of the Virgin in the oratory, where it remained visible to pay the debt.[64] The lead figure and the silver-covered wax effigy worked as mediators between the living image and the faithful in need of a miracle; they were also mimetic and stood in for the Virgin and the sick child. As observed in several miracle-stories throughout Guizzelmi's collection, images made in the similitude of the Virgin had the same effect as the actual image, an effect that was amplified if the avatar had touched the prototype. As we have seen, the mimetic strategies were carried out at several levels, calling upon a multitude of concepts that were available within the cultural repertoire of the participants.

At one level we find a chain of material replications: the miraculous image was made in the similitude of the true, biblical, Virgin; the lead figures were made in the similitude of the living image; and the wax effigies were made in the similitude of the recipient of the Virgin's aid. Other objects such as bandages and olive branches were simply re-used as ex-votos that made the votary and the miraculous occurrence perpetually present. Other types made the votary present through weight or length. At another level, we find chains of actions where inanimate objects stand in for animate beings in an exchange of verbal and tactile communications. On both levels, inanimate matter mimicked persons (human and divine) and mediated between them, and between the worldly and heavenly spheres. Ultimately, the miracle narratives and the dissemination of the cult relied primarily on circulation and exchange of favours (miracles and public displays of thankfulness) and of images and objects that acted on behalf of their divine and human prototypes as extensions able to distribute their personhood.

## Assembling personhood

When then the personhood of human and divine actors were obtained in objects and images and distributed, they were typically assembled together within the sanctuary. This way, the distributed personhoods were multiplied, grouped together, and the exchanges between humans and the divine were encapsulated, enhanced and perpetuated materially as an ever-growing mass of signs that underlined and confirmed the reality of the miraculous occurrences. The very act of giving a physical manifestation of one's hope or thankfulness underlined the agency, efficacy and potency of the living image, confirming its ability to live and act. Moreover, the assembly of ex-votos within the sanctuary mapped out generations of followers of the cult, making it a site of social bonds as well as competition. All of this made the sanctuary an assemblage of working, living and acting materials that communicated with each other and with spectators. Furthermore, the images, figures and other objects were often composite; assembled from different materials carrying particular meanings and abilities. The living image and its surrounding ex-votos were thereby turned into an assemblage that was composed of credible living entities.

Although the examples above include a multitude of different objects acting as ex-votos, the most common types were wax or terracotta replicas of whole persons or body parts (limbs, organs) and votive panels featuring either whole miracle narratives or particular extracted scenes. Both these types of ex-votos use verisimilitude in form as their chief communicative strategy. By way of artistic and painterly techniques they constructed physical manifestations of the votaries' bodies making them palpable presences in the vicinity of the living image.[65] Wax was the main medium for veristic effigies and is therefore associated with the rise of portraiture in Renaissance Italy.[66] The medium of wax was particularly suitable because of its plasticity enabling it to mimic the human form and produce a skin-like surface. Its association with memory and authority through its impressionability gave it further symbolic resonance.[67] This combination of physical abilities and symbolic efficacy made wax an ideal medium for establishing a direct link between the physical bodies of the votaries and their ex-votos.

Its impressionability meant that wax could absorb the essence of votaries and the sacred presence of relics and cult images, which effectively made the wax effigies at the Sanctuary in Prato into composite amalgamations of the distributed personhoods of votaries, the living image and its sacred prototype. Thus, they were essentially vessels able to absorb and transmit personhoods and mix them together in symbiotic entanglement. Wax could also absorb and transmit actions and occurrences, enabling it to contain and express the ephemeral act of giving and counter-giving, thereby supplying the reciprocal relationship between the human and divine actors with a physical expression. If given as a work of art, usually in the form of an effigy or body part, the votive offering would be very durable and could encapsulate the miraculous occurrence beyond the organic memory of votary and community. If, however, wax was given in its ephemeral form as either raw material or candles, it could transmit personhood, agency and intentions in a different way.

When wax was transformed into liturgical candles, the votary would implicitly partake in the rites of the church through their distributed personhood. If candles were given to be burned in front of the living image, the personhood of the votary alongside their prayers would rise towards heaven as smoke. With reference to the visions of Nicolo described above, we can assume that a vast amount of candles were burning in the proximity of the living image in Prato at all times, although probably at an accelerated rate during ecclesiastical feasts and votive processions. Indeed, as Richard Trexler has once put it: 'one could measure the miracles an image had allegedly performed by the smoke from candles that devotees had purchased and lit before it'.[68] This way, the constant burning of candles bore witness to the efficacy of the image and confirmed that it and its cult were alive and working. It was thus the malleable character of wax and its ability to contain humanity and divinity, perpetuity and ephemerality, action and stationarity that made it such a popular material for votive offering.

Votive effigies were composite in their material construction and wax was mainly used for heads and hands which were the parts that showed visible skin and needed to mimic a real human with the most accuracy. The rest of the construction could consist in a variety of materials. The inside was for instance usually made up of a wooden 'skeleton' which could be covered by different other materials, mainly cloth or paper plastered in gesso (plaster based on burned and grinded limestone).[69] This composite body would be covered by clothes that usually came from the votaries own wardrobe and often, as seen above, was worn by the votary at the time a miraculous cure took place. Some votive effigies offered by the very rich were covered in precious metals and/or had precious stones or other ostentatious materials attached to them. This is exemplified by Guizzelmi's donation of his nephew's effigy in silver and even more ostentatiously by the diamond and niello inlay-decorated silver votive effigy given by Piero de' Medici (1416–1469) to the Santissima Anunziata in Florence in 1465 that showed his son, Giuliano, kneeling in prayer in thankfulness to the Virgin for his recovery from illness.[70]

The materials themselves played a significant role in the presentation of the votary in the vicinity of the living image. Wood mediated presence as living matter.[71] Precious metals were widely used in medieval sculpture to elevate the portrayed saint or sacred person from humanity and underscore their divinity.[72] Perhaps this strategy of representation was also used to elevate the votaries' presence in the nearness of the living image. Gemstones, moreover, were not only symbols of conspicuous consumption but also potential conveyers of life and sacred presence. Conceived as living entities, the talismanic efficacy of gemstones rested on their ability to link the heavenly and earthly spheres and make cosmic operations work on the operations that were carried out in the body.[73] This only enhanced the effect of surrogate bodies of the votaries.

The use of *exuviae* (often biographical objects or 'ego documents'[74]), like the use of a shirt that was worn by the beneficiary of the miracle when it happened further underlines the private as well as public aspects of votive offering; votaries needed a way both to establish personal closeness to the sacred and to manifest it in a publically visible way. These aspects appear over and over again in Guizzelmi's collection, often through a public proclamation that this offering was made to satisfy a vow and in thankfulness for a miracle performed by the Santa Maria delle Carceri.[75] Biographical elements like Simone's shirt mentioned above are well-documented in fifteenth- and sixteenth-century Italy in general and could be shrouded in some rather theatrical modes of expression. Indeed, Giorgio Vasari (1511–1574) described how one of the votive effigies of Lorenzo de' Medici (1449–1492) in the Santissima Annunziata Basilica in Florence made by Orsino Benintendi (1440–1498) was wearing the same clothes as Lorenzo when he was sought assassinated in 1478.[76]

As mixed media artworks, wax effigies were able to amalgamate symbolic meanings, veristic visual strategies (to varying degrees) and biographical elements into powerful avatars that were able to answer the votaries' needs for continuous physical nearness to the sacred presence. The personhoods of votaries and their avatars could be so interlinked that votive effigies could be punished or executed in the place of their prototype like the famous 'killing' ('*l'ammazzorno*') of votive images at the Santissima Annunziata Basilica in Florence on several occasions during times of strife in the first half of the sixteenth century.[77] The amalgamation of prototype and image, moreover, certifies the social authority that the gathering of votive images within sanctuaries carried. When all of these manifestations of personhood were grouped together, they created a mini-community of avatars that represented several generations, living as well as dead, and mirrored the surrounding society of the living. Distributing their personhood, articulating their power and mapping out networks within sacred spaces through generations, votive images of all kinds were important social markers able to forge and confirm as well as contest allegiances and social rank, especially among the highest on the social ladder. Who got the most prominent pieces placed in the most prominent places within the sacred space was a field of competition[78], but also a dynamic field of communication between human and nonhuman actors and communities.

In order to control the social competition and prestige aspects of the offering of votive effigies, the Florentine commune forbad those who were not Florentines or a member of one of the greater guilds to display figurative ex-votos in Florentine houses of worship on the 20 January 1401.[79] This not only underlines the power that such figures held, but also reveals that they were instrumental in the construction of town identity. With this mixture of religious, political and social agendas that all overlapped, the sanctuary functioned like a three-dimensional *Liber Vitae*[80] that contained, distributed, structured and re-structured the personhoods of the community of the faithful through their avatars (whole, fragmented/anatomized or indexical/by association) in the presence of the living image. The malleable materials were thus able to continuously (re-)negotiate positions and agendas within the community of the faithful in a dynamic communication between many different actors.

The multitude of materials, images, figures and *exuviae* grouped within the walls of the sanctuary amplified each other and gave each other meaning, agency and life. In combination, they turned into one organism, vibrant with life. It also radiated life, which extended into the images and objects that had touched it and was circulated far and near. In that way, the centrally planned sanctuary with its living image and surrounding votive offerings made an assemblage of living materials that communicated together across social as well as dimensional spheres. It contained and assembled the multiple personhoods that had been absorbed and distributed in matter and enabled them to function together. It represented and was able to contain the individual agendas as well as the universal principles and the paradoxes and polarities they offered on each their level. This dynamism was crucial for the efficacy of the cult and was the direct result of its composite nature.

## Conclusion

Throughout this chapter I have identified occasions of exchange between humans and the divine via material and pictorial means. Focusing on the interconnectedness and dynamic relationship between the living image, its distributed personhood in the form of its *exuviae* and the practice of votive offering within the communicative situation of exchange, I have analysed the processes by which matter could obtain personhood, distribute it through and to other materials, and assemble these many distributed personhoods together within one sanctuary. Throughout my analysis, I have focused on the chains of actions and reactions that allowed both human and nonhuman actors endowed with the ability to change the cause of events. I have shown that the animation of the image of the Santa Maria delle Carceri was not a single event, but a culmination of a chain of events that involved the agencies and actions carried out by the place, its surroundings, and many different human and nonhuman actors.

The miraculous animation of the image was not an event that happened only once. Rather, the life and agency of the image were continuously produced, affirmed, reproduced and enhanced through the circulation and cultic use of many replicas in paper or lead, many of which had touched the living image. It was, moreover, not only the divine that could distribute its personhood through surrogate materials and gain agency through contagious and sympathetic strategies carried out in matter. The same system of contagious and sympathetic production and reproduction was carried out by human actors when their personhoods were divided, distributed and transferred to different types of matter and given as votive offerings. These were truly mixed-media vessels that combined a great number of materials and elements in order to act as surrogates for their giver. In these multitudes of animated matter the earthly and the heavenly spheres could thereby exist on the same plane and symbiotically melt together as one organism within the sanctuary. Within this melting pot of materials and communicative strategies, a variety of individual and collective agendas were able to converge, compete and communicate in a dynamic interplay between the materials that were put on display and the practices that took place in their proximity, inside and around the sanctuary, as well as in the region by way of the material avatars that were circulating.

Humans and the divine were able to transfer their personhood to matter, distribute it and thereby communicate through and in various forms of material media. Via this continual communication, the life of the Santa Maria delle Carceri itself and of its cult would be perpetuated and confirmed throughout generations. The central element that set all of these communications across social and dimensional borders in motion was exchange; it created a chain of actions and reactions that gave both humans and nonhumans (i.e. images, objects) agency and enabled them to act and make changes in the world on a multitude of levels (i.e. physical changes in the body, material and spatial transformations, social changes) which all affected the lived reality of people in fifteenth- and sixteenth-century Italy.

## Notes

1   Erik Thunø, 'The Miraculous Image and the Centralized Church Santa Maria Della Consolazione in Todi', in *The Miraculous Image in the Late Middle Ages and Renaissance*, ed. Erik Thunø and Gerhard Wolf (Rome: L'erma di Bretschneider, 2004), 29.

2   Georges Didi-Huberman, 'Ex-Voto: Image, Organ, Time', *L'Esprit Créateur* 47:3 (2007): 9. See also Christopher S. Wood, 'The Votive Scenario', *Res: Anthropology and Aesthetics* 59–60 (2011): 206–27; Christopher S. Wood, 'Public and Private Dimensions of Votive Giving', in *Agents of Faith: Votive Objects in Time and Place*, ed. Ittai Weinryb (Bard Graduate Center: New York, 2018), 67–86 for the many forms ex votos could take.

3   Anna Benvenuti, *Santa Maria delle Carceri a Prato: Miracoli e devozione in un santuario toscano del Rinascimento* (Florence: Mandragora, 2005). The older miracle collection, Biblioteca Roncioniana, MS. 86 (Q.II.6), is transcribed on pp. 104–34, Guizzelmi's miracle collection, Biblioteca Roncioniana, MS. 87 (Q.II.5), is transcribed on pp. 135–53.

4   See Robert Maniura, 'The Images and Miracles of Santa Maria delle Carceri', in *The Miraculous Image in the Late Middle Ages and Renaissance*, ed. Erik Thunø and Gerhard Wolf (Rome: L'erma di Bretschneider, 2004), 81–95 for a source critical description.

5   Ittai Weinryb, 'Introduction: Ex-voto as Material Culture', in *Agents of Faith: Votive Objects in Time and Place,* ed. Ittai Weinryb (Bard Graduate Center gallery: New York, 2018), 8; Giorgio Antei, 'Grazie al cielo: Pratiche votive a Firenze fra Medio Evo e Rinascimento', in *Grazie al cielo: repertorio di ex voto messicani, Fontanellato*, ed. Elin Luque Agraz and Giorgio Antei (Parma: Franco Maria Ricci, 2018).

6   See Megan Holmes, 'Ex-votos: Materiality, Memory and Cult', in *The Idol in the Age of Art: Objects, Devotions and the Early Modern World*, ed. Michael Cole and Rebecca Zorach (Aldershot: Ashgate, 2009), 160–1 esp. n. 3 and 4 for fifteenth- and sixteenth-century discourses, see also Lee Palmer Wandel, *Voracious Idols and Violent Hands: Iconoclasm in Reformation Zurich, Strasbourg, and Basel* (Cambridge: Cambridge University Press, 1999), 190, 196 for protestant attitudes. For the destruction of ex-votos during the Enlightenment see Julius von Schlosser, 'Geschichte der Porträtbildnerei in Wachs. Ein Versuch', *Jahrbuch der Kunsthistorischen Sammlungen des Allerhöchsten Kaiserhauses* 29 (1911): 77 and Lenz Kriss-Rettenbeck, *Ex Voto: Zeichen, Bild und Abbild im christlichen Votivbrauchtum* (Zürich: Atlantis Verlag, 1972). See also Bernadette Filotas, *Pagan Survivals: Superstitions and Popular Cultures in Early Medieval Pastoral Literature* (Toronto: Pontifical Institute of Mediaeval Studies, 2005), 65–119 and Robin Lane

Fox, *Pagans and Christians* (Harmondsworth: Penguin, 1988), 677 for continuities in the use of images between pagan and Christian times.

7   Aby Warburg, *Bildniskunst und florentinisches Bürgertum* (Leipzig: H. Seemann, 1902); Richard Andree, *Votive und Weihegaben des katholischen Volks in Süddeutschland* (Braunschweig: F. Wieweg und Sohn, 1904); Schlosser, 'Geschichte der Porträtbildnerei', 171–258; Rudolf Kriss, *Das Gebärmuttervotiv, Ein Beitrag zur Volkskunde nebst einer Einleitung über Arten und Bedeutung der deutschen Opfergebräuche der Gegenwart* (Augsburg: G. Filser, 1929); Kriss-Rettenbeck, *Ex Voto*; Manfred and Hildegard Brauneck, *Religiöse Volkskunst: Votivgaben, Andachtsbilder, Hinterglas, Rosenkranz, Amulette* (Cologne: DuMont, 1978).

8   Michael Camille, *The Gothic Idol: Ideology and Image-Making in Medieval Art* (Cambridge: Cambridge University Press, 1989), 4, 27–49; Stuart Weeks, 'Man-Made Gods? Idolatry in the Old Testament', in *Idolatry: False Worship in the Bible, Early Judaism and Christianity*, ed. Stephen C. Barton (London: T & T Clark, 2007), 15; Caroline Walker Bynum, *Christian Materiality: An Essay on Religion in Late Medieval Europe* (Brooklyn: Zone Books, 2011), 44–52, 162, 212, 223, 253, 270, 277; Sarah Salih, 'Idol Theory', *Preternature: Critical and Historical Studies on the Preternatural* 4:1 (2015): 13–36.

9   Bynum, *Christian Materiality*, 15–18; Megan Holmes, 'Miraculous Images in Renaissance Florence', *Art History* 3 (2011): 435.

10  Hannah Baader and Ittai Weinryb, 'Images at Work: On Efficacy and Historical Interpretation', *Representations* 133:1 (2016): 8–12.

11  Ragnhild M Bø, 'Sculptures and Accessories: Domestic Piety in the Norwegian Parish around 1300', *Religions* 10:640 (2019): 3; Mads Vedel Heilskov, 'Living Matter in Medieval Denmark', in *Materiality and Religious Practice in Medieval Denmark*, ed. Mads Vedel Heilskov and Sarah Croix (Turnhout: Brepols, 2021), 147–80.

12  See also Sari Katajala-Peltomaa, 'Demoniac's Gratitude: Corporeality and Materiality of Votive Offerings to St Nicholas of Tolentino (1325–1550)', this volume.

13  André Vauchez, *Les laïcs au Moyen Âge: Pratiques et expériences religieuses* (Paris: Cerf, 1987); André Vauchez., *Contrat et dévotion: les transformations du voeu: La Sainteté en Occident aux derniers siècles du Moyen Âge d'après les procès de canonisation et les documents hagiographiques* (Rome: École française de Rome, 1981), 530–40; André Vauchez., *Sainthood in the Later Middle Ages* (Cambridge: Cambridge University Press, 1997), 455–8; Jean-Claude Schmitt, 'Religion populaire' et culture folklorique', Annales, histoire, sciences sociales 31 (1976): 941–53; Jean-Claude Schmitt, 'Les superstitions', in *Histoire de la France religieuse*, vol. 1, ed. Jacques Le Goff (Paris: Seuil, 1988), 425–53; Jean-Claude Schmitt, 'Rituels de l'image et récits de vision', in *Testo e immagine nell'alto medioevo: 15–21 aprile 1993 (Settimane di studio del Centro italiano di studi sull'alto Medioevo)*, vol. 1, ed. col. Fondazione Cisam (Spoleto: Centro italiano di studi sull'alto Medioevo, 1994), 419–62; Jean-Claude Schmitt, *Religione, folklore e società*

nell'Occidente medievale (Rome: Biblioteca Universale Laterza, 2000); Jean-Claude Schmitt, *Le corps des images: essais sur la culture visuelle au Moyen Âge* (Paris: Gallimard 2002); Jean-Claude Schmitt, *La représentation de l'espace et l'espace des images au Moyen Âge* (Geneve: Haute École d'Art et de Design 2011).

14  David Freedberg, *The Power of Images* (Chicago: Chicago University Press, 1989), 27–40, 99–160.
15  Didi-Huberman, 'Ex-voto', 7.
16  Hans Belting, *Bild und Kult: eine Geschichte des Bildes vor dem Zeitalter der Kunst* (Munich: C.H. Beck Verlag, 1990), 510–12.
17  Weinryb, 'Introduction', 18.
18  Thunø, 'The Miraculous Image', 29–30. These new breakthroughs were in fact contested, especially within the religious sphere. See Ronald F.E. Weissman, 'Sacred Eloquence: Humanist Preaching and Lay Piety in Renaissance Florence', in *Christianity and the Renaissance: Image and Religious Imagination in the Quattrocento*, ed. Timothy Verdon and John Henderson (Syracuse, NY: Syracuse University Press, 1990), 250–71. Indeed, in religious art in particular, stylistic continuities held significant cultural capital. See Kathleen Giles Arthur, 'Cult Objects and Artistic Patronage of the Fourteenth Century Flagellant Confraternity Gesù Pellegrino', in *Christianity and the Renaissance*, 336–60.
19  This tendency can also be traced in other fields and on other research topics, see Anna Boeles Rowland, '"With This Rynge": The Materiality and Meaning of the Late Medieval Marriage Ring', this volume.
20  Newer studies are Sara Lipton, 'The Sweet Lean of His Head: Writing about Looking at the Crucifix in the High Middle Ages', *Speculum* 80:4 (2005): 1172–1208; Christopher Swift, 'Robot Saints', *Preternature: Critical and Historical Studies on the Preternatural* 4:1 (2015): 52–77; Johannes Tripps, *Das handelnde Bildwerk in der Gotik, Forschungen zu den Bedeutungsschichten und der Funktion des Kirchengebäudes und seiner Ausstattung in der Hoch- und Spätgotik* (Berlin: Gebr. Mann Verlag, 1998); Johannes Tripps, 'Der Kirchenraum als Handlungsort', in *Kunst und Liturgie im Mittelalter: Akten des internationalen Kongresses der Bibliotheca Hertziana und des Nederlands Instituut te Rome, Rom, 28. - 30. September 1997*, ed. Nicolas Bock (Munich: Hirmer, 2000), 235–47; Kamil Kopania, *Animated Sculptures of the Crucified Christ in the Religious Culture of the Latin Middle Ages* (Wydawn:Neriton, 2010); Robert Maniura, 'Agency and Miraculous Images', in *The Agency of Things in Medieval and Early Modern Art: Materials, Power and Manipulation*, ed. Grażyna Jurkowlaniec, Ika Matyjaszkiewicz and Zuzanna Sarnecka (New York: Routledge, 2017), 63–72; Jacqueline Elaine Jung, 'The Tactile and the Visionary: Notes on the Place of Sculpture in the Medieval Religious Imagination', in *Looking Beyond: Visions, Dreams, and Insights in Medieval Art and History*, ed. Colum Hourihane (Princeton: Princeton University Press, 2010), 203–40.

21  For an additional review of recent trends, see Lars Kjær, 'Introduction: The Matter of the Gift', this volume.

22  In the study of medieval religion, the growing interest in materiality has largely been influenced by the concepts of 'object agency' (material things and humans are connected in a collective web of humans and nonhumans where both act), see Bruno Latour, 'A Collective of Humans and Nonhumans: Following Daedalus' Labyrinth', in *Pandora's Hope: Essays on the Reality of Science Studies*, ed. Bruno Latour (Cambridge, MA: Harvard University Press, 1999), 174–21, 'technologies of enchantment' (particular objects hold power because they fascinate with technological skill) see Alfred Gell, *Art and Agency: An Anthropological Theory* (Oxford: Oxford University Press, 1998), 68–9 and 'thing-power' (the ability of inanimate things to animate, act and produce effects) see Jane Bennett, *Vibrant Matter: A Political Ecology of Things* (Durham, NC: Duke University Press, 2010), 6. See the studies cited above in n. 18 for their application.

23  Susanne Lettow, 'Turning the Turn: New Materialism, Historical Materialism and Critical Theory', *Thesis Eleven* 140:1 (2017): 111–12.

24  See Peter N. Miller, 'Introduction: The Culture of the Hand', in *Cultural Histories of the Material World*, ed. Peter N. Miller (Ann Arbor: The University of Michigan Press, 2013), 2–6; Christy Anderson, Anne Dunlop and Pamela H Smith, 'Introduction', in *The Matter of Art: Materials, Practices, Cultural Logics, c. 1250–1750*, ed. Christy Anderson, Anne Dunlop and Pamela H Smith (Manchester: Manchester University Press, 2014), 5–6, 14 for useful historiographical overviews of the debates concerning the connection between art, consumption and the construction of social class.

25  Holmes, 'Ex-votos', 172; Eckhart Marchand, 'Material Distinctions: Plaster, Terracotta, and Wax in the Renaissance Artist's Workshop', in *The Matter of Art: Materials, Practices, Cultural Logics, c. 1250–1750*, ed. Christy Anderson, Anne Dunlop and Pamela H. Smith (Manchester: Manchester University Press, 2014), 166–8. See also Sabine Sommerer, 'Of Ivory, Gold and Elephants: Materiality and Agency of Pre-modern Chairs as Gifts', this volume, for an additional discussion on the charisma of ostentatious and exotic materials.

26  The exception is Robert Maniura's work, see e.g. 'The Images and Miracles'; 81–95; 'Persuading the Absent Saint: Image and Performance in Marian Devotion', *Critical Inquiry* 35:3 (2009): 629–54; 'Ex votos, Art and Pious Performance', *Oxford Art Journal* 32:3 (2009): 409–25. Although Robert Maniura has dealt with many of the themes and sources dealt with in this chapter there are considerable differences between his and my approach since he works from the viewpoint of historical anthropology and sees human activity as his sole object of study. He furthermore does not consider objects and images acting agents and sees Guizzelmi's collection's claim that miraculous occurences happened as pure pretense on the part of all involved parties, see 'Persuading the absent saint': 650.

27  The date of the sixth of July is according to Guizzelmi; the older collection only states the year 1484.
28  The papal bull is transcribed in Pietro Morselli and Gino Corti, *La Chiese di Santa Maria delle Carceri in Prato: Contributo Di Lorenzo de' Medici e Giuliano da Sangallo alla Progettazione* (Florence: Societa Pratese Di Storia Patria, 1982), 83–4.
29  Paul Davies, 'The Madonna delle Carceri in Prato and Italian Renaissance Pilgrimage Architecture', *Architectural History* 36 (1993): 3.
30  See Thunø, 'The Miraculous Image', 33.
31  Benvenuti, *Santa Maria delle Carceri*, 104.
32  See Davies, 'The Madonna delle Carceri in Prato', 14.
33  Benvenuti, *Santa Maria delle Carceri*, 135. On the Bianchi devotions see Daniel Ethan Bornstein, *The Bianchi of 1399: Popular Devotion in Late Medieval Italy* (Ithaca: Cornell University Press, 1993).
34  Thunø, 'The Miraculous Image', 36.
35  Benvenuti, *Santa Maria delle Carceri*, 135.
36  Benvenuti, *Santa Maria delle Carceri*, 136.
37  Benvenuti, *Santa Maria delle Carceri*, 136–7.
38  In contagious magic efficacy is transferred through contact; in sympathetic magic it is transferred through morphologic resemblance. See Michael T. Taussig, *Mimesis and Alterity: A Particular History of the Senses* (New York: Routledge, 1993), 44–58; Gell, *Art and Agency*, 99–101; Weinryb, 'Introduction', 10; Jacqueline Marie Musacchio, 'Imaginative Conceptions in Renaissance Italy', in *Picturing Women in the Renaissance and Baroque* ed. Geraldine A. Johnson and Sara F. Matthews Grieco (Cambridge: Cambridge University Press, 1997), 42.
39  Michael Uebel, 'Medieval Desert Utopia', *Exemplaria* 14:1 (2002): 1–45.
40  F.ex. Mark 1:13: 'Et erat in deserto quadraginta diebus, et quadraginta noctibus: et tentabatur a Satana: eratque cum bestiis, et angeli ministrabant illi' ('And he was there in the wilderness forty days, tempted of Satan; and was with the wild beasts; and the angels ministered unto him').
41  On contact relics, see Rebecca Browett, 'Touching the Holy: The Rise of Contact Relics in Medieval England', *The Journal of Ecclesiastical History* 68:3 (2017): 493–509, esp. 494.
42  Phrases such as 'gloriosissima vergine maria del carcere', 'gloriosissima vergine Maria del carcere di Prato' and 'gloriosissima madonna del carcere di Prato' are used throughout Guizzelmi's collection. Benvenuti, *Santa Maria delle Carceri*, 144, 150.
43  Gell, *Art and Agency*, 21, 104, 231–2.
44  Benjamin John Nilson, *Cathedral Shrines of Medieval England* (Woodbridge: Boydell Press, 1998), 168–91, see also Ittai Weinryb, 'Votive Materials: Bodies and Beyond', in *Agents of Faith: Votive Objects in Time and Place*, ed. Ittai Weinryb (New York: Bard Graduate Center, 2018), 47.

45  This testifies to the dual private and public aspects of gift-giving within what we may call the 'lived religion' of the late Middle Ages that has been identified by several authors in this volume. See Gustavs Strenga's, Sari Katajala-Peltomaa's, and Philipp Höhn's contributions in particular.
46  The importance of witnesses in the medieval legal culture and its impact on personal relationships and transactions are underlined in Boeles Rowland's and Strenga's contributions in this volume.
47  Vauchez, *Sainthood*, 455–8.
48  Indeed, as is shown by Boeles Rowland in 'With This Rynge', this volume, objects had the ability to activate and actualize particular occurences.
49  Benvenuti, *Santa Maria delle Carceri*, 140.
50  See also Boeles Rowland's remarks on objects or tokens as manifest signs of particular intentions or internal states of being in 'With This Rynge', this volume.
51  In another example the paper image that has touched the image was put inside the mouth of the person in need of miraculous recovery (Benvenuti, *Santa Maria delle Carceri*, 145).
52  Benvenuti, *Santa Maria delle Carceri*, 143.
53  Benvenuti, *Santa Maria delle Carceri*, 144.
54  Benvenuti, *Santa Maria delle Carceri*, 144.
55  Benvenuti, *Santa Maria delle Carceri*, 150.
56  Benvenuti, *Santa Maria delle Carceri*, 148.
57  As Sommerer remarks in 'Of Ivory, Gold and Elephants', this volume, materials could allude to and manifest the presence of their giver.
58  Benvenuti, *Santa Maria delle Carceri*, 146–7.
59  Benvenuti, *Santa Maria delle Carceri*, 148.
60  In other instances the transaction between votary and image was much more direct and took the form of a payment in money or livestock in exchange of a miracle. See, for example, the two miracles from May 1486, Benvenuti, *Santa Maria delle Carceri*, 148.
61  Freedberg, *Power of Images*, 136–60.
62  Benvenuti, *Santa Maria delle Carceri*, 150.
63  After Maniura, 'Persuading the Absent Saint', 638.
64  Benvenuti, *Santa Maria delle Carceri*, 150. In Guizzelmi's *Memoriale* the expenditure for the votive effigy is also mentioned, see Maniura, 'The Images and Miracles', 89.
65  Holmes, 'Ex-votos', 160.
66  Freedberg, *Power of Images*, 156–9; Hugo van der Velden, 'Medici Votive Images and the Scope and Limits of Likeness', in *The Image and the Individual: Portraits in the Renaissance*, ed. Luke Syson and Nicholas Mann (London: British Museum Press, 1998), 126–37.

67 Marchand, 'Material distinctions', 166–8.
68 Richard C. Trexler, 'Being and Non Being: Parameters of the Miraculous in the Traditional Religious Image', in *The Miraculous Image in the Late Middle Ages and Renaissance*, ed. Erik Thunø and Gerhard Wolf (Rome: L'erma di Bretschneider, 2004), 27.
69 Guido Mazzoni, *I boti della Santissimo Annunziata in Firenze: Curiosità storica* (Florence: Le Monnier, 1923), 22–3; Holmes, 'Ex-votos', 171.
70 Described in Holmes 'Ex-votos', 167. See also Katajala-Peltomaa, 'Demoniac's Gratitude', this volume, for further examples of the use of ostentatious materials for ex-votos in late medieval and renaissance Italy.
71 Michael Baxandall, *The Limewood Sculptors of Renaissance Germany* (New Haven: Yale University Press, 1980), 27–49; Michel Pastoureau, 'Introduction á la symbolique médiévale du bois', in *Les Cahiers du Léopard d'or: L'arbre Histoire naturelle et symbolique de l'arbre, du bois et du fruit au Moyen-Âge*, vol. 2, ed. Michel Pastoureau (Paris: Léopard d'or, 1993), 25–40, esp. 26–28; Christina Neilson, 'Carving Life: The Meaning of Wood in Early Modern European Sculpture', in *The Matter of Art: Materials, Practices, Cultural Logics, c. 1250–1750*, ed. Christy Anderson, Anne Dunlop and Pamela H. Smith (Manchester: Manchester University Press, 2015), 275.
72 Thomas Raff, *Die Sprache der Materialien: Anleitung zu einer Ikonologie der Werkstoffe* (Munich: Waxmann Verlag, 1994), 30–4; Cynthia Hahn, *Strange Beauty: Issues in the Making and Meaning of Reliquaries*, 400-circa 1204 (University Park, PA: Penn State University Press, 2012), 122; Assaf Pinkus, 'Transformations in Wood: Between Sculpture and Painting in Late Medieval Devotional Objects', *Viator* 48:3 (2017): 278–80.
73 Stefania Gerevini, 'Sicut crystallus quando est obiecta soli: Rock Crystal, Transparency and the Franciscan Order', *Mitteilungen des Kunsthistorischen Institutes in Florenz* 1:3 (2014): 272; Martina Bagnoli, 'The Stuff of Heaven: Materials and Craftsmanship in Medieval Reliquaries', in *Treasure of Heaven: Saints, Relics and Devotion in Medieval Europe*, ed. Martina Bagnoli, Holger A. Klein, C. Griffith Mann and James Robinson (New Haven: Yale University Press, 2010), 138; Tanja Klemm, 'Life from Within', *Reperesentations* 133:1 (2016): 110–23.
74 See Strenga's contribution in this volume for further information on ego documents.
75 In the example on pp. 146–7 we find the phrase 'sodisfé al suo voto', on p. 148 the phrase 'sodisfé al voto' and on pp. 150–1 the phrase 'per sodisfare al voto offerirlo, secondo promissi'. On the cultural significance of public vows in Renaissance Tuscany see Richard C. Trexler, *Public Life in Renaissance Florence* (Ithaca: Cornell University Press, 1980), 173, 248, 351.

76 Giorgio Vasari, *Le Vite de' più eccellenti pittori, scultori ed architettori*, vol. 3, ed. Gaetano Milanesi (Florence: G. C. Sansoni, 1906), 374.
77 Holmes, 'Ex-votos', 177–8 (esp. note 49).
78 See Wood, 'Public and Private', 67–86. See also Ruth Sargent Noyes, '"The Polar Winds have driven me to the conquest of the Treasure in the form of the much-desired relic." (Re)moving relics and performing gift exchange between early modern Tuscany and Lithuania', this volume, for further discussion on the political intricacies attached to the layout of sacred spaces and the placement of various inventory with ties to individual patrons within them.
79 Guiseppe Richa, *Notizie istoriche delle Fiorentine*, vol. 3 (Florence: Viviani, 1754–1762), 12.
80 The lists of living and dead members of the Christian community used in the *memento etiam* following the Eucharistic sacrifice. See Arnold Angenendt, 'Theologie und Liturgie der mittelalterlichen Totenmemoria', in *Memoria: Der geschichtliche Zeugniswert des liturgischen Gedenkens im Mitte Mittelalter*, ed. Karl Schmid and Joachim Wollasch (Munich: Vilhelm Fink Verlag, 1984), 185–8, 198–9.

6

# Demoniac's gratitude: Corporeality and materiality of votive offerings to St Nicholas of Tolentino (1325–1550)

Sari Katajala-Peltomaa

Saints were active agents in the medieval world and interaction with them was an important element of lived religion. Saints had power over nature: they could heal and protect in a situation beyond human help. Their intercessory powers were sought for among daily troubles; to plead for a miracle was a coping mechanism available for all Christians. Yet, heavenly intercessors needed to be invoked in a proper way. In addition to a prayer of help, a successful invocation included a vow: the petitioner promised to offer a counter gift in return for recovery or rescue. Hence, gift-exchange was an important part of the interaction with a saint. Offerings could have been material – like various wax objects, painted tablets or even jewellery – or corporeal, like ascetic pilgrimages and other penitential acts. All of them were, nevertheless, communication: the message addressed to the saint was one of gratitude and devotion, but the offerings functioned as messages on the social level, too, manifesting the beneficiary's position as a receiver of divine grace, his or her firm faith, and piety.[1]

The ritualistic offering of ex-votos was a way to personalize religion, give meaning to past experiences and narrate them to the surrounding community.[2] The petitioner had some flexibility to choose the counter gift, but they demanded time, money and effort and hence needed to be pondered carefully. They were evaluated by the surrounding community, their careful recording and depicting testifies to the importance given to the offering on both individual and communal levels. Lived religion forms the conceptual frame for this chapter; by 'lived religion' is meant something people do, feel and sense. Religion-as-lived was encapsulated in performances, rituals and narrations. Faith, theology and theory were commingled with elements of daily life. From this perspective, gift-exchange with a saint offered people a performative space in which to participate in their community and manifest their position in it. Gift-exchange as an element of lived religion was simultaneously personal, private even and shared, public and visible to others.³

This chapter explores both the narrative forms of offerings and actual material donations to St Nicholas of Tolentino.⁴ Nicholas' canonization process was carried out in the cities of Marches of Ancona in 1325.⁵ Canonization processes were judicial inquiries into the sanctity, the meritorious life and miracles, of the candidate. They were carried out by papal commissioners, in St Nicholas's case they were Federico, Bishop of Senigallia and Tomasso di Cesena. Altogether 371 depositions and 301 miracles were recorded in the dossier. In order to testify to the miracle-working powers of St Nicholas the witnesses had the opportunity to narrate of their rituals and offerings promised in exchange for a recovery or protection. Nicholas' hearing was not as meticulously carried out as some other contemporary canonization processes, but it did, too, follow the regulations of canon law. *Interrogatorium* – the papal ruling concerning the validation of information given by witnesses as well as their ways of knowing – specifically instructed to interrogate the exact words of invocation.⁶ This means that *votum*, prayer for help and promise of a counter-gift, was carefully recorded in the records often in a form of direct quotation.

On a general level, Italian urban sphere was a fertile field for various lay rituals. The interaction with St Nicholas is an eminently suitable context to study lived religion in the context of gift-exchange since a vast array of votive offerings are found in the records and the cult continued to be active after the canonization hearing and official canonization (1446). The devotees brought offerings to the shrine well into the nineteenth century.

Depositions in the canonization process and later votive tablets form the empirical evidence for this chapter. The canonization dossier of Nicholas presents a wide variety of offerings enabling a scrutiny of oblations and their background motivation in a narrative form. Among the promised offerings pilgrimages to the shrine and various wax objects, figures of different body parts, strings and candles, were the most typical, as they were in other canonization processes of the era as well.⁷ Such offerings, or the promise to make such a gift, were given on a special occasion; to receive a divine grace. The majority of them were not luxurious status manifestations but they cannot be defined as 'everyday objects', either.⁸ Already within the depositions recorded in 1325, there are mentions of painted images as votive offerings, but depicted ex-voto tables are thought to become more popular from the end of fifteenth century on. Altogether 394 votive tablets offered to St Nicholas are preserved. They date from the fifteenth to nineteenth centuries; the majority is from the seventeenth century. The preserved collection is clearly a sample and likely an arbitrary one; we do not know how many votive panels of the whole or of certain type has been preserved.[9]

On a general level, the content of the collection is rather formulaic; more than half, 233 images depict the votary praying, either on one's knees, in *oranti* position or as lying in bed. Votive panels offered to St Nicholas support the findings of Fredrika Jacobs. According to her, three dominant features can be deduced from votive panels in Renaissance Italy: standardized imagery, remarkably rudimentary style and conspicuously poor state of preservation in many cases.[10] On occasion, the poor state of preservation hinders us, for example, reading the writing added to the painted tablets. Nevertheless, the message of style and imagery will be analysed: the 'language' of votive tablets is different from the narrations found in depositions of a judicial hearing but they both deliver similar messages. Tablets, too, offer a view to the background situation: the need for cure, accident for example, was often depicted in them or a plate of writing inserted in the image could have clarified the situation.

From this vast corpus of depositions and tablets the gifts promised and given in cases of demonic possession have been chosen for closer scrutiny. Driving out malign spirits was a traditional manifestation of saintly powers with biblical prototypes. Nevertheless, cases do not tend to be particularly numerous in canonization processes or miracle collections with the exception of the Italian material.[11] In Italian hagiography they are rather numerous and Nicholas' miracles are no exception: nine (out of 301) cases were recorded in Nicholas' canonization process and eight (out of preserved 394) tablets depicting a demoniac, that is someone believed to have been possessed by a demon, were offered to the shrine. The intention is to scrutinize the social processes the offerings – whether in narrated form in the depositions or depicted in votive tables – reveal. How was the gratitude of a demoniac expressed? Intermingling of materiality and gift-exchange illuminate how the miracle beneficiaries saw themselves in their communities. Votive offerings cut across various social and cultural levels; they were personal responses to everyday needs as well as social and religious structures and forces.

## On gifts, saints and demons

General tendencies of gift-exchange with a saint follow the basic notions set out by Marcel Mauss: the importance of reciprocity and constrained and interested nature of gifts.[12] The vow was the first turning point in the relationship of the petitioner with the saint. It was considered a binding moral contract; the petitioners' obligation was to fulfil the promise given in the vow. One needed to seek absolution from the papal curia after leaving a vow unfulfilled.[13] Quite often this was not necessary: the saints were eager to punish negligent petitioners by a renewed illness. The *topos* of the punishment miracle was well known from Antiquity on, and lay people were familiar enough with its logic to be able to put their personal experiences within this hagiographic frame.[14] Therefore, one needed to ponder carefully what to promise to a saint. The offering needed to be important enough to make a saint to act favourably yet simultaneously something the petitioner could afford – economically, socially and emotionally. All promises required time, money and effort, and some could have been socially demanding. Various methods of paying one's due and manifesting gratitude created a performative space for lay devotees underlining the interested nature of gifts.

The cultural ideas regulating the interaction with a saint were a mixture of social control and room to manoeuvre. Even if the idea of reciprocity was well established, the initiative to it came from the petitioner and there were ample options for them to fulfil their part of the interaction. The whole process was ritualistic: the idea of reciprocity and the outspoken conventions of things donated as well as the actual giving were recognized and were enforced by cultural patterns and traditions. Nevertheless, the offerings were not merely barter or a loan. Therefore, votive offerings do not follow the logic of the critics of Mauss' theories claiming that barter or a loan is an inevitable outcome of a gift-exchange when the need for and modes of reciprocity are regulated.[15] Enhanced devotion was an indispensable outcome of a miracle and inner spirituality was an essential element in votive offerings. Piety as well as social conventions demanded that gratitude was manifested. Divine grace could not be remunerated by Christians, an opinion which became further stressed during the Renaissance. Thus, there was no risk of an offering to a saint becoming a culturally unaccepted bribe,[16] but negotiating the line between piety and superstition was relevant in this context. Crucial in this sense was the question of control: the gift or the rituals of offering were not obligating for a saint but rather manifestations of need, devotion and gratitude. The offering did not bring about the miraculous intervention, but the God's secret judgement and grace worked through the saint.

According to Mauss' theory, the gifts to a deity followed a *do ut des* principle and he categorized them as contract sacrifice and as such as a subcategory of reciprocal gift-exchange. In premodern societies gift reciprocity and formal contract shared some of the same moral ground; both were also forms of bonding.[17] In the context of interaction with a saint, the contractual nature of gifts should not be understood in purely judicial, calculated or cynical terms, as elements of faith, devotion and emotions were crucial. Gift-exchange with a saint functioned in the social sphere but inner spirituality was a prerequisite for a successful invocation and enhanced devotion an indispensable outcome of grace bestowed: social and spiritual aspects were entangled and mutually reinforcing making votive offerings an illustrative example of how religion was 'lived out' in the daily life.[18]

In gift-giving to a saint the spiritual infused the material with new meaning. A similar comingling of spheres can be seen in cases of demonic possession where the material was the demoniac's body and the spiritual was of malign kind. Demonic possession was a spiritual state; an overpowering evil spirit took hold of a Christian. Since the demon was thought to dwell in the body, not in the soul, it was also a corporeal condition with essentially physical symptoms. Many of the victims were out of their minds and raving mad which added an aspect of mental disorder to demonic presence. Aggression and general unrest were often thought to be the most aggravating symptoms making demonic possession an essentially social phenomenon. The diagnosis was always a result of communal negotiation that originated within the needs and expectations of local community.[19]

Deliveries from demonic possession form a specific subcategory within the interaction with a saint. They had a biblical prototype and exorcising malign spirits was often regarded as a traditional manifestation of saintly powers. Because of their condition and its debilitating symptoms, the demoniacs themselves were not often active agents in the interaction: a vow was often made by others, and they were taken to the shrine by others, sometimes by force. A partial recovery or at least a lucid interval was a prerequisite for a demoniacs' independent participation. As noted, this kind of cases tend to be more numerous in the Italian hagiographic material; furthermore, another specific feature for Italian cases is that demoniacs often testified themselves in canonization hearings. This is the case also in Nicholas' canonization process. Clearly, their testimonies, as well as those of other witnesses, were regulated by the demands of canon law, the framework of hagiographic genre, the act of interrogation and oral memories of the community prior to the hearing.[20] Nevertheless, the deposition and votive tablets enable a view to religion-in-action of demoniacs and their communities; gift-giving as a means of interaction with the divine to overcome the demonic.

## Offering one's body

Demonic possession was a spiritual state, but it was understood and conceptualized by concrete, material ways. The terms used to describe the situation, like *obsessio*, meant also trapping, besieging or imprisoning, and *rapere* was also a word for rape.[21] The malign spirit was literally thought to penetrate the body of his victim. Similarly, the exit was concrete; in many depositions it is described how something came out of the body, be it black coal, smoke, vomit or just air.[22] The signs evaluated by the community were physical and mental and contextualized in the social sphere; the spiritual, physical and social intermingled. In the votive offerings, in turn, corporeality and materiality were hardly separate from one another.

Regularly, the counter-gifts were donated to the shrine only after the recovery; only a promise was uttered before the hoped-for cure.[23] The deliveries from malign spirits seem to form an exception to this, however. In these cases, the vow was often made at a distance, but the final liberation took place at the shrine. An illustrative example was given by Mancinus from Forti de Castro Sancti Angeli. In his deposition he described, how, five years prior to the interrogation, a possessed man was carried to St Nicholas' chapel in Tolentino. He had lost the ability to speak or move; thus, his friends and relatives took the initiative and carried him, tied up and mute, to St Nicholas' shrine where he recovered.[24] At first glance, the possessed himself seems to be a passive object in the rituals. In the context of gift-exchange, however, it can be argued that he had crucial role in the chain of events.

On a lucid interval this unnamed man had personally made a vow to St Nicholas. The journey itself was a meaningful act and a way to render homage to the heavenly intercessor. Furthermore, his bodily presence was a crucial element in the gift-exchange. Scholars of votive cultures argue for a connection between the votary's body and the votive object. Wax figures in particular held connotations of resemblance and equation; it was a substance of similitude and simulacra.[25] Here more than just a connection is seen: the beneficiary himself became a material donation to the saint. Obviously, the person and his or her body were not the same thing, but spirit or mind and body should not be seen as distinct, either. Body was the site where religion was experienced and the body affected the way religion was felt and practised, making corporeality crucial in the interaction with a saint.[26]

The materialization of the demoniac as a gift is even more pronounced in the case of Salinbena Vissanucii. She had been possessed for several months when she recovered at St Nicholas' shrine after sleeping a night there. This took place on Nicholas' feast day. Since the commissioners conducting the hearing were in Tolentino at the same time, Salinbena and her pilgrim companions were interrogated on the matter immediately after the recovery. Two of them, namely Gentile Nugarelli and Mathiola Corraducii, corroborated Salinbena in the details of vow: Mathiola testified that in a lucid interval Salinbena promised, if St Nicholas delivered her from the malign spirits, to visit her shrine and always be devoted to him.[27]

Gift-exchange was a transaction creating and maintaining relationships: gift-giving was a social strategy, a mechanism of social bonding.[28] This notion is particularly valid for devotion as a votive offering; the aim was to form a perpetual bond with the heavenly intercessor and maintain it with repeated oblations. The promise of perpetual devotion may have implicitly included repeated pilgrimages, fasts, vigils and material gifts. This was not obligatory, but customary, nonetheless. Perpetual devotion was simultaneously abstract, intimate and material as an offering. It was both a formation and an affirmation of a special connection between the petitioner and the saint. The amalgam of repeated corporeal and spiritual practices was a constant reminder of the grace gained and of the bond between the petitioner and the saint.

Embodied devotion was in the heart of Philippucia's offering, too. Philipucia was a nun in the Cistercian convent of Santa Lucia in San Ginesio. Her affliction was public knowledge in the convent; it lasted for five years with particularly visible and disturbing signs. She called the Devil to come to her, walked on her hands and did other unnatural things. She also talked like a prostitute causing a scandal. During lucid intervals she invoked several saints for help but in vain. She recovered only after she promised to visit the shrine of St Nicholas bare feet with hands tied making her body a gift to the saint.[29] On a symbolic level, this kind of servitude was eminently suitable in this situation: Philippucia had been enslaved by malign spirits and consequently she promised herself to the saint's service.

Once she gained the control of herself, at least temporarily, she embarked on a pilgrimage to the sacred place, to the shrine of St Nicholas. Gift-exchange was materialized in the body of the pilgrim and former demoniac. To be successful, personal and intimate votive offerings required recognition of cultural categories and values. They were constructed by the corporeality of the beneficiary – doing, feeling and sensing – infused with materiality: the donated object, which could have been the beneficiary herself, and the beneficiary's physical presence at the shrine. The holistic nature of gift is evident in the interaction with a heavenly intercessor.

The gift-like nature of Philippuccia's pilgrimage and especially her body was particularly highlighted in some of the depositions to the case. For example, sister Iohannucia Servidei testified that Philippuccia promised to travel to the shrine and sort of, *quedam*, offer [herself] there.[30] *Quedam* could mean both something and sort of. It was not regularly used in depositions of Nicholas' process, only on rare, specific occasions. The words *quedam offerre* were used only in the promises of a pilgrimage made with hands tied, making a connection between ascetic pilgrimages and the body of the pilgrim as an offering.

Bodies were crucial in religious practices and religion produced and defined bodies: both the unruly body of a demoniac and humble and devout body of a pilgrim were recognized and identified via religion. The body and the material surroundings were part of what bridged individuals and communities, and transformed one-time actions into rituals and eventually social structures. A promise of a demoniac was turned into a culturally sanctioned practice; the materiality of a gift concretized the cult. Salinbena's and Philippucia's gifts also fit into the pattern of keeping-while-giving aspect of gift-exchange; they offered their bodies to the saint to be able to return to their former position in the community.[31] The offering was simultaneously symbolical as well as material and concrete, including repeated performances of gratitude and devotion. The result was not only integration back into the community – which can be certified by the fact that both women testified in the hearing themselves[32] – but also a change in identity: former demoniac became a miraculé, a beneficiary of divine grace.

Pilgrimages were a concrete sign of gratitude and devotion; at the same time, they were a way to emphasize the successful invocation and grace gained. All pilgrimages were public deeds and corporeal manifestations of devotion, but by ascetic practices, such as walking barefoot and with hands tied, like Philippucia, the bodily aspect was further highlighted. Bare feet also enhanced devotion as they enabled fuller contact with the sacred sphere. Tied hands, on the other hand, were a rare sign of humility and gratitude – a practice particularly favoured by the devotees of St Nicholas, since examples are thus far found only in this process. The journey performed with hands tied may have been a symbolic way to proclaim, among other things, that the pilgrim was bound by an obligation: she had received divine grace and was obliged to pay tribute to St Nicholas. Only after the promise was fulfilled were petitioners such as Philippucia free from the responsibility to offer a counter-gift to St Nicholas, a counter-gift that she herself had become.

## Objects as gifts

In cases of demonic possession, the beneficiaries' presence at the shrine was crucial; it was often the prerequisite for the recovery and an indispensable part of interaction. The pilgrimage and the pilgrim were part of the gift-exchange. Demoniacs' presence at the shrine was the spatiotemporal location where she or he was transformed from a victim of malevolent spirits to the beneficiary of a miracle. The materiality, both of the mundane within the body of the demoniac and of the sacred within the relics and the shrine of a saint, a concrete building block within this process.

The afore-mentioned anonymous man who was brought tied up to the shrine of St Nicholas valued also the material side of interaction. He was apparently unable to make the pilgrimage on his own, but on a lucid interval he had promised to offer ten libras wax to the shrine. He was cured after he had spent a night at the shrine: he did not offer the promised wax, though. Instead, he gave hundred *solidi*, a considerable sum of money – and sent another hundred *solidi* after arriving home. As the walls of the church were at that time immured, there was likely a concrete need for the money. If the donated sum was used in building the walls, the possessed man became memorized not only in a wax image at the shrine but rather in the building itself – at least in the mind of Mancinus, a witness to the case, who was immuring the walls while witnessing the demoniac's arrival, cure and donation.

Another nun from the same convent of San Lucia, named Anthonia, was also possessed. She was afflicted soon after the afore-mentioned Philippucia and her torments lasted for a year. Active participants in her case were her family members; they promised to take her to the shrine and offer her clothes and a wax image, if she was cured.[33] The recovery took place after her relatives had made Anthonia lay at the shrine a whole night. Used clothes were not a particularly luxurious gift but they were important elements of the interaction since they bore a strong connotation of the donor. They were left at the shrine as a token a recovery but also to symbolically represent the beneficiary at the healing presence of relics. Used clothes materialized the beneficiary's presence at the shrine, even if they lacked the veristic effect of an anatomical wax figure or votive paining depicting the beneficiary; however, at the same time clothes were more intimately connected with the donor. Clothes worn by the beneficiary did not only represent her at the sacred space but contain more clearly, in Maussian sense, a quasi-spiritual power that binds receiver and giver together. Following this line of thought, the strict line between humans and donated objects was blurred; the donations were not completely separated from the donors. Because of their intimate nature clothes worn by the beneficiary were active, animated and sentient; more than being mere objects they had agency giving value to the interaction, arousing emotions in the participants and spectators and creating social relations.[34] In addition to clothes, the family of Anthonia also promised a wax image to St Nicholas; its symbolic power remains obscure since it was not identified as certain figure.

## Gifts in/as votive tablets

Votive figures and *tavolette* were a conspicuous part of Renaissance culture in Italy. Many were the shrines where offerings amassed. Cultic excess was encapsulated in abundance of ex-votos, which became a target of the criticism of Catholic and Protestant reformers. St Nicholas' shrine was no exception even if it was not among the most popular cultic centres. The testimonies in canonization process reveal the copiousness of offerings and the cult continued to flourish after the inquiry. After the hearings and especially the official canonization there was not such a need to register the miracles and written sources are fewer. However, from the end of fifteenth century actual material ex-votos to St Nicholas has been preserved.

As noted, many votive panels offered to St Nicholas are quite formulaic in their imagery. It may point to a standardized method of production, but it also creates a recognizable language of suffering. A patient lying in bed, for example, was a situation familiar enough to the spectators; the category was grasped and the message comprehended by the other pilgrims at the shrine.[35] *Tavolette* were visual narrations of a familiar event, yet the votive tablets were not only meant to be looked at, they were not sheer decorative artefacts. Their materiality was part of the narration which was meant to be an agent in enhancing devotion. *Tavolette* were materialized prayer: their standardized outlook did not exclude their personal and even intimate nature.[36] The style may have been a result of mass production, which was not too uncommon at pilgrimage sites, particularly production of anatomical wax images was typical. Little, however, is known of the concrete production of Renaissance *tavolette* in general and of those offered to St Nicholas in particular. They may have been produced near-by and purchased in shops close to the shrine as in other places. Many of the early panels offered to St Nicholas are accredited to *scuola marchigiana*, local production typical enough so that it can be labelled as a 'school'. Majority of the donators may have been of modest background as the miracle scenes do not portray affluence. However, the material and visual language may have also been purposefully humble.[37] Tempera painting on wood or wax figures mentioned earlier were not luxurious items but conveyed deliberate message: humility was essential when approaching the divine. Similarly, the ascetic practices, barefoot and tied hands, adopted for the travel as well as lying at the shrine humbly waiting for the saint's power to work and force out the malign spirits, point to hierarchy and submissiveness of the petitioner in the interaction. This corroborates with cultural patterns: God gives grace to the humble (James 4:6). These practices also show the ways spirit and matter were fused together.

Humility and submissiveness were further underlined in cases of demonic possession. Demoniacs' presence at the shrine was crucial for the recovery, as noted. Many demoniacs were unable to perform the pilgrimage by themselves and thus were taken to the shrine. Family, for example, led, *ducerent*, the aforementioned Anthonia to the shrine and they made her lay there for the night, *fecerunt eam iacere tota una nocte*. Hers was the patient waiting. Narrative methods within images were different from the deposition but they both point to the same direction, since more than half of the votive panels depict the beneficiary praying for help.

Not all offerings were humble, though. Some of them were of precious material which was revealed in a noticeable manner; the intention was to manifest the value of the offering made to the sanctuary.[38] Silver and even golden objects were not unknown in medieval shrines; either and objects of precious metal were offered to St Nicholas, too. One hundred and forty later silver ex-votos are preserved in the museum of the sanctuary. At the time of the canonization hearing, golden or silver objects were not particularly popular votive offerings, though. Promises of precious metal were not numerous in the depositions and they tend to be strings of gold or silver circled around the shrine.[39] Similar promises were given of wax strings as well. The ritual practice accompanying material oblation gave meaning to the donation. Circling the shrine was a method to determine the important essence, mark out the core of the sacred place. A circle could keep the beneficial effect of the relics within and transfer their power to the one circling: by the act of circling the donors enclosed themselves within the sacred power focussed in and radiating from the shrine.[40]

Out of eight *tavolette* depicting a delivery from demonic possession, three votive panels are chosen for closer scrutiny; they date to the end of fifteenth or beginning of sixteenth century. These three are all rather rudimentary in style but vary in their size and content. The smallest is 17.7 cm x 17 cm while the largest is nearly three times its size: 59 cm x 41.5 cm. They are all painted with tempera method, that is a painting technic using (typically) egg-yolk as binder medium of paint, and they are accredited to Marchesian origin. All demoniacs were women and the force driving out the malign spirits was obviously St Nicholas. He was depicted in all the examples. In the deposition, the exit of malign spirits was often something quite concrete, as noted. As demonic possession was understood in concrete physical terms, the delivery followed similar logic. This detail was particularly emphasized in *tavolette* where the most telling element was the exiting demon(s), often depicted as an imp-like figure, sometimes also as a herd of insects. On a general level, deliveries from demonic possession in votive panels offered to St Nicholas follow standardized imagery. Unlike many other types of miracles, where the prayer or the moment of accident was depicted, the very moment of delivery was the core message in them.[41]

Often the delivery from malign spirits was dynamic, aggressive or even violent situation. In the didactic miracle narrations, the demoniac was clearly out of his or her mind, typically held still by other people. This element can also be found in votive panels. The biggest panel depicts the most typical scene; the recovery takes place at the shrine; a swooning rather than violently resisting demoniac is being held by a group of clerics, while a priest at the high altar exorcizes the demons. A herd of them is flying away from the demoniac. St Nicholas with the Virgin Mary and a male figure with bishop's attributes appear in the upper part of the panel while the family of the victim pray in front of the altar at the centre of the panel. The procedure of exorcism changed during this time: it was not anymore understood to be a divine grace performed via a saint but rather a priestly ordained ceremony. Nancy Caciola links this development to other administrative and political changes within Christianity: the Western Schism and its aftermath and reform movements from below in the fifteenth century.[42] Moshe Sluhovsky, in turn, argues that the roots of changes can be found in the fourteenth century but major shifts took place only in the second half of the sixteenth century. He sees the changes as a regulatory effect; the aim was to replace the diverse methods of individual practitioners, priests and lay healers, with one standardized liturgical rite performed by selected and trained group of exorcists. Sluhovsky also links these changes to a campaign to control the miraculous.[43] This process was not, however, highlighted in the eight votive panels of St Nicholas as only in three of them was a priest performing an exorcism.

Likely this *tavolette* depicts a similar chain of events as was depicted in Anthonia's case: the family was active in invoking the saint, took the demoniac to the shrine where she was cured. The role of the priest seems to have been the clearest difference; there is no mention of exorcism rituals in any of the deposition of Nicholas' canonization process. It may well be that the family members were responsible also for the votive offering as their central role in the panel indicates. More of this situation is not known; the text in the upper left corner of the panel would give more details to the case, but unfortunately, it is so poorly preserved that it is not readable. On a general level, writing within votive tablets added details to the experience, like dates and names and individualized the visual expression. A blank space, a panel or scroll within the panel, could be left in the standard image for the votary to add essential details, which were the same as in written miracle testimonies: name and identification (like place of origin) of the beneficiary, the ailment and the date. Mary Laven, for example, argues that the tone of some inscriptions is that of an official declaration and votive panels had a certificatory role making them a form of miracle records.[44] 'Per gratia ricevuta' or 'ex-voto' was often added to the text certifying the tablet's role as a token of successful interaction with St Nicholas. Such personal details gave the formulaic 'language' of a panel an individual voice regarding devotion and memory of the grace bestowed. It enabled claiming presence at the shrine in a way the standard visual imagery did not enable. When a votive panel was hung among others on the wall, it transformed personal gratitude to a collective collaborative act. Both images and the short declarations in them become integrated into a shared history.[45] They linked demoniacs to other devotees and personal experiences into cultural patterns.

The other two panels differ from the largest one in their content; the situation depicted does not take place in a church. In the other one there is only the petitioner and St Nicholas who drives out one demon – of quite robust stature – flying out of small window in the upper right corner. The woman is depicted as tranquilly praying, on her knees and hands united. The third panel depicts a similar kind of setting: a woman is praying outdoors, on her knees with a rosary in her hands. Her husband is praying on one knee and a herd of miniature demons, barely visible more than black spots, is hovering around her head. Bright-faced and young-looking St Nicholas appears in the right corner taking one third of the space. In these *tavolette*, the humility is stressed by several elements, the relatively small size (17.7 cm × 17 cm and 20.8 cm × 27 cm) and lacking details in the background as well as the mere black spots instead of more elaborate imagery of malign spirits point to this direction.

Elisabeth Antoine argues that a gender-based imagery can be found in the tablets offered to St Nicholas in the fifteenth and sixteenth centuries; votive panels offered by women were more detailed and personal. Women often also prayed for others and in these pictures writings and other explanations can be found while men were often depicted praying alone and mute.[46] The votive panels offered for a cure of a demoniac fit into this frame only partially; the two cases which were likely donated by the former demoniac herself are scare with details and lack text. The third example with exorcizing priest in the church accords better with the model set out by Antoine, but one can question whether it was offered by the demoniac herself or rather by the relatives depicted as active participants in the centre of the panel.

Another significant feature in the two smaller panels is the tranquillity; the exit of malign spirits is not violent or aggressive, rather the grace is bestowed upon a humble, praying petitioner. The message of panels is of resorted harmony and proper order. Whatever problems the demonic presence may have caused, it was over. The women in the images were already transforming or transformed from a demoniac into a miraculé. This accords with the rhetoric chosen by Philippucia in her deposition. She had been possessed for five years and the depositions of other sisters argue for a severe disruption in the life of the convent due to her affliction. Philippucia's narrative strategy was, in addition to emphasizing the experience of infirmity – not of demonic presence–, to argue firmly for the manifestation of her devotion. She claimed, and other witnesses corroborated her statement, that she had made, and made good, a promise to embark barefoot with hands tied on an ascetic pilgrimage to the shrine of St Nicholas. She also separately mentioned that she had requested permission for her pilgrimage both from the mother house of her convent and from her abbess stressing her submission to hierarchy and rules. Philippucia reclaimed successfully her position as a pious nun, thus restoring and confirming the peace and harmony of the community.

## Conclusions

Gifts to a saint were a way to manifest gratitude and devotion but also a way of creating identity and interacting with the divine. Offerings were symbolic communication; they were a way to tell others (and oneself) of personal experiences, of past tribulations as well as received divine grace. The gifts were both public and intimate; they were posited above the shrine or hung on the walls of the chapel. They were meant to be inspected by other pilgrims and devotees to enhance their devotion and contribute to the construction of the sacred; they reflected shared cultural values. Part of their power, however, came from their personal, intimate nature which stressed their persuasive, intensive message.[47]

A tendency to favour certain kind of offering in cases of demonic possession cannot be deduced from the canonization process of Nicholas. Similarly, later votive panels differed in size and content. The offerings were connected by various ways to social processes. Ritualistic gift-exchange with a saint was a way to contribute to the culture and community as well as to the construction of the sacred. The object-like status of a demoniac was stressed in the typical imagery of exorcism; demoniacs were seen as a battleground of supernatural forces while the saint (and sometimes exorcizing priest) and exiting demons were the crucial features. These elements can be found in some of the votive panels offered to St Nicholas. Depositions given by the victims themselves and some votive panels offer different kind of view to the phenomenon; in them the agency of the demoniac was not shunned, they were active participants contributing to their personal cures by invocation and rituals as well as to the social and religious discussions and structures, like construction of the sacred, by their rituals and votive offerings.

In addition to manifestation of gratitude, the gift-exchange was also a method of integration. The votaries were no longer demoniacs but beneficiaries of divine grace. The materiality of the gift was essential in manifesting gratitude, but it was also a way to posit oneself in the closeness of a sacred space. The bodies of demoniacs, which used to be the dwelling place of malevolent spirits, could become the material tokens of gratitude by performing ascetic pilgrimages. Other kind of material donations, money, wax or clothes were important in the gift-exchange while the materiality of the shrine was a concrete element in the interaction with the heavenly intercessor.

Demoniac's gratitude, the ritualized gift-exchange with St Nicholas was also a way to claim agency, to manifest regained proper order and one's position in the community. Religion-as-lived offered a coping mechanism; it offered an explanation to extraordinary situation and a means to ameliorate it. The material donated was an integral part of social processes, a way to tell a story of oneself to the community. These processes were partly restrictive; their sharedness meant that the form of interaction and objects donated had to be at least partly approved of by others. In cases of demonic possession, they were also clearly empowering and constructive, as they allowed a negotiation and manifestation of individual and communal identity; they represented the victory over malign spirits. A gift to a saint was holistic phenomenon including and infusing the cognitive and the somatic – deliberate pondering, emotions and embodied practices – as well as the spiritual, social and cultural.

## Notes

1. On interaction with a saint studied via hagiographic material, see Pierre-André Sigal, *L'Homme et le miracle dans la France médiévale (xie–xiie siècle)* (Paris: Éditions du Cerf, 1985); Ronald C. Finucane, *Miracles and Pilgrims: Popular Beliefs in Medieval England* (London: J. M. Dent & Sons, 1977); Michael E. Goodich, *Violence and Miracle in the Fourteenth Century: Private Grief and Public Salvation* (Chicago: University of Chicago Press, 1995); Christian Krötzl, *Pilger, Mirakel und Alltag: Formen des Verhaltens im skandinavischen Mittelalter (12.–15. Jahrhundert)* (Helsinki: SHS, 1994); Didier Lett, *L'Enfant des miracles: Enfance et société au Moyen Âge (xiie–xiiie siècle)* (Paris: Aubiers, 1997); Sari Katajala-Peltomaa, *Gender, Miracles, and Daily Life: The Evidence of Fourteenth-Century Canonization Processes* (Turnhout: Brepols, 2009); Jenni Kuuliala, *Childhood Disability and Social Interaction in the Middle Ages: Construction of Impairments in Thirteenth- and Fourteenth-Century Canonization Processes* (Turnhout: Brepols, 2016).

2. On votive offerings, see Giovanni Battista Bronzini, '"Ex voto" e cultura religiosa popolare', *Rivista di storia e letteratura religiosa* 15:1 (1979): 3–27; Giovanni Battista Bronzini, 'Fenomenologia dell'ex voto', *Lares*. Organo dell'instituto di storia delle tradizioni popolari dell'universta di Bari e della federazione italiana tradizioni popolari E.N.A.L. 44:1 (1978): 143–66; and Anne-Marie Bautier, 'Typologie des Ex-voto mentionnés dans des textes antérieurs a 1200', in *La Piété Populaire au Moyen Âge*. Actes du 99e Congrès National des Sociétés savantes (Besançon 1974), (Paris: Bibliothèque nationale, 1977), 238–82; Sigal, *L' homme et le miracle*, 88–91. On votive images in the Renaissance see especially Fredrika Jacobs, *Votive Panels and Popular Piety in Early Modern Italy* (Cambridge: Cambridge University Press, 2013); Fredrika Jacobs, 'Humble Offerings: Votive Panel Paintings in Renaissance Italy', in *Ex Voto: Votive Giving Across Cultures*, ed. Ittai Weinryb (New York: Bard Graduate Center, 2016), 140–65; Fredrika Jacobs, 'Votive Culture and Purposeful Destruction', *Source. Notes in the History of Art* 36:3/4 (2017): 212–22; Megan Holmes, 'Ex-votos: Materiality, Memory and Cult', in *Objects, Devotions and the Early Modern World*, ed. Michael W. Cole and Rebecca Zorach (Aldershot: Ashgate, 2009), 159–81.

3. On conceptualizations of lived religion, see, for example, Meredith B. McGuire, *Contested Meanings and Definitional Boundaries: Historicizing the Sociology of Religion* (Oxford: Oxford University Press, 2008); R. Ruard Ganzevoort and

Srdjan Sremac, ed., *Lived Religion and the Politics of (In)Tolerance* (Cham: Palgrave Macmillan, 2017); John H. Arnold, 'Histories and Historiographies of Medieval Christianity', in *The Oxford Handbook Medieval Christianity*, ed. John H. Arnold (Oxford: Oxford University Press, 2014), 23–41; Sari Katajala-Peltomaa, *Demonic Possession and Lived Religion in Later Medieval Europe* (Oxford: Oxford University Press, 2020), 2–4, and Sari Katajala-Peltomaa and Raisa Maria Toivo, *Lived Religion and Gender in Late Medieval and Early Modern Europe* (London: Routledge, 2021), 1–21.

4   Nicholas of Tolentino (1245–1305) was an Augustinian friar of humble origin, born after his parents' invocation to his namesake, Nicholas of Bari. In the depositions, St Nicholas was described as humble ascetic, a devoted and understanding confessor. He gained the fame of sanctity already during his lifetime and performed several *miracula in vita*. Miracles started at the shrine immediately after his death. The main promoters of St Nicholas' cult were the Augustinian friars and the inhabitants of Tolentino. Domenico Gentili, 'Introduzione', in *Il Processo per la Canonizzazione di S. Nicola da Tolentino*, ed. Nicola Occhioni O.S.A. (Rome: Padri Agotiniani di Tolentino, École française de Rome, 1984), IX–XXVII.

5   *Il processo per la canonizzazione di s. Nicola da Tolentino*. On organization of this canonization process, see Gentili, 'Introduzione', IX–XXVII and especially Didier Lett, *Un procès de canonisation au Moyen Âge: Essai d'histoire sociale. Nicolas de Tolentino, 1325* (Paris: Presses universitaires de France, 2008).

6   The seminal work in the field of canonization processes is still André Vauchez, *La Sainteté en Occident aux derniers siècles du Moyen Âge. D'après les procès de canonization et les documents* hagiographiques (Rome: École française de Rome, 1988). On practicalities in canonization hearings, see Thomas Wetzstein, *Helige vor Gerich. Das Kanonisationsverfahren im europäischen Spätmittelalter* (Köln: Böhlau, 2004), 337–41. This set of questions contains standard-elements that every witness should be asked in any lawful process following the romano-canonical procedure. They generally applied to the person of the witnesses and to the circumstances of the event about which the witness was interrogated. Sari Katajala-Peltomaa and Christian Krötzl, 'Approaching Twelfth–Fifteenth-Century Miracles: Miracle Registers, Collections and Canonization Processes as Source Material', in *Miracles in Canonization Processes: Structures, Functions, and Methodologies*, ed. Christian Krötzl and Sari Katajala-Peltomaa (Turnhout: Brepols, 2018), 1–39.

7   Katajala-Peltomaa, *Gender, Miracles, and Daily Life*, 161–246.

8   The seminal work in medieval materiality is Tara Hamling and Catherine Richardsson, ed., *Everyday Objects: Medieval and Early Modern Material Culture and Its Meanings* (Farnham: Ashgate, 2010). Tara Hamling and Catherine Richardson (Tara Hamling and Catherine Richardsson, 'Introduction', in *Everyday Objects,* 1–23) argue for the centrality of materiality to shaping experiences and regulating life. At the same time these objects of everyday life are hard to scrutinize

since they were not always consciously considered. On relationship between documents and materials they depict, see Rachel M. Delman and Anna Boeles Rowland, 'Introduction: People, Places, and Possessions in Late medieval England', *Journal of Medieval History* 45:2 (2019): 129–44. On interconnection between intercessory prayers and almsgiving and especially changes in these customs after Reformation, see the article of Poul Grinder-Hansen in this volume.

9   Images of the votive tablets are published in a catalogue: *Gli ex voto per San Nicola a Tolentino* (Basilica di San Nicola Tolentino 1972), see also Mario Massacesi, 'La raccolta degli ex voto nel santuario di S. Nicola a Tolentino', in *Gli ex voto per San Nicola a Tolentino*, 45–50 and Domenico Gentili, 'Il Santo e il suo santuario', in *Gli ex voto per San Nicola a Tolentino*, 15–44.

10  Jacobs, 'Votive Culture and Purposeful Destruction'.

11  Katajala-Peltomaa, *Demonic Possession and Lived Religion*.

12  Marcel Mauss, *The Gift. The Form and Reason for Exchange in Archaic Societies* (London: Routledge, 1990 [orig. 1924]). On historiographical analysis of the use of Mauss's theories in the gift-exchange in historical and sociological studies, see Arnould-Jan A. Bijsterveld, 'The Medieval Gift as Agent of Social Bonding and Political Power: A Comparative Approach', in *Medieval Transformations. Texts, Power, and Gifts in Context*, ed. Esther Cohen and Mayke B. De Jong (Leiden: Brill, 2001), 123–56.

13  Vauchez, *La Sainteté en Occident*, 530–1. On this kind of supplications in papal penitentiary, see Kirsi Salonen, *The Penitentiary as a Well of Grace. The Example of Province of Uppsala 1448–1527* (Helsinki: Academia Scientiarum Fennica, 2001), 153–6.

14  On punishment miracles Gábor Klaniczay, 'Miracoli di punizione e maleficia', in *Miracoli. Dai segni alla storia*, ed. Sofia Boesch Gajanao and Marilena Modica (Rome: Viella, 2000), 109–35. On lay witnesses' conceptualizations of punishing ability, see Sari Katajala-Peltomaa, 'Narrative Strategies in the Depositions: Gender, Family and Devotion', in *Miracles in Medieval Canonization Processes: Structures, Functions, and Methodologies*, ed. Christian Krötzl and Sari Katajala-Peltomaa (Turnhout: Brepols, 2018), 227–56.

15  Alan Schrift, 'Introduction: Why Gift?' in *The Logic of the Gift. Toward an Ethic of Generosity*, ed. Alan Schrift (New York: Routledge, 1997), 1–22. On further analysis of gift-exchange and critic towards Mauss's theories, see the whole volume Schrift (ed.), *The Logic of the Gift*. On Mauss's theories' social and intellectual context as well as their aim to criticize modern capitalism, see Patrick Geary, 'Gift Exchange and Social Science Modelling. The Limitations of a Construct', in *Negotiating the Gift. Pre-Modern Figurations of Exchange*, ed. Gadi Algazi, Valentin Groebner and Bernhard Jussen (Göttingen: Vandenhoeck Ruprecht, 2003), 129–40 and Beate Wagner-Hasel, 'Egoistic Exchange and Altruistic Gift. On the Roots of Marcel Mauss's Theory of the Gift', in *Negotiating the Gift*, 141–71.

16  On gift-giving and limit of acceptable behaviour in Early modern English political context, Felicity Heal, *The Power of Gifts. Gift Exchange in Early Modern England* (Oxford: Oxford University Press, 2014).
17  Mauss, *The Gift*, 17. Natalie Zemon Davis, *The Gift in Sixteenth Century France*. The Curti Lectures (Oxford: Oxford University Press, 2000), 21.
18  The offerings were significant in several different perspectives. This seems to accord with Marcel Mauss's notion of gifts as 'total social activities'. According to Mauss, gifts were simultaneously, for example, economic, moral, aesthetic and religious phenomena. Mauss, *The Gift*, 3, 79–80. See also Ilana Silber, 'Gift-giving in Great Traditions: The Case of Donations to Monasteries in Medieval West', *Archives européennes de sociologie* 36 (1995): 209–43.
19  Katajala-Peltomaa, *Demonic Possession and Lived Religion*.
20  On methodology of canonization processes, see the chapters in Krötzl and Katajala-Peltomaa, ed., *Miracles in Medieval Canonization Processes*.
21  Dyan Elliott, 'The Physiology of Rapture and Female Spirituality', in *Medieval Theology and the Natural Body*, ed. Peter Biller and A. J. Minnis (Bury St Edmunds: York Medieval Press, 1997), 141–73.
22  Katajala-Peltomaa, *Demonic Possession and Lived Religion*, 122–7.
23  On increase of distance miracles, see Christian Krötzl, 'Miracles au tombeau—miracles à distance: approches typologiques', in *Miracle et Karama. Hagiographies médiévales comparées* 2, ed. Denise Aigle (Turnhout: Brepols, 2000), 557–76.
24  *Il processo per la canonizzazione di San Nicola da Tolentino*, testis LXXXVIII, 259–60. Mancinus is the only witness to the case.
25  Holmes, 'Ex-votos: Materiality, Memory and Cult', and Jacobs, 'Votive culture and Purposeful Destruction'.
26  A 'corporeal turn' has been substantial especially among literary criticism during recent decades. The field is too vast to be cited here in full. For the study of body in medieval religiosity, the work of Caroline Walker Bynum has been seminal. See, for example, her *Fragmentation and Redemption. Essays on Gender and the Human Body in Medieval Religion* (New York: Zone Books, 1991) and *The Resurrection of the Body in Western Christianity, 200–1336* (New York: Columbia University Press, 1995) and *Christian Materiality: An Essay on Religion in Late Medieval West* (New York: Zone Books, 2011), esp. 31–3 for a caveat against taking the body as a synonym for a person or individual.
27  *Il processo per la canonizzazione di San Nicola da Tolentino*, testis CCII, 445–6; testis CCIX, 452–3; testis CCX, 453–4; testis CCXI, 454–5.
28  Bijsterveld, 'The Medieval Gift', 143. See Davis, *The Gift in Sixteenth Century France*, 45–7.
29  The witnesses to this case are *Il processo per la canonizzazione di San Nicola da Tolentino*, testis XX–XXII, 135–42 and testis CXXIII–CXXVI, 322–31. Philippucia's invocation according to her deposition. 'Et ipsa testis voverat se in

corde suo, aliquando quando erat in non tanta mala dispositione, beato Venantio de Camereno et beato Claudio de Macerata et pluribus aliis sanctis et tandem vovit se beato Nicholao predicto promittens, si liberaretur a dicta infirmitate seu stupefactione, accedere Tholentium ad archam dicti beato Nicholay ligatis manibus et discalciata pedibus', testis XX, 137.

30 *Il processo per la canonizzazione di San Nicola da Tolentino*, testis CXXV, 328: 'Et postea audivit dici ab ipsa sorore Philippucia quod voverat se beato Nicholao predicto ire Tholentinum ad archam dicti beati Nicholai, et ibi quedam offerre, ut sibi testi videtur, si liberabatur de predictis'. For another case, see testis CIII, testis CIV, 296.

31 On this theoretical framework in Oceanian societies, see Annette B. Weiner, *Inalienable Possession. The Paradox of Keeping-While Giving* (Berkeley: University of California Press, 1992); on criticism towards her arguments, see Mark S. Mosko, 'Inalienable Ethnography: Keeping-While-Giving and the Trobriand Case', *Journal of the Royal Anthropological Institute* 6:3 (2000): 377–96. On body and materiality within lived religion producing 'experience', see Katajala-Peltomaa & Toivo, *Lived Religion and Gender*, 129 et passim.

32 Canon law forbade the testimony of people with *infamia*. Especially in Nicholas' hearing the floor was reserved for the wealthy and respectable political elite of the communities. On the canon law regulations in selection of the witnesses in canonization hearings, see Christian Krötzl, 'Prokuratoren, Notare und Dolmetscher. Zu Gestaltung und Ablauf der Zeugeneinvernahmen bei spätmittelalterlichen Kanonisationsprozessen', *Hagiographica* V (1998): 119–40. Didier Lett has shown (Lett, *Un procès de canonisation* and Didier Lett, 'La parole des humbles comme resource. L'utilisation de la procedure inquisitoire par les postulateurs de la cause dans la procès de canonisation de Nicolas de Tolentino (1325)', in *Agiografia e culture popolari –Hagiography and Popular Cultures. In ricordo di Pietro Boglioni*, ed. Paolo Golinelli (Bologna: Clueb, 2012), 233–40 that local Ghuelp families dominated Nicholas' hearing.

33 The witnesses to this case are *Il processo per la canonizzazione di San Nicola da Tolentino*, testis XX–XXII, 135–42 and testis CXXIII–CXXVI, 322–31; testis XX, 136: 'voverunt eam beato Nicholao predicto quod, si liberaret eandem sororem Anthoniam idem beato Nicholao predicto a tentatione predicta demonis, quod ducerent ipsam Tholentinum ad tumulum seu archam dicti sancti Nicholay et ibidem offerrent vestimenta ipsius monialis Anthonie et unum cereum; et parentes ipius sororis Anthonie et alii consagunei ipius, emisso dicto voto, extraxerunt eandem de dicto monasterio et duxerunt eam ad dictam terram Tholentini ad archam predictam, et fecerunt eam iacere tota una nocte in ecclesia Sancti Augustini de Tholentino ante tumulum supradictum'.

34 On these characteristics of 'things', see Kellie Robertson, 'Medieval Things. Materiality, Historicism, and the Premodern Object', *Literature Compass*

5/6 (2008): 1060–80; things in social relations in general Arjun Appadurai, *The Social Life of Things, Commodities in Cultural Perspective* (Cambridge: Cambridge University Press, 1988); Christopher Tilley, *Metaphor and Material Culture* (Oxford: Blackwell, 1999); Hamling and Richardsson, 'Introduction'. On interconnection of gender, emotions and materiality, see Jacqueline Van Ghent and Raisa Maria Toivo, 'Introduction. Gender, Material Culture and Emotions in Scandinavian History', *Scandinavian Journal of History* 41:3 (2016): 263–70; on the relationship between documents and objects Delman and Rowland 'Introduction: People, Places, and Possessions'. The meaning of and emotions attached to a gift could vary over time as Anna Boeles Rowland argues in her article in this volume.

35 See also Jenni Kuuliala, 'Infirmity and the Miraculous in the Early Seventeenth century. The San Carlo cycle of paintings in the Duomo of Milan', in *Representing Infirmity. Diseased Bodies in Renaissance Italy, The Body in the City*, ed. John Henderson, Fredrika Jacobs and Jonathan K. Nelson (London and New York: Routledge, 2021), 213–32 who argues that sufferings and ailments were more emphasized in textual than image forms of recovery miracles of Carlo Borromeo.

36 On material and hermeneutical mutability of relics as gifts exchanged see Ruth Sargent Noyes's article in this volume.

37 The collection of votive panels at the museum of sanctuary in Tolentino has even been depicted as the 'Sistine Chapel of the Poor'. Mary Laven, 'Recording Miracles in Renaissance Italy', *Past & Present*, 230:11 (2016): 191–212. https://doi.org/10.1093/pastj/gtw026 (accessed 29 January 2021). On the messages of visual objects of different materials, see Bynum, *Christian Materiality*, esp. 28.

38 Holmes, 'Ex-votos: Materiality, Memory and Cult', 159–81.

39 While men tended to favour sheer money (*Il processo per la canonizzazione di San Nicola da Tolentino*, testis CLV, 375; testis CCXXIII, 491), sometimes even large sums, like the unnamed demoniac, women offered St Nicholas strings of silver (testis CXI, 305–6) or gold (testis LIII, 187; testis CCLV, 534; testis CCXCIII, 585). *Gli ex voto per San Nicola a Tolentino*, 44.

40 Many rituals involved in votive offerings bear resemblance of magic. Bautier, 'Typologie des Ex-voto', 250–2.

41 While many panels depict the generic condition of infirmity, moments of crisis such as accidents were also typical motifs. A specific sub-category found by Fredrika Jacobs is the 'purging' image of usually vomiting patient depicting the start of a recovery process. These images can be seen to be parallel to 'purging' from impure spirits of demoniacs. Fredrika Jacobs 'Infirmity in Votive Culture. A Case Study from the Sanctuary of the Madonna dell'Arco, Naples', in *Representing Infirmity*, 191–212.

42 Nancy Caciola, *Discerning Spirits: Divine and Demonic Possession in the Middle Ages* (Ithaca: Cornell University Press, 2003), 225–73.

43 Moshe Sluhovsky, *Believe Not Every Spirit: Possession, Mysticism, and Discernment in Early Modern Catholicism* (Chicago: University of Chicago Press, 2008), 61–8.
44 According to her, ex-votos played a certificatory role, not far removed from that of the written legal or statutory records found in notarial archives. Laven, 'Recording Miracles in Renaissance Italy'.
45 Jane Garnett and Gervase Rosser, 'The Ex-voto between Domestic and Public Space: From Personal Testimony to Collective Memory', in *Domestic Devotions in Early Modern Italy*, ed. Maya Corry, Marco Faini and Alessia Meneghin (Leiden: Brill, 2019), 45–62. The collective nature of the miraculous is more emphasized or even the core message in images commissioned collectively or by authorities, like in the San Carlo cycle in the Duomo of Milan. See Kuuliala, 'Infirmity and the Miraculous'.
46 Élisabeth Antoine, 'L'Image d'un Saint Thaumaturge: les ex-voto de Saint-Nicholas de Tolentino (XVe–milieu XVIe siècle)', *Revue Mabillon*. Revue international d'histoire et de littérature religieuses. Nouvelle série 7:68 (1996): 183–208.
47 On power of objects in creating identities, see Ryan Perry, 'Objectification, Identity and the Late Medieval Codex', in *Everyday Objects*, 309–19.

7

# Alms boxes and charity: Giving to the poor after the Lutheran Reformation in Denmark

Poul Grinder-Hansen

Near the exit door in the nave of many old Danish Lutheran church buildings stands an alms post, often carved out of solid oak and protected by heavy iron bands. On the top is an iron protected slit for coins (Figure 7.1).[1] The dates of such iron bound posts are from the sixteenth to the eighteenth century, while alms posts from the nineteenth century typically have a less stout construction. The posts had a common purpose: to collect donations for the poor. Some of the posts are still used each Sunday to collect donations for charitable or diaconal purposes but in most churches small collection boxes of brass mounted on the wall or on a pew are used instead and the old posts serve as historical monuments. The offertory boxes as well as the related collection plates are significant testimonies of an important aspect of Lutheran post-Reformation charitable gift-giving.[2] In some cases their iconography and inscriptions point to the dilemmas and theological considerations that the Lutheran Church had to face when it came to the promotion of charitable donations. Martin Luther stated that God bestowed his gifts on human beings quite gratis without any expectance or need of reciprocity. It was not, anyway, possible for a human being to give God anything that he wanted or needed.[3] This idea had fundamentally questioned the idea of doing good works in return for a divine reward. Almsgiving could thus no longer be interpreted as an efficient way of doing penance. It might seem a tempting assumption that the Lutheran Reformation which lead to the demolition of monasteries and religious institutions in Denmark, also lead to a reduced willingness to donate gifts to the poor and needy. Such an assumption has been promoted from time to time by various Danish scholars during the last century.[4] This interpretation is, however, questionable.[5]

**Figure 7.1** Alms box Svendborg St Nicolai Church. © Arnold Mikkelsen, National Museum of Denmark, Creative Commons.

## Alms before the Reformation

The word 'alms' (German *Almosen*, Danish *almisse*) originates in the Greek word for compassion, eleemosyne, (ἐλεημοσύνη), and denotes a work of mercy, usually in the sense of a charitable gift to the poor.[6] The medieval, Roman Catholic church emphasized that almsgiving was one of the most effective acts of penance which would lead to absolution.[7] Therefore almsgiving was a natural part of life for well-to-do people in the Middle Ages.[8] In the doctrine of

Purgatory almsgiving was considered an effective means of shortening the stay of the soul in the purifying fires of Purgatory.[9]

Wills benefiting ecclesiastical institutions would often include an explicit wish that some of the means should be used for donations to the poor, both in connection with death and burial and later on the anniversary of the benefactor's death.[10] The motivations given for the almsgiving in wills could vary but they expressed the same fundamental idea that almsgiving washed away sins and secured God's goodwill for the repentant sinner.[11] The poor gained a special importance in relation to gift-giving simply by their mere existence which made it possible to do good works. When the mayors and council of the Danish town Faaborg in 1477 supported the founding of a hospital in the city in the form of a Monastery dedicated to the Holy Ghost, the reasons they offered were not the need for care of the infirm but that within a distance of three to four miles from the town there was not 'a monastery or an indulgence which we can enjoy to benefit the salvation of our souls'.[12]

The concept of intercessory prayers and requiems was the driving force behind most donations to churches and religious institutions in the late Middle Ages. This was also the case with almsgiving, since the grateful intercessory prayers offered by poor gift-recipients were supposed to carry a special weight.[13] Anonymous donations could not be reciprocated in the same way by the recipients, but still there would be an indirect reciprocity, since God would in the end reward the good works.[14] The system of reciprocal relations can, with a Latin phrase from Roman law, be described as 'do ut des' (I give so that you shall give).[15] The donation of material gifts to poor people or to ecclesiastical institutions thus deserved a spiritual gift from God in return, with the clergy as intermediaries.[16]

In late medieval Denmark most donations were given directly to religious institutions (Figure 7.2). Some of them, especially monasteries in the countryside and town-based institutions like Houses of the Holy Spirit or leper hospitals, contributed greatly to the care of poor and needy people with the use of such donations. But poor relief was not the main task of most ecclesiastical institutions, and in addition a great deal of the donations which were described as 'alms' were not aimed at ordinary poor and needy people. Large-scale alms were collected by mendicant friars of the Franciscan, Dominican and other orders, by pilgrims and school children and by collectors of contributions for various good and pious causes like church building or indulgences.[17]

**Figure 7.2** Late-medieval collection plate from Brændekilde Church, Fyn.
© Arnold Mikkelsen, National Museum of Denmark, Creative Commons.

## Luther and almsgiving

From 1517 onwards Martin Luther fundamentally contested the Catholic 'do ut des' logic of religious and charitable gift-giving. He had come to the conclusion that the justice of God was quite different to earthly justice, and that no human being could justify themselves in the eyes of God through their own efforts. God acted through forgiveness, and the gift of God was free since it was not possible for anyone to give God anything in return.[18] The only thing that was demanded from human beings was faith or rather confidence in the power of God. Luther always stressed that this faith should not be a measurable effort since this would imply that human beings could reciprocate the gift from God. In Luther's view the Holy Spirit 'teaches mankind to understand this deed of Christ which has been manifested to us, helps us receive and preserve it, use it to our advantage and impart it to others, increase and extend it'.[19] One of the logical reactions to the reception of the gift of grace from God thus was to pass it on to others. This was not only a spiritual matter of preaching and teaching, but also of using the temporal and physical blessings, that God bestows upon mankind in the right manner.[20] Almsgiving could be one of the ways of doing this. The human reaction to the reception of God's gifts should be to become a giver yourself, not to God, but to someone else.

This kind of reciprocity was something quite different than the 'do ut des' – concept of the medieval Catholic church. First of all, it was impossible to donate something in order to receive God's reciprocity. The initiative always came from God. Without God's free gift of faith and grace, man was helpless. Secondly, the reciprocity from humans to God had no tangible or material character. It was individual, elusive and invisible. Good works could according to this line of thought no longer contribute to the salvation of a donor's soul. They could only be seen as a natural reaction by a good Christian who could not help passing on some of the gifts that God had already given.

## Poor relief after the Lutheran Reformation in Denmark

In 1536 the Danish king Christian III (1534–1559) implemented a Lutheran Reformation. The king took over the role of protector of the church, and the bishops were replaced by Lutheran 'superintendents'. The episcopal estates were confiscated for the crown, and king Christian declared the official dissolvement of monasteries and religious institutions which had already gradually begun in the previous, turbulent years of religious unrest and civil war.[21] The poor relief which used to be the responsibility of ecclesiastical institutions would from now on be a public obligation of the state with a secular management, yet under supervision by representatives of the new Lutheran Church.[22] Income from landed property, which had been given as frankalmoign to ecclesiastical institutions and had formed the economic basis of their charitable activities, was now transferred to new, public hospitals.[23] The new church law (*kirkeordinans*) which was published in Latin in 1537 and in Danish in 1539[24] described the new

**Figure 7.3** The interior of the fifteenth-century Holy Ghost House in Copenhagen which after the Reformation was turned into a hospital. © Wikimedea, Creative Commons.

hospitals as a natural part of a Christian, Lutheran state. Most of the new state hospitals were installed in converted monastic building complexes (Figure 7.3).[25]

The head of a hospital was allowed to provide additional funding for the institution by sending a wagon around the county in order to beg for food and provisions that could be useful for the hospital. The procedure of sending a wagon to collect alms in the countryside was a direct imitation of the practice of the late medieval mendicant friars who maintained their convents through begging. The reformers, however, found it much easier to justify a collection of alms in this way since the outcome was used directly for the poor inhabitants of the hospitals.[26]

The aim of the new Lutheran authorities was to improve the charitable work. This seemed to be an achievable goal since the collected income could now go directly to needy people instead of being used for religious purposes. The local vicars in the countryside and town authorities in urban areas were entrusted with the right to assign poor people as inmates of the hospitals. The criterion was a distinction between deserving poor who could not live without help, as opposed to people who were fit to work and should be self-supporting. This distinction which was introduced into Danish legislation before the Lutheran reformation, in Christian II's (1481–1559) city-law from 1522, had also been known in other Europeans countries since the early sixteenth century.[27]

The new hospitals were far from able to cover the need for social assistance, and alms remained the foundation of poor relief after the Reformation. To make sure that only deserving poor received alms, a control system was introduced in 1537. Two citizens appointed by the town council or the vicars in each country parish were told to issue small control badges of lead, beggar's badges, which the lawful beggars should carry as a visible sign of their status.[28] The beggars were only allowed to beg inside their own parish or town. Besides these legitimate beggars, school children were also allowed to receive alms. Frederik II's statutory instrument from 1587 developed the system further and described among other things that lists should be kept of all beggars in Denmark to make sure that beggar's badges were handed over to the authorities after the user's death in order to avoid fraud.[29] People who had been struck by accidents such as fire, disease or the loss of a ship could be provided with a special beggar's letter that requested everyone to give a donation to the holder of the letter. Holders of such a letter were entitled to beg outside their own town or parish, for example, in a whole region.[30]

The church law from 1537 impressed on the vicars that they should encourage their parishioners to give alms.[31] But a challenge remained. How could the parishioners be convinced that it was a good and necessary thing to give alms, whether directly to a beggar or in an alms post or a collection tray in the church, if there was not a direct divine reward to the giver? Various arguments for almsgiving were repeatedly presented by the religious authorities of Lutheran Denmark.

## Arguments for almsgiving

Around 1541 the new Lutheran superintendent (bishop) of Roskilde diocese Peder Palladius (1503–1560) wrote a manuscript which he could use as an inspiration for speeches to the parishioners during his pastoral visitations in the parish churches of Sjælland (Figure 7.4).[32] The manuscript testifies to the attitudes towards alms from a prominent Danish Lutheran and reveals how these attitudes were communicated and used to motivate parishioners. There are five things, Palladius said, that you shall do in your parish church: pray, listen to God's words, receive the Eucharist, praise and thank God and finally give alms

**Figure 7.4** Lutheran service depicted on a painted alterfrontal from Torslunde Church on Sjælland 1561. © Lennart Larsen, National Museum of Denmark, Creative Commons.

to the poor. The post for the poor stands right inside the door of the church so that no one can miss it, because in that way

> my friend.... when you come to make up your account at judgement day you cannot excuse yourself and say that you have not seen the poor Lazarus laying before your eyes; as clearly as you see their post there inside the church door, you must remember that there are poor people in this parish who are in need of your alms.[33]

Palladius listed several kinds of poor people who might need help and added in this connection a further argument: 'We never know what might happen to each of us before we leave this world.' He stressed that the people in charge of poor relief should carry the collections plate for the poor among the congregation in the same way as the church wardens carried the collection plate for the church. He even argued that they should visit dying people and that after some encouraging words about the expected eternal life they should ask them to give a gift to benefit their soul (*sjælegave*) 'as it is called', preferably while they still lived rather than in a will after their death.

Palladius obviously found it necessary to use both the stick and the carrot to convince parishioners that they should give alms. Apparently there were problems. The superintendent noted that many people now suffered more poverty and misery than they had done before the Reformation. But he rejected the assertion that the 'new teachings' were the cause of this calamity. First of all it was not 'new teachings' but the oldest possible, based directly on the words of the Bible. The reason for the misery of the poor was that people

> will not obey the words of God... nor act towards their neighbours and the poor as they should; they will not touch the alms box of the poor when they enter the church door as they did previously with the salt-box and the holy-water font; they will not put the gifts on the plate of the poor, which they used to place in abundance on the monks' altar.

Palladius threatened the tight-fisted parishioners that the punishment of God would strike them if they despised the poor and did not bring money to the church for alms. On the other hand, he promised a reward for the cheerful givers:

> What you give to the poor does not disappear. You get 20 coins for one; indeed, even if you just give a cup of cold water, you shall not lose your reward, says he, who cannot lie, he who is named Our Lord Jesus Christ... But if you walk empty handed to and from this church, God will surely empty your hands in your own house so that you shall not have as much as you can hold between your fingers and put in your mouth, because... as you act towards God and the poor, so will he act against you.

If it is heard that poor people or smallholders freeze or starve in your neighbourhood, Palladius warned, 'it is a sure sign that God will curse and damn all of you'.[34]

Palladius didactically listed five groups of poor people and gave examples how it was possible to help them. The first group was the poor and sick people in the hospitals. 'It might as well be you!', he warned. When the wagon from the hospital came, the parishioners should not only donate food, money and grain but also bedclothes and bedlinen. They could for example strip the now superfluous side altars of their altar clothes and give them to the hospitals. The second group was the young scholars who were allowed to go begging or to sing at the doors for eggs, paper, shoes and books. They deserved help because they would afterwards become vicars who would spread the word of Christ. The third group was homeless or foreigners. People should open the doors for them, wash their weary feet and offer them something to eat and drink, on condition that they demonstrated knowledge of the Ten Commandments and the Lord's Prayer. The fourth group of potentially poor people comprised vicars and clerks. They took care of the souls of their parishioners and therefore the parishioners should take care of their bodies in times of need. The fifth and last group comprised the homeless and poor in the parish. The churchgoers should give alms in the alms box and on the collection plate in the church but they should also be willing to donate food to the poor at home. 'Pick out a Lazarus whom you can send something good when you brew, bake or get food; this person can later on bring you along into Heaven.' It was a total mistake to make pilgrimages to dead saints instead of living fellow human beings. A true pilgrimage was to attend the service in the parish church and afterwards to go and visit the living James, Severin or Anne on their sickbed and to offer them bread, butter, cheese or milk, if they were poor.[35]

Palladius wrote his manuscript just five years after the Reformation in a time of transition, and it was an obvious challenge that alms could no longer be motivated as good works to benefit the donor's salvation, if you stuck to Luther's interpretation. Palladius was a very committed Lutheran, but he used reciprocity on several levels in his arguments. According to Palladius, it was, first of all, a common condition or human life that you should be willing to give now, since you never knew if you might yourself be struck with misfortune and poverty. But he also promised a divine reward. The gifts for the poor would be reciprocated twentyfold by God, and the poor person who had received your help could later on help the donor into Paradise. On the other hand, you would be struck by God's punishment both on this earth and on Judgement Day if you did not give alms to destitute people. Palladius referred several times to Jesus' parable about the rich man who ends in hell and the poor Lazarus who ends in the lap of God (Luke 16:19–31). As it appears from the quotation above, he occasionally used the name Lazarus simply as another word for a beggar.

Related messages about the right Lutheran way of living and giving reached another and more aristocratic audience in the funeral sermons for members of the Danish nobility. Such sermons, which were held in the church at the funeral but normally were also printed and published afterwards, were introduced after the Reformation by university educated, classically schooled Lutheran clergymen. They were modelled according to a fixed pattern.[36] The orator began by describing the relationship of the deceased to fatherland, parents and lineage. He continued with a description of the course of life and the virtues of the deceased, and he ended with a detailed description of a peaceful, serene and pious death. The sermons typically described the deceased as a devoted gift giver, especially to the poor. Considering the purpose of the genre this may not necessarily be an objective description, but it testifies to the ideals for a good life which the vicar and his audience shared. In the sixteenth century the Lutheran vicars rarely spoke of the good works of the deceased as something that could clear the way for a well-deserved salvation. On the contrary, the good works were seen as the natural manifestation of faith. The sermon could thus comfort the bereaved that the deceased had really lived as a good Christian who could rest in peace in hopeful expectation of an eternal life with God.

The sermon for Karine Knudsdatter Gyldenstierne 1596 states that 'she proved her Christian love and charity in many ways, and she let especially the want and need of the poor go to her heart and helped them willingly'.[37] Anders Bing, who died in 1589, had helped the impoverished peasants in the Danish province of Halland after the war with Sweden 1563–1570 by donating grain and seed corn: 'by this he has proven his faith in God: by love to the poor subjects, by diligence and care in his office and by allegiance to his king'.[38] Similarly Holger Rosenkrantz, who died 1575, 'had proven his faith through alms to the poor'.[39]

Since the beginning of the seventeenth century the official Danish Church was totally dominated by a rigid Lutheran orthodoxy which claimed to be based directly on the writings of Luther.[40] It stressed the active interference by God through punishment and – logically enough – also by rewards. Sermons from this century are more explicit about divine reciprocity. The sermon over Kaj Bredesen Rantzov from 1623 thus states: 'The late man has not willingly declined the begging of the poor but has always been generous and shared with others. For that reason God has also been with him and will reward him on judgement day.'[41] Or the sermon from 1647 for Hans Tygesen Krabbe: 'He who takes pity on the despised, he gives a loan to God who shall repay him what he should have.'[42]

In the seventeenth century the beggar's letters that were issued to people who had been struck by accident used the same arguments to persuade people to give alms. A letter issued in 1630 to Anders Hansen from Fyn, who had lost his livestock, requested alms from all kind-hearted Christians who could in return expect 'wages from God the Almighty who will reward all good works'.

## The testimonies of alms boxes

Solid alms post near the entrance door was clearly already an established fact a few years after the Reformation, when their position and use are mentioned as a given thing by Peder Palladius in his journal of pastoral visitations.[43] The first reference in official sources is an announcement from Peder Palladius to the deans of his diocese from 1553 which stated that each church should have two collection posts, one near the altar for donations to the church and the vicar, and one near the entrance door for alms to the poor and needy. Money should also be collected during the services by the use of a collection plate which had a handle and could be carried around by the parish clerk or other authorized collectors. Each church should have two plates, one for the church and one for the poor.[44] This was accomplished, but while the solid alms posts in the west end of the church still survive, most of the more fragile wooden collection plates have been damaged and have at some point been discarded, especially after a law from 1856 banned the carrying around of collections plates during the services since it disturbed the grave attention of the churchgoers.[45]

The concept of offertory boxes and collection plates in churches was known before the Reformation, but it seems that donations for the fabric of the church, for the poor and for the vicar were delivered in the same box or on the same collection plate,[46] and that the focus point of collection was the east end of the church, not near the entrance door. In some churches the pedestals of a chancel-arch crucifix served as a collection post so that donations were given at the feet of the crucified Saviour. In other churches monstrance tabernacles could serve as collections posts. There are several examples of this phenomenon from medieval Denmark (Figure 7.5).[47] All of these collection boxes were, however, at some point after the Reformation moved from their original position, re-shaped and reused as alms posts in the west end of the church. Specific alms boxes and collection plates for the poor is a post-Reformation phenomenon.

The coins that were donated through the slit on top of the alms post or placed on the collection plate were managed by the local authorities in charge of poor relief and were distributed among the deserving poor of the parish with the intention to centralize and optimize the use of alms. Alms could be given directly to the needy in kind or in cash, but the placing of alms boxes inside the church door as well as the use of collection plates during services points to the fact that churchgoers could be expected to bring some coins along with them, just as Palladius in his book of pastoral visitations urged people not to walk empty-handed to church.[48]

The collection plates would usually have an ornamented vertical board with a depiction or inscription indicating the purpose of the collected money, either for the church or for the poor.[49] The collection plates for the maintenance of the church and donations for the vicar often displayed a picture of its patron saint. This was a tradition from Catholic times, as a few late medieval examples indicate, e.g. the painting on the collection plate from Sneslev Church on Sjælland which depicts St Anne with Madonna and Child, each with a halo, arranged according to typical medieval iconography.[50] Other 'examples are the collection plates from Brændekilde Church on Fyn with a painting of a bishop's

**Figure 7.5** A medieval monstrance tabernacle in Kerteminde Church on Fyn reused as alms box. © Arnold Mikkelsen, National Museum of Denmark, Creative Commons.

saint,[51] and the one from Sønder Asmindrup Church on Sjælland with a painted depiction of Mary standing with the infant Jesus in her arms, both with a halo.[52] After the Reformation the patron saints might still be depicted yet now without a halo. Examples of this are the mid-seventeenth-century collection plate from Ganløse depicting Mary with the Child as the Apocalyptical Madonna yet without a halo,[53] and the collection plate which was donated to St Nicolai Church in Copenhagen in 1637 has a wood carving of the standing bishop's saint on the vertical board.[54] A collection plate from 1596 for Tikøb Church depicts a woman with her hands crossed in front of her breast, with a Scripture text from the Acts of the Apostles 20, verse 35: 'Det er saligere at give end at tage' (it is more blessed to give than to receive).⁵⁵

Three Danish churches have a post-Reformation block at the west end of the nave where collections both for the church and for the poor could be given. The iron-bound post from 1624 in Fuglse Church on the island of Lolland has two slits for money on its top, separated by a profiled, chequered board. There is no inscription over the slit for money to the church, while the inscription over the slit for alms states: 'Give some of your bread to the poor, then you shall sit in Abraham's bosom' (*Gif de fattig af dit brød, saa skalt du sidde i Abrahams skød*).⁵⁶ A painting from 1633 over the collection box in Næstved St Peder's Church shows on one side a prospect of the church, on the other side an almost naked old beggar sitting on the ground with his staff and lifting a bowl to receive alms (Figure 7.6). The inscription over his head reads: 'Help the poor in their distress/ then God will bless your daily bread/ 'cause never have I seen the one forsaken/ who fears God and does good works' (*Di fattige hielp i deris Nød/ Saa velsigner Gud dit daglig Brød/ ti aldrig haffuer ieg sett den forlatt/ som frøgter Gud oc giører gott*).⁵⁷ In 1717 the church warden in Tingsted on the island of Falster Hans

**Figure 7.6** Painting from a collection box for the church and for the poor 1633 in St Peter's Church, Næstved, Sjælland. © Museum Southeast Denmark/Jens Olsen.

Lauritzen Brygger and his wife Karen Pedersdatter donated a new collection box with two slits on either side of a vertical, artfully forged copper lattice. A painting above depicts the exterior of the church to the left of the latticework and on the other side a sitting beggar with a clutch in his right hand and the other hand stretched out in an appealing gesture. A tiny dog is licking his leg. The inscription above is a short poem in Danish: 'Give to the church, the needy and poor/ then God will have mercy on you' (*Giver til kircken, nødlidende og arme/ saa vil sig Gud over Eder forbarme*). An inscription commemorating the donors is painted on three sides of the frame around the painting.[58] Both in Fuglse and Tingsted there is a promise of divine reward for the alms giver.

Similar messages of reciprocity are expressed on Danish collections plates for the poor. The plate from the German Lutheran congregation in St Mary's Church in Helsingør (Elsinore) from 1577 declares in a Low German poem: 'Endow and give to the poor/then God will have mercy on you' (Bedencket und gebit den Armen/ so wyl sych Got aver Evch erbarmen).[59] Danish versions of the same text may be found on the collection plates from 1578 in Slangerup,[60] from 1595 in Søborg,[61] from 1599 in Birkerød[62] and from the early eighteenth century in Sengeløse.[63] An inscription from 1688 on a tablet over the alms block in Rørvig Church adds a slight theological touch to the same message: 'Come hither, wanderer, give what you like to the poor. In the distress over you, God will then have mercy' (*Kom hid du Vandringsmand/ gif huad du vilt den Arme/I Nøden ofver dig/ Gud vil sig da forbarme*) (Figure 7.7).[64]

In contrast the inscription on a plate over the alms box from 1616 in the palace church of Frederiksborg simply states: 'For homeless people, destitute poor, school children and other poor children of God who need help and alms here in the neighbourhood of Frederiksborg Palace' (*Til Huusarme Folk, Nødtørftige Stakkele, Skolebørn og andre fattige Gudslemmer, som Hiælp og Almisse behøve Heromkring Frederiksborg Slot*).[65] It would probably have been offensive to suggest that the Lutheran king and his court would need persuasion and arguments for giving alms.

Similarly the seventeenth-century collection plate for alms in the town church of Slangerup restricts itself to a request without a promise of reward yet with a reference to Christ: 'Think of your Saviour's death, think of the distress of the poor and give him something for bread' (*Betænk din frelsers død betænk den armes nød oc gif ham lidt til brød*).[66]

In some cases pictures were used to emphasize the purpose of the collection plate or the alms box. An atypical iconography is found on the abovementioned collection plate in Birkerød.[67] The plate from 1599 for the need of the church

**Figure 7.7** Inscription over the alms box in Rørvig Church on Sjælland, 1688. © National Museum of Denmark.

depicts the old patron saint of the church St Nicolaus – which is not unusual – but the collection plate for the poor depicts a bearded St Laurentius (St Lawrence) standing with his grill and a spear. Since the inscription mentions the reward for those who give to the poor, it is clearly a plate for alms collection, but the use of Laurentius in this connection is unique in a Danish Lutheran context. The explanation may be that the person who ordered the plate, probably the local vicar, knew the medieval legend of St Laurentius, including the episode where the Roman emperor ordered Laurentius to bring him all the treasures of the Church. Laurentius agreed and returned after a while with a crowd of poor and humble people since they were the true treasure of the Church.[68] Laurentius, who acted as treasurer for the congregation in Rome, may at the same time have been interpreted as a kind of forerunner of the overseer of the poor in Birkerød who administered the money that was donated on the collection plate.

Another rare motif is found on a collection plate made for St. Nicolai Church in Copenhagen in 1672.[69] The costly plate of tortoiseshell and ivory has a relief in silver of the good Samaritan, a well-suited topic which is however not found on any other Danish collection plates or alms boxes, perhaps because it does not refer directly to the giving of alms.

Otherwise the iconography of the collections trays and the occasional tablets over the alms boxes fall into two slightly overlapping groups: (1) a contemporary beggar, always a male, (2) Lazarus, usually depicted on his own, sitting on the ground while one or more dogs lick his wounds. Only very few examples illustrate the whole story of the rich man and Lazarus as told in St. Luke 16, verses 19–31. But a seated beggar with dogs can with reasonable certainty be identified as Lazarus since the biblical text emphasizes that the dogs came and licked the poor man's wounds.

The most expressive depiction of a contemporary beggar is found on a collection plate from about 1600 in the Renaissance collection at the National Museum of Denmark (Figure 7.8).[70] It has an uncertain provenance but may have come from the royal chapel in Copenhagen Castle. The standing board has a wooden relief where a bare-footed beggar with a staff and an outstretched hand receives alms from a well-dressed man. The pantomimic scene is in itself a demonstration of gift-giving for the poor. The gestures of the two persons reflect their roles and status: the beggar slightly crouching and in a lower position than the gently and elegantly forward-moving alms giver.[71]

A similar example is a landscape painting from Kerteminde Church from 1767 where a rich man with a walking stick in his hand and a tiny black dog at his feet places alms in the hat of a humbly dressed beggar with a beggar's staff in one hand and a purse in his belt. The inscription lets the beggar speak: 'The smallest coin you give to me/ will make me grateful/and be of joy to you in Heaven' (*Den ringeste Skierv du giver mig/ skal gøre mig taknemmelig/ og glæde dig i Himmerig*).[72]

Usually the beggar is, however, depicted on his own but clearly recognizable as a beggar by holding a staff or eventually a crutch. He will stretch out his hand, either empty with the palm turned upwards or holding a collection bowl or a hat. A wooden relief on a collection plate from Stenløse from *c*. 1650 presents a beggar with staff and bowl seated on a stone outside the gates of a building with

**Figure 7.8** Danish collection plate from *c*. 1600 from an unknown church. © National Museum of Denmark.

ashlar walls, which probably represent the church, since the same building is depicted on the matching collection plate for the church, where a man with keys, undoubtedly the church warden, is unlocking its gate (Figure 7.9).[73] A collection plate from Slangerup from *c*. 1650 depicts a well-dressed beggar with solid boots on his feet standing erect and not especially humbly, but recognizable from his rugged beggar's staff and the empty bowl in his hand (Figure 7.10). The inscription stresses the message further. Over the almsbox in Højrup Church, Southern Jylland, hangs a tablet with a seventeenth- or early eighteenth-century painting of a beggar, walking in a landscape with a stick and hat in hand under

**Figure 7.9** Collection plate from Stenløse Church, Sjælland, c. 1650. © National Museum of Denmark.

the inscription 'Endow the poor' (*Betenck dend Arme*).[74] The collection plate from the middle of the eighteenth century in Hornbæk Church, North Sjælland, depicts a rather well-dressed standing beggar with slightly bent knees, holding a staff in one hand and a hat or bowl in the other. The inscription reads 'Give and you shall be given to' (*Giver saa skal Eder givis*). A more active beggar is shown on an early eighteenth-century silver plate at the alms box in Sengeløse where a half-naked beggar is limping on one leg through a door way, supported by a crutch under his left arm while holding a bowl in his right (Figure 7.11).[75] The accompanying poem promises God's mercy to the alms giver.

**Figure 7.10** Collection plate from Slangerup Church, Sjælland, c. 1650. © National Museum of Denmark.

A step down the ladder of misery is represented in depictions of a seated or lying beggar, often half-naked, yet still holding a beggar's staff, and with a bowl or a hat in his hand. Two very similar examples are found in Raklev[76] and Kirke Helsinge,[77] both of them from the last quarter of the seventeenth century and possibly painted by the same artist. The abovementioned painting over the alms block in Tingsted depicts a seated beggar with clutches and a begging bowl, yet a closer look reveals a tiny white dog licking his leg as an indication that this beggar belongs to the second large group of motives: Lazarus.

**Figure 7.11** Silver plate from an alms box in Sengeløse Church, Sjælland, from the early seventeenth century. © National Museum of Denmark.

Sometimes the name Lazarus is written beside the picture, as on the collection plate from 1595 in Søborg Church (Figure 7.12). But even without the written name the identification of the seated beggar with two dogs licking his bare legs and two crutches would have been certain. Lazarus is depicted with these recognizable features on several collection plates, e.g. the wood carved reliefs in the Church of St Mary in Helsingør from 1575,[78] in Slangerup from 1578,[79] in Ganløse from 1625 to 1650 (Figure 7.13),[80] in the city church of Sæby from the end of the seventeenth century[81] and in Vig from 1702.[82] On top of the

**Figure 7.12** Two collection plates from 1595 in Søborg Church on Sjælland, one for the church with a depiction of its medieval patron saint, the other for the poor with a picture of Lazarus. © National Museum of Denmark.

costly collection plate which was made for St Nicolai Church in Copenhagen in 1672, above the previously described scene with the good Samaritan, is a wooden sculpture of the lying Lazarus with two dogs. The use of Lazarus for alms boxes and collection plates was a way to connect the actual poor people of the parish to a biblical parallel, and the name Lazarus could in the sixteenth and seventeenth centuries be used simply to denominate a poor person, such as Peder Palladius did several times in his text for pastoral visitations from 1541 where he encourages the parishioners e.g. to 'Pick out a Lazarus whom you can send something good...'[83] The name of Lazarus did not necessarily involve the whole biblical context. So there is an overlap between the contemporary beggars and Lazarus. You might have suggested that the contemporary beggar represented the appeal for donations out of a good, Christian heart, while the Lazarus depictions would promise a divine reward or at least a divine punishment if almsgiving was ignored. But the occasional written texts and poems reveal that there is not such a clear connection between motive and message.

In Borup Church in Jylland there is a rather damaged collection plate with a wood carving of the whole story of Lazarus set on a theatrical stage subdivided by columns. A rich dinner with several participants seated around a table is

**Figure 7.13** Lazarus on the collection plate from Ganløse Church on Sjællland, 1625–1650. © National Museum of Denmark.

found in the centre. Lazarus is lying on the left side of the stairs to the dinner hall in the company of dogs. On the other side of the hall there is a scaring vision of hell including a terrible devil's head in the middle of the blazing fire. Above it all Lazarus rests in the bosom of Abraham surrounded by clouds. In this case the moralizing message cannot be overlooked.

A synthesis of the contending arguments for almsgiving is found in the Church of St Mary in the medieval Danish town Helsingborg (now Sweden). In the west end of the church hangs a painting on wood mounted in a classically inspired, yet rather simplified, Renaissance architectural frame (figure 7.14). Two biblical

**Figure 7.14** Painting over the alms box in Helsingborg St Mary's Church, Scania, present day Sweden, dated 1583. © Poul Grinder-Hansen.

quotations in Latin are painted on the frame. The upper one reads 'blessed is he who considers the poor Psalm. 41.' (*beatvs qvi intellegit svper pavperem XLI Psalm*), the one the pedestal 'Whoever shuts their ears to the cry of the poor will also cry out and not be answered Proverb. 21 1583' (*qvi obtvrat avrem svam ad clamorem pavperis et ipse clamabit et non exavdietvr*, Proverb.21.13). The year 1583 is the date of the painting. The first quotation promises a reward if you give alms, the second one threatens with divine punishment if you do not. The upper part of the central painting is a detailed depiction of the story of Lazarus set in a sixteenth-century Danish context. A rich couple dressed in the latest fashion are sitting at a well-provided table. The golden chains around their necks prove them to be of noble birth, and the round pendant hanging from the chain on the nobleman's breast is undoubtedly meant to be a gold medal with a portrait of the king. Frederik II (1559–1588) who ruled Denmark at that time was known to use such golden chains with portrait medals as gifts to his trusted noblemen.[84] Beside them are scenes shown in a smaller scale. The poor Lazarus sits on the ground beside the table with his hat and a crutch lying behind him. Dogs lick the wounds of the handicapped man who seems to be missing his right hand and left leg, perhaps a war injury. The rich couple do not pay any notice to the beggar. In the background the consequences are shown. The naked soul of the rich man burns in the flames of hell while the poor Lazarus rests in Abraham's bosom in the eternal golden light over the white clouds. The detailed Lazarus story with its focus on divine justice in connection with almsgiving – or rather the lack of almsgiving – goes well with the two verses from the Bible telling of reward and retribution.

The lower part of the painting displays a long inscription in the shape of a poem in Danish. The poem is written as one long text without any attempt to place the rhymes at the end of each line, but the line breaks are marked in the following rendering:

*I CRISTNE SOM GVDT HAFVER GIFVET NOCK*
*BETENCKER DE ARME NOGET I DENE BLOCK*
*SOM LIDE SORRIG SIVGDOM IAMMER OG NØDT*
*ARMODT FATIGDOM OC HVNGER FOR BRØDT*
*BEVISER EDERS TRO MED GIERNINGER SKØNNE*
*DE VIL GVD I HIMMERIGE EDER VEL BELGNE*
(You Christians whom God has given enough
Give something to the poor in this box,
who suffer sorrow, disease, misery and need,
destitution, poverty and hunger for bread.
Prove your faith through wonderful works,
such will God in Heaven repay you well for)

It is clear from the text that the alms post originally stood immediately below the painting ('in this box') so that the painting with its clear message was directly linked to almsgiving. The somewhat primitive, yet expressive painting dares to use two representatives of people from the highest stratum of Danish society as a warning against indifference to the sufferings of the poor. The Danish text manages to combine the various Lutheran arguments for almsgiving: that people who have received sufficient blessings and gifts from God are obliged to pass some of it on to the poor, and that if you prove your faith by giving, God will reward you afterwards.

## Almsgiving in practice

Alms were donated to the poor by people on all levels of society in the centuries after the Lutheran Reformation. The subject is too extensive to cover in the present context, but some examples can be given. Funeral sermons for noble men and women did not only praise the generosity of the deceased in general terms but sometimes gave so precise description of their almsgiving activities that they are likely to be reliable. Chancellor Christian Friis (1556–1616) thus provided for thirty homeless people at his manor Borreby and gave each of them a yearly gift of 12 Daler, he provided for sixteen persons at his other manor, Hagested, along the same lines. Besides that, he distributed 360 Daler annually to homeless people through the learned men and professors of the university.[85] Birgitte Axelsdatter Brahe (1576–1619) to Turebygaard fed everyone who came to her gates, helped orphans with food and clothes and gave alms to poor homeless. In winter she used to talk to the vicar to hear how many deserving poor there were in the neighbouring parish of Dalby while she knew herself all the poor ones in her own parish Tureby, since they received daily help from her. And then she gave the vicar a large sum of money to distribute among the poor. Besides she had wagons sent out with rye as a gift to the poor according to their need.[86]

Account books of kings and noblemen reveal that almsgiving was indeed one of the recurring expenses. Christian III, who was the leading force behind the Lutheran Reformation in Denmark and a devout Lutheran himself, showed the way and demonstrated the expected generosity towards the deserving poor. Coins 'to place on the plate of the poor' in the church was a constant expense in the royal account books, besides coins that were given directly to beggars inside or outside the church.[87] First secretary to king Frederik II Arild Huitfeldt kept an account book from September 1577 to December 1578 which likewise contains many examples of gift-giving, including alms. He rarely placed coins on the collection plates of the churches but apparently preferred to give coins directly to needy persons.[88] The account books of the noblewoman Sophie Brahe, who was married to the pious and learned nobleman Holger Rosenkrantz, testify to a large-scale charitable activity in the years 1627–1640 through gifts to hospitals and poor people in the shape of fixed annual interests from investments as well as direct gifts to individuals and large-scale donations at various occasions, e.g. during the large yearly fair in Viborg.[89]

Outside the circles of king and nobility almsgiving was also an established activity, as convincingly proven by the account books of the hospital in Malmø during the latter half of the sixteenth century.[90] Nobility and wealthy citizens naturally gave the largest single amounts to the hospital but artisans, widows and even unnamed servants such as 'Hans Tinker's maid' donated money as well. Alms collection in the churches produced a further significant income to the hospital. In the year 1588–1589, 47 Mark and 11 shilling were put on the collection plates for the hospital, while the alms box in the church gave no less than 233 Mark and 2 shilling.[91] It seems that the concept of donations to the poor and even gifts in collection plates and alms boxes was not languishing after the Reformation.

So alms were given, but it is hardly possible to search the hearts and reins of sixteenth- and seventeenth-century Danes to find out *why* they gave alms. The arguments that were put forward as well in the sermons of the vicars as on the pictures and inscriptions of alms boxes and collection plates will probably have made an impression. But sometimes you get a sense that the concept of do-ut-des was not quite forgotten. It is noteworthy that when king Christian III in 1558 felt that his death was approaching he had 64.000 two-shillings coins struck for the sole purpose of distribution as alms to the poor during the king's journey through Fyn and Jylland in the summer of 1558.[92] Did he after all feel that a charitable donation would be useful for the salvation of his soul?

Other impulses may have been at stake. The iron-bound alms box in Melby Church in North Sjælland from 1629 stood at the usual spot near the entrance to the door. In 1750 the bishop noted during his pastoral visitation: 'Here is a box in which donations are put (by people coming) from far away when someone is ill or has some kind of trouble.'[93]

## Conclusion

The Lutheran Reformation in Denmark meant a break of the medieval system that considered almsgiving as an efficient way of doing penance which involved a retribution of the charitable gift either through interecessory prayers from the side of the poor recipients or through a subsequent divine indulgence. It was the intention of the Lutheran reformers that almsgiving should be given out of pure love for your neighbour as a natural part of the life of any good Christian. As it appears from Peder Palladius' book of pastoral visitations this ideal could be difficult to realize if there was not at least a tiny reward for the giver involved in the transaction. The depictions and inscriptions on alms boxes or collection plates contain references to this quandary, sometimes stressing the act of giving in accordance with Luther's intention, sometimes pointing to an expectance of a divine reward to the alms giver. The most common motive was Lazarus, sometimes on his own accompanied by dogs, rarely as part of the whole story about the rich man and the beggar, who ended up after life in Hell or Heaven respectively, thus pointing to the aspect of God's divine reaction to human behaviour. This sense of God's direct interference in the life of each human being in order to punish sins and reward good works lived on well into the nineteenth century, although it was not quite in accordance with Luther's description of God's unconditional gifts to mankind.

The arguments for almsgiving seem to have been successful. At least alms were quite as important in the life of well-to-do people and even ordinary citizens and peasants as had been the case in the late Middle Ages. Admittedly it was a subtle distinction if almsgiving paved the way to salvation, or if it was simply the visible result of a true Christian faith. Good works towards the poor made the pious soul of the donator visible, not only to God who could be expected to see and know everything, but even to the surrounding society, which was probably at least as important to people living a society based on honour, rank and social status such as Renaissance Denmark. Inside the churches everyone present could witness the acts of charitable giving when generous people placed their donations in the alms box at the church door or on the collection plate during services.

# Notes

1. Marie-Louise Jørgensen, 'Pengeblokke', in *Synligt og usynligt. Studier tilegnede Otto Norn*, ed. Hugo Johannsen and Hans Stiesdal (Herning: Poul Kristensens Forlag, 1990), 71.
2. Hans Christian Johansen and Søren Kolstrup, 'Dansk fattiglovgivning indtil 1803', in *Dansk velfærdshistorie*, ed. Jørn Henrik Petersen, Klaus Petersen and Niels Finn Christiansen (Odense: Syddansk universitetsforlag, 2010), 161–75.
3. Bo Kristian Holm, *Gabe und Geben bei Luther. Das Verhältnis zwischen Reziprozität und reformatorischer Rechtfertigungslehre* (Berlin: De Gruyter, 2006).
4. E.g. Harald Jørgensen, Studier over det offentlige fattigvæsens historiske udvikling i Danmark i det 19. aarhundrede, Copenhagen: Gyldendal 1940), 3; Svend Cedergreen Bech, *Reformation og renæssance 1533–1596*, Copenhagen: Politikens Forlag 1970), 163–4; Kåre Johannessen, *Magt og mennesker i Danmarks middelalder* (Copenhagen: Turbine, 2020), 357.
5. Troels Dahlerup, 'Den sociale forsorg og reformationen i Danmark', *Historie/Jydske Samlinger*, Ny række, vol. 13, 1979, 194–207; Peter Wessel Hansen, 'Almissekultur og gavegivning i Oplysningstidens København', *Historiske Meddelelser om København* 2007–08, 5–62.
6. Troels Dahlerup, 'Eleemosyne', in *Kulturhistorisk Leksikon for Nordisk Middelalder*, vol. 3., ed. John Danstrup (Copenhagen: Rosenkilde og Bagger, 1956–1978), 583–6.

7 Anne Riising, *Danmarks middelalderlige prædiken* (Copenhagen: Gad, 1969), 203-5.
8 Eamon Duffy, *The Stripping of the Altars. Traditional Religion in England 1400-1580* (New Haven and London: Yale University Press, 1992), 354-66; Per Ingesman, 'Spiritualitet og fromhed i senmiddelalderen', in *Kirkens historie I*, ed. Per Ingesman and Nils Arne Pedersen (Copenhagen: Hans Reitzels Forlag, 2012), 717-45.
9 Jacques le Goff, *The Birth of Purgatory* (Chicago: The University of Chicago Press, 1984), 292-5, 356-7; Susanne Wegmann, *Auf dem Weg zum Himmel. Das Fegefeuer in der deutschen Kunst des Mittelalters* (Köln: Böhlau Verlag, 2003), 12-13.
10 Otto Gerhard Oexle, 'Memoria als Kultur', in *Memoria als Kultur*, ed. Otto Gerhard Oexle (Göttingen: Vandenhoeck & Ruprecht, 1995), 9-78; Arnoud-Jan A. Bijsterveld, *Do ut des. Gift Giving, Memoria, and Conflict Management in the Medieval Low Countries* (Hilversum: Verloren, 2007), 158-87.
11 Dahlerup, 'Eleemosyne', 585.
12 Lasse Bendtsen and Thomas Bertelsen, 'Helligåndskirken Faaborg. Historisk Indledning', in *Danmarks Kirker. Svendborg Amt* (Copenhagen: Nationalmuseet/Syddansk Universitetsforlag, 2014), 612.
13 Joel M. Rosenthal, *The Purchase of Paradise. Gift Giving and the Aristocracy 1307-1485* (London: Routledge and Kegan Paul Limited, 1972), 9-10; Carsten Selch Jensen, 'Byerne og de fattige - den internationale baggrund for den danske udvikling', in *Middelalderbyen*, ed. Søren Bitsch Christensen (Aarhus: Aarhus Universitetsforlag, 2004), 311-2.
14 Natalie Zemon Davis, *The Gift in sixteenth-Century France* (Oxford: Oxford University Press, 2000), 26.
15 Bijsterveld, *Do ut des*, 7.
16 Philippe Jobert, *La notion de donation, Convergences 630-750* (Paris: Societé les belles lettres 1977), 184-5.
17 Dahlerup, 'Den sociale forsorg og reformationen i Danmark', 196-7.
18 Risto Saarinen, *God and the Gift. An Ecumenical Theology of Giving* (Collegeville: Liturgical Press, 2005), 52, 56; Holm, *Gabe und Geben bei Luther* 2006).
19 Saarinen, *God and the gift*, 46.
20 Niels Henrik Gregersen, 'Radical Generosity and the Flow of Grace', in *Word - Gift - Being*, ed. Bo Kristian Holm and Peter Widmann (Tübingen: Mohr Siebeck 2009), 117-44.
21 Paul Douglas Lockhart, *Denmark 1513-1660. The Rise and Decline of a Renaissance Monarchy* (Oxford: Oxford University Press, 2007), 58-77.
22 Martin Schwarz Lausten, *Biskop Peder Palladius og kirken (1537-1560)*. (Copenhagen: Akademisk forlag 1987), 176-7; Peter Henningsen, 'Misericordia. Tiggere, husarme og andre fattige i København, 1500-1800', *Historiske Meddelelser om København* 2005, 22-3.

23 Hans Krongaard Kristensen, *Klostre i det middelalderlige Danmark* (Aarhus: Aarhus Universitetsforlag 2013), 435–8.
24 *Kirkeordinansen 1537/39*, ed. Martin Schwarz Lausten (Copenhagen: Akademisk Forlag 1989).
25 Kristensen, *Klostre i det middelalderlige Danmark*, 436–8.
26 *Kirkeordinansen* 1537/39, 217.
27 Selch Jensen, 'Byerne og de fattige', 295.
28 Christian III's second Copenhagen recess 24 August 1537, see *Danske Kirkelove*, vol. 1, ed. Holger Frederik Rørdam (Copenhagen: G. E. C. Gad, 1883), 13.
29 Frederik II's statutory instrument 27 December 1587 about beggars, see *Danske Kirkelove*, vol. 2, ed. Holger Frederik Rørdam (Copenhagen: G.E.C. Gad, 1884), 420–31.
30 Troels Dahlerup, 'Bidrag til tryglebrevsinstitutionens historie i 17. århundrede', *Bol og By*, 4, Copenhagen 1963, 7–10; *Danske Kirkelove*, vol. 2, 425.
31 Dahlerup, 'Den sociale forsorg og reformationen i Danmark', 198.
32 Peder Palladius, 'Visitatsbog 1541', in *Peder Palladius' Danske Skrifter*, vol. 5, ed. Lis Jacobsen (Copenhagen: H.H. Thiele 1925–1926), 1–240.
33 Palladius, 'Visitatsbog', 73.
34 Palladius, 'Visitatsbog', 76.
35 Palladius, 'Visitatsbog', 127–35.
36 F.J. Billeskov Jansen (ed.), *Humanitas christiana. Mindetaler over Herluf Trolle af Niels Hemmingsen og Christian Machabæus* (Copenhagen: C.A. Reitzel, 1990), 13–30; Elisabet Holst, 'Kvindedyd og kvindedød i danske ligprædikener 1550–1700', in *Svøbt i mår*, ed. Flemming Lundgreen-Nielsen and Hanne Ruus, vol. 1 (Copenhagen: C. A. Reitzel, 1999), 281–5; Grethe Jacobsen, 'Danske ligprædikener 1565–1610. Køn, 'stand og embede i en litterær genre', *Historisk Tidsskrift* 115:1 (2015): 1–36.
37 C. F. Bricka and S.M. Gjellerup, *Den danske Adel i det 16de og 17de Aarhundrede. Samtidige Levnetsbeskrivelser uddragne af trykte og utrykte Ligprædikener, Første Samling* (Copenhagen: Rudolph Klein, 1874–1875), 132.
38 Bricka and Gjellerup, *Den danske Adel i det 16de og 17de Aarhundrede*, 186.
39 Bricka and Gjellerup, *Den danske Adel i det 16de og 17de Aarhundrede*, 85.
40 Lockhart, *Denmark 1513–1660*, 173–8.
41 Bricka and Gjellerup, *Den danske Adel i det 16de og 17de Aarhundrede*, 423.
42 Bricka and Gjellerup, *Den danske Adel i det 16de og 17de Aarhundrede*, 512.
43 Palladius, 'Visitatsbog', 73.
44 *Danske Kirkelove*, vol. 1, 348.
45 Sven Rask, 'Kollekter', in *Dansk Kulturhistorisk Opslagsværk*, vol. 1, ed. Erik Alstrup and Poul Erik Olsen (Højbjerg: Dansk Historisk Fællesforening 1991), 468–9.

46  Gustav Berg, 'Pengeblok', in *Kulturhistorisk Leksikon for Nordisk Middelalder*, ed. John Danstrup (Copenhagen: Rosenkilde og Bagger 1956–78), vol. 13, 172–4.
47  Jørgensen, 'Pengeblokke', 72–7.
48  Palladius, Peder Palladius' Danske Skrifter, vol. 5, 76.
49  Jørgensen, 'Pengeblokke', 79.
50  National Museum of Denmark, Medieval and Renaissance Collection, inventory number D2537.
51  National Museum of Denmark, Medieval and Renaissance Collection, inventory number D1318; David Burmeister, *Danmarks Kirker. Odense Amt. Brændekilde Kirke. Inventar* (Copenhagen: Nationalmuseet/Syddansk Universitetsforlag, 2015), 3035.
52  National Museum of Denmark, Medieval and Renaissance Collection, inventory number D9557.
53  Hugo Johannsen, 'Ganløse Kirke. Inventar', in *Danmarks Kirker. Frederiksborg Amt* (Copenhagen: Nationalmuseet, 1975), 2467.
54  National Museum of Denmark, Medieval and Renaissance Collection, inventory number D3138; Poul Grinder-Hansen, 'Arresthusets Kirkesal II', in *Danmarks Kirker. København* (Copenhagen: Nationalmuseet, 1987), 104.
55  Erik Moltke, 'Tikøb Kirke. Inventar', in *Danmarks Kirker, Frederiksborg Amt* (Copenhagen: Nationalmuseet, 1967), 710.
56  Erik Skov, 'Fuglse Kirke. Inventar', in *Danmarks Kirker, Maribo Amt* (Copenhagen: Nationalmuseet, 1948), 726–7.
57  Christian Axel Jensen, 'Næstved Skt. Peders Kirke. Inventar', in *Danmarks Kirker, Præstø Amt* (Copenhagen: Nationalmuseet, 1935), 103.
58  Otto Norn, 'Tingsted Kirke. Inventar, in *Danmarks Kirker, Maribo Amt* (Copenhagen: Nationalmuseet, 1951), 1323.
59  Erik Moltke, 'Helsingør S. Marie Kirke, Inventar', in *Danmarks Kirker, Frederiksborg Amt* (Copenhagen: Nationalmuseet, 1964), 130.
60  Marie-Louise Jørgensen, 'Slangerup Kirke. Inventar', in *Danmarks Kirker, Frederiksborg Amt* (Copenhagen: Nationalmuseet, 1970), 2076.
61  Erik Moltke, 'Søborg Kirke. Inventar', in *Danmarks Kirker, Frederiksborg Amt* (Copenhagen: Nationalmuseet, 1967), 1137.
62  Erik Moltke, 'Birkerød Kirke. Inventar, in *Danmarks Kirker, Frederiksborg Amt* (Copenhagen: Nationalmuseet, 1967), 952–3.
63  Erik Moltke, 'Sengeløse Kirke. Inventar', in *Danmarks Kirker, Københavns Amt* (Copenhagen: Nationalmuseet, 1944), 563–4.
64  Marie-Louise Jørgensen, 'Rørvig Kirke. Inventar', in *Danmarks Kirker, Holbæk Amt* (Copenhagen: Nationalmuseet, 1990), 2079.
65  Marie-Louise Jørgensen, 'Frederiksborg Slotskirke, Inventar', in *Danmarks Kirker, Frederiksborg Amt* (Copenhagen: Nationalmuseet, 1970), 1849.

66  Jørgensen, 'Slangerup Kirke, Inventar', 2076.
67  Moltke, 'Birkerød Kirke. Inventar', 952–3.
68  Jacobus de Voraigne, *Legenda aurea. Die Heiligenlegenden des Mittelalters*, ed. Matthias Hackemann (Köln: Anaconda Verlag, 2008), 189–95.
69  Jan Steenberg, 'Helligåndskirken', in *Danmarks Kirker, København* (Copenhagen: Nationalmuseet, 1958), 690–2.
70  National Museum of Denmark Medieval and Renaissance Collection, inventory number D9216.
71  Poul Grinder-Hansen, 'Gavegivningens gestik i 1500-tallets Danmark', *Iconographisk Post. Nordisk tidsskrift för bildtolkning* 2015:2: 25–6.
72  Rikke Ilsted Kristiansen, 'Skt. Laurentii Kirke, Kerteminde. Inventar', in *Danmarks Kirker, Odense Amt* (Copenhagen: Nationalmuseet, 1999), 2001–2.
73  Hans Stiesdal, 'Stenløse Kirke. Inventar', in *Danmarks Kirker, Frederiksborg Amt* (Copenhagen: Nationalmuseet, 1975), 2390–1.
74  Erik Moltke, 'Højrup Kirke. Inventar', in *Danmarks Kirker, Tønder Amt* (Copenhagen: Nationalmuseet, 1957), 278.
75  Erik Moltke, 'Sengeløse Kirke. Inventar', 563–4.
76  Marie-Louise Jørgensen, 'Raklev Kirke. Inventar', in *Danmarks Kirker, Holbæk Amt* (Copenhagen: Nationalmuseet, 1986), 1396.
77  Marie-Louise Jørgensen, 'Kirke Helsinge Kirke, Inventar', in *Danmarks Kirker, Holbæk Amt* (Copenhagen: Nationalmuseet, 1982), 1281.
78  Moltke, 'Helsingør S. Marie Kirke. Inventar', 130.
79  Jørgensen, 'Slangerup Kirke. Inventar', 2076.
80  Johannsen, 'Ganløse Kirke. Inventar', 2467.
81  National Museum of Denmark, Medieval and Renaissance Collection, inventory number D6336.
82  Marie-Louise Jørgensen, 'Vig Kirke. Inventar', in *Danmarks Kirker, Holbæk Amt* (Copenhagen: Nationalmuseet 1990), 2467.
83  Palladius, 'Visitatsbog', 127–35.
84  Poul Grinder-Hansen, *Frederik 2. Danmarks renæssancekonge* (Copenhagen: Gyldendal, 2013), 241–2.
85  Bricka and Gjellerup, *Den danske Adel i det 16de og 17de Aarhundrede*, 175.
86  Bricka and Gjellerup, *Den danske Adel i det 16de og 17de Aarhundrede*, 104–5.
87  *Christian III.s Rentemesterregnskaber 1551,1554, 1556, 1557–1558*, I-IV, ed. Søren Balle Søren and Niels Geert Bolwig (Copenhagen: Selskabet for udgivelse af kilder til dansk historie, 1999).
88  Poul Grinder-Hansen, 'Aspects of Gift Giving in Denmark in the Sixteenth Century and the Case of the Rose Flower Cup', *Journal of Medieval History* 37:1 (2011): 114–24.
89  *Sophie Brahes regnskabsbog 1627–40*, ed. Henning Paulsen (Viborg: Jysk Selskab for Historie, Sprog og Litteratur, 1955).

90 Åke Norström, *1500-talets Malmö. Om människor i en stad* (Malmö: 2012), 98–9, 235–6, 268.
91 Norström, *1500-talets Malmö*, 236.
92 Niels Geert Bolwig and Ebbe Yndgaard, *Christian III.s Rentemesterregnskaber. Analyser og oversigter*, Copenhagen 2007. www.kildeskriftselskabet.dk/analyser (accessed 10 January 2021), section: Udbetalinger.
93 Erik Moltke, *Danmarks Kirker, Frederiksborg Amt, Melby Kirke, Inventar* (Copenhagen: Nationalmuseet, 1970), 1628.

8

# Taken objects and the formation of social groups in Hamburg, Gdańsk and Lübeck

Philipp Höhn

In his *Chronicles* Jean Froissart recounted an intriguing anecdote that supposedly took place in in 1382, in the aftermath of the Battle of Roosebeke, when the French had defeated the Flemish towns under Philipp van Artevelde. On this occasion, so Froissart, the French king Charles VI (r. 1380–1422) was told about the existence of a chapel in the Church of St Mary in Kortrijk, in which five hundred spurs of French knights that the Flemish had killed eighty years earlier were on display. As Froissart would have it, the king decided that the Flemish should pay for these actions and burnt Kortrijk to the ground. These spurs and their ostentatious display in the Church of St Mary are one among many examples of spoils that were exhibited as trophies in late medieval cities in Europe. The *Banderia Prutenorum*, the flags of the Teutonic Order taken by the Polish and Lithuanians in the Battle of Grunwald/Tannenberg in 1410, which hung in the churches of Crakow and Vilnius for nearly 400 years, and the harbour chain of Pisa, which the Genoese seized in 1290, broke into its links and exhibited on municipal and religious buildings all over the town are but the most famous examples of this practice.[1] This chapter examines such ostentatiously displayed spoils as a particular modality of circulating objects, and it inquires into the role that these objects played in the constitution of social groups in these towns. Its central argument is that the urban elites of north European towns repeatedly invoked their shared experience and practice of violence as a way to constitute themselves and the towns in which they lived as coherent communities. As such, this chapter investigates the social dimensions of taking

I owe great thanks to Georg Jostkleigrewe and Klaus Krüger for discussing my ideas, to Juhan Kreem and Gadi Algazi who gave me very helpful advices and especially to my courses taught in the summer terms of 2019 and 2020 at the University of Halle-Wittenberg.

and of taken objects in particular; it inquires how these objects could be used to both question and evoke social bonds.²

As is well known, endowments and gifts played a crucial role in the formation of social groups in medieval towns. Visitors to such towns in norther Europe encountered the self-representation of urban elites in objects scattered throughout the urban landscape. Just consider the different gifts and endowments that contemporaries would have been able to observe as they entered fourteenth-century Lübeck through the town's northern gates. In front of the gates visitors would have passed a chapel that the town council had endowed after the Black Death. In this chapel visitors would also have been able to see a set of relics of Thomas Beckett that two members of the council had received from King Edward (r. 1327–1377) on the intervention of the bishops of Herford, Durham and Lincoln and the archbishop of Canterbury in 1375: a small piece of a bone, a part of the robe that Beckett had supposedly worn when he was killed and a piece of shrub that had allegedly turned green in the midst of Winter during his martyrdom. In 1396 the council added to this display the corpse of one of the children that Herod had murdered and a painting of the confrontation between emperor Frederik Barbarossa (r. 1147/55–1190) and pope Alexander III (1159–1181).³ Immediately after the gate any visitors would have seen the Dominican abbey of St Mary Magdalen, which the town council had endowed after its victory over the Danish king Waldemar II (r. 1202–1241) in 1227. Further along their way into the center of town they would have seen the hospital of the Holy Spirit that a group of rich merchants had set up in the early thirteenth century BCE. While many of these buildings and objects were indeed gifts and endowments, some objects that the urban elite put on display in Lübeck had also been taken by force. By thus pointing to the violence that these urban elites practised, these objects confound the image of the supposedly peaceful merchant elite that ruled these towns. As I hope to show, both the experience and the practice of violence played a crucial part in how these elites represented themselves; in the late Middle Ages, then, not only noble warriors but also urban elites used violence as a way to articulate and shape their identities.

Concretely put, the chapter analyses the histories of three taken objects that were set up in churches in Gdańsk, Hamburg and Lübeck respectively. As I hope to show, these three objects⁴ – just like endowments or donations on display in these towns – were of crucial importance for the practices of individual and collective *memoria* within these towns. These objects existed physically; they were visible in the urban space. At the same time, I contend, these objects can also readily be understood as 'imagined objects'.⁵ They and their violent histories were socially interpreted, memorialized, performed and narrated. As a result, we should not only imagine that violent seizures were omnipresent in the economic and legal practices of urban elites in Northern Europe;⁶ such actions also played an important part in the formation of social groups and the negotiation of power and status in urban contexts.

This chapter departs from recent discussions in the rich field of studies on gift-giving and other premodern economic practices that were not market exchange.⁷ Following a suggestion by Jan Rüdiger,⁸ I see practices of taking as a complementary phenomenon to the practices of late medieval gift-giving.⁹ According to Gadi Algazi gift-giving was not a prototype for archaic economic and social interaction but a configuration and social negotiation of a broad set of transactions beyond the realm of market-exchange.¹⁰ While this argument makes transactions and their social meanings a promising area of historical research, practices of taking have rarely been investigated from this perspective. However, as I hope to show, acts of taking created social bonds comparable to those that arose from gift-giving or endowment practices, and as such these bonds were crucial for the coherence of social groups in late medieval towns. As I hope to show, the groups that were constituted around these objects gained at least some of their coherence from violence, both practised and suffered; the objects in question and the authenticating powers that their materiality held helped these group narrate and memorialize this violence and thus also themselves.¹¹ In short, taken objects and their materiality helped urban elites in northern European towns to represent themselves as 'communities of violence', as communities that jointly suffered and perpetrated violence – a dynamic that has arguably not yet received the scholarly attention it deserves.

## Hamburg in 1525: Spoils, executions and the staging of the town as a community of violence

In 1525 an urban fleet under the command of Ditmar Koel and Simon Perseval returned to Hamburg from Frisia. Koel and Perseval brought with them many captives, among them a certain Claus Kniphof, whom they displayed prominently as part of their triumphal entry into the city. The processions from the port and the ensuing revelry lasted several days. The city celebrated the victory over Kniphof and his comrades at Greetsiel in Frisia by staging large-scale displays of violence and executions. Koel and Perseval had already executed many of their captives back in Frisia; they were sea-robbers, and this was their adequate punishment – or so they claimed. In Hamburg they now grouped the remainder of Kniphof's crew by rank, tied them up with ropes and led through the town while musicians played. Two days later they brought Kniphof's banner that they had captured in a procession to the cathedral. This episode nicely illustrates the interplay between the narration and justification of violence and plunder on the one hand and the self-representation of urban social groups on the other. The banner that Koel and Perseval brought back could be conceptualized as a trophy, not least in a contemporary chronicle written by Adam Tratzinger:

> In this year [1526] Clawes Kniphof took to the sea with four ships that king Christian and the Burgundians had provided to him. He did great harm to the common merchant from the Hanse towns. Thus the Hamburgers equipped four ships around Pentecost. Those ships came from the river Elbe to search for Kniphof, but they came back to the Elbe, because they did not find him. The city council equipped them once again around 3rd October and added two smaller vessels. These ships found Kniphof in the eastern arm of the Ems [the mouth of a river in Northern Frisia], they fought him with strength, and they captured him together with 162 of his men, whom they all brought to Hamburg. Kniphof and 73 of them were beheaded, their heads were speared and exhibited on stacks

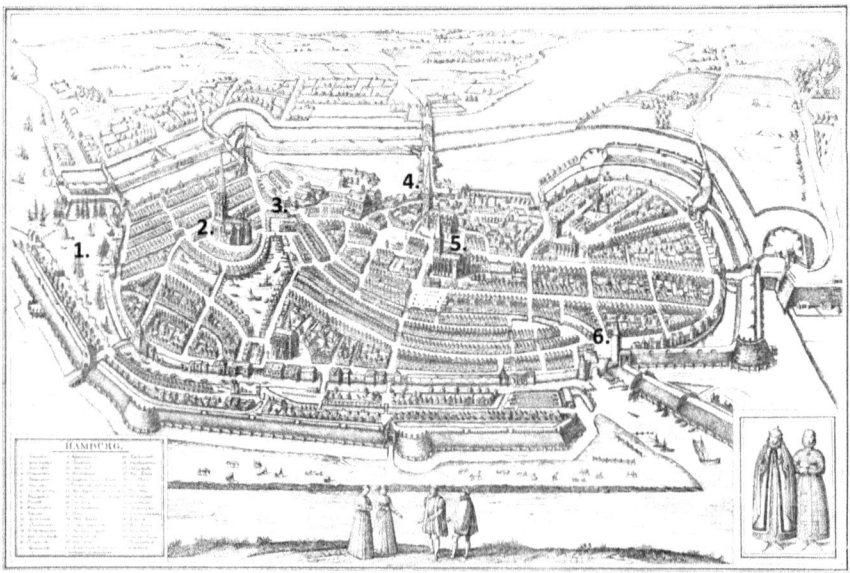

**Figure 8.1** Map of Hamburg, originally from around 1570. 1. Port, 2. St Nicolai, 3. Townhall, 4. St. Petri, 5. Cathedral, 6. Winsertor. © Wikimedia Commons (public domain).

at the Brook [the island on which the execution took place] and their banners where hung up in the tower over the pulpit in Hamburg.[12]

Bernd Gyseke, the cities' scribe for the *Bierprobe* and a further writer of a chronicle, also mentioned Kniphof's banner: 'Anno 1525 on the Thursday before All Saint's Day (26 October), Kniphof's banner was hung over the pulpit in the cathedral.' Kniphof and his crew fared less well; the council of Hamburg executed them as sea-robbers, although Kniphof's father, a mayor of Malmö, had interceded for them.[13] The council immediately started to appropriate the plunder including the captured men that the two captains had taken: they exhibited the objects in the building and organized processions of the captives through the town accompanied with pipers and drummers and five urban banners.[14] The treatment of Kniphof, his crew and their possessions in early sixteenth-century Hamburg would thus appear to be prototypical for the dynamic outlined above: the taking of objects and its interpretation through which social ties were invoked. The exhibition of the spoils and the slaughter aimed to include the whole urban community in the acts of taking and triumphing. From our records, we can hardly decide which exact way the procession made through the town, but according to one of the first maps of Hamburg (*c*. 1570), we can make some plausible suggestions. We know from Gyseke that the captives were led through the city from the port to the townhall, probably passing the parish churches of St Nicolai and St Petri and the cathedral to the Winsertor, where they were held as prisoners.[15] The procession with Kniphof's banner probably also passed the important parish churches of St Nicolai and St Petri, the townhall, the hop market and the central market – the economic and political symbolical centre of the town.[16] The city's successful violence was finally performed in the cathedral. The cathedral was not only the formal seat of the archbishop of Bremen who was also the bishop of Hamburg, but also the central church in which the council held its rituals and memorial practices. In the cathedral relics of Matthew, the evangelist and apostle, of Saint Laurence, Saint Sigismund of Burgundy, and Saint Eustache, and parts of the Holy Cross were on display.[17] In the central choir contemporaries could also see the cenotaph of pope Benedict V (r. 964), who had been exiled by emperor Otto I (r. 962–973) and died in Hamburg in 965/6 and remained an important point of reference for the urban elites even after reformation, which started in Hamburg during the 1520s.[18] Within this memorial context Kniphof's banner was exhibited over the pulpit, which became the focal point of the liturgy during the Reformation because of the rising importance of the sermon in liturgy. In short, the banner and its capture seem to have been staged in the centre of Hamburg's sacral and political topography.

By engineering this *mise en scène* in 1525 the council of Hamburg construed the town as a community united around violence, as a fictive unit that stood to suffer violence at the hands of pirates but also joined in committing such violence to ward off the threat that emanated from these pirates. By this point the chancelleries of Hanse towns had been invoking threatening heterotopias of 'pirates' and their supporters that had to be fought in defence of the 'common merchant' (*gemene copman*) for about one hundred years.[19] Behind this narrative, however, lurked a set of strategic interests that Hamburg's leading burghers had in Frisia and beyond. To understand these interests, some details about Hans Kniphof and his supposed 'piracy' are required.

In a document from 15 August 1525, Kniphof described himself as 'captain of his royal majesty of Denmark'.[20] Just like Hamburg's designation of him as 'sea-robber', this was a controversial claim because at the time Kniphof was acting in the service of Christian II (r. 1513–1523/59) – he was carrying out Christian's feuds – after the Danish Council of the Realm had deposed Christian as king in 1523. In 1525, when Hamburg's triumphal celebrations took place, Christian II was in the Netherlands, where he had found support with his brother-in-law, emperor Charles V and Margarethe, the stadtholder of the Netherlands.[21] From there he carried out feuds against Frederik I (r. 1523–1544), the man whom the Danish Council of the Realm had made his successor, and these were the feuds in which Kniphof acted as his agent. After his capture Kniphof repeatedly invoked the privateering licences that Christian II had granted him as well as the guarantee of safe conduct he had received from the count of Eastern Frisia.[22] While these legal arguments were to no avail, they do provide the background against which we can begin to understand the enmity between Kniphof and Hamburg, but also the role, the banner had in legitimizing the expeditions of the city council against Kniphof.

This legitimation was crucial for at least two reasons, which resulted from struggles for the control over economic and political power in the North Sea region in 1525. Firstly, the battle cry to fight alleged pirates allowed the council to persecute its economic interests and to legitimate its intervention in the conflicts over the Danish crown. Frederik I formally was the territorial lord of Hamburg and the town nominally feuded in his name.[23] Self-interest however very likely also motivated the decision of the council to side its lord. Hamburg and Lübeck were keen to concentrate the trade between the Baltic and the North Sea onto the land route between both towns and away from sea route via the Øresund, which Christian II had privileged.[24] Lastly, the merchant elites of Hamburg had also economic interests in Frisia, where Kniphof was under the safe conduct of the count.²⁵ Gyseke even argued that the expeditions against Kniphof potentially allowed to intervene against the count of Frisia. He mentioned that the burghers demanded that the count of Frisia should be treated like Kniphof, since the receiver of stolen goods ('heler') should be treated like the stealer ('steler'). Overall, then, it seems safe to say that the town's claim to pacify the sea overlapped with the structural interests of its elite. As Hamburg ramped up its propagandistic efforts against Kniphof, a range of circumstances conspired to ultimately make even Christian II renounce his agent.²⁶ Charles V, Margarethe and the Dutch towns distanced themselves from Kniphof, essentially delivering him to the attacks of Hamburg, and in 1525 Christian II followed suit: he denied that he had licensed Kniphof, and in September of that year Kniphof was publicly declared a sea-robber in Antwerp.²⁷ Thus the claims of Hamburg, controversial though they may have been, ultimately prevailed. Kniphof was stigmatized as a pirate and the ostentatious exhibition of the spoils in the religious centre of the town manifested the actions of the council as legitimate counter-piracy for the common good of the town as a sacred commune.

Secondly, in Hamburg itself these propagandistic claims and the spectacular performance of the captured seamen and the spoils very likely were intended to have a stabilizing effect. For one, in the decades before 1525 urban revolts and riots had taken place in Hamburg; the position of the council in Hamburg had not been uncontested. In 1483, for instance, riots had broken out, when members of the city council were suspected of hoarding grain at a time of food shortage with a view to selling at profit at a later stage, not least by participating in the forbidden Iceland-trade. Furthermore, rumours that members of the council had prolonged expensive feuds because they had equipped the warships used to carry them out were also circulating at the time.²⁸ The well-edited correspondence between the councils of Hamburg and Lübeck around Kniphof and the attacks contains mentions of rumours circulating in the town – rumours that could potentially question the local government through its subversive subtexts.²⁹ In the early sixteenth century the Reformation provided yet another source of instability in Hamburg. In 1525 the council was still Catholic but by 1529 the first Lutheran church order was declared in the town. Also, Stephan Kempe, Kniphof's confessor, was a prominent protagonist of the Reformation in Hamburg,³⁰ and Dietmar Koel, who captured Kniphof, was another proponent of the religious reform. Two years later, he was elected as a councillor, and in 1548 he became burgomaster.³¹ Because Christian II himself was an early proponent of the Lutheran faith, Kniphof's execution did not align completely with confessional battlelines. At the same time, it seems safe to say that it took place during a period when Hamburg, the city and its government, was embroiled in religious and economic conflicts.[32] Recent studies on the ways how urban elites dealt with religious objects and memorial practices that had become obsolete due to the Reformation have stressed the pragmatism by which urban elites still referred to Catholic practices to stabilize its power or created new according to the new faith to represent the social hierarchy in the sacral space. Because of the Lutheran networks that I have sketched and the prominent place over the pulpit, I would put the exhibition of Kniphof's banner into the context of the Reformation, yet not as subversive act, but as a stabilizing and inclusive act, connecting the legitimation and identity of the urban community as a just community fighting its enemies with the new confession. Within this context the celebrations and staging of the victory over Kniphof performed the town as one unified community, rallying around a common threat and uniting in the fight against it. The performance of the town's violence in the processions, the exhibitions of the plunder and the staged executions provided avenues for creating inclusive social bonds by invoking an 'imagined community', or more specifically an 'imagined community of violence'.[33]

Three surviving songs written shortly after the event testify to this dynamic.[34] Jelle Haemers and Jan Dumolyn have stressed the importance of songs for rebellious speech in communal communication.[35] The three songs in question, however, formulated no subversive ideas but legitimized the town's government and its violence because – so the songs claimed – Hamburg had defended the interest of the 'common merchant', a vague, yet inclusive collective singular. The songs appeal to solidarity within the urban community but also between towns in general, the autonomy of which the princes supposedly threatened. Overall, the composers of these songs – one anonymous, the second Stephan Kempe, Kniphof's confessor, and the third Hans von Göttingen, who had also written a song about Martin Pechlin, another partisan of Christian II, killed by the *Bergenfahrers* from Lübeck – they all agreed that Kniphof had to be executed as a sea-robber.

To illustrate, in Göttingen's song the Hamburgers attacking Kniphof shouted: 'Slaughter them all. Stab them, beat them all over board and let none of them survive. They brought many to poverty. May God forgive them.'[36] In Kempe's song, the connection between a divine authorized urban community and its just violence dominates. Kempe, who had been Kniphof's confessor, had pity with the alleged sea-robber, but he did not question the council's verdict: The town had to sharpen its sword to protect itself and the 'common merchant' against the nobility and thus took the 'right of the sword'.[37] Instead, he depicted Hamburg as a peace-loving town of great honour and stylized the body of Kniphof as a trophy of the city's conquest. In Kempe's depiction, Kniphof played his role well in the theatre of the city's violence. Sentenced to death, he showed no fear and accepted the verdict. Then, he was guided again through the city. He took the sacraments with peace in his heart before Saint Catherine's church and pleaded for forgiveness as a faithful sinner.[38] Kempe and Kniphof thus acted according to an ideal that emerged in the context of the Reformation, wherein the task of the confessor was to admonish the convicted to act as a good Christians and 'to perform a felicitous execution'[39] which did not threat the social order but expressed God's mercy instead. Kempe emphasized that Kniphof's life was taken by the sword, but that his soul went to God.[40] He thus connected the legitimation of the city's violence with Kniphof's execution as a humble sinner. In Kempe's example, materiality was crucial to create a 'community of violence'. However, rather than highlighting the spoils, he focused on Kniphof's body, whom he performed as a trophy demonstrating the rightful and divinely ordained urban violence.

In sum, in 1525 in Hamburg urban elites used the taking of objects and of lives to create and reinforce social bonds. In particular, they used the public display of spoils such as the banner and the public execution of enemies and opponents as a means to unify the town around the threat of violence and the claim to have jointly perpetrated such violence. The fact that a set of strategic interests, both internal and external, on the part of Hamburg, its merchants and its council underpinned these performances does nothing to lessen their historical importance. While the mass execution of Kniphof and his associates was profoundly tied up with their stigmatization as sea-robbers and pirates, the display of banners and other taken objects was a widespread phenomenon in late medieval political culture. In the case study from Hamburg we can trace that flags became trophies through a range of practices, including processions, displays and songs, which all gave these objects meaning. It is however difficult to estimate whether these objects encapsuled its stories and told it to the following generations. Although Tratzinger and Gyseke memorated the story in their chronicles, I have found no evidence that the flag was part of any post-Reformation civic ceremony, although its prominent place might suggest this. This speculation illustrates however a crucial point: the objects themselves were hardly meaningful without being interpreted in relation to memorial practices and other objects. Through these acts of interpretation the objects received a new role: their materiality and the authenticity it invoked allowed these objects to serve as witnesses and proof of the city's history and identity.[41] The following example from sixteenth-century Gdańsk, where the taking of one particular object arguably was forgotten and elided, helps to underline the importance of such memorial practices as a precondition for the materiality of objects to unfold its power.

## Gdańsk before and after 1550: The story of an altar repressed and remembered

Around 1635 Bartholomäus Milwitz portrayed the interior of St Mary's church in Gdańsk in a well-known painting (see figure 8.2). An altar depicting the last judgement in bright tones dominates the picture while the other objects in the church fade in the background. The history of this altar is as complex, as it is tantalizing. Commissioned by Angelo Tani, a business partner of the Medici, for a chapel in Fiesole, the Flemish master Hans Memling (c. 1435–1494) painted 'The Last Judgement' in the second half of the fifteenth century. In 1473 the painting was placed on a galley owned by Tommaso Portinari, the lead banker of the Medici branch in Bruges, which sailed under the flag of the Duke of Burgundy. At the time the Anglo-Hanseatic War (1467–1474) was underway, and as part of this conflict a group of mercenaries from Gdańsk under the leadership of Paul Benenke seized the galley of Tommaso Portinari together with Memling's painting that was on it, and brought them to Gdańsk.[42] 'The Last Judgement' remains in this city to this day. In nineteenth- and twentieth-century Gdańsk, Memling's masterpiece became a focal point of urban and national pride.[43] By contrast, in late medieval and early modern Gdańsk the painting garnered no comparable attention; only a few people recounted its history. Examining these accounts, as I will go on to do, illustrates how the relationship between taken objects and social groups could not only be narrated and commemorated but also masked, repressed and elided, when these taken objects were potential 'dangerous' trophies, when they were not includable into historical narratives or even endangered the coherence of urban elites like 'The Last Judgement' probably did in the late fifteenth century.

In the second half of the sixteenth century Stenzel Bornbach, the town's scribe of the Great Mill, compiled several chronicles and historical notices from Gdańsk. While copying out the texts, Bornbach added what he found in other manuscripts to those that he copied. In a passage that Caspar Weinreich, a shipmaster, had written at the end of the fifteenth century, Bornbach added a description of the prominent object on Milwitz's painting. Bornbach's witness

**Figure 8.2** St Mary's church in Gdańsk by Bartholomäus Milwitz (*c.* 1635). © Wikimedia Commons (public domain).

Weinreich was interested in Beneke's attack on the galley, but he did not mention the altar that had been captured as part of the attack. As a seaman, he focused on the monetary value of the plunder and was fascinated by Beneke's ship, the 'Peter von Danzig,' supposedly 'a great caravel'. By contrast, in the late sixteenth century Bornbach connected Beneke's attack on the Florentine galley with the altar:

'On this galley there was the tablet, that is set on St. George's altar, a beautiful, old, and artfully painting of the last judgement. Down, by the right wing of the angel, there shall be written the name of the master: Jacob and ANNO DONI. CCCLXVII.'[44]

Here we can begin to see that taken objects cannot be understood in their own right; instead they need to be analysed as part of an 'assemblage,'[45] as part of a network of objects, practices and texts, in which the object was integrated and interpreted. In his writings Bornbach included the altar in a new network of meaning. Nearly hundred years after the attack, he was one of the first men on record to connect the altar with the attack in 1473. We can only speculate how the altar piece came to Gdańsk. It seems likely that the syndicate, which had bought Beneke's ship, shortly before the attack, donated it. It was exhibited in the chapel of the St George-brotherhood. Probably the members of the syndicate, all members of the brotherhood, donated the painting for the chapel.[46] But this is not mentioned in contemporary sources. According to the editions in the *Scriptores rerum Prussicarum*, only two other texts connected the painting with Beneke, the chronicle of Christoph Beyer (1458–1518) and the chronicle of Georg Mehlman (1521–1566).[47] The chronicle of Beyer has not survived in the original version. Instead, the editor Theodor Hirsch posited that Beyer had been one of Weinreich's sources – a conclusion at which he arrived based on Bornbach's copy of Weinreich. Hirsch's attribution of the story about the altar to Beyer is thus speculative and can be neither verified nor falsified. Quite likely, then, Mehlman's account dating to the middle of the sixteenth century was the source that Bornbach copied into the chronicles of Beyer and Weinreich.[48] More generally, I am inclined to think that chronological anecdotes connecting the altar piece with Paul Beneke's attack did not exist before the middle of the sixteenth century. Aby Warburg dated the creation of the altar to 1467. His main argument was the identity of the donors, who were depicted on the outward-facing tables of the altar.[49] Since Mehlman and Bornbach focused their dating efforts on 1367 on the Roman numeral written by an angel's wing, it seems likely by the time that they were writing – almost one hundred years after the object's creation and subsequent seizure – many aspects of its history were not known in Gdańsk. Arguably, some parts of this history had been actively elided or forgotten, before Bornbach wrote it into the 'assemblage', and as will be shown below, this probably happened for good reason.

In 1473, when the altar arrived in Gdańsk, its status as a taken object was profoundly problematic. For one, the violent seizure of sacral objects posed problems for their integration into liturgical processes.[50] Secondly, and maybe even more importantly: despite nationalistic historians' attempts to instrumentalize Benecke's actions, this seizure was not an act of national heroism; instead, it gave rise to a diplomatic problem.[51] Already Bernd Pawest, Beneke's predecessor as a captain of the ship, had quarrelled with his seamen about their pay. The attack on the galley was a consequence of a structural lack of resources in medieval warfare, and from a legal point of view it was at best controversial. The claims and counterclaims surrounding the seizure of the galley only came to an end in 1499 when the city of Bruges agreed to pay a compensation to Portinari.[52] As part of the conflict, clerics and pilgrims from

Lübeck were arrested in Florence, and the pope excommunicated the city of Gdańsk.[53] The city councils of most Hanseatic towns feared that they too might be held accountable. Consider the council of Hamburg, which prevented Beneke and his financiers from pawning off their plunder in the town so as to avoid liability for his actions. Similarly, the city council of Lübeck forbade the burghers from making deals with the plunderers when they relocated to Stade in the territory of the archbishop Bremen.[54] That being said, Beata Mozejko has argued that in spite of these efforts much of the plunder will have made its way into the hands of Lubeckians, albeit through clandestine channels.[55] Gdańsk's council was keen to distance itself from these actions.

Unlike in Hamburg in 1525, then, in the case of Beneke's seizure of the Medici galley, political circumstances did not conspire to render these actions widely acceptable. Instead, the representatives of the Hanse towns had to go to great lengths to excuse the behaviour of Beneke and his financiers from Gdańsk. During the Anglo-Hanseatic peace negotiations in Utrecht in 1474 they apologized for having been unable to prevent the seizure from taking place while also excusing and legitimizing it. They argued that in the fog Beneke had not been able to identify the Burgundian flag and that the attack had happened in the waters of the English king, with whom the Hanseatic cities had been at war.[56] In short, this was not a context in which the city council of Gdańsk or any of its members stood to gain much from memorializing Beneke's actions by purposefully parading and staging any of the objects that he had taken. Furthermore, the political changes in Gdańsk in the second half of the fifteenth century very likely also played a part in eliding the altar's presence and its violent history in the city's memorial practices.

At the end of the fifteenth century, Gdańsk's urban space was shaped by spoils of war that were readily interpreted as an 'assemblage' of trophies and objects commemorating the town's violence. Those material objects were crucial for the self-awareness of the urban corporations and the representation of their social status after the Thirteen Years War 1454–1466, in which Gdańsk had changed its overlord from the Teutonic Order to the Polish king.[57] As a result of this conflict, the former common frame of historical narratives among the urban elites was contested. The St George-brotherhood, which shared its patron with the Order, commemorated the common struggle of the Order and the burghers against the 'heathens.' Other social groups however commemorated the fight against the Order. In the chapel of the Holy Cross in St Mary's the burghers of Gdańsk could admire a relic of the Holy Cross, which had been taken from Marienburg's castle chapel to Gdańsk in 1457, after the mercenaries of the Order gave the castle to the

Prussian estates. After a fire in 1477, the Artushof was rebuilt on the foundations of the Great Hall of the destroyed castle of the Order in Gdańsk and some of the pillars were reused. This set the re-erection of this central meeting place of merchants in Gdańsk explicitly into the context of the victory over the former territorial lord. The corporation of the 'Marienburger Bank' set up in Artushof even commemorated this fight by celebrating the conquests of Marienburg in 1457 and 1460. In the Artushof they could also see a painting depicting the siege of Marienburg as well as weapons of slaughtered and captured knights of the Order and a sail of the Order taken in a battle in 1463, which was also mentioned in a poem defaming the Teutonic Order. In 1487 the 'Marienburger Bank' even came into conflict with the St George-brotherhood because the latter positioned some of the armors in a way which hindered visitors to see the painting of the siege of Marienburg.[58] For Gdańsk's elites violence was a pivotal part of the city's history. However, memorial practices and rituals were shifting in the last quarter of the fifteenth century and they were conflicting between a long tradition evoking the fight against pagans together with the knights of the Teutonic Order and the new narrative of self-confident town fighting for its right against the tyranny of the Order. This might give an additional explanation why 'The Last Judgement' was not performed as a trophy of the town's violence and fall into oblivion. It did not fit into any of these two frameworks.

In the second half of the sixteenth century, Stenzel Bornbach and Georg Mehlmahn were in a different situation when they wrote the altar piece into the city's history of Gdańsk and into a network of objects and texts. The city was at its height of power, an economic and cultural hub in the Baltic, and enjoyed great autonomy within the Polish kingdom.[59] The conflict with the Teutonic Order had lost its relevance. In Gdańsk the Lutheran faith spread quickly even though the Polish king only recognized it in the city in 1557.[60] This environment allowed contemporaries to integrate the altar into an anti-Catholic narrative. Lübeck's chronicler Reimar Kock (†1569) was one of the first to integrate if not the altar itself but Beneke's attack on the galley into such narrative. He was a supporter of the Reformation in Lübeck in the 1530s and was a Lutheran pastor on a warship in the wide-reaching, disastrous military actions of Jürgen Wullenweber in the Count's Feud between 1534 and 1536. In his chronicle, finished after 1550, he depicted Beneke as a tough 'German sea-hero,' who defeated the arrogant (and Catholic) Italians.[61] This narrative was not only about the fight against Catholics. When Kock, Mehlmann and Bornbach wrote, the political landscape of the Baltic had changed fundamentally. By the middle of the sixteenth century memories of past violent actions by members of urban elites also served as important reference points in these urban elites' current struggles against territorial lords more generally.

Bornbach probably shared this interpretation of Beneke's attack on the galley, and he also emphasized that the family to which he was now connected by marriage had played a prominent part in this fight. Bornbach was a son of a Warsaw burgomaster and married the daughter of a Gdańsk city councillor.[62] He had married into the family of Christoph Beyer, whose wife was probably a godchild of the wife of Paul Beneke.[63] In the sixteenth century the boundaries between urban chronicles (*Chronik*), the chronicles of patrician families and houses (*Hausbücher*) and merchant accounts (*Handelsbücher*) were fluid.[64] Bornbach integrated this family history into an urban chronicle, and his text had probably several functions; it reflected individual and collective practices of accounting, legitimation and historical narration. His compiled texts transformed a taken object into a trophy that featured prominently in the town's history of violence, which just so happened to also feature friends and relatives of the family into which he had married. The altar still on display in St Mary's church could now be read as a visible and tangible testament to this history. Its materiality helped Bornbach authenticate his narrative.

What conclusions, then, might we draw from this history of Memling's altar in the memorial landscape of Gdańsk? As Michael Jucker has suggested, taken objects could be separated from the history of their violent appropriation only with great difficulty.[65] However, the history of Memling's altar illustrates that histories of violent appropriation could be forgotten or elided by those who saw these objects in daily life. Without explicit practices of memorialization and their integration into the 'assemblage', their stories could lose prominence, and at times this was exactly what was desired. More generally, 'The Last Judgement' from Gdańsk confronts us with a methodological problem. In our written sources we find either the narrative appropriation of things, the intended elision of an object's history or the forgetfulness of contemporaries.[66] The latter two went hand in hand quite readily. In the first case objects were truth-makers; they validated the authenticity of stories told.[67] In these contexts they received their meaning in a network of practices, including (written) texts. Regarding the formation of groups the example of the 'Last Judgement' does, however, highlight a crucial point: taken objects could not only manifest and create groups; they could also pose a challenge to the coherence of the urban community itself.[68] This was a consequence of the fact that they had to be integrated into often vague yet conflicting narratives and into networks of objects and texts. The last case study will elucidate still more aspects of this dynamic.

## Lübeck before 1942: A patchwork of plunder

In 1942 a British bombardment heavily damaged St Mary's church in Lübeck. While many of the art objects were evacuated beforehand, some were destroyed together with the church.[69] Photographs from the pre-war period show an interior of the church that differed wildly from the architectural purity that is on display today. Overall, signs of violence and warfare from different periods were omnipresent. For instance, flags from the wars against Napoleon hung in the choir. But also older trophies were on display. Over the chapel of the *Bergenfahrer* corporation, the merchants trading with Bergen in Norway, the flag of Martin Pechlin, a partisan of Christian II could be admired. It had been brought to Lübeck in 1526 when *Bergenfahrer* killed Pechlin, drowned some of his crewmembers and executed the survivors. In chronicles and material objects, the Bergenfahrer represented themselves as strong 'pirate-hunters' who commemorated their members and seamen who had died at sea with votive paintings and messes.[70] The different flags and banners in the church were related to other taken objects that had been placed there, of which more below. As the vivid sixteenth-century chronicles of Lübeck's burghers show, such objects also featured in annual processions and celebrations in the city.

The case study of Lübeck shows an additional dynamic to the 'assemblages' studied in the previous sections. It reveals that such taken objects were part of networks or ensembles of objects, texts, practices and interpretations that were not intentionally created and changed their social meanings. Instead, they emerged from overlapping and sometimes even conflicting interpretations of urban violence, which created narratives that legitimized different configurations of power. The example from Lübeck thus sheds light on the 'social life' of these objects in relation to other objects. A social history approach towards circulating objects can hardly be a history of objects but has to be a history of the practices of appropriations, negotiations and interpretations.[71] These happened in a network with other objects, practices and texts. One can hardly understand them without contextualizing them in a reconstructed topography of objects. Within these 'patchworks' of objects, texts and practices different, ambiguous or even contradictory voices overlapped as they told and re-told anecdotes that framed the representation and self-conception of social groups and allowed the urban community to imagine itself as a unified community.

The prime example for such ever-changing patchworks is a banner hung in the choir of St Mary's, which was a patchwork in itself. The city's records mention its existence for the first time in 1571, when the council asked a painter to repair it.[72]

As it was destroyed in the fire in 1942, we rely on a pre-war photograph to describe its appearance (Figure 8.3). The banner was composed of three parts that were stitched together. One part depicted St Mary and St Jacob. The second was divided into quarters by a cross comparable to the Dannebrog, the Danish national flag. In each quarter the coats of arms of different political powers were on display – of the Danish, Swedish and Norwegian realms, which were united in the Calmar Union in 1397, and of Erik of Pomerania (1397/1412–1439/59), who was the first ruler of that Union. The third part of the banner showed two red plates, separated by a white line; probably it was younger than the other two.[73] We do not know how this banner came into existence or how it made its way to Lübeck. This circumstance did not stop late nineteenth-century scholars from elaborating their interpretations of the object – interpretations that in themselves constituted yet another network of texts, practices and interpretations.

In a period of nationalistic tensions between Denmark and the German Empire the flag inspired the phantasies of both German and Danish scholars. Erich Christian Werlauff (1781–1871), historian from Copenhagen saw the banner as the oldest surviving Dannebrog and as a crucial part of Danish national heritage. According to Werlauff, soldiers from Lübeck took the banner from a Danish ship in the Øresund in 1427 when Erik of Pomerania inflicted a disastrous defeat on a Wendish fleet. He based this interpretation on the writings of Ernst Deecke (1805–1862), who had only mentioned the capture of a Danish and a Swedish ship on that occasions; indeed, nothing more was written in the fifteenth-century chronicles, on which Deecke based his account.[74] Still, Werlauff's interpretation gained a prominent following. When the archaeologist Henry Petersen (1849–1896) visited St Mary's church in 1879 and saw the banner in such a 'hostile' environment, he asked the authorities of Lübeck to allow him

**Figure 8.3** Danish Flag from 1427. Published in Henry Petersen, 'Et dansk Flag fra Unionstiden i Maria-Kirken i Lübeck', Aarbørger for nordisk oldkyndighed og historie 1882, 57. © Public domain.

to paint a copy to be exhibited in Frederiksborg. His perspective of the flag as a symbol of humiliation corresponded with the chauvinistic attempts of German historians after the German-Danish war (1864). Leading Hanse historian Dietrich Schäfer (1845–1929), a prominent supporter of German imperialism, published a popular history of the Hanse, in which a drawing of the banner was identified as a trophy from the Danish-Wendish war from 1426/7 to 1435.[75] Overall, then, Werlauff, Petersen and Schäfer agreed that the banner symbolized the triumph of the German Hanse and the humiliation of the Danish nation. They saw the flag as a trophy in the framework of nationalistic monumental practices. Not least because written sources from the period do not mention this object, one should however be sceptical. We have no evidence about how contemporaries interpreted this banner in the fifteenth and sixteenth centuries. Still, the composite nature of the middle part of the banner might offer some clues as to such interpretations.

To begin with, most likely Werlauff and others were correct in dating the appropriation of the banner's second part – the one that resembled the Dannebrog – to 1427. Based on the pictorial programme it seems plausible that this part of the banner came to Lübeck as a result of a violent conflict between the town's inhabitants and the subjects of Erik of Pommerania. Banners with such a programme as the middle part were probably used in military settings, meaning that it might indeed have been the case that the second part of the flag in St Mary's Church was captured at the Battle of Øresund in 1427.[76] At any rate, it will have come to Lübeck as part of the city's conflict with the Calmar Union and Erik of Pomerania. The other two parts of the flag were very likely taken during different, chronologically later military conflicts. More generally, the positioning of the banner in the most prominent place – the choir – in Lübeck's most prominent church at the time speaks to the importance that the object held in the town's memorial practices. The meetings of the city council started with a service in St Mary, which was followed by a procession to the neighbouring town hall. St Mary's was also the place where the city's archive was situated.[77] Lastly, the church was also a communications hub between the inhabitants of the town, the council and foreign visitors. To illustrate, in 1439 the council of the Danish realm published their revocation of loyalty to Erik of Pomerania in a letter attached to the doors of St Mary's, and the election of Erik's successor Christian II also took place in this church.[78] Moreover, St Mary's was also a crucial staging ground for the memorial practices of Lübeck's urban elites.[79]

In the environment of St Mary's Church and the townhall, an environment that arguably constituted Lübeck's socio-political centre in the fifteenth century, other objects were used to tell the city's history, thus providing a ready context in which the tripartite banner might have been read. In the *Hörkammer*, a representative room in the townhall that was probably reserved for city councillors and noble guests, visitors could admire painted scenes from the city's history.[80] These paintings had been installed in the first half of the fifteenth century, so precisely at the time when the second part of the banner might have arrived in Lübeck. By and large, these paintings depicted the city's history as a struggle for autonomy in which the conflict with the Danish king was key. This conflict culminated in the Battle of Bornhöved in 1227 when Lübeck defeated the Danish king Waldemar II (r. 1202–1241), who had previously been their overlord. Five of the fifteen paintings in the *Hörkammer* focused on this conflict, as a result of which the Emperor Friedrich II (r. 1212/20–1250) granted Lübeck the privilege of imperial immediacy. The first four of these paintings show the council's interactions with Mary Magdalen, who supposedly supported Lübeck in the conflict against the Danish king. The fifth depicts a scene from 1375, when the emperor Charles IV (1346/1355–1378) visited Lübeck. According to the chronicle of Detmar, Charles called the city's councillors 'Herren' on that occasion, adding that they were to be honoured in the same way as princes.[81] Overall, these paintings illustrate several ways in which the council legitimized its socio-political prominence. The legal privileges that the town had received from the emperors and the high regard in which they held the councillors were key among them. At the same time, these paintings also provided an explanation for how these imperial privileges and recognition had been obtained: through Lübeck's own valiant fights against its enemies, first among them the Danish king.

In the first half of the fifteenth century these paintings were not alone in highlighting Lübeck's ferocious and successful warfare. Since the middle of the fourteenth century the city council marked the anniversary of the battle of Bornhöved by distributing food to the urban poor. On the Sunday after the Day of Maria Magdalene (July 22) a service was celebrated in recognition of what she had done for the town, a practice that continued even after the reformation.[82] The commemoration of the city's successful military conflicts also shaped contemporary historiography. Chronicles from the fourteenth and fifteenth centuries included small anecdotes illustrating how the city enforced its interests over the previous centuries. For instance, Detmar reported that in 1249 the burghers equipped ships, conquered and burned Copenhagen, took rich plunder and captured many noblemen. In the same year, they also attacked Stralsund, which would subsequently become part of the Hanse.[83] Hermann Korner told the heroic tale of Alexander van Soltwedel, a pious, brave man, who led Lübeck's forces in the battle of Bornhöved and gained the exclusive right to sit with his brother in Lübeck's city council. While it is commonly agreed that Soltwedel and his role in Lübeck's history as depicted by Korner were historical fiction, such fiction nevertheless did fit into the vision of Lübeck as a community that enforced its interests with rightful violence, a vision to which the evidence assembled here amply testifies.[84]

Intriguingly, Lübeck's elite articulated this vision in a moment of crisis. Recent scholarship no longer sees the early fifteenth century as the heyday of the Hanse, highlighting instead the profound economic and political transformations that were underway at the time.[85] Ever since the 1370s many Hanse towns had witnessed a set of rebellions and riots. In Lübeck the conflicts first escalated in the *Knochenhaueraufstand* of 1384. In 1406/8 many members of the council fled and a new council was constituted. Ten years later the exiles were restored, and the reconciliation was celebrated ostentatiously, not least in an annual procession.[86] In 1427 the disastrous defeat in the Øresund shook up the balance of power in Wendish towns yet again.[87] The economic consequences of the defeat were severe: many merchants lost their goods, and others had to be ransomed. In the aftermath of the defeat the mayor of Wismar, who had commanded the town's fleet, was executed, and the opposition party took over the town until 1430. In Hamburg a councillor was executed in 1428, accused of failing to seize Flensburg when he had the chance.[88] In Lübeck the mayor Tidemann Steen, who commanded the Wendish fleet, seemingly faced a similar fate. The Wendish towns were blaming the defeat on him, and the city's council had already begun to distance itself from him by claiming that he had acted contrary to the council's orders. In March 1427 the city council of Hamburg wrote to Lübeck that its burghers would not continue the war until Steen was executed. Steen only avoided execution because the emperor Sigismund (1411–1437), a set of noblemen, and the towns of Braunschweig, Göttingen and Lüneburg intervened on his behalf.[89] Beyond these pressures that resulted from the defeat in the Øresund the council of Lübeck and other Wendish towns were also under pressure from the emperor himself, who urged them to make peace with Erik and join his crusades against the Hussites.[90] Moreover, mercenaries of Wismar had also captured one of the servants of Nikolaus Stock, Sigismund's representative in Northern Europe.[91] Stock now confronted the council of Lübeck with serious accusations: the town had broken its friendship with Erik, caused murder, fire, bloodshed and other un-Christian actions and had encouraged the infamous Vitalian brethren. Overall, then, it seems fair to conclude that in 1427 and 1428 the Wendish towns were in a position of weakness, confronted with both urban opposition and the Emperor's attempts to label them as wrongdoers in order to achieve their support in the war against the Hussites.

Within this context, in January 1428, the representatives of the Wendish towns agreed to equip a second fleet against Erik. They set strict rules. Mercenaries who stole objects from churches should be executed. The burghers of each town should hold weekly religious services, in which they prayed for military fortune. When the fleet left, they should also hold a procession. Additionally, every ship should have a light blue cross sown into its sail.[92] In making these provisions, the Wendish towns, including Lübeck, performed their war as a just war according to divine law. By declaring the war against the Danish king as a holy war, they justified the reluctance of the delegates of the councils to join the actions against the Hussites. Against the opposition in their respective towns, they underlined that the war against Erik of Pomerania was fought in defence of the *bonum commune*. Furthermore, the processions also created the towns, including Lübeck, as a 'communities of violence' and evoked their unity in a situation of crisis. At the same time, the defeat in the Øresund was thoroughly blamed on Steen. Several chronicles written immediately after the events by authors close to the council argued that he had transgressed the explicit orders of the council, thus causing harm, disgrace, and destruction to the Hanse towns.[93] Lubeckians and other common soldiers were depicted as brave and heroic fighters; the shameful behaviour of their captain made sure that their efforts were to no avail.[94]

While these chronicles remain silent about the banner of the Danish king in St Mary's, the presentation of the banner, stitched together with two other flags that had probably been captured in warfare, can readily be seen as telling the same story as the paintings, rituals and chronicles that I have discussed here so far. This was the story of Lübeck as a sacred 'community of violence' with a long history that stretched back into the thirteenth century. In contrast to the paintings in the *Hörkammer* and the urban chronicles the flag was not only accessible to a limited circle of people who were close to the council; instead, everyone who came into the church could see it. Comparable to the chain links of Pisa's harbour chain, which Genoa destroyed in 1290 and subsequently exhibited all over its own religious and communal buildings, this composite flag was hard to miss.[95] Arguably, the banner integrated large parts of Lübeck's inhabitants into an imagined 'community of violence'. Very likely, the banner memorialized not only a specific victory but Lübeck's victoriousness more generally, not least against the Danish kings, whom the town chronicles made out to have been Lübeck's enemies all throughout the thirteenth, fourteenth and fifteenth centuries.

In the first two case studies taken objects were part of networks of texts and practices. The example of the patchwork-flag in St Mary's church shows additional characteristics which differ from the examples from Hamburg and Gdańsk. Its patchwork character likely fit to its memorial function since the three parts symbolized not concrete events but a narrative of a constant struggle for urban autonomy in itself. Thus it is not surprising that we have no concrete evidence about the conflicts in which the council took the other parts of the banner. It was however also part of an urban memorial landscape, in which it very likely was one among many objects entangled in the story of Lübeck's fight for autonomy. The flag was part of an urban ensemble of objects depicting the council's violence as continuously just violence practiced for the benefit of the town. It was however not just the council depicting itself as a 'community of violence'. In Lübeck, different 'communities of violence' overlapped and historical narratives emerged around objects that were part of different, even conflicting narrations of violence. In the sanctuary of St Mary's church for example laid the tomb slab of Brun Warendorp, who died during the successful siege of Helsingborg in 1369 in the war against the Danish king Waldemar IV. In the inscription, he was remembered as a mayor, as the captain of the Hanse towns, but also as the son of *dominus* Gottschalk Warendorp.[96] *Memoria* practices of the council and the family overlapped. Thus, it is complicated to reconstruct if and how people after 1427 created relations between the tomb slab and the banner of Erik of Pomerania. The trophies and symbols of urban violence offered loose associations to narrate histories of violence and to create cohesion among social groups. Over these narrations, the urban elites of towns such as Lübeck, Hamburg and Gdańsk imagined social coherence, not by an elaborated pictorial programme, but by the fluid patchwork of taken objects with the narratives into which they were integrated.

## Conclusion

This chapter has examined the histories of three material objects that had once been violently taken and subsequently were put on display in the urban spaces of Hamburg, Gdánsk and Lübeck respectively. My goal was to inquire how these objects evoked social bonds and what role their materiality played in this process. Some preliminary conclusions can now be state.

Medieval towns in Northern Europe were shaped by a topography of circulating objects, that both represented and created social bonds. Some of these objects were gifts, some were endowments; others, yet again, were taken objects – plunder, spoils and trophies – and it's this last group on which I have focused here. This chapter suggests that the narratives of violence that centred around these objects were used to evoke social coherence and social bonds in phases of crises. As I hope to have shown, these narratives shaped the negotiation of power relations within the towns in ways that had not been recognized before. By evoking a fiction of cohesion among social groups, they helped stabilize the often fragile oligarchic government of the towns. The evidence of taken objects shaping the town's political and sacral landscape challenges traditional views that have stressed the peaceful habit of mercantile communities in contrast to noble habits. Towns such as Hamburg, Gdańsk and Lübeck not only imagined themselves as communities of violence; as historians today we should probably see and analyse them from this perspective as well.

More generally, I also hope to have shown that taken objects had histories, but that they did not tell these histories on their own; instead, such histories had to be constantly interpreted and narrated, or else they were elided and forgotten. This finding might be seen to point to a fundamental problem in studies on materiality. At least in the examples that I have presented here, a focus on 'object biographies' alone would seem to constitute an incomplete perspective on the social dimension of the agency of material objects in premodern societies. Although I have taken material objects as a starting point for my chapter, I have found that their agency can hardly be comprehended without the textual and praxeological networks in which they were appropriated. At the same time, materiality clearly mattered – but as a marker of historical truth for the larger narratives in which the objects were inscribed, not least by being integrated into larger assemblages of other objects, texts and performances. Medievalists should thus concentrate on the reconstruction of 'object topographies' that were open to situated interpretations. Such object topographies can be read as manifestations of complex and conflicting social relations and narrations. Their reconstruction might offer new perspectives on the social history of urban elites in the late medieval period.

# Notes

1  Jean Froissart, *Chronicles*, trans. Geoffrey Brererton (London: Penguin Books, 1978), 251; Sven Ekdahl, *Die 'Banderia Prutenorum' des Jan Dlugosz, eine Quelle zur Schlacht bei Tannenberg 1410: Untersuchungen zu Aufbau, Entstehung und Quellenwert der Handschrift* (Göttingen: Vandenhoeck & Ruprecht, 1976);

Rebecca Müller, *Spolien und Trophäen im mittelalterlichen Genua: sic hostes Ianua frangit* (Weimar: VDG, 2002).

2   Cf. William I. Miller, 'Gift, Sale, Payment, Raid: Case Studies in the Negotiation and Classification of Exchange in Medieval Iceland', *Speculum* 61 (1986): 18–50.

3   Wilhelm Mantels, 'Die Reliquien der Rathskapelle zu St. Gertrud in Lübeck', *Hansische Geschichtsblätter* 2:1 (1872): 139–54; for the role of gifts in urban political culture cf. the contribution of Gustavs Strenga in this volume.

4   On memorial practices in the Baltic space cf. Gustavs Strenga, *Remembering the Dead: Collective Memoria in Late Medieval Livonia*, (PhD Thesis, Queen Mary University of London, 2013); Heinrich Dormeier, 'Das laikale Stiftungswesen in spätmittelalterlichen Pfarrkirchen. Kaufleute, Korporationen und Marienverehrung in Lübeck', in *Die Pfarrei im späten Mittelalter*, ed. Enno Bünz, Gerhard Fouquet (Ostfildern: Thorbeke, 2013), 279–340; Stefanie Rüther, *Prestige und Herrschaft: Zur Repräsentation der Lübecker Ratsherren in Mittelalter und Früher Neuzeit*, Köln et al., 2003. For spoils in medieval towns cf. Klaus Graf, 'Schlachtengedenken in der Stadt', in *Stadt und Krieg*, ed. Bernhard Kirchgäßner, Günter Scholz (Sigmaringen: Thorbeke, 1989), 91.

5   For a comparable phenomen cf. the elephant chair in the Benedictine Abbey of Kremsmünster in the contribution of Sabine Sommerer in this volume.

6   Philipp Höhn, Kaufleute im Konflikt. Rechtspluralismus, Kredit und Gewalt im spätmittelalterlichen Lübeck (Frankfurt: Campus, 2021), 281–349.

7   Miller, *Gift*, 22–8.

8   Jan Rüdiger, 'Eine Geschichte mittelalterlichen Nehmens. Zur Einführung', *Geschichte in Wissenschaft und Unterricht* 65 (2014): 525–39; for the noble world Andrew Cowell, *The Medieval Warrior Aristocracy. Gifts, Violence, Performance, and the Sacred* (Cambridge: Cambridge University Press, 2007), 3, 8 offers a comparable approach.

9   For recent literature cf. Lars Kjaer, *The Medieval Gift and the Classical Tradition: Ideals and the Performance of Generosity in Medieval England, 1100–1300* (Cambridge: Cambridge University Press, 2019); Arnoud-Jan Bijsterveld, *Do ut des: Gift Giving, Memoria and Conflict Management in the Medieval Low Countries* (Hilversum: Verloren, 2007); Valentin Groebner, *Liquid Assets: Dangerous Gifts, Presents and Politics at the End of the Middle Ages* (Philadelphia: University of Pennsylvania Press, 2002).

10   Gadi Algazi, 'Introduction: Doing Things with Gifts', in *Negotiating the Gift. Pre-Modern Figurations of Exchange*, ed. Gadi Algazi, Valentin Groebner and Bernhard Jussen (Göttingen: Vandenhoeck & Ruprecht, 2003), 9–27.

11   For the history of the term 'communities of violence' and its critique cf. David Nirenberg, *Communities of Violence: Persecution of Minorities in the Middle Ages* (Princeton: Princeton University Press, 2015), preface. For my use of this term cf. Philipp Höhn, '"Fighting pirates" as a paradigm: conflict, competition and

criminalization in fifteenth and sixteenth century Lübeck and the North European trade', in *Annales HSS* (forthcoming); for the noble aristocracy in the high middle ages cf. Cowell, Aristocracy, 57–63.

12  Johann M. Lappenberg, ed., *Tratziger's Chronica von der Stadt Hamburg* (Hamburg: Perthes, Besser & Mauke, 1865), 261; for the historiography of Hamburg in the sixteenth century cf. Susanne Rau, 'Städtische Erinnerung im Spiegel des Hamburger Reformationsgedenkens in Chroniken der frühen Neuzeit', *Zeitschrift des Vereins für Hamburgische Geschichten* 87 (2001): 1–48.

13  HR III, 9, 339 fn. 1; James A. Larson, *Reforming the North: The Kingdoms and Churches of Scandinavia, 1520–1545* (Cambridge: Cambridge University Press, 2010), 50.

14  Johann M. Lappenberg, ed., *Hamburgische Chroniken in niedersächsischer Sprache* (Hamburg: Perthes, 1861), 32.

15  Hamburgische Chroniken, 31.

16  Volker Plagemann, ed., *Die Kunst des Mittelalters in Hamburg: Aufsätze zur Kulturgeschichte* (Hamburg: Dölling & Gallitz, 1999), book end paper; cf. also Volker Plagemann, 'Die spätmittelalterliche Sakraltopographie', in ibid., 144–51.

17  Ralph Knickmeier, *Der vagabundierende Altar* (Berlin: Mann, 2004), 87–8.

18  Ralf Busch, 'Benedikt V.: Ein Papst in Hamburg und sein Grabmal im Hamburger Dom', in *Kunst*, 81–4.

19  Höhn, *Fighting*.

20  J. L. van der Gouw, 'Claes Kniphof: Kaperkapitein van Christian II in 1525 voor de Hollandse kust', *Bijdragen en Medelingen van het Historisch Genootschap* 67 (1949): 65.

21  HR III, 9, no. 77, 107, 132 § 95, 160, p. 165 fn. 3; Larson, *Reforming*, 135.

22  HR III, 9, no. 17, 21, 177, p. 320 fn. 4, 198, 199, 205, 210, 228; van der Gouw, Claes Kniphof; Larson, *Reforming*, 175–6; HR III, 9, p. 313 fn. 1.

23  Erich Hoffmann, *Geschichte Schleswig-Holsteins, vol. 4: Spätmittelalter und Reformationszeit* (Neumünster: Wachtholtz 1986), 325–33.

24  Philipp Höhn, 'Entscheidungsfindung und Entscheidungsvermeidung: Das Beispiel der Sunddurchfahrt um 1440', in *Entscheidungsfindung in spätmittelalterlichen Gemeinschaften*, ed. Wolfgang Eric Wagner (Göttingen: Vandenhoeck & Ruprecht, forthcoming).

25  Gregor Rohmann, 'The Making of Connectivity: How Hamburg Tried to Gain Control over the Elbe River (13th–16th Centuries)', in *Merchants, Pirates and Smugglers: Criminalization, Economics and the Transformation of the Maritime World (1200–1600)*, ed. Thomas Heebøll-Holm, Philipp Höhn and Gregor Rohmann (New York: Frankfurt a. M., 2019), 235–42.

26  Larson, *Reforming*, 89–97, 143, 148–51, 197–9.

27  HR III, 9, no. 93, §§ 104–114; no. 94 §§ 33, 41, 44, 46, 47, no. 131 § 78, no. 132 § 144, 167–171, no. 134; 145 §§ 2, 9; no 203, 247 § 8, no. 632 §§ 59, 84, 89, 94;

cf. Louis H. J. Sicking, 'Die offensive Lösung wird fortgesetzt: Das holländische Eingreifen im Ostseeraum vom 15. bis zum 18. Jahrhundert', in *Hansestädte im Konflikt. Krisenmanagement und bewaffnete Auseinandersetzung vom 13. bis zum 17. Jahrhundert*, ed. Ortwin Pelc (Wismar: Callidus, 2019), 220.

28  Gerhard Theuerkauf, 'Hinrich Murmester und Hermann Langenbeck, Bürgermeister von Hamburg (1467–1517)', in *Akteure und Gegner der Hanse: Zur Prosopographie der Hansezeit*, ed. Detlef Kattinger, Ralf-Gunnar Werlich and Horst Wernicke (Weimar: Böhlau 1998), 178–80.

29  Cf. Christopher D. Fletcher, 'Rumour, Clamour, Murmur and Rebellion: Public Opinion and It Uses before and after the Peasant's Revolt (1381)', in *La communidad medieval como esfera pública*, ed. Hipólito Rafael Oliva Herrer (Sevilla: Universidad de Sevilla Publicaciones, 2014), 193–210.

30  Helga-Maria Kühn, 'Kempe, Stephan', in *Neue Deutsche Biographie*, vol. 11 (Berlin: Duncker & Humblot, 1977), 483.

31  Werner von Melle, 'Kohl, Ditmar', in *Allgemeine Deutsche Biographie*, vol. 16 (Leipzig: Duncker & Humblot, 1882), 422–3.

32  Rainer Postel, *Die Reformation in Hamburg*, (Gütersloh: Gütersloher Verlagshaus Mohn, 1986).

33  Benedict Anderson, *Imagined Communities: Reflections on the Origin and Spread of Nationalism* (London and New York: Verso, 1983); Nirenberg, *Communities*.

34  Johann M. Lappenberg, 'Des Hans von Göttingen Lied von Klaus Kniphof', *Zeitschrift des Vereins für Hamburgische Geschichte* 2 (1847): 141–56; Johann M. Lappenberg, 'Des Stephan Kempe Lied von Klaus Kniphof', in *Zeitschrift des Vereins für Hamburgische Geschichte* 2 (1847): 118–40; Johann M. Lappenberg, 'Des Hans von Göttingen Lied vom Seeräuber Martin Pechlin', in ibid., 141–56.

35  Jan Dumolyn, Jelle Haemers, 'A Bad Chicken Was Brooding': Subversive Speech in Late Medieval Flanders, in *Past and Present* 214 (2012): 45–86.

36  Lappenberg, *Des Hans von Göttingen Lied vom Claus Kniphof*, 584.

37  Lappenberg, *Stephan Kempe*, 131–2.

38  Lappenberg, *Stephan Kempe*, 137–9.

39  Peter Schuster, *Verbrecher, Opfer, Heilige: Eine Geschichte des Tötens 1200–1700* (Stuttgart: Klett Cotta, 2015), 256–65.

40  Lappenberg, *Stephan Kempe*, 139.

41  For the discussion of the agency of material objects cf. the introduction of this volume by Lars Kjaer.

42  Beata Mozejko, *Peter von Danzig: The Story of a Great Caravel, 1462–1475* (Leiden: Brill, 2019), 200–8.

43  Beata Mozejko, 'Ein Bild als Zeugnis der maritimen Gewalt', in *Störtebeker & Konsorten. Piraten der Hansezeit?* ed. Europäisches Hansemuseum (Neumünster: Wachholz, 2019), 109–11.

44  Hirsch (ed.), *Caspar Weinreichs*, 13–14.

45  Hans Peter Hahn, 'Dinge sind Fragmente und Assemblagen: Kritische Anmerkungen zur Metapher der Objektbiografie', in *Biography of objects: Aspekte eines kulturhistorischen Konzepts*, ed. Dietrich Boschung, Patric-Alexander Kreuz and Tobias L. Kienlin (Paderborn: Schöningh, 2015), 23–5. For the inscription of the history into an object cf. the contribution of Rowland in this volume; for the manipulative dimension of such inscription cf. the example of the elephant chair in the contribution of Sommerer in this volume.
46  Stephan Selzer, *Artushöfe im Ostseeraum: Ritterlich-höfische Kultur in den Städten des Preußenlandes im 14. und 15. Jahrhundert* (Frankfurt: Peter Lang 1996), 115; Mozejko, *Peter von Danzig*, 225; Willi Drost, *Die Marienkirche in Danzig und ihre Kunstschätze* (Stuttgart: Günther & Co, 1963), 136.
47  Theodor Hirsch ed., 'Einleitung zu Christoph Beyers des Älteren Chronik', in *Scriptores rerum Prussicarum. Die Geschichtsquellen der preußischen Vorzeit bis zum Untergange der Ordensherrschaft 5* (Leipzig: Hirzel 1874), 441–2.
48  Cf. Theodor Hirsch, *Die Ober-Pfarrkirche von St. Marien in Danzig in ihren Denkmälern und in ihren Beziehungen zum kirchlichen Leben Danzigs überhaupt* (Danzig: Anhuth 1843–1847), 261.
49  Barbara G. Lane, 'The Patron and the Pirate: The Mystery of Memling's Gdańsk Last Judgement', *The Art Bulletin* 73 (1991): 623.
50  Michael Jucker, 'Rauben, Plündern, Brandschatzen. Kriegs- und Fehdepraxis im Spannungsfeld von Recht, Ökonomie und Symbolik', in *Fehdeführung im spätmittelalterlichen Reich: Zwischen adeliger Handlungslogik und territorialer Verflechtung*, ed. Julia Eulenstein, Christine Reinle and Michael Rothmann (Affalterbach: Dydimos, 2013), 281–2.
51  Mozejko, 'Bild', 109–11.
52  Mozejko, *Peter von Danzig*, 208–75; Lane, 'Patron', 632–5.
53  Tobias Daniels, 'Kooperation und Konflikt im hansischen Mittelmeerhandel zwischen Spätmittelalter und Früher Neuzeit', in *Hansischer Handel im Strukturwandel vom 15. zum 16. Jahrhundert*, ed. Rolf Hammel-Kiesow and Stephan Selzer (Trier: Porta Alba, 2016), 137–60.
54  Mozejko, *Peter von Danzig*, 211–16.
55  Mozejko, *Peter von Danzig*, 212–14.
56  Mozejko, *Peter von Danzig*, 211–20.
57  Blazej Sliwinski, Beata Mozejko, 'The Political History of Gdańsk from the Beginning to the Sixteenth Century', in *New Studies in Medieval and Renaissance Poland and Prussia,* ed. Beata Mozejko (London: Routledge, 2017), 33–7.
58  Stephan Selzer, 'Bürger an König' Artus Tafel: Gemeinschaft und Erinnerung in den Artushöfen des Preußenlandes', in *Gemeinschaft und Geschichtsbilder im Hanseraum*, ed. Thomas Hill and Dietrich W. Poeck (Frankfurt a. M: Peter Lang, 2000), 136–9; Weinreich, ed., *Caspar Weinreichs*, 52–3; Paul Simson, *Der Artushof in Danzig und seine Brüderschaften, die Banken* (Gdańsk: Bertling, 1900), 32–66.

59  Justyna Wubs-Mrozewicz, 'Danzig (Gdańsk): Seeking Stability and Autonomy', in *The Routledge Handbook of Maritime Trade around Europe 1300–1600*, ed. Justyna Wubs-Mrozewicz, Wim P. Blockmans and Michail M. Krom (London: Routledge, 2017), 248–72.
60  Slawomir Koscielak, 'Religion in Gdańsk in the Middle Ages and Early Modern Times: From St. Adalbert's Mission to the Reformation Victory', in *New Studies*, ed. Mozejko London: Routledge, 2017, 93–6.
61  The text is printed in passages – Ferdinand H. Grautoff, ed., *Chronik des Franciscaner Lesemeister Detmar, nach der Unterschrift und mit Ergänzungen aus andern Chroniken* (Hamburg: Perthes, 1830), vol. 2, 701–8.
62  Cf. Julia Mozdzen, 'Das Geschäftsbuch des Danziger Schiffers Caspar Weinreich (1461–1496). Ein Beitrag zur Arbeitstechnik von Stenzel Bornbach', in *Schriftlichkeit im Preußenland*, ed. Marie-Luise Heckmann and Jürgen Sarnowsky (Osnabrück: Fibre, 2020), 233–57. Caspar Weinreich's chronicle is edited – Caspar Weinreich, *Danziger Chronik, Ein Beitrag zur Geschichte Danzigs, der Lande Preußen und Polen, des Hansabundes und der nordischen Reichen*, ed. Theodor Hirsch and Friedrich August Voßberg (Berlin: Stargardt, 1855). The editions of Hirsch are problematic – Julia Mozdzen, '"Merke auff Lieber leser wy woltadt gelonet wirt mit arge". Die Danziger Chronik Bernt Stegemanns (1528) als Beispiel bürgerlicher Moralliteratur', *Jahrbuch des Wissenschaftlichen Zentrums der Polnischen Akademie der Wissenschaften in Wien* 8 (2017): S. 111–16.
63  Hirsch, ed., *Caspar Weinreichs*, xxiv–xxv.
64  Julia Mozdzen, 'Handelsbuch – Hausbuch – Gedenkbuch: Bücher mit gemeinsamer Genese oder mit heterogenen Schrifttumsformen? Das Beispiel einiger Danziger Handelsbücher', in *Selbstzeugnisse im polnischen und deutschen Schrifttum im Spätmittelalter in der Frühen Neuzeit (15–18. Jahrhundert)*, ed. Renata Skowronska et al. (Torun: Wydawnictwo Naukowe Uniwersytetu Mikolaja Kopernika, 2014), 133–50.
65  Jucker, 'Rauben', 265.
66  On processes of differing interpretations and processes overwriting interpretations in the conversion of objects cf. Philippe Buc, 'Conversion of objects', *Viator* 28 (1997), 102–9, 115.
67  Algazi, 'Introduction', 18–19; Buc, 'Conversion', 125.
68  Michael Jucker, 'Geraubte Gaben, Verschwiegene Vergangenheit: Hoch- und spätmittelalterliche Geschenk- und Kirchenpolitik mit Objekten aus Byzanz und Burgund', in *Geschenke erhalten die Freundschaft: Gabentausch und Netzwerkpflege im europäischen Mittelalter*, ed. Michael Grünbart (Berlin: Lit Verlag, 2011), 88.
69  Thorsten Albrecht, 'Palmarum 1942: Der Bombenangriff auf Lübeck und der Kunst- und Kulturgüterschutz', in *Palmarum 1942. Neue Forschungen zu zerstörten Werken mittelalterlicher Holzskulptur und Tafelmalerei aus der Lübecker Marienkirche*, ed. Ulrike Nürnberger and Uwe Albrecht (Kiel: Ludwig, 2015), 11–72.

70  Fritz Hirsch and Friedrich Bruns, ed., *Die Bau- und Kunstdenkmäler der Freien und Hansestadt Lübeck*, vol. 2 (Lübeck: Nöhring, 1906), 445; Höhn, 'Fighting Pirates'.
71  Arjun Appardurai, 'Introduction: Commodities and the Politics of Value', in Arjun Appardurai, *The Social Life of Things. Commodities in Cultural Perspective* (Cambridge: Cambridge University Press, 1988), 3–63.
72  Hans Horstmann, 'Die Dänische Flagge von 1427 in der Marienkirche zu Lübeck', *Deutsches Schiffahrtsarchiv* 2 (1978): 191.
73  Horstmann, *Flagge*, 192.
74  Erich C. Werlauff, *Om Danebrog og Danebrogsordenen: En historisk Undersøgelse* (Copenhagen: Glydenhalske, 1872), 18; Ernst Deecke, *Lübeckische Geschichten und Sagen* (Lübeck: Boldemann, 1852), 200–3.
75  Petersen, 'Et dansk Flag fra Unionstiden i Maria-Kirken i Lübeck', *Aarbørger for nordisk oldkyndighed og historie 1882*, 1–2; Dietrich Schäfer, *Die Deutsche Hanse* (Leipzig: Velhagen & Klassing, 1914), 95.
76  Horstmann, *Flagge*, 193.
77  Friedrich Bruns, Hugo Rathgens and Lutz Wilde, ed., *Die Bau- und Kunstdenkmäler Lübecks vol. I, 2: Rathaus und öffentliche Gebäude* (Lübeck: Schmidt-Römhildt, 1939); Dietrich Poeck, *Rituale der Ratswahl: Zeichen und Zeremoniell in Europa (12.-18. Jahrhundert)*, (Wien: Böhlau, 2003).
78  Ernst Daenell, *Die Blütezeit der Deutsche Hanse* (Berlin: De Gruyter, 2001) (first published 1905/06), vol. 1, 303–4.
79  Rüther, *Prestige*, 62–71, 178–203.
80  Sascha Möbius, *Das Gedächtnis der Reichsstadt: Unruhen und Kriege in der lübeckischen Chronistik und Erinnerungskultur des späten Mittelalters und der frühen Neuzeit* (Göttingen: Vandenhoeck & Ruprecht, 2012), 154–5.
81  Ibid.
82  Möbius, *Gedächtnis*, 133–4.
83  Karl Koppmann, ed., *Die Chroniken der niedersächsischen Städte: Lübeck I* (Die Chroniken der deutschen Städte vom 14. bis ins 16. Jahrhundert 19) (Leipzig: Hirzel, 1884, 92–3); Möbius, *Gedächtnis*, 152.
84  Wilhelm Brehmer, 'Der Ratsherr Alexander von Soltwedel in Sage und Geschichte', *Zeitschrift des Vereins für Lübeckische Geschichte und Altertumskunde* 4 (1884): 213–15; for the attack on Copenhagen Maria R. D. Corsi, 'Piracy or Policy? Lübecks 1249 Attack on Copenhagen', *Viking and Medieval Scandinavia* 8 (2012): 53–70.
85  Ulla Kypta, 'Aufstieg, Blüte, Niedergang – Entstehung, Krise, Übergang: Von der bürgerlichen zur postmodernen Hanseforschung?' in *Hansegeschichte als Regionalgeschichte: Beiträge einer internationalen und interdisziplinären Winterschule in Greifswald 2012*, ed. Oliver Auge (Frankfurt: Peter Lang, 2014), 422–4.
86  Rotz, *Lübeck Uprising*.

87 HR I, 8, no. 214, 234, 259, 261, 287, 288, 289; *Urkundenbuch der Stadt Lübeck* (abbreviated as UBStL), ed. Johann F. Böhmer et al., 11 vols. (Lübeck: Aschenfeldt 1843–1905), vol. 7, no. 67, 68, 70, 76, 96, 100, 101.

88 Cornelia Neustadt, *Kommunikation im Konflikt: König Erik VII. von Dänemark und die Städte im südlichen Ostseeraum (1423–1435)* (Berlin: De Gruyter, 2019), 139–6, 316–19.

89 UBStL 7, no. 68, 76, 78, 104, 105, 106, 114, 119, 125, 156, 170, 234, 339, 390, 404, 419.

90 Stephan Selzer, 'Die Hanse in den Hussitenkriegen', in *Hansestädte*, 106–7.

91 Neustadt, *Kommunikation*, 194–6.

92 UBStL 7, no. 101.

93 Karl Koppmann, ed., *Die Chroniken der niedersächsischen Städte: Lübeck*, vol. 3 (Leipzig: Hirzel, 1902), 268–74, 386–8.

94 Jacob Schwalm, ed., *Die Chronica Novella des Hermann Korner* (Göttingen: Vandenhoeck & Ruprecht, 1895), 549. Koppmann, *Lübeck*, vol. 3, 271–2.

95 Müller, *Spolien*.

96 Rüther, *Prestige*, 181.

# Gifts: Concluding Remarks

Miri Rubin

Revisiting a lively workshop for the purpose of reflecting on its findings is always a form of time travel where temporalities mix: the memories of chapters delivered and conversations enjoyed, with the polished chapters that resulted from those communions. In 2021 this is an even stranger experience. For many of us the workshop on gift-giving in Tallinn, organized by Gustavs Strenga, was one of the last conferences attended in person before the Covid-19 pandemic. Most of us combined scholarship and tourism, and enjoyed the summer in the beautiful Baltic city, so redolent of medieval culture and traces in particular of social forms developed within it: guildhalls and parish churches. Memories of the reciprocities of academic life, the ways we learn from each other – by giving and receiving – fit well into the subject of this volume, as you have read and seen.

\*\*\*

Let us begin with some history, personal and historiographical. My own interest in gift-exchange developed when I was conducting doctoral research on chartable activity in medieval Cambridge and its region in the 1980s. Inspired by scholars of the *Annales* School, I sought to understand the ideas and objectives that underpinned the wave of foundation in the new and growing urban centres of a whole array of foundations – leper houses, hospitals and in Cambridge, soon academic colleges too.[1] I sought an approach which would not take charity as performed Christian faith, but rather to treat it as an *explanandum,* something requiring explanation, as part of a system of social relations.

It was a time of fervent rapprochement between historians and anthropologists, when theories about gift-exchange seemed of particular interest. Structuralist frames of explanation were attractive, as they offered models that were based on extensive ethnography distilled into elegant and universal formulations. Marcel

Mauss' *Essai sur le don (The Gift)*, first published in 1925,[2] was the inspiration for what followed, hence I read it first. I found the precise formulation of his way, to venture behind 'formal pretence and social deception', to be just what I was hoping to achieve.[3] Indeed, I soon found in my sources the very principle Mauss had identified, that 'generosity is necessary because otherwise Nemesis will take vengeance upon the excessive wealth and happiness of the rich by giving them to the poor and the Gods'.[4] However prudently those who might save wealth in land and objects acted, it was always towards the end of using it – the superfluous – as well-chosen gifts.[5] However widely comparative was his use of the ethnography available from across the globe, Mauss always insisted that the gift was a social relationship. And like all true relationships it held – even if tested – over stretches of space and time.

Marcel Mauss's insight inspired a generation of anthropologists who took the idea of gift, as a meme for the whole system of social relations. Indeed, Claude Lévi-Strauss (1908–2009) even saw it as the very basis of his own wide-ranging mapping of social relations through structuralism.[6] What had been a very precise social relationship – the gift – was made to offer the key to all social relations, through the concept of exchange.[7] Historians did not, on the whole, take to fully flung structuralism, but found the concept of the gift as cast by Mauss to be useful, as did scholars of other disciplines.[8]

Historians have mapped out the networks of exchange in the many contexts created by complex societies: gifts in war and diplomacy, in marriage and conviviality. Clearly this was far from Mauss' image of 'archaic' societies where all relations were compressed into the gift, and where economies were made up of gift-exchanges. So anthropologists extended Mauss' insight, and were moved to develop from the all-encompassing gifts, an approach to social relations that is seen as series of 'reciprocities', some more some less clearly defined.[9] Yet even those who dealt with more differentiated societies still find the gift a useful concept, in identifying particularly freighted relations. Mauss had always expected his question to provoke historians and ethnographers rather than as a model; his essay offered lines for research. He sought to follow where historians would lead.[10] Natalie Zemon Davis did so in her analysis of sixteenth-century France through the gift.[11]

What historians appreciated was the deliberation Mauss saw invested in the gift, and his observation that the gift-giving was a form of self-expression.[12] For historians of the material this is a point of particular interest, which invites us to look closely at the gift, at its symbolic value as well as at its inherent value. This close look means appreciating so much about what contemporaries saw, heard, felt, conveyed with gifts given and received. In his introduction, Lars Kjær reminds us that beyond their intrinsic value and their location within a symbolic order, gifts prompt us to appreciate the emotions they carry and transmit. We may think of the gifts given by royal fathers to their daughters at marriage – objects imbued with diplomatic purpose and marks of power – which also bespoke an emotional relationship with a daughter whose marriage also marked separation.[13]

Here the contributions to this volume display how much can be learned about gift-giving when we attend to the materials given and received. This inflection of theories of gift-giving through a material turn is fruitful indeed. And it is material in the broadest sense – including living and dead things; human, mineral and animal. These are now appreciated for a wide range of sense experiences they offer users: touch, smell, shimmer, texture. Historians have learned to appreciate the material, even when all their sources allow is a description in words. So for historians, and especially those of earlier centuries, attention to the material refocuses efforts at careful reading of texts. This meant a renewed engagement with inventories, wills, chronicles and meticulous command of specialist vocabularies, in search of the fullest image of a depicted object.[14]

The turn to materiality has opened historians to materials from the past which lay in cabinets, museums, and archives, perhaps not unexplored, but unused by historians. The turn to the material has brought the different fields of history closer together, all bringing to the study of things their perspectives: archaeological and economic, artistic and codicological.[15] And beyond historical inquiry are other humane disciplines: philosophy and anthropology, literary theory and economics. And further afield, historians and material scientists have resolved mysteries of provenance, authorship, use and reuse.[16]

Historians do particularly well when they attend to the 'biographies' of things.[17] This is particularly true of gifted things. This means treating an object not as a thing made with its meaning, value, shape and, if gifted, intent already fixed. Rather, circulation, bequeathing, repurposing, theft, purloining – and other acts of kindness as well as meanness – make the life of an object continuous and full of possibilities for change.[18] Anna Boeles Rowland demonstrates this well in her study of rings within disputes over intimate relationships. A single object could be thought a token of sincere affection, as well as reward for sexual favours. Objects can contain as many narratives as those authorized to speak and recount can make. The relatives authority, rhetorical ability, privileged knowledge – and in the cases Anna discusses, the disposition of the law – determine who will triumph in writing a gift's next life-chapter.

Imagining that next chapter could occupy gift-givers as they assembled their gift packages for the most auspicious fit to those flowing their way. Ruth Noyes shows how carefully the exchange between the Medici and Lithuanian courts were prepared, as gift-exchanges always are. But as they sent relics of precious saints, they also knew that these would be treated appropriately. Trust that the narrative associated with a thing – that which made it a gift – was essential for the life and hence its biography to continue to its next chapter.

The ring was a privileged form in medieval cultures, one 'routinely invested with special powers'.[19] In that sense it was 'gifty', to invoke here again Chris Wickham's term, discussed by Lars Kjær in the Introduction to this volume.[20] Bettina Bildhaeur discusses the rich possibilities with which certain types of objects were endowed: rings, mirrors, nets, treasure, grail/cup. Around these have developed some of the most enduring myths, and in them the thing is an actor; to it is imputed agency.[21] Yet all these possibilities existed as long as they were embedded into narratives, as Höhn shows in the case of things 'taken' in the heat of battles – that made sense afresh to every generation.

In tracing the lives of things, and of those very special things – gifts – we are almost always in a ritual present, or attending a rite of passage. The chapters assembled here have recorded gift giving as part of marriage (Rowland), of treaty making (Noyes), of entry into office (Strenga), of thanks-giving at a shrine (Peltomaa, Heilskov) and as the very act of almsgiving (Grinder-Hansen). We rightly attend to these symbolically rich, usually public, and hence well-documented rituals through the display and performance of gifted objects. The gift's life continued in liturgy, office-holding and personal relations, of which the gifts formed part of a routine, as reminder of moments of passage and change.

Yet what of longer aftermaths? Is there a history of forgotten gifts, of discarded offerings? I am thinking here of the material legacies which we all inherit and which we may revere but also resent. I am prompted to consider legacies of this kind by Ann Laura Stoler's exploration of 'Imperial debris'.[22] Even after the passage of colonial rule, buildings built under it still remained standing, and were even deemed to be useful, however powerful were the messages of domination by Europeans that they conveyed. Of course, appropriation is a type of victory, but does that mean that every gift – even one forced in an unequal relationship – can be remade into a useful, even desired, thing?

These innovative and reflective essays indicate some of the ways that gifts understood in their full materiality are informing areas of historical inquiry, and of the Humanities more broadly, that have traditionally privileged texts above all. One good example is the intersection of gifts, materiality and diplomacy in the exciting field of New Diplomatic History (a good example of which are the articles by Noyes and Strenga here). In 2020 the new journal *Diplomatica* dedicated its second issue to 'Gift and Tribute in Early Modern Diplomacy: Afro-Eurasian Perspectives'. Here the materiality of gifts is also an occasion to open our studies to global perspectives, as Lars Kjær noted in his introduction, for gifts givers sought out precious, rare and unusual materials, and this meant involvement in travel and commerce, commerce implicated in markets formed through conquest and domination.

Similarly, the materiality of gifts also invites reflection on emotions, memory and heritage. From Anna Rowland's treatment of rings to Philipp Höhn's of spurs as booty, emotions and the treatment of gifts will reveal relations between individuals and gifted things, as well as communities and their memories of gifts. Here historical work and the skills of curators and heritage experts are increasingly meeting fruitfully. Heritage too is a sphere of great controversy and debate. Hence in this volume, the gift is explored alongside booty, mementos, keepsakes, tribute, encompassing a whole range of relations associated with fresh and urgent calls for social justice.

Gifts and their materiality thus take us to the heart of questions that currently animate humanities scholars as both academics and as citizens. Free or coerced, given or expected, lasting or ephemeral – gifts lead us into human relations in their fullest complexity, inviting our fullest commitment and compassion.

# Notes

1. This was published as Miri Rubin, *Charity and Community in Medieval Cambridge* (Cambridge: Cambridge University Press, 1987).
2. Marcel Mauss, 'Essai sur le don. Forme et raison de l'échange dans les sociétés archaïques', *Annee sociologique* (1923–1924): 30–186.
3. Marcel Mauss, *The Gift: Forms and Functions of Exchange in Archaic Societies*, trans. Ian Cunnison (Glencoe: The Free Press, 1954), 1. [*Essai sur le don: forme et raison de l'echange dans les societes archaiques* (Paris: Presses Universitaires de France, 1950)].
4. Mauss, *The Gift*, 15.
5. Mauss, *The Gift*, 73.
6. Claude Lévi-Strauss, 'Introduction a l'oeuvre de Marcel Mauss', in *Sociologie et anthropologie*, ed. Marcel Mauss (Paris: Presses Universitaires de France, 1950), xxiii–xxv.

7   Claude Lévi-Strauss, *La pensee sauvage* (Paris: Plon, 1962).
8   See the essays collected in *The Question of the Gift: Essays across Disciplines*, ed. Mark Osteen (London: Routledge, 2002).
9   Marshall Sahlins, *Stone Age Economics* (Chicago: Aldine, 1972), especially chapters 4 and 5.
10  Mauss, *The Gift*, 98, 100.
11  Natalie Zemon Davis, *The Gift in Sixteenth-Century France* (Oxford: Oxford University Press, 2000).
12  Mauss, *The Gift*, 30–3, 37, 56, 75.
13  See, for example, Jitkse Jasperse, *Medieval Women, Material Culture, and Power: Matilda Plantagenet and Her Sisters (*Leeds: ARC Humanities Press, 2020), chapter 2. See also Jitske Jasperse, 'Women, Courtly Display and Gifts in the *Rolandslied* and the *Chanson de Roland*', *Mediaevistik. International Journal of Interdisciplinary Medieval Research* 30 (2017): 125–41.
14  This is evident in the work of the research project led by Dan Smail, Documentary Archaeology of Late Medieval Europe (DALME).
15  *Scraped, Stroked, and Bound. Materially Engaged Readings of Medieval Manuscripts*, ed., Jonathan Wilcox (Turnhout: Brepols, 2013).
16  See, for example, the collaboration between Dr Eyal Poleg and Dr Paola Ricciardi. https://theconversation.com/how-thomas-cromwell-used-cut-and-paste-to-insert-himself-into-henry-viiis-great-bible-143765 (accessed 23 May 2021). See also, *The Art and Science of Illuminated Manuscripts*, ed. Stella Panayatova (London: Harvey Miller, 2020).
17  For an introduction to 'thing' biographies, see Bettina Bildhauer, *Medieval Things. Agency, Materiality, and Narratives of Objects in Medieval German Literature and Beyond* (Columbus, OH: Ohio State University Pres, 2020), chapter 3.
18  The biography of an object – an accordion – was powerfully realized in E. Annie Proulx, *Accordion Crimes* (New York: Scribner, 1996).
19  Bildhauer, *Medieval Things,* 131; see the whole chapter 4.
20  Above, p. 2.
21  Bildhauer, *Medieval Things,* 8–13.
22  Anne Laura Stoler, 'Introduction. "The Rot Remains": From Ruins to Ruination', in *Imperial Debris. On Ruins and Ruination* (Durham, NC: Duke University Press, 2013), 1–39.

# Index

*adventus* ceremony 51–3, 77–93
alms 11–12, 185–212, 249
amber 10, 74 n. 80, 110–19
animals
    birds, American 6
    deer 111
    elephants 6–9, 43–7, 50–64, 113–14, 201
    horses 110–11
    polar bears 111–16
    squirrels 88
    walrus 113

banners 222–8, 234–40
Barcelona 48–62
Bible, the 4–5, 12, 48, 50, 141, 173, 197–8, 209
    Dives and Lazarus 12, 192–4, 201, 204–9, 211

chairs 8, 43–65
charity *see* alms
Charlemagne, Frankish emperor 54
Charles the Bald, Frankish emperor 8, 48–9, 54, 59
Charles V, Hapsburg emperor 6, 51–2
cloth and clothes
    associated with donor 151–2, 171–2
    as gifts 54, 88, 90, 151–2, 193, 210
community-creation
    and gifts 11–12, 34, 141, 153, 163–70, 192–3
    and taken objects 240–1
Cosimo III de Medici, Grand Duke of Tuscanny 9, 103–21
Counter-reformation, *see* reformation
cups 3, 101, 251

Denmark 13, 185–212, 220–4, 235–40

Edward I, king of England 49

food and drink 193–4, 210, 237
    parmesan 10, 111
    wine 84, 88–90
fur 111–13
*see also* animals

Gdańsk 228–33
Germany 219–41
gifts
    and distance 6, 51, 82–3, 103–21
    and exoticism 6, 56–7, 110, 137
    manufacture of 7, 22, 51–2, 172–3
    and marriage 7, 18–35, 251
    material value of 6, 22–3, 80, 88, 149
    and memory 30–4, 44–5, 50, 52–8, 251
    and sex 29–30

Hamburg 221–8

images 133–54, 172–8, 228–33
India 6, 51
Italy 9–10, 103–21, 133–54, 163–71
ivory, *see* animals, elephants; walrus

jewels 24, 85, 89, 109, 115, 117–19, 151–2
Joanna, princess of Portugal 6, 51, 55
John, king of England 3

Kazimierz Jagiellończyk, saint 104–21
Konrad von Erlichshausen, Grand Master of the Teutonic Order 8, 78–86

Lithuania 10, 103–21
Livonia 78–93
London 18–34, 49
Louis VII, king of France 58
Lübeck 234–40
Luther, Martin 5, 48–9, 188–9, 212

Maria Maddalena de' Pazzi, saint 104–21
Martin I 'the Humane', king of Aragon 8, 50, 55, 60–62

matter, *see also* new materialism
    agency of 43–65, 137–54, 172, 241, 252
    living 133–54
Mauss, Marcel 1, 44, 78, 165–7, 249–51
Maximilian II, Hapsburg emperor 6, 51–7
medicine 103, 108–9

new materialism 2, 136–7
Nicholas of Tolentino, saint 163–78

Ottoman Empire 6, 107–8

paintings, *see* images
pearls 46
Pippin, king of the Franks 54
plunder 45–6, 108–10, 219–41
Prato 133–54
Prussia 78–83

reciprocity 3, 44, 78, 92, 166–7
    anxiety about 4, 187–9
reformation 103–6, 135, 185–212, 232

relics 9–11, 48, 85–6, 103–8, 113–14, 133–54, 171–3, 220 223
Riga 77–93
rings 3, 7–8, 17–35, 89, 252
romance literature 31–22, 43
Rome 47–8

Saints, *see also* relics
    gift exchange with 34, 47, 133–54, 163–78
Santa Maria delle Carceri ` 10–11, 134–54
Seneca the younger 4–5
Silvester Stodewescher, archbishop of Riga 8, 77–93
slavery 108, 169

Tolentino 163–78

vases 58
Vienna 51–6
Vilnus 103–21

wax 11, 147–53, 171–2

www.ingramcontent.com/pod-product-compliance
Lightning Source LLC
Chambersburg PA
CBHW062128300426
44115CB00012BA/1849